BRAIN POWERED

ALSO AVAILABLE FROM TOKYOPOP®

MANGA

.HACK//LEGEND OF THE TWILIGHT (September 2003)
@LARGE (COMING SOON)
ANGELIC LAYER*
BABY BIRTH* (September 2003)
BATTLE ROYALE*
BRAIN POWERED*
BRIGADOON* (August 2003)
CARDCAPTOR SAKURA
CARDCAPTOR SAKURA: MASTER OF THE CLOW*
CHOBITS*
CHRONICLES OF THE CURSED SWORD
CLAMP SCHOOL DETECTIVES*
CLOVER
CONFIDENTIAL CONFESSIONS*
CORRECTOR YUI
COWBOY BEBOP*
COWBOY BEBOP: SHOOTING STAR*
DEMON DIARY
DIGIMON*
DRAGON HUNTER
DRAGON KNIGHTS*
DUKLYON: CLAMP SCHOOL DEFENDERS*
ERICA SAKURAZAWA*
FAKE*
FLCL* (September 2003)
FORBIDDEN DANCE* (August 2003)
GATE KEEPERS*
G GUNDAM*
GRAVITATION*
GTO*
GUNDAM WING
GUNDAM WING: BATTLEFIELD OF PACIFISTS
GUNDAM WING: ENDLESS WALTZ*
GUNDAM WING: THE LAST OUTPOST*
HAPPY MANIA*
HARLEM BEAT
I.N.V.U.
INITIAL D*
ISLAND
JING: KING OF BANDITS*
JULINE
KARE KANO*
KINDAICHI CASE FILES, THE*
KING OF HELL
KODOCHA: SANA'S STAGE*
LOVE HINA*
LUPIN III*
MAGIC KNIGHT RAYEARTH* (August 2003)
MAGIC KNIGHT RAYEARTH II* (COMING SOON)

MAN OF MANY FACES*
MARMALADE BOY*
MARS*
MIRACLE GIRLS
MIYUKI-CHAN IN WONDERLAND* (October 2003)
MONSTERS, INC.
PARADISE KISS*
PARASYTE
PEACH GIRL
PEACH GIRL: CHANGE OF HEART*
PET SHOP OF HORRORS*
PLANET LADDER*
PLANETES* (October 2003)
PRIEST
RAGNAROK
RAVE MASTER*
REALITY CHECK
REBIRTH
REBOUND*
RISING STARS OF MANGA
SABER MARIONETTE J*
SAILOR MOON
SAINT TAIL
SAMURAI DEEPER KYO*
SAMURAI GIRL: REAL BOUT HIGH SCHOOL*
SCRYED*
SHAOLIN SISTERS*
SHIRAHIME-SYO: SNOW GODDESS TALES* (Dec. 2003)
SHUTTERBOX (November 2003)
SORCERER HUNTERS
THE SKULL MAN*
THE VISION OF ESCAFLOWNE
TOKYO MEW MEW*
UNDER THE GLASS MOON
VAMPIRE GAME*
WILD ACT*
WISH*
WORLD OF HARTZ (COMING SOON)
X-DAY* (August 2003)
ZODIAC P.I. *

For more information visit www.TOKYOPOP.com

100% AUTHENTIC MANGA

*INDICATES 100% AUTHENTIC MANGA (RIGHT-TO-LEFT FORMAT)

CINE-MANGA™

CARDCAPTORS
JACKIE CHAN ADVENTURES (COMING SOON)
JIMMY NEUTRON (September 2003)
KIM POSSIBLE
LIZZIE MCGUIRE
POWER RANGERS: NINJA STORM (August 2003)
SPONGEBOB SQUAREPANTS (September 2003)
SPY KIDS 2

NOVELS

KARMA CLUB (April 2004)
SAILOR MOON

TOKYOPOP KIDS

STRAY SHEEP (September 2003)

ART BOOKS

CARDCAPTOR SAKURA*
MAGIC KNIGHT RAYEARTH*

ANIME GUIDES

COWBOY BEBOP ANIME GUIDES
GUNDAM TECHNICAL MANUALS
SAILOR MOON SCOUT GUIDES

6-5-03

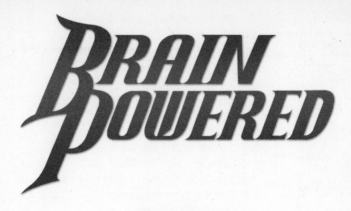

BRAIN POWERED

Volume 2

Art by
YUKIRU SUGISAKI
Story by
YOSHIYUKI TOMINO

TOKYOPOP®
LOS ANGELES • TOKYO • LONDON

Translator - Aya Matsunaga
English Adaptation - Ross Richie
Layout and Lettering - Anna Kernbaum
Additional Design & Lettering - Mark Paniccia
Cover Layout - Aaron Suhr

Editor - Mark Paniccia
Managing Editor - Jill Freshney
Production Coordinator - Antonio DePietro
Production Manager - Jennifer Miller
Art Director - Matthew Alford
Editorial Director - Jeremy Ross
VP of Production - Ron Klamert
President & C.O.O. - John Parker
Publisher & C.E.O. - Stuart Levy

Email: editor@TOKYOPOP.com
Come visit us online at www.TOKYOPOP.com

A ⊙ **TOKYOPOP** Manga
TOKYOPOP® is an imprint of Mixx Entertainment, Inc.
5900 Wilshire Blvd. Suite 2000, Los Angeles, CA 90036

ISBN: 1-59182-390-0

First TOKYOPOP® printing: August 2003

10 9 8 7 6 5 4 3 2 1
Printed in the USA

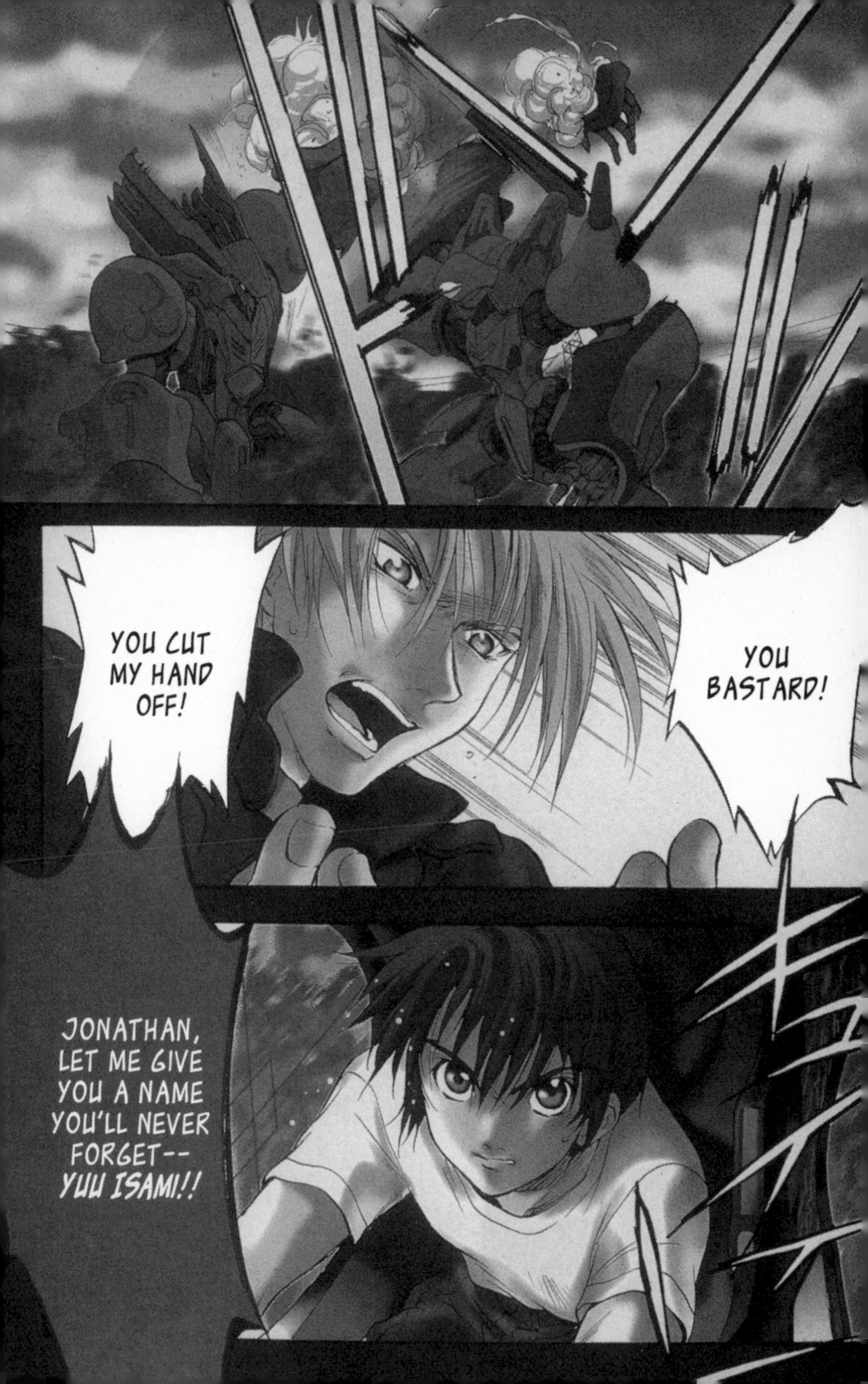
YOU BASTARD!
YOU CUT MY HAND OFF!
JONATHAN, LET ME GIVE YOU A NAME YOU'LL NEVER FORGET-- YUU ISAMI!!

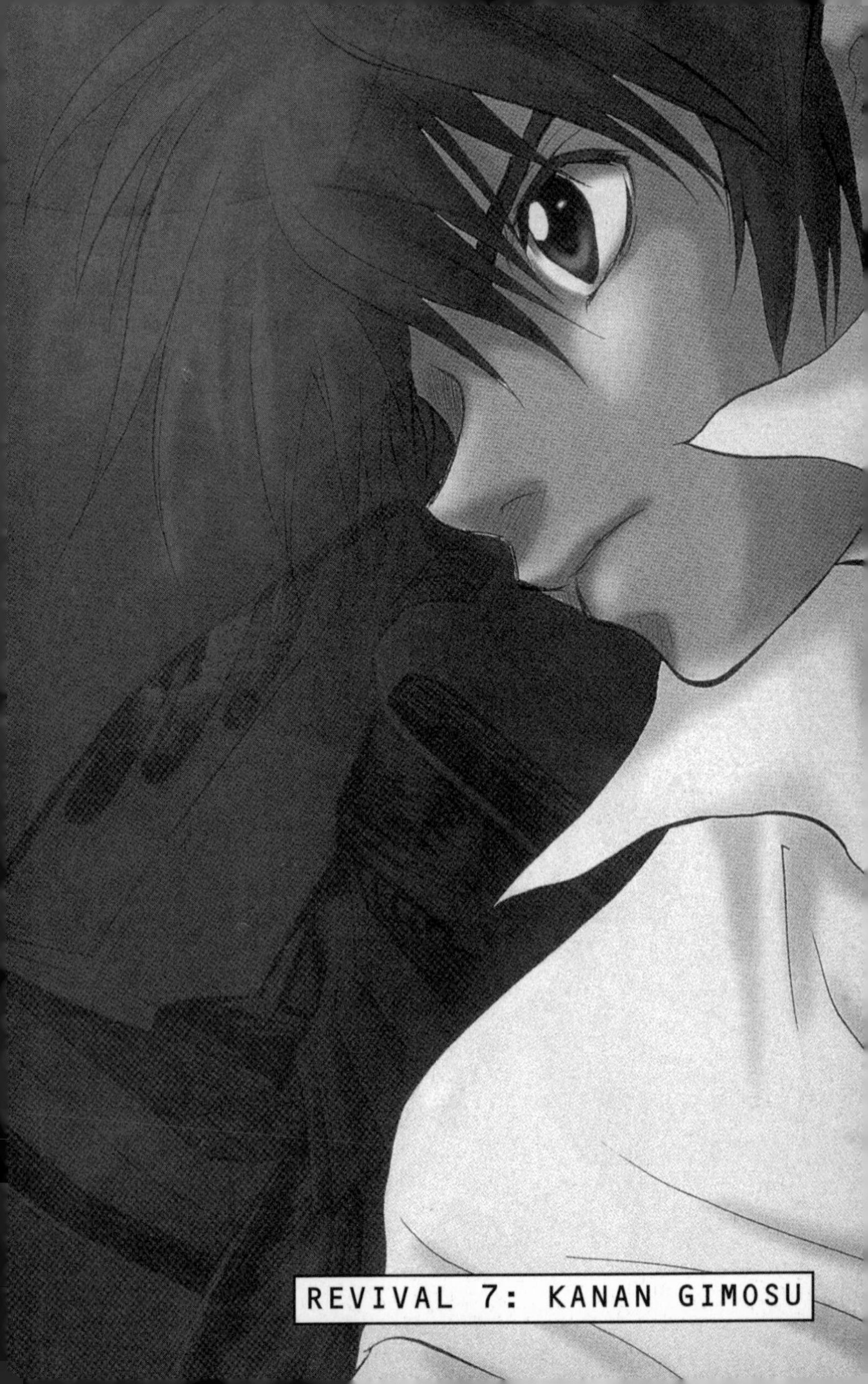
REVIVAL 7: KANAN GIMOSU

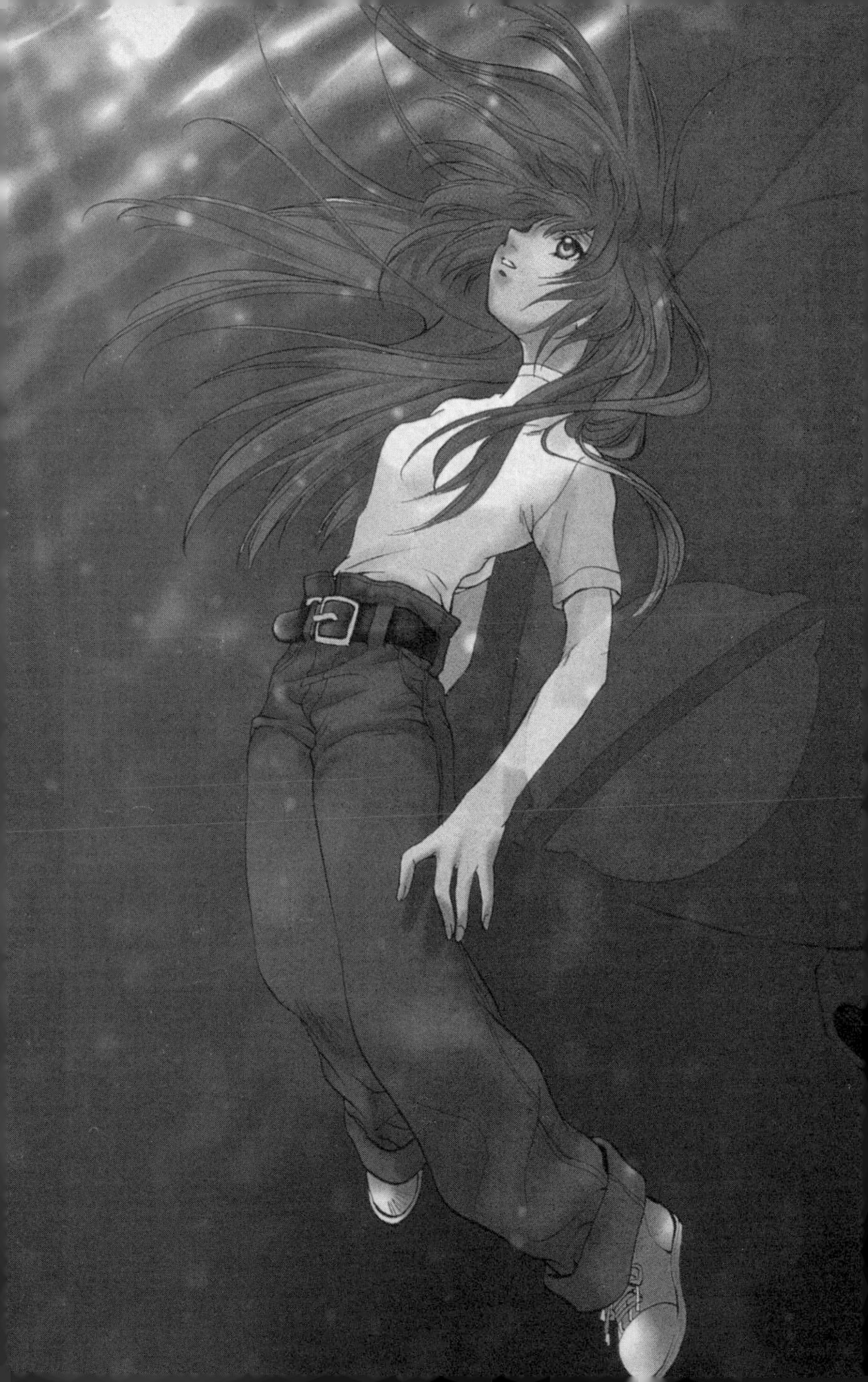

BRAIN POWERED

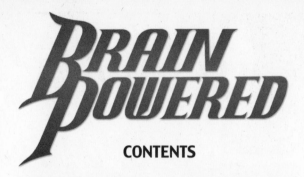

CONTENTS

2

THE STORY SO FAR

THE FUTURE: When the mysterious undersea base Orphan is discovered, it polarizes the world. Scientists migrate to the base, piloting its Grand Cher mecha suits and pursuing Orphan's mysterious agenda. Meanwhile, the United Nations becomes nervous about the possible threat that Orphan represents and creates the Novis Noah, a ship designed to be a resistance force and a shelter against this possible danger.

Young Grand Cher pilot Yuu rebels against his scientist parents and flees Orphan in an organic Brain Powered mecha armor. Fearing that Yuu will share valuable information with the U.N., Orphan has sent its deadliest Grand Cher pilots to bring Yuu back, dead or alive. Too rebellious for his own good, Yuu refuses to join the Novis Noah, certain he can fight Orphan on his own. Or can he? With the fate of the world hanging in the balance, it's time for Yuu to pick a side—and a cause.

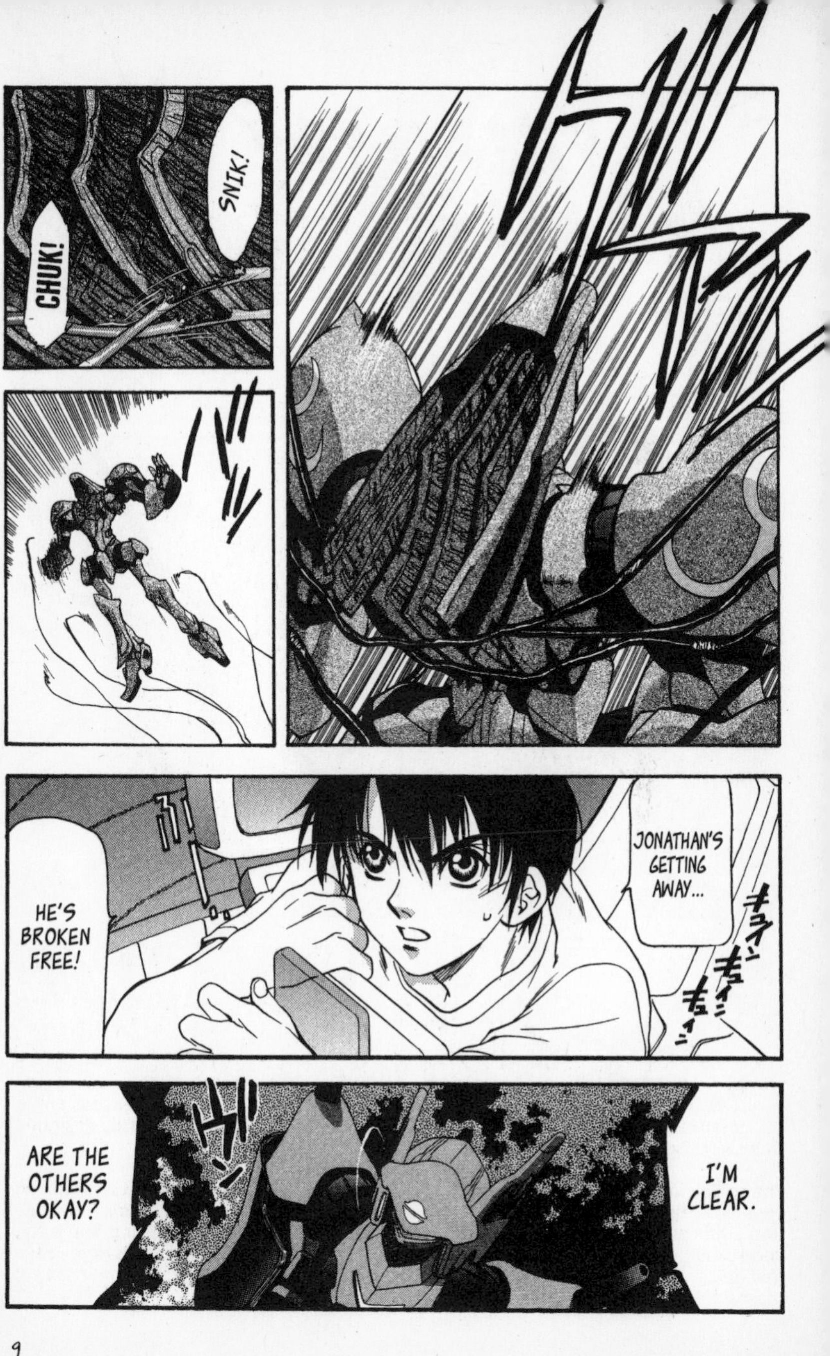
SNIK!
CHUK!
JONATHAN'S GETTING AWAY...
HE'S BROKEN FREE!
I'M CLEAR.
ARE THE OTHERS OKAY?

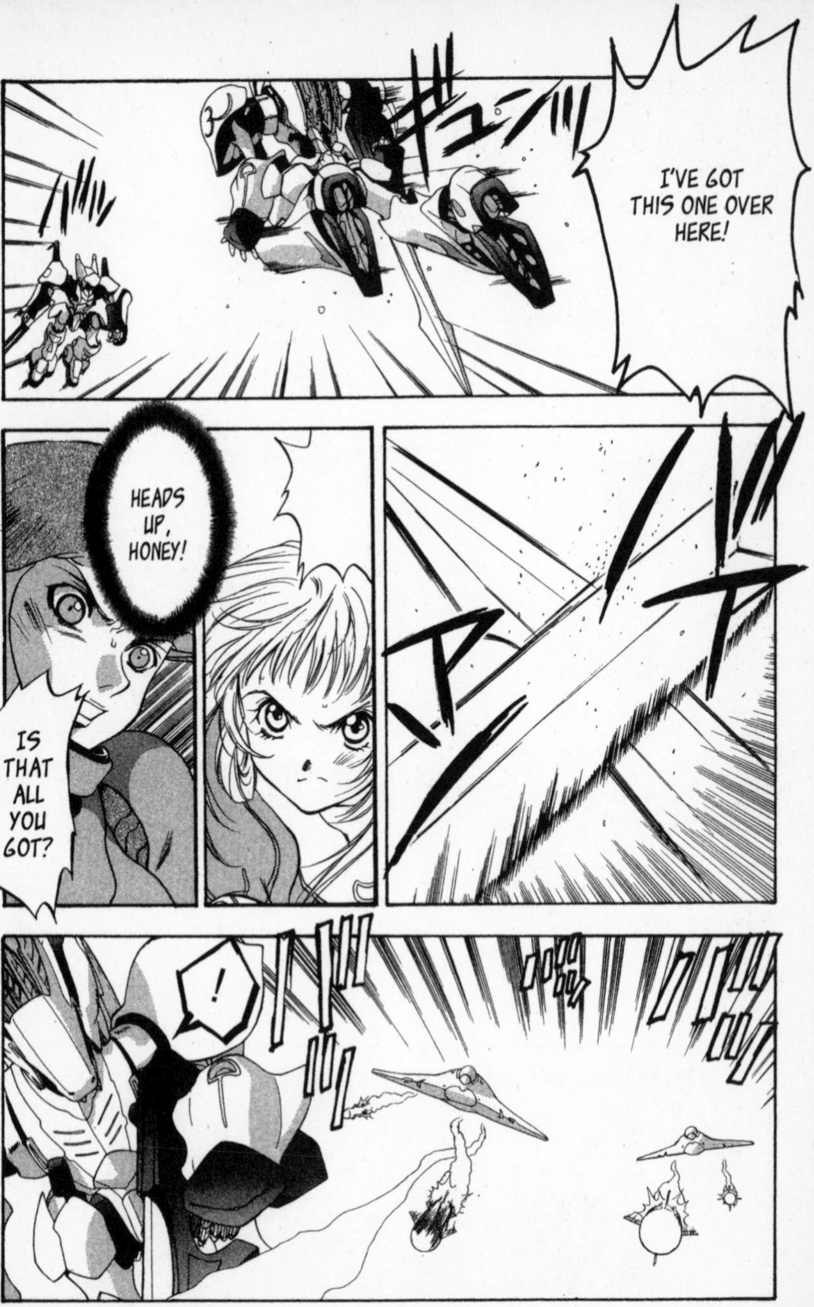
I'VE GOT THIS ONE OVER HERE!
HEADS UP, HONEY!
IS THAT ALL YOU GOT?
!

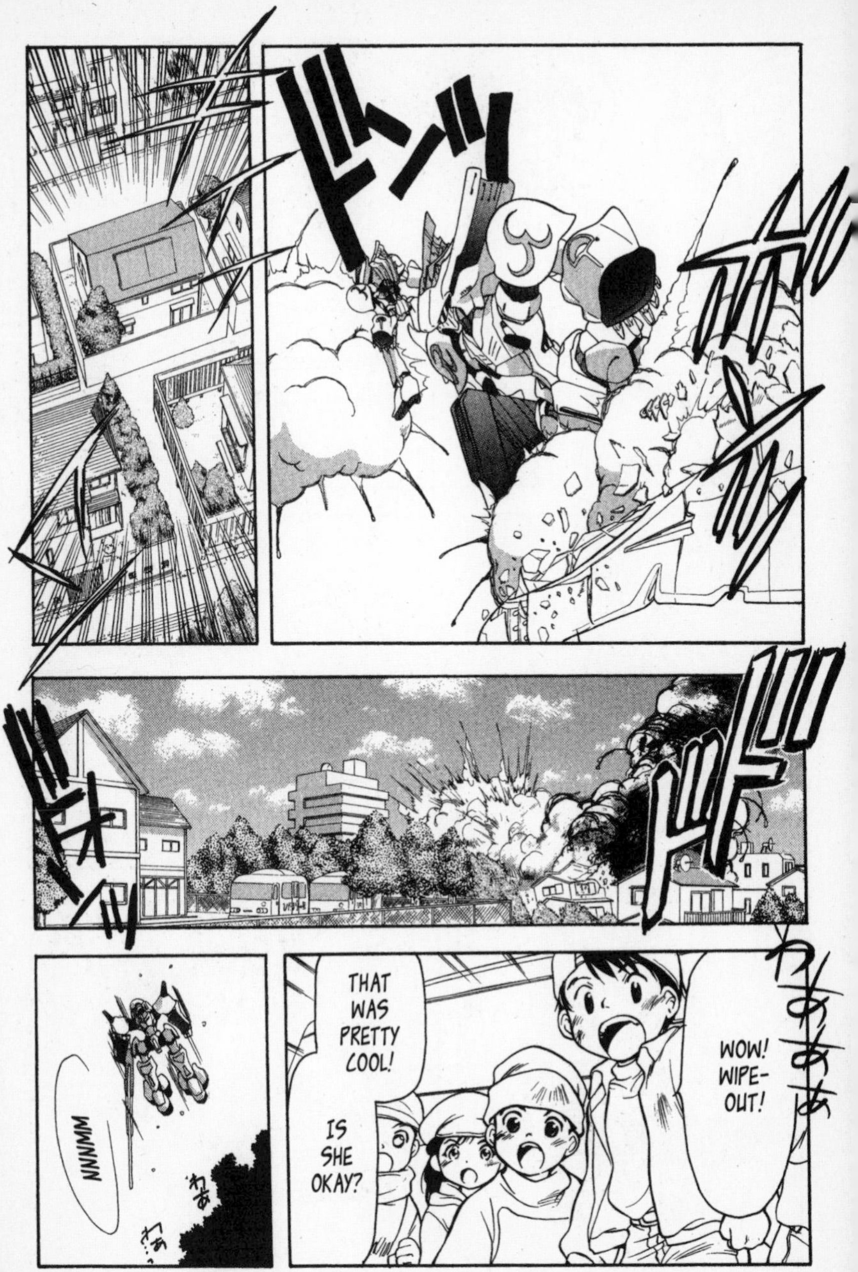
WOW! WIPE-OUT!
わあああ
THAT WAS PRETTY COOL!
IS SHE OKAY?
NNNNMM
わあ
わあ…

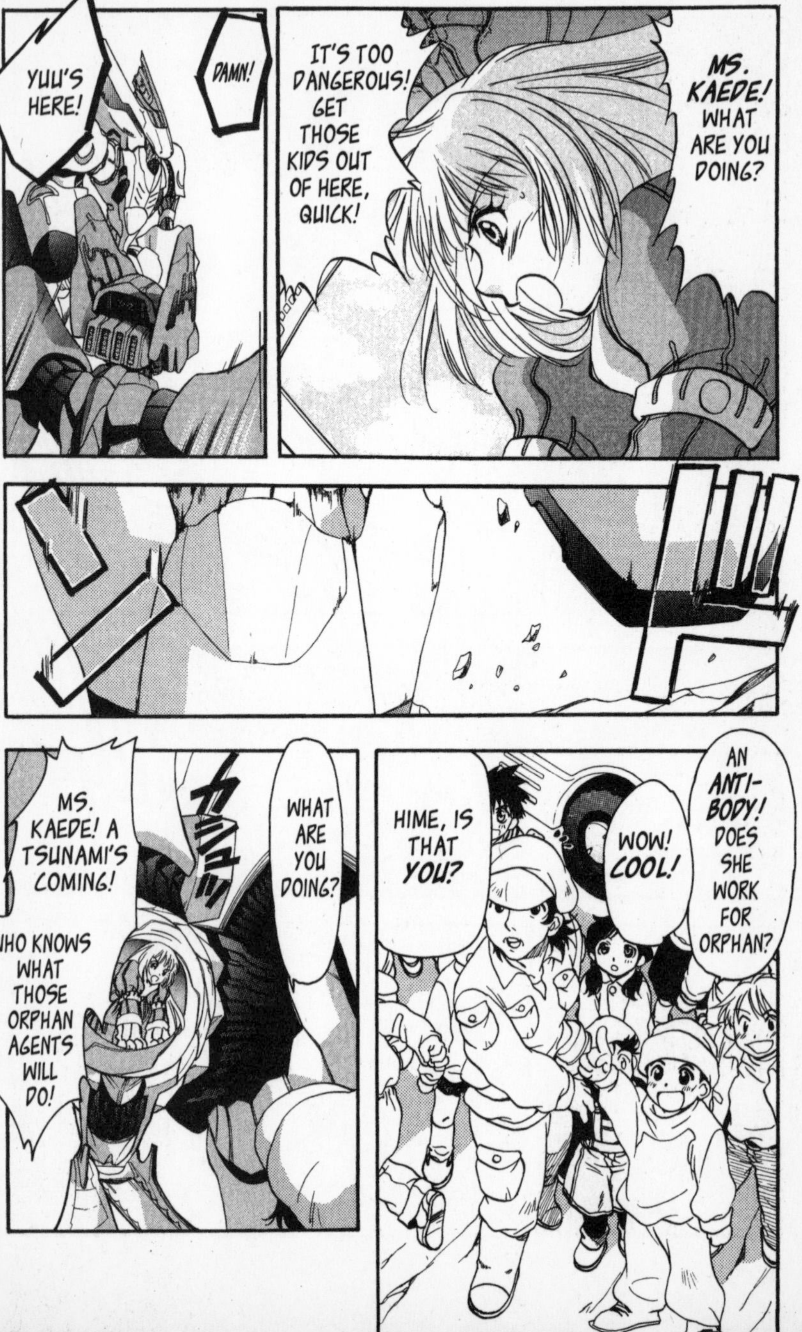
MS. KAEDE! WHAT ARE YOU DOING?
IT'S TOO DANGEROUS! GET THOSE KIDS OUT OF HERE, QUICK!
DAMN!
YUU'S HERE!
AN ANTI-BODY! DOES SHE WORK FOR ORPHAN?
WOW! COOL!
HIME, IS THAT YOU?
WHAT ARE YOU DOING?
MS. KAEDE! A TSUNAMI'S COMING!
WHO KNOWS WHAT THOSE ORPHAN AGENTS WILL DO!

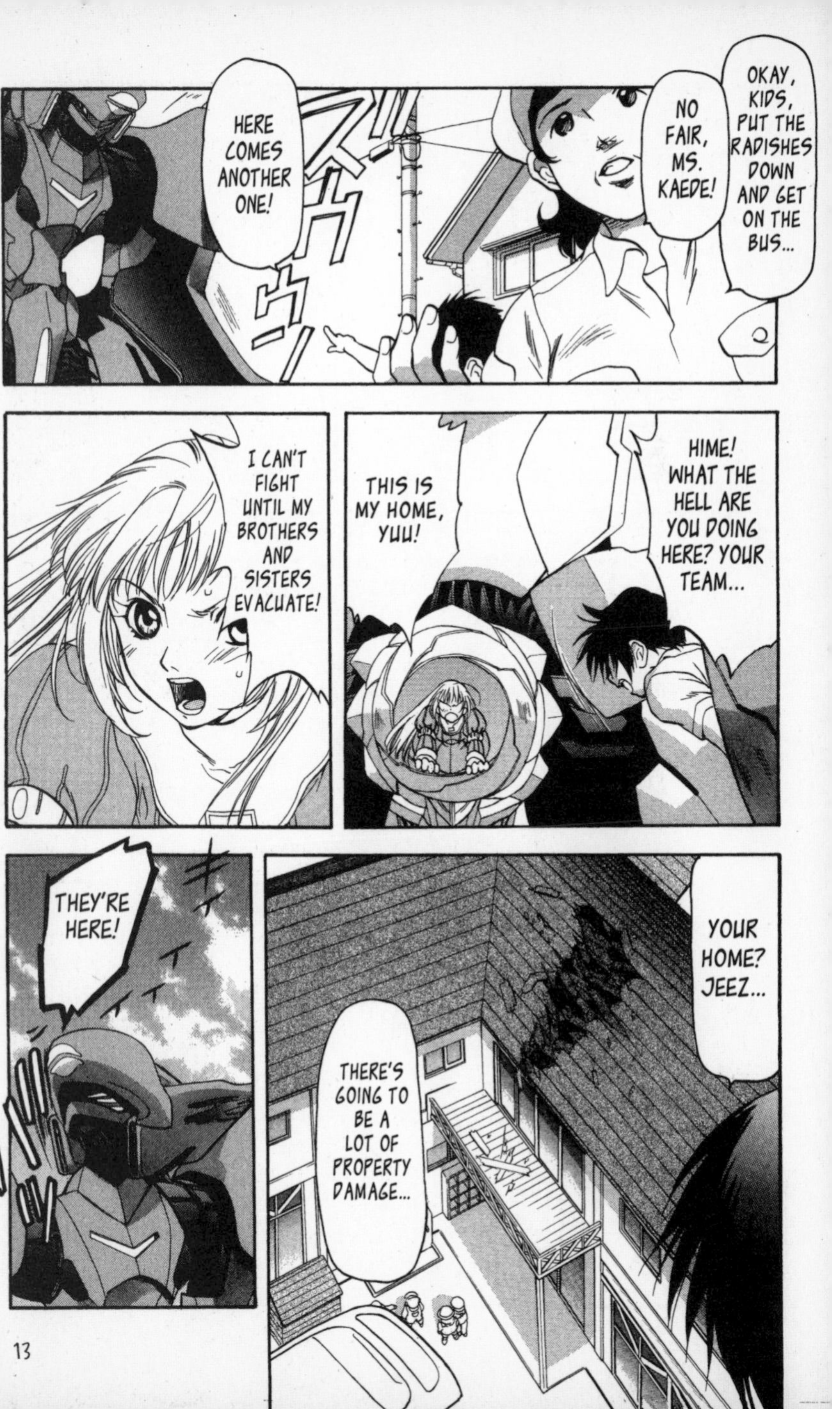
OKAY, KIDS, PUT THE RADISHES DOWN AND GET ON THE BUS...
NO FAIR, MS. KAEDE!
HERE COMES ANOTHER ONE!
HIME! WHAT THE HELL ARE YOU DOING HERE? YOUR TEAM...
THIS IS MY HOME, YUU!
I CAN'T FIGHT UNTIL MY BROTHERS AND SISTERS EVACUATE!
YOUR HOME? JEEZ...
THERE'S GOING TO BE A LOT OF PROPERTY DAMAGE...
THEY'RE HERE!

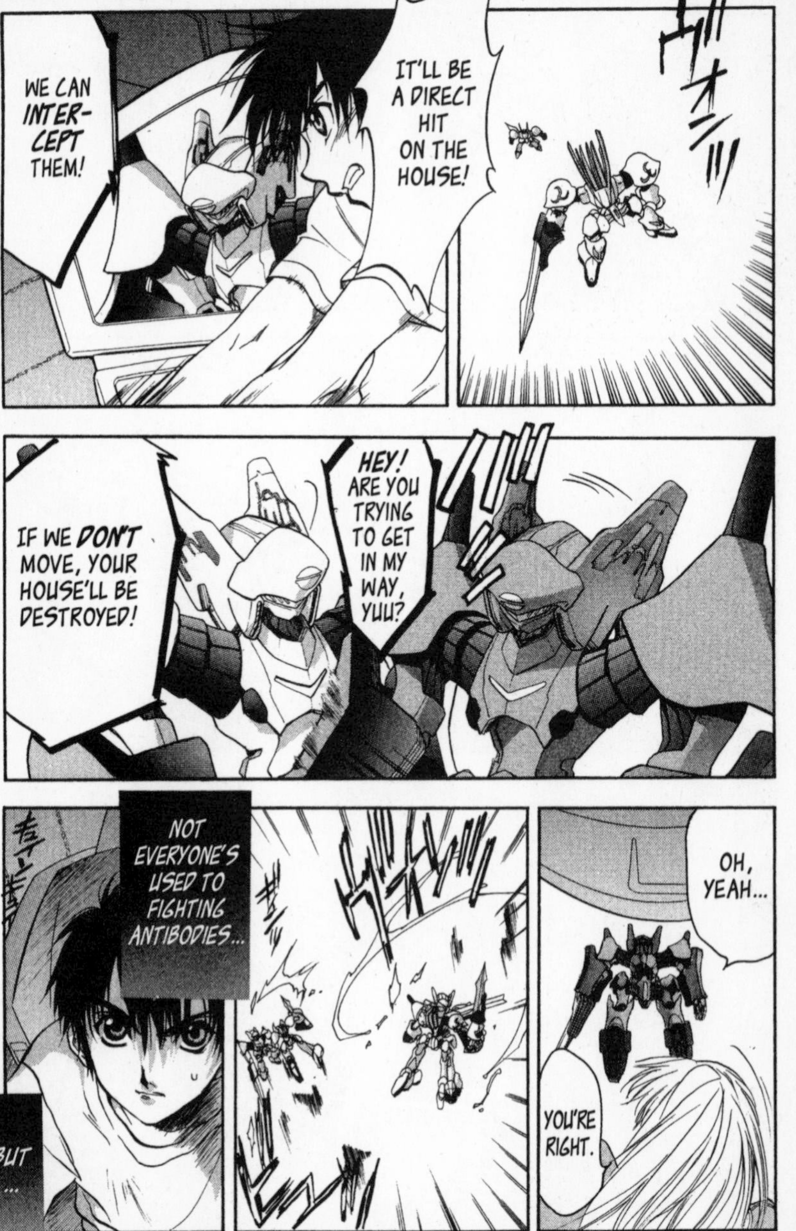
IT'LL BE A DIRECT HIT ON THE HOUSE!
WE CAN INTER-CEPT THEM!
HEY! ARE YOU TRYING TO GET IN MY WAY, YUU?
IF WE DON'T MOVE, YOUR HOUSE'LL BE DESTROYED!
OH, YEAH...
YOU'RE RIGHT.
NOT EVERYONE'S USED TO FIGHTING ANTIBODIES...
BUT ...

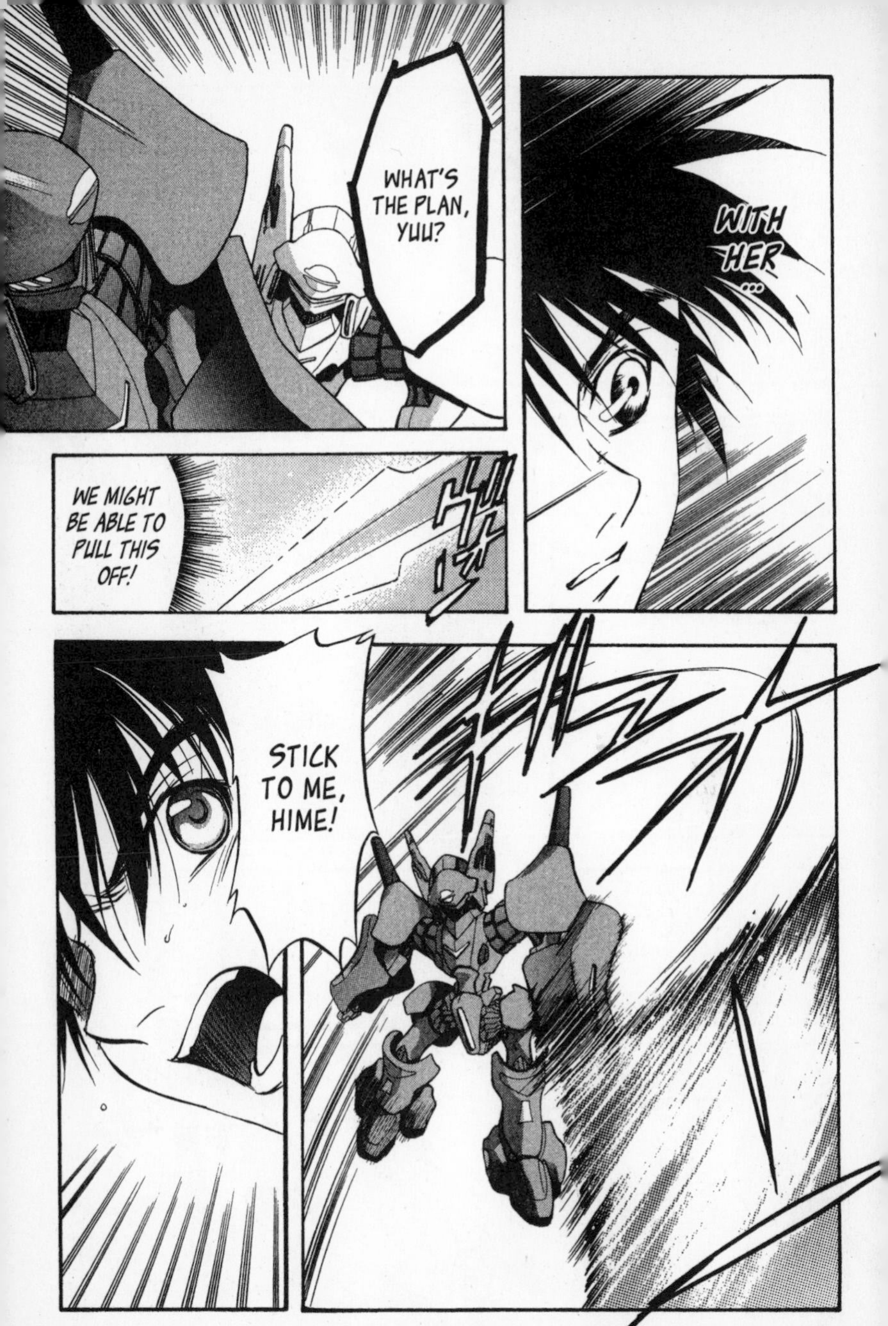
WITH HER...
WHAT'S THE PLAN, YUU?
WE MIGHT BE ABLE TO PULL THIS OFF!
STICK TO ME, HIME!

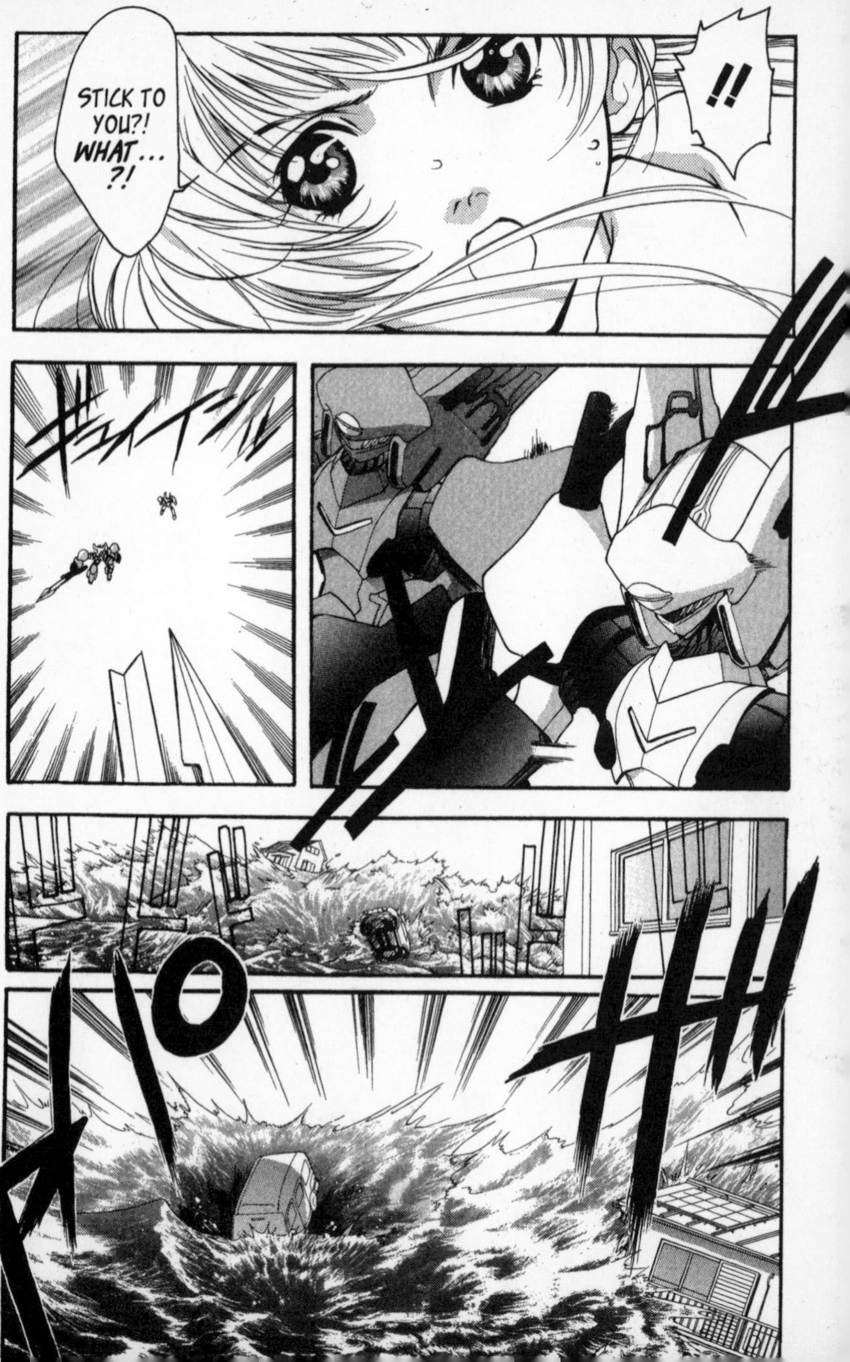
!!
STICK TO YOU?! WHAT... ?!

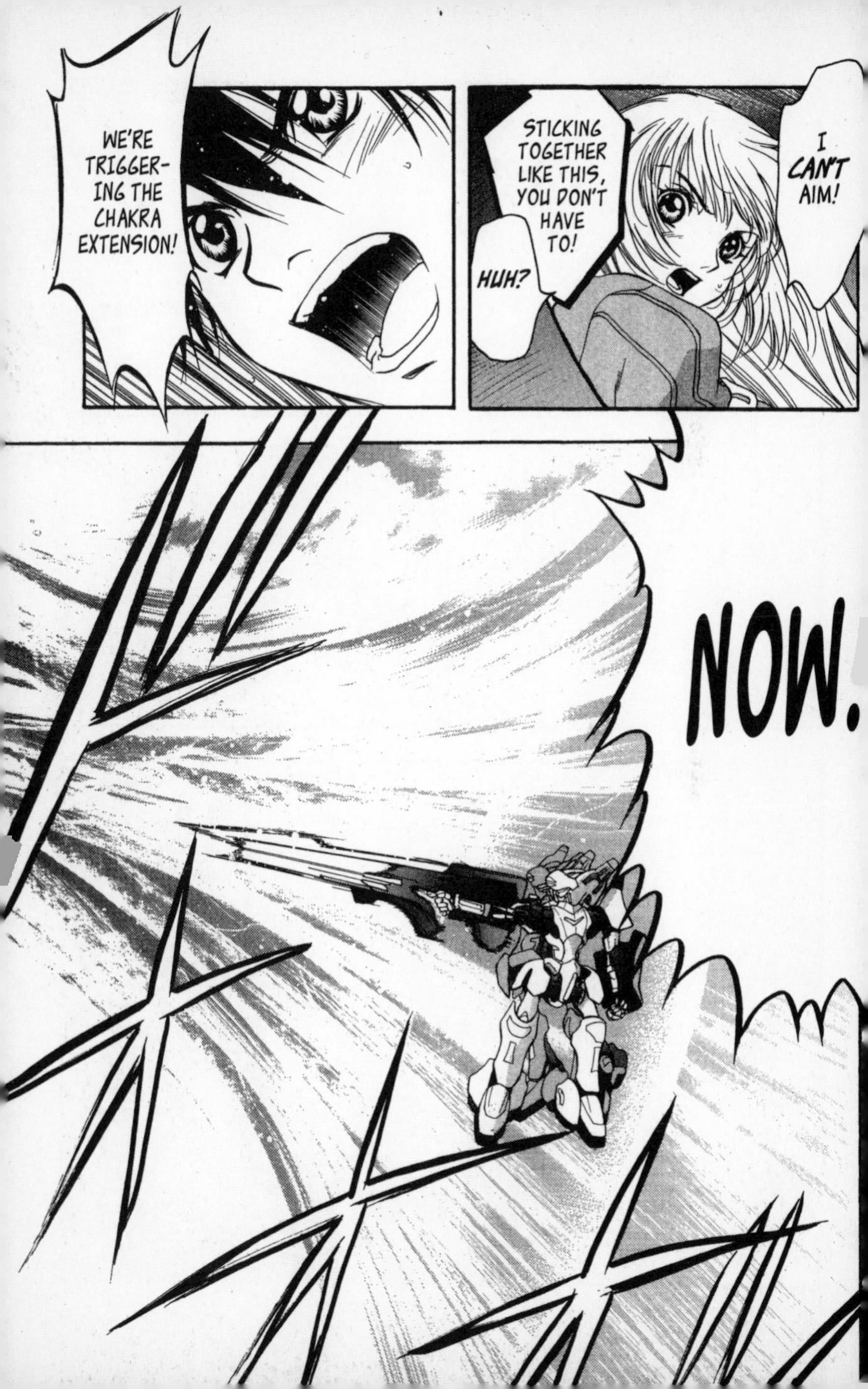
I CAN'T AIM!
STICKING TOGETHER LIKE THIS, YOU DON'T HAVE TO!
HUH?
WE'RE TRIGGER-ING THE CHAKRA EXTENSION!
NOW.

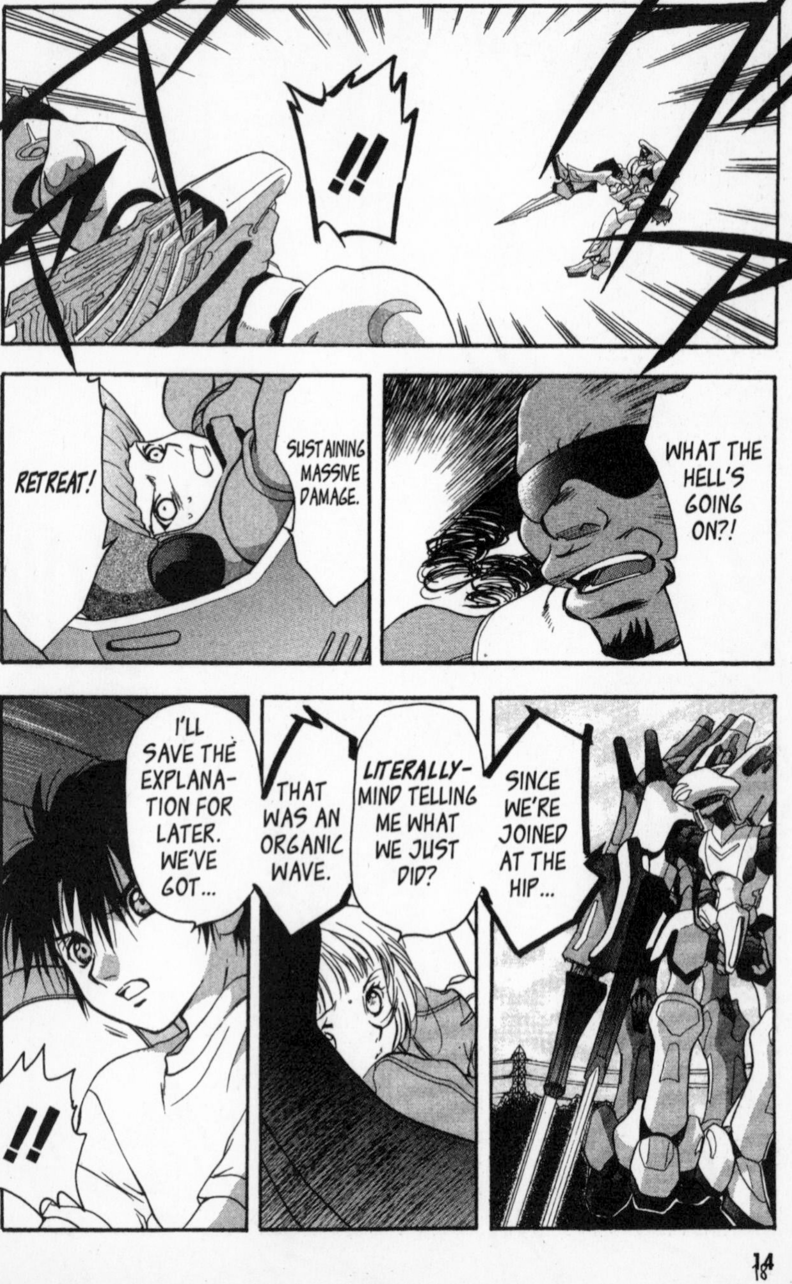
!!
WHAT THE HELL'S GOING ON?!
SUSTAINING MASSIVE DAMAGE.
RETREAT!
SINCE WE'RE JOINED AT THE HIP...
LITERALLY- MIND TELLING ME WHAT WE JUST DID?
THAT WAS AN ORGANIC WAVE.
I'LL SAVE THE EXPLANATION FOR LATER. WE'VE GOT...
!!

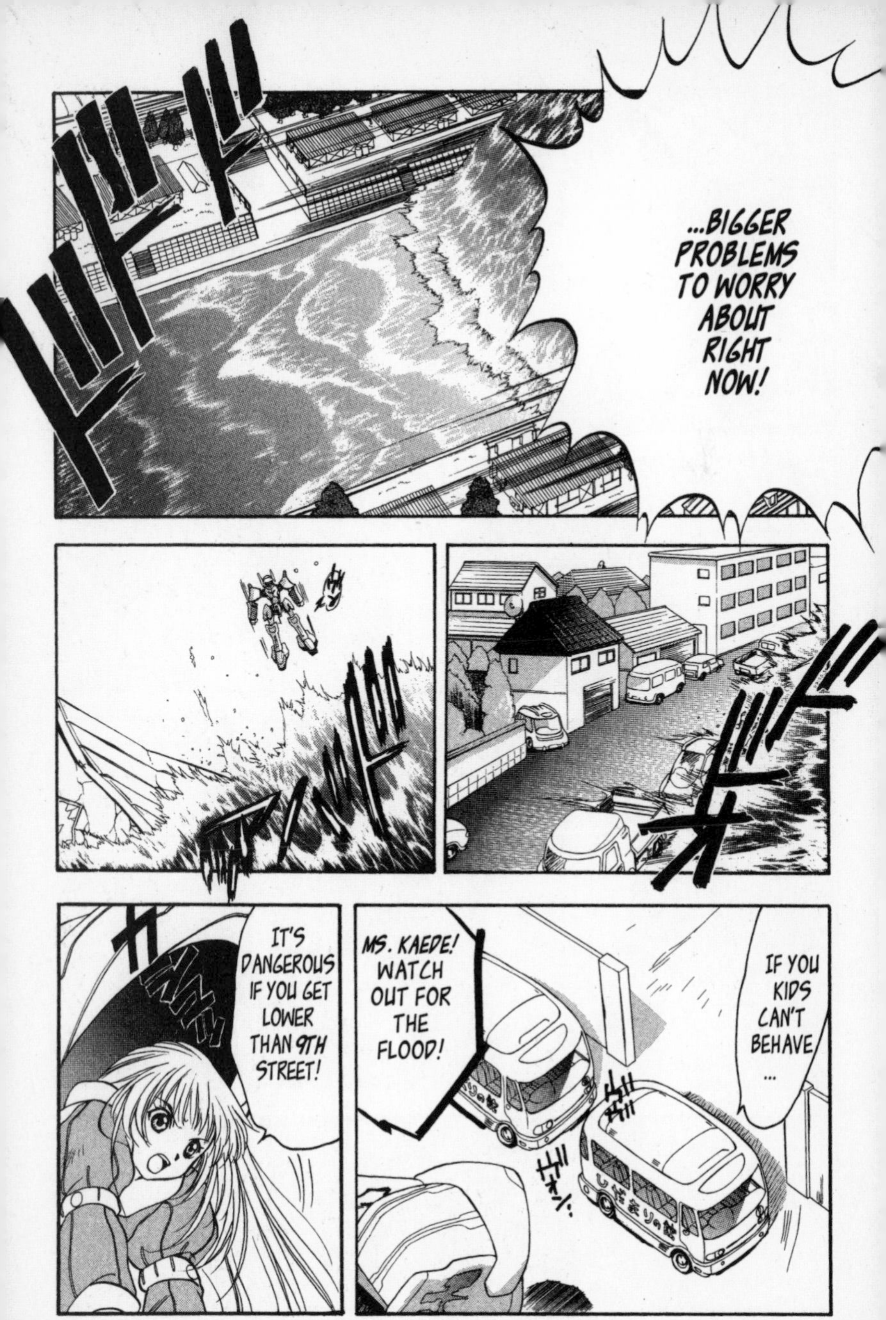
...BIGGER PROBLEMS TO WORRY ABOUT RIGHT NOW!
IF YOU KIDS CAN'T BEHAVE ...
MS. KAEDE! WATCH OUT FOR THE FLOOD!
IT'S DANGEROUS IF YOU GET LOWER THAN 9TH STREET!

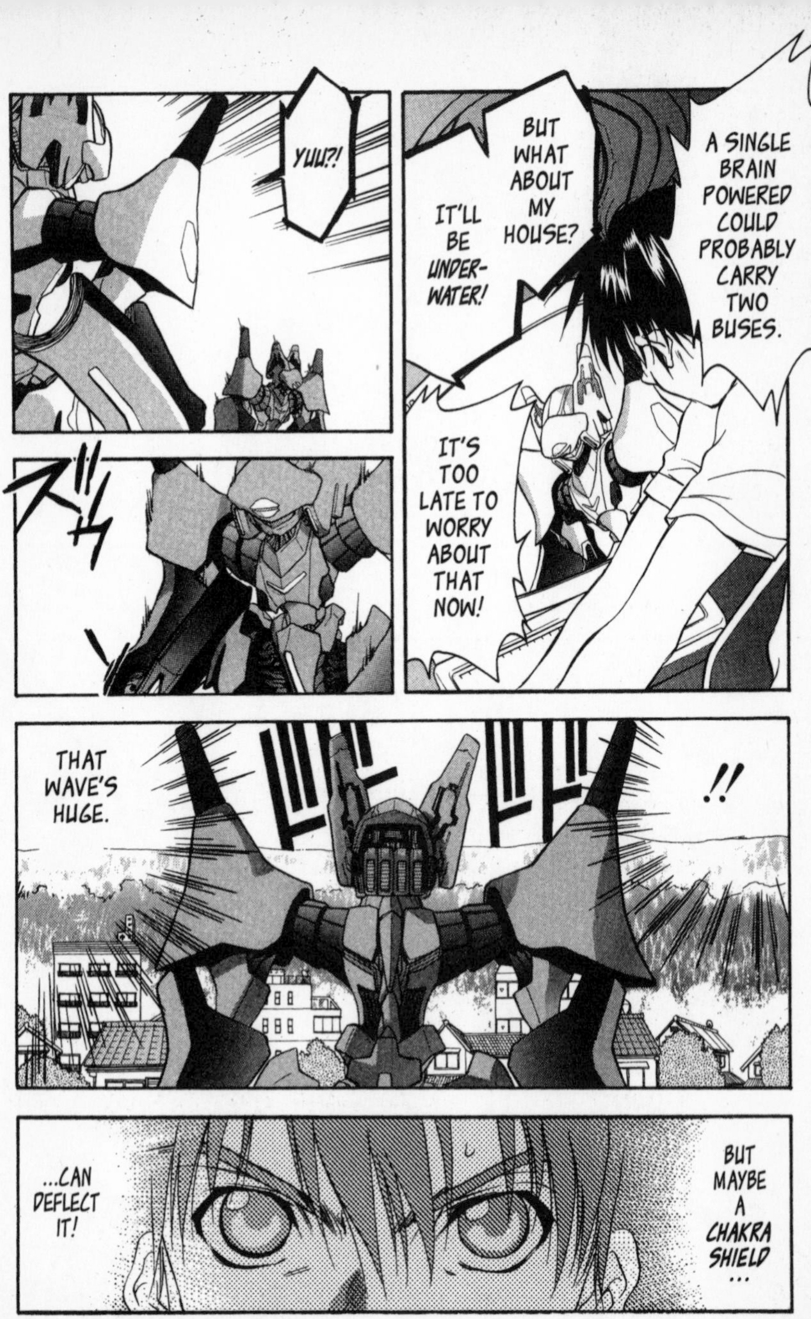
A SINGLE BRAIN POWERED COULD PROBABLY CARRY TWO BUSES.
BUT WHAT ABOUT MY HOUSE?
IT'LL BE UNDER-WATER!
IT'S TOO LATE TO WORRY ABOUT THAT NOW!
YUU?!
ズル
!!
THAT WAVE'S HUGE.
BUT MAYBE A CHAKRA SHIELD...
...CAN DEFLECT IT!

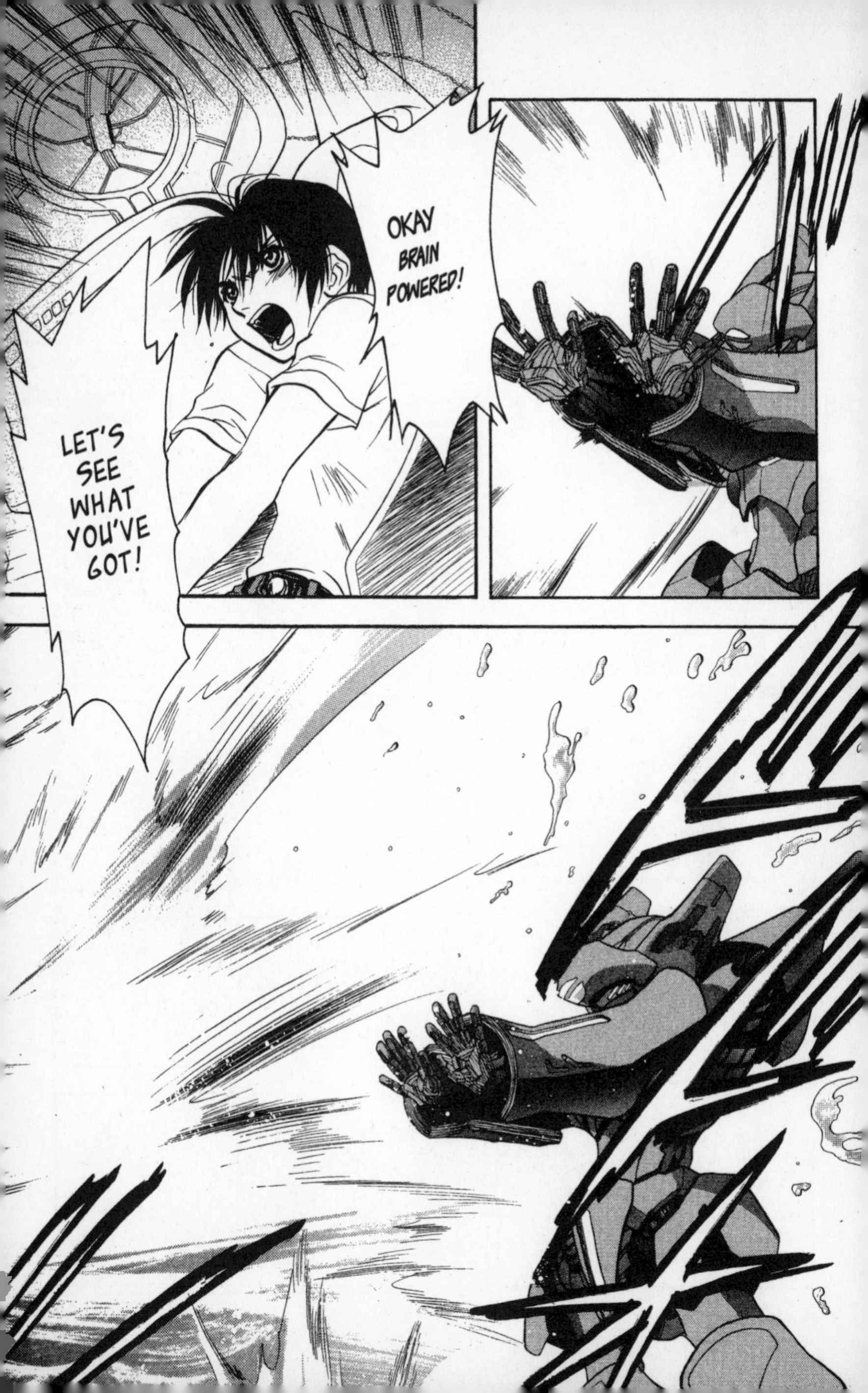
OKAY BRAIN POWERED!
LET'S SEE WHAT YOU'VE GOT!

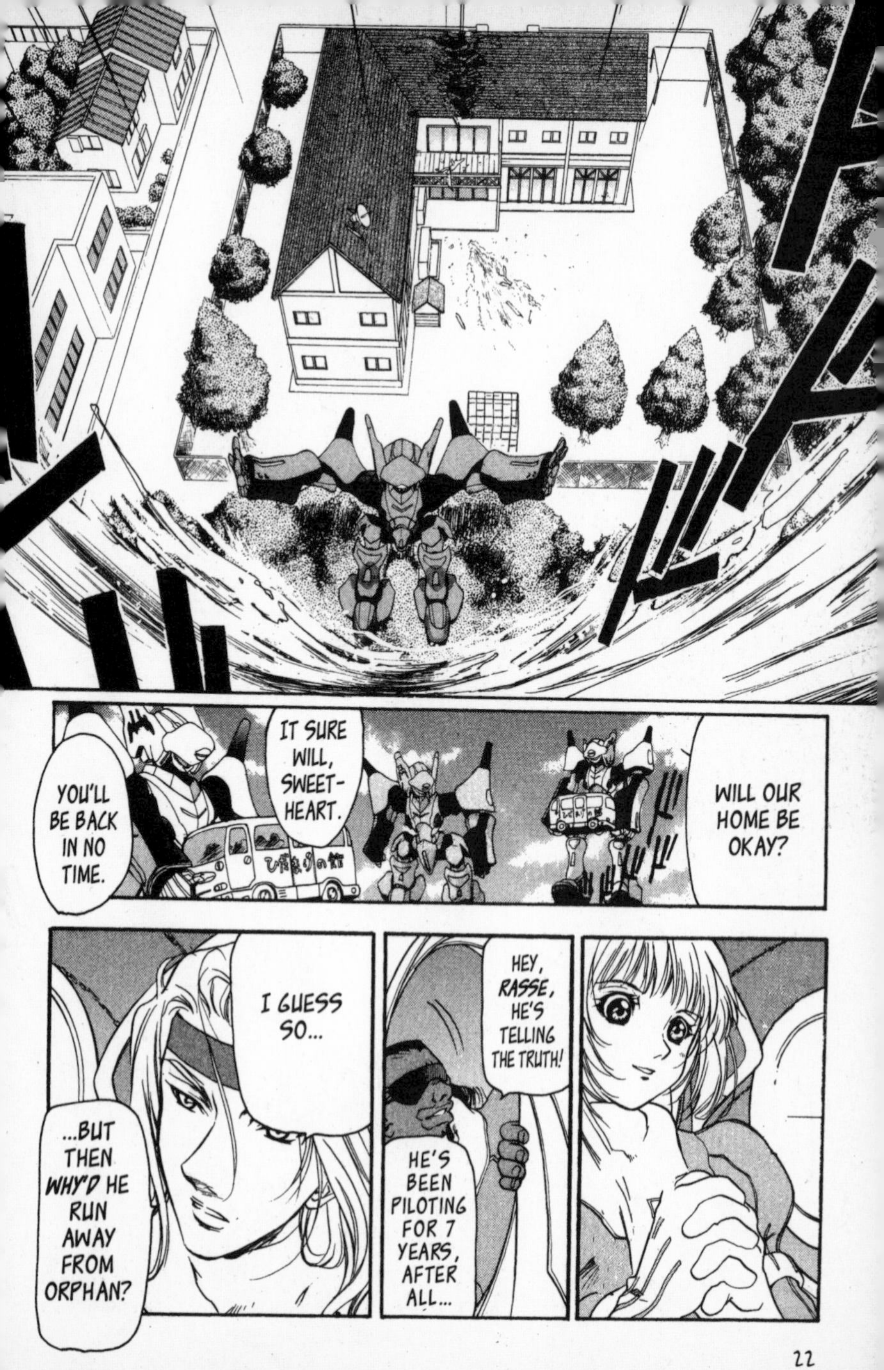
WILL OUR HOME BE OKAY?
IT SURE WILL, SWEET-HEART.
YOU'LL BE BACK IN NO TIME.
HEY, *RASSE*, HE'S TELLING THE TRUTH!
HE'S BEEN PILOTING FOR 7 YEARS, AFTER ALL...
I GUESS SO...
...BUT THEN *WHY'D* HE RUN AWAY FROM ORPHAN?

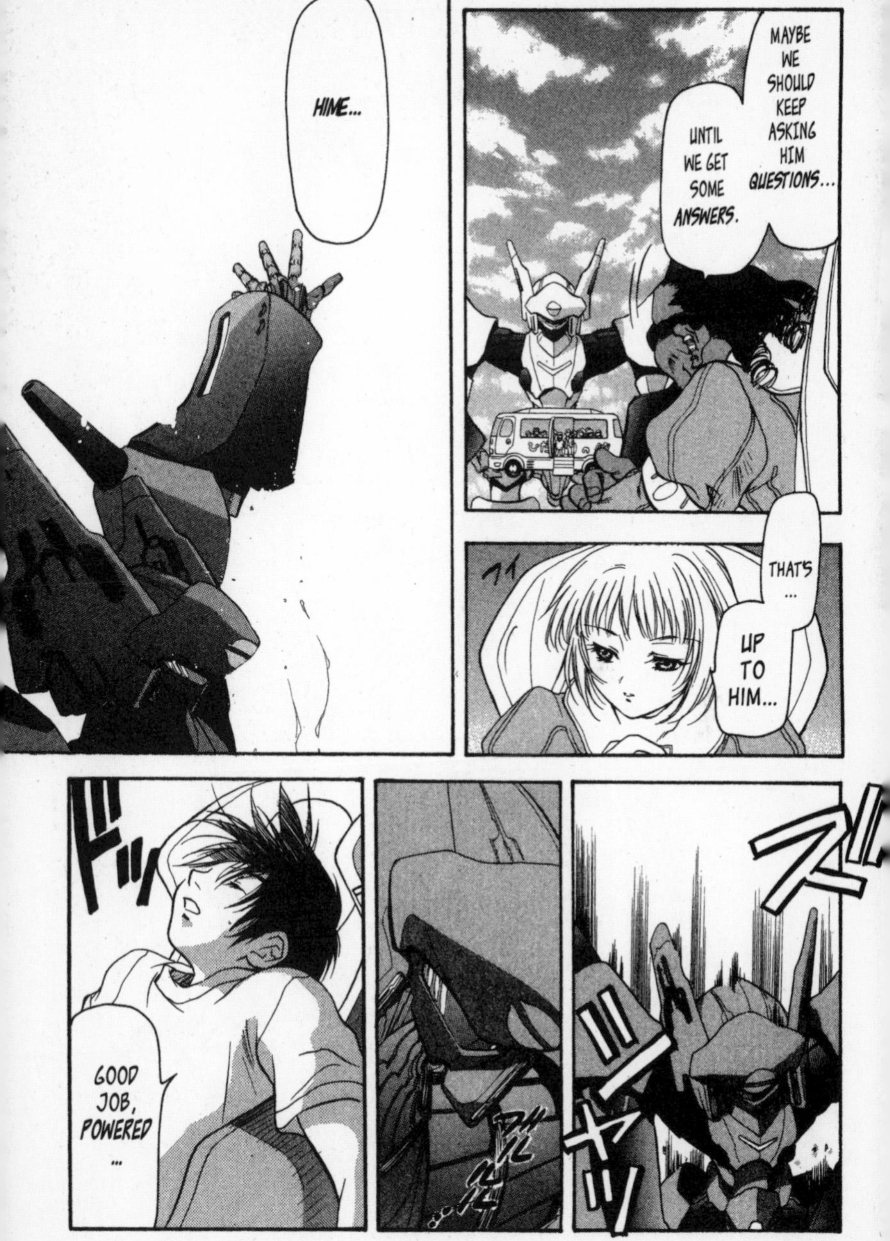
MAYBE WE SHOULD KEEP ASKING HIM QUESTIONS...
UNTIL WE GET SOME ANSWERS.
THAT'S ...
UP TO HIM...
HIME...
GOOD JOB, POWERED ...

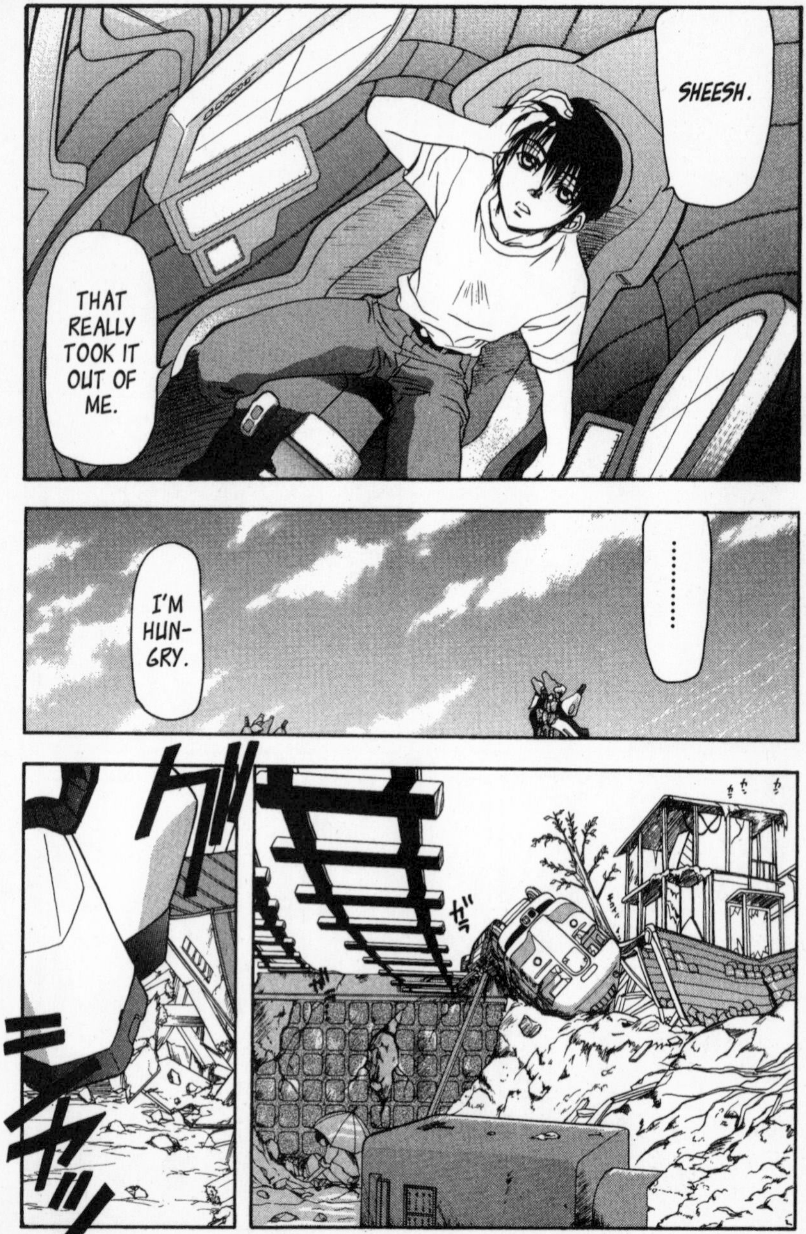
SHEESH.
THAT REALLY TOOK IT OUT OF ME.
....
I'M HUN-GRY.

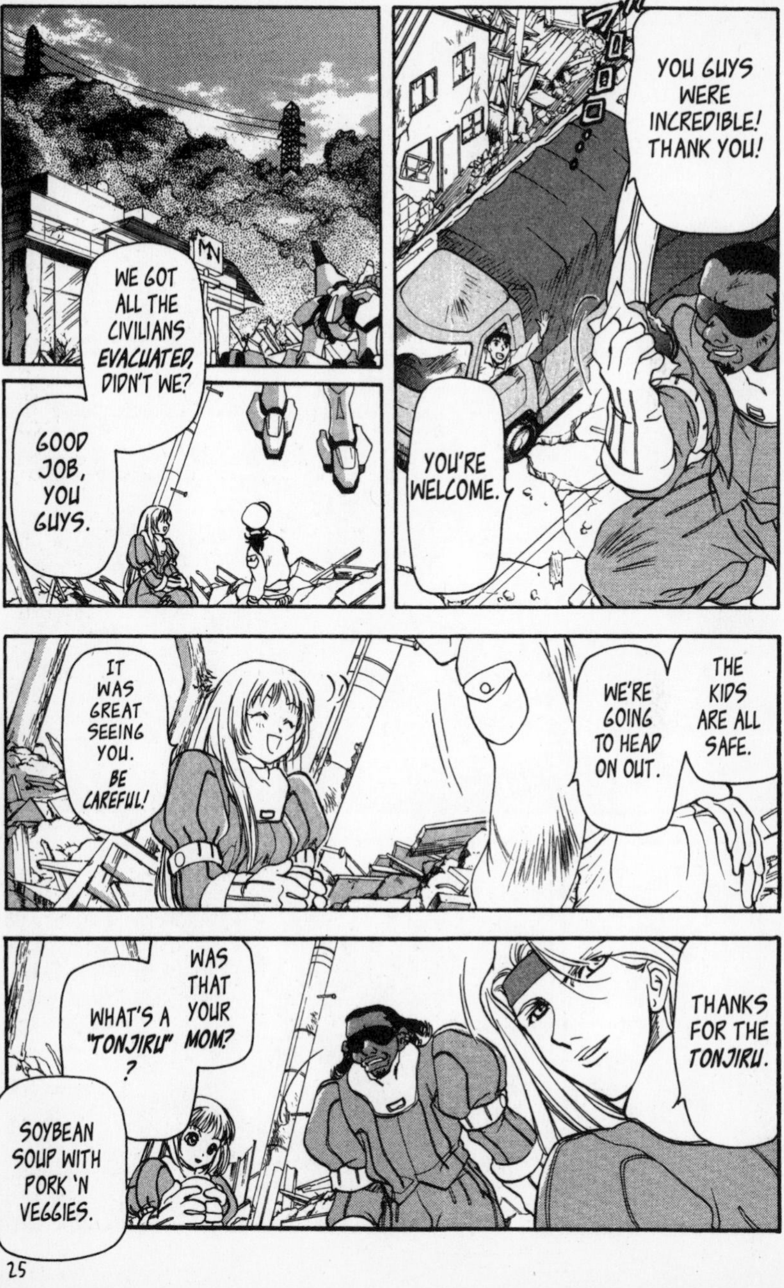
YOU GUYS WERE INCREDIBLE! THANK YOU!
YOU'RE WELCOME.
WE GOT ALL THE CIVILIANS EVACUATED, DIDN'T WE?
GOOD JOB, YOU GUYS.
THE KIDS ARE ALL SAFE.
WE'RE GOING TO HEAD ON OUT.
IT WAS GREAT SEEING YOU. BE CAREFUL!
THANKS FOR THE TONJIRU.
WAS THAT YOUR MOM?
WHAT'S A "TONJIRU"?
SOYBEAN SOUP WITH PORK 'N VEGGIES.

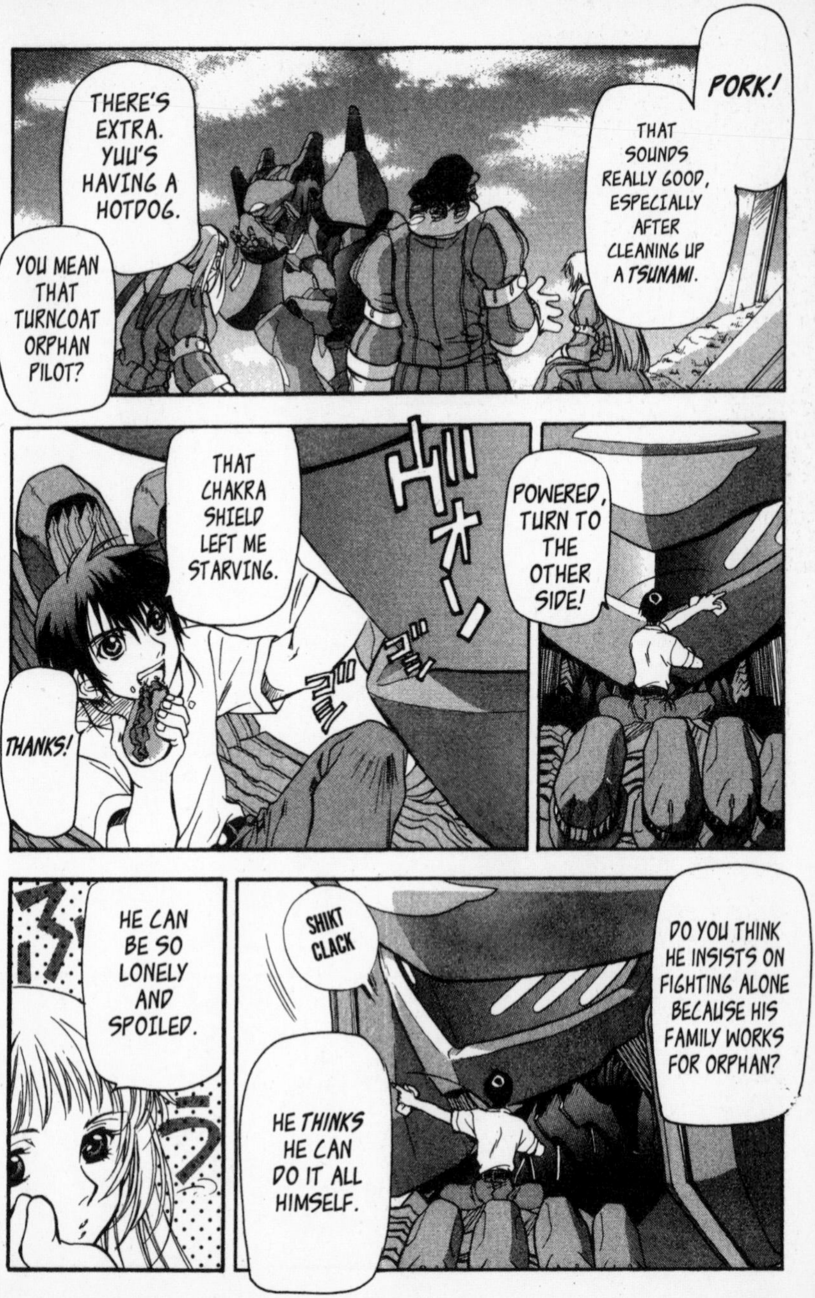
PORK!
THAT SOUNDS REALLY GOOD, ESPECIALLY AFTER CLEANING UP A TSUNAMI.
THERE'S EXTRA. YUU'S HAVING A HOTDOG.
YOU MEAN THAT TURNCOAT ORPHAN PILOT?
POWERED, TURN TO THE OTHER SIDE!
THAT CHAKRA SHIELD LEFT ME STARVING.
THANKS!
DO YOU THINK HE INSISTS ON FIGHTING ALONE BECAUSE HIS FAMILY WORKS FOR ORPHAN?
SHIKT CLACK
HE THINKS HE CAN DO IT ALL HIMSELF.
HE CAN BE SO LONELY AND SPOILED.

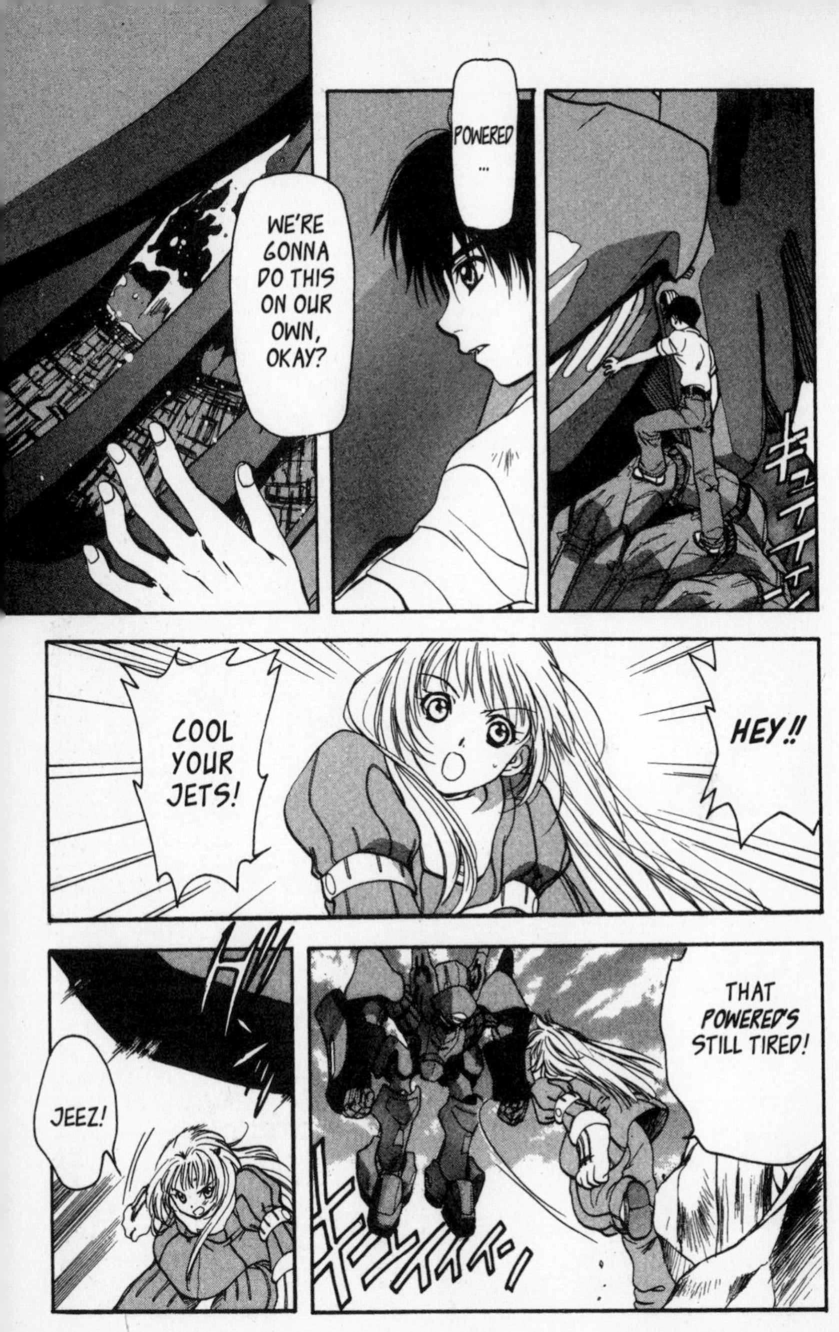
POWERED ...
WE'RE GONNA DO THIS ON OUR OWN, OKAY?
HEY!!
COOL YOUR JETS!
THAT POWERED'S STILL TIRED!
JEEZ!

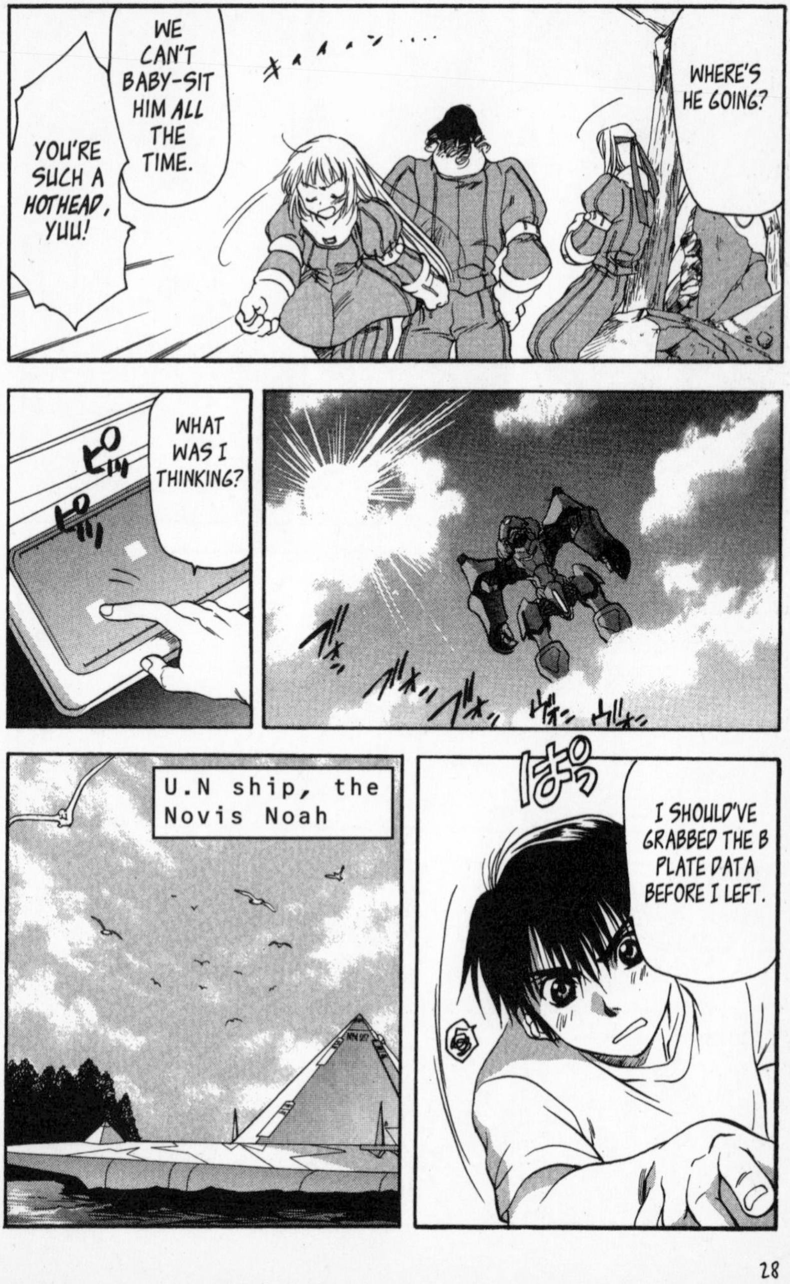
WHERE'S HE GOING?
WE CAN'T BABY-SIT HIM ALL THE TIME.
YOU'RE SUCH A HOTHEAD, YUU!
WHAT WAS I THINKING?
ぱっ
I SHOULD'VE GRABBED THE B PLATE DATA BEFORE I LEFT.
U.N ship, the Novis Noah

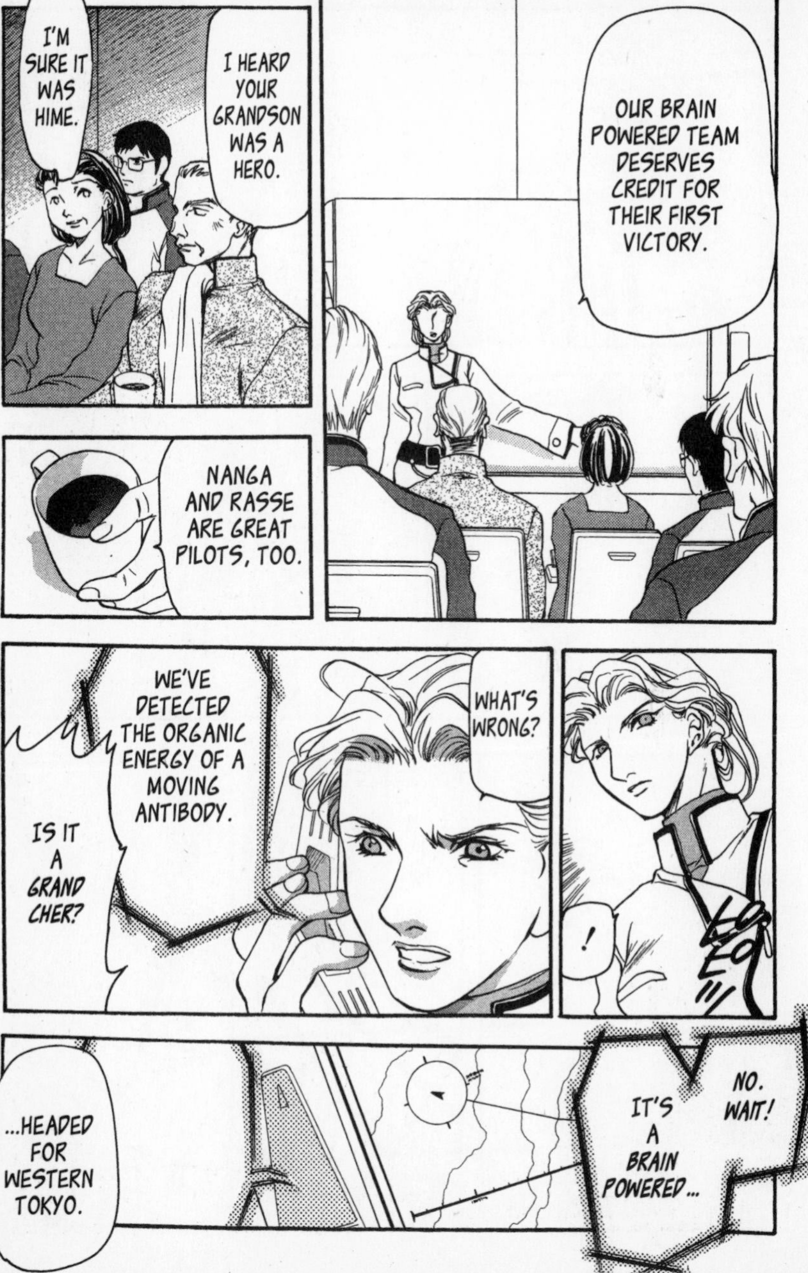
OUR BRAIN POWERED TEAM DESERVES CREDIT FOR THEIR FIRST VICTORY.
I HEARD YOUR GRANDSON WAS A HERO.
I'M SURE IT WAS HIME.
NANGA AND RASSE ARE GREAT PILOTS, TOO.
!
WHAT'S WRONG?
WE'VE DETECTED THE ORGANIC ENERGY OF A MOVING ANTIBODY.
IS IT A GRAND CHER?
NO. WAIT!
IT'S A BRAIN POWERED...
...HEADED FOR WESTERN TOKYO.

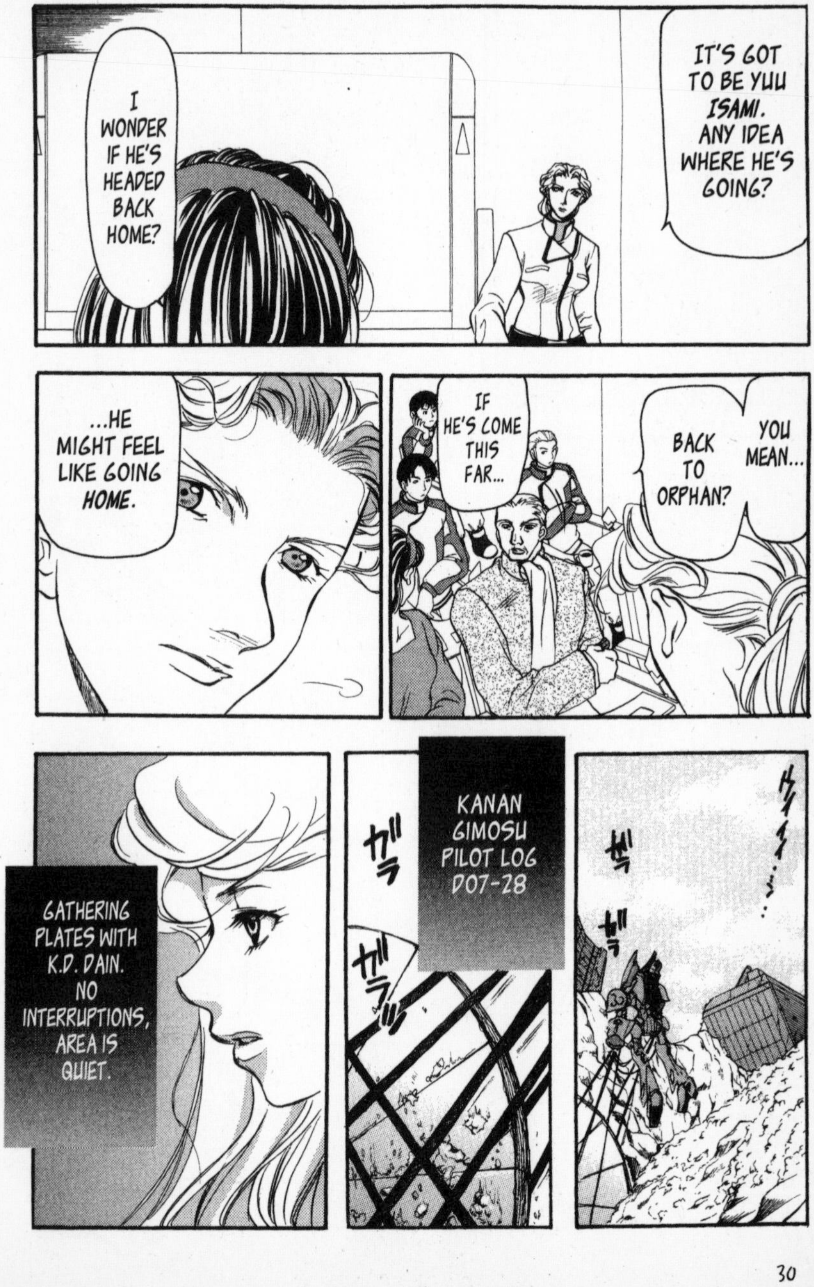
IT'S GOT TO BE YUU *ISAMI*. ANY IDEA WHERE HE'S GOING?
I WONDER IF HE'S HEADED BACK HOME?
YOU MEAN...
BACK TO ORPHAN?
IF HE'S COME THIS FAR...
...HE MIGHT FEEL LIKE GOING *HOME*.
KANAN GIMOSU PILOT LOG D07-28
ガラ
ガラッ
GATHERING PLATES WITH K.D. DAIN. NO INTERRUPTIONS, AREA IS QUIET.

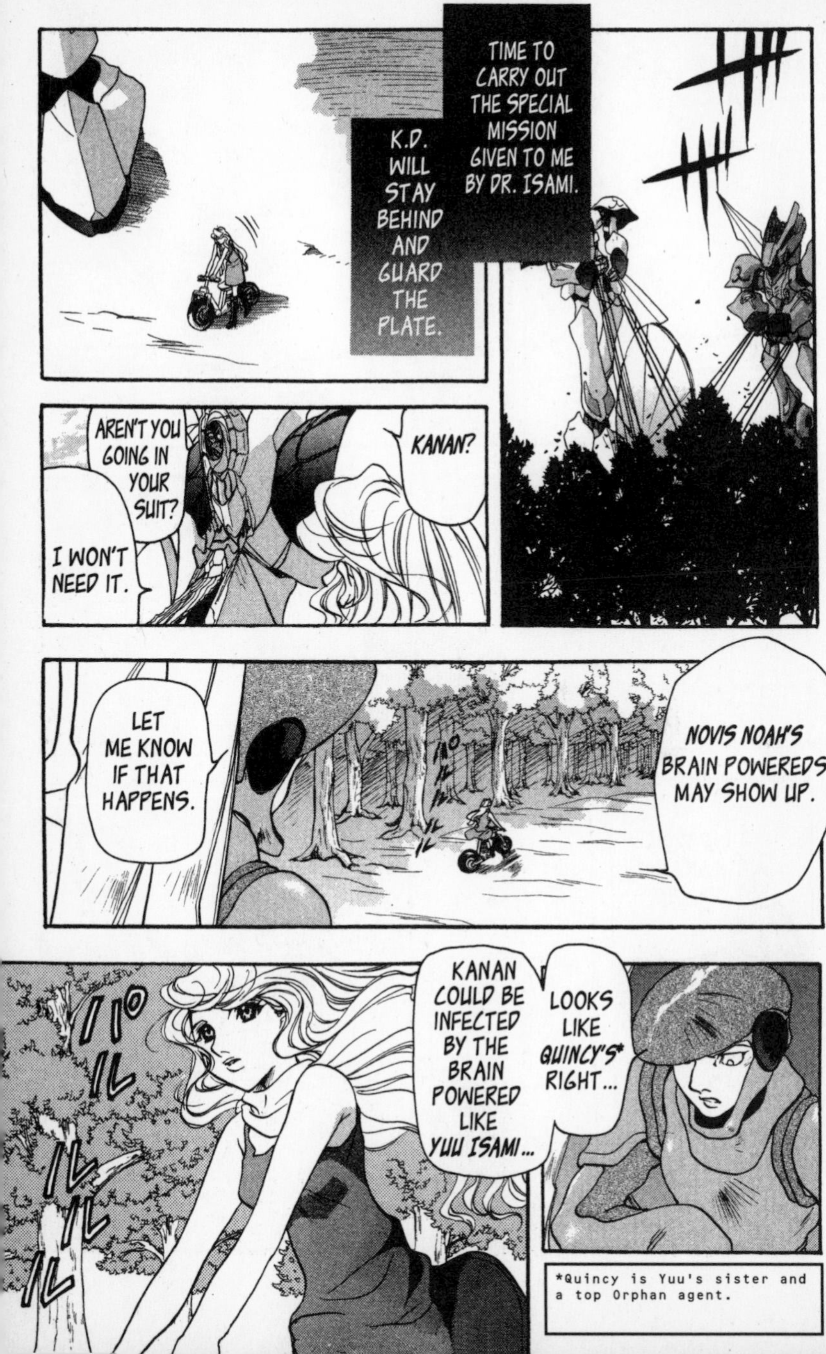
TIME TO CARRY OUT THE SPECIAL MISSION GIVEN TO ME BY DR. ISAMI.
K.D. WILL STAY BEHIND AND GUARD THE PLATE.
KANAN?
AREN'T YOU GOING IN YOUR SUIT?
I WON'T NEED IT.
NOVIS NOAH'S BRAIN POWEREDS MAY SHOW UP.
LET ME KNOW IF THAT HAPPENS.
LOOKS LIKE QUINCY'S* RIGHT...
KANAN COULD BE INFECTED BY THE BRAIN POWERED LIKE YUU ISAMI...
*Quincy is Yuu's sister and a top Orphan agent.

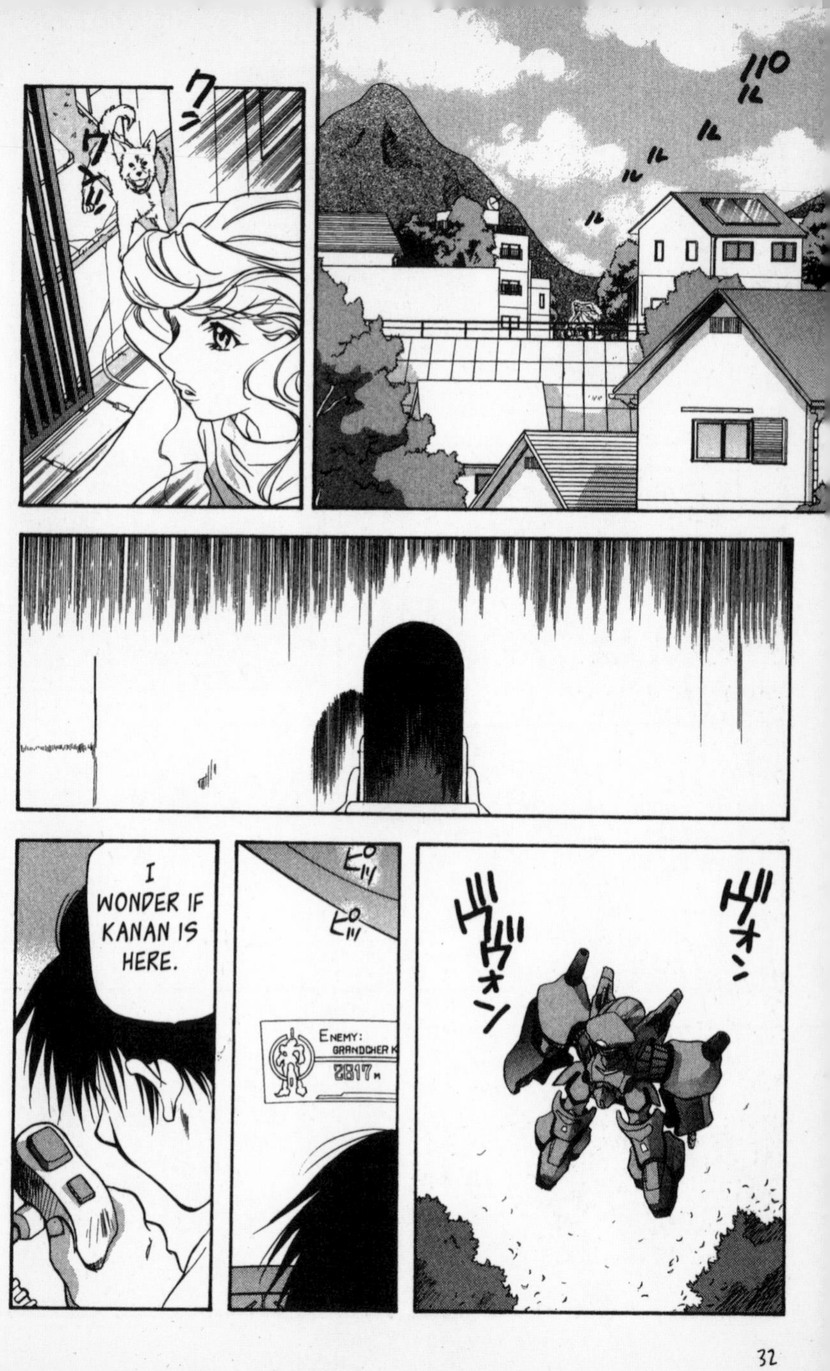
パルルルル
ヴォン
ヴヴォン
ENEMY:
GRANDCHER K
2817 M
I WONDER IF KANAN IS HERE.

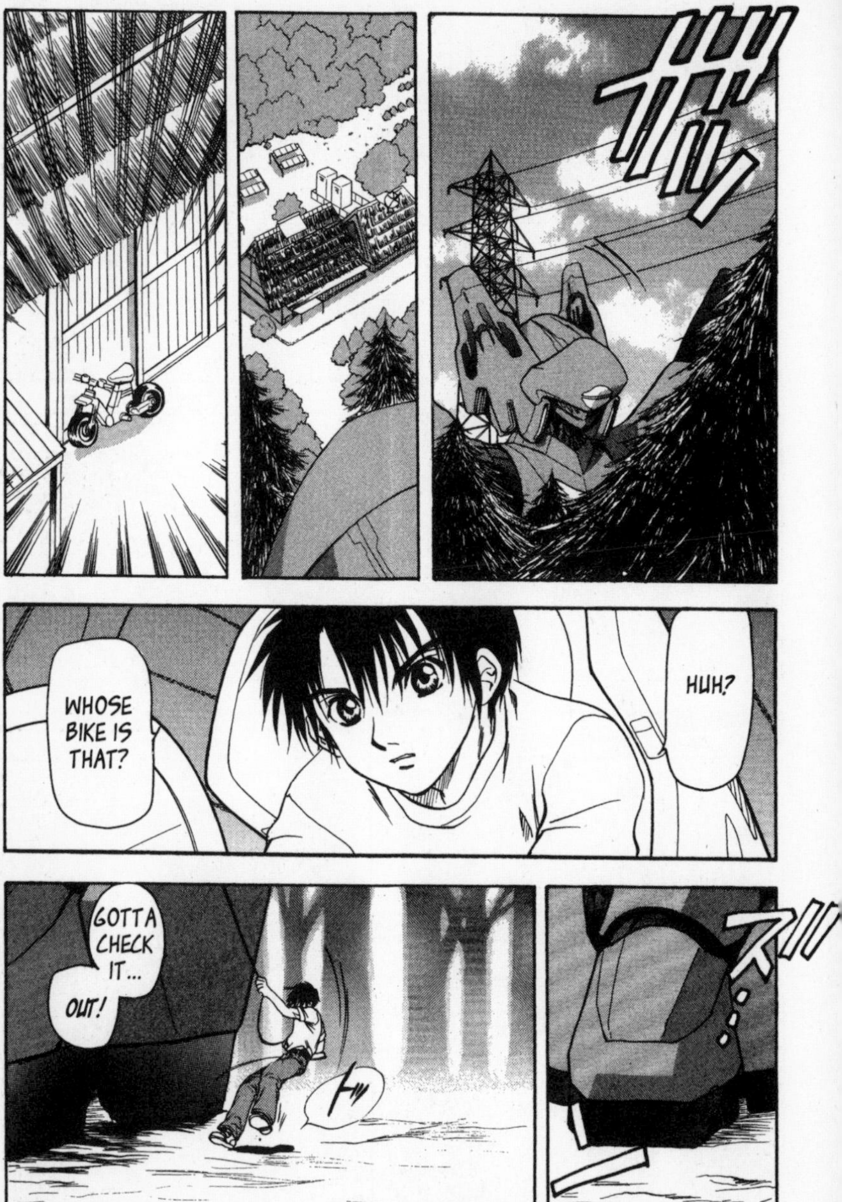
HUH?
WHOSE BIKE IS THAT?
GOTTA CHECK IT...
OUT!

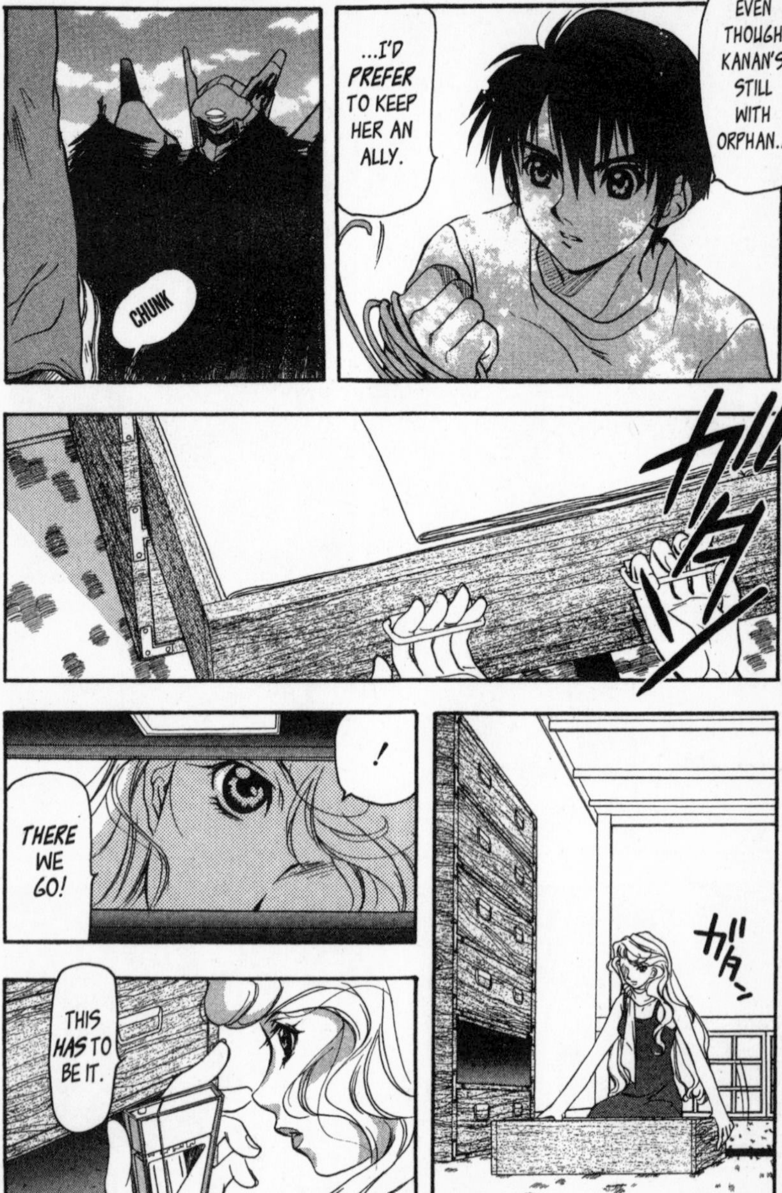
EVEN THOUGH KANAN'S STILL WITH ORPHAN...
...I'D PREFER TO KEEP HER AN ALLY.
CHUNK
ガタン
ガタ〜ン
!
THERE WE GO!
THIS HAS TO BE IT.

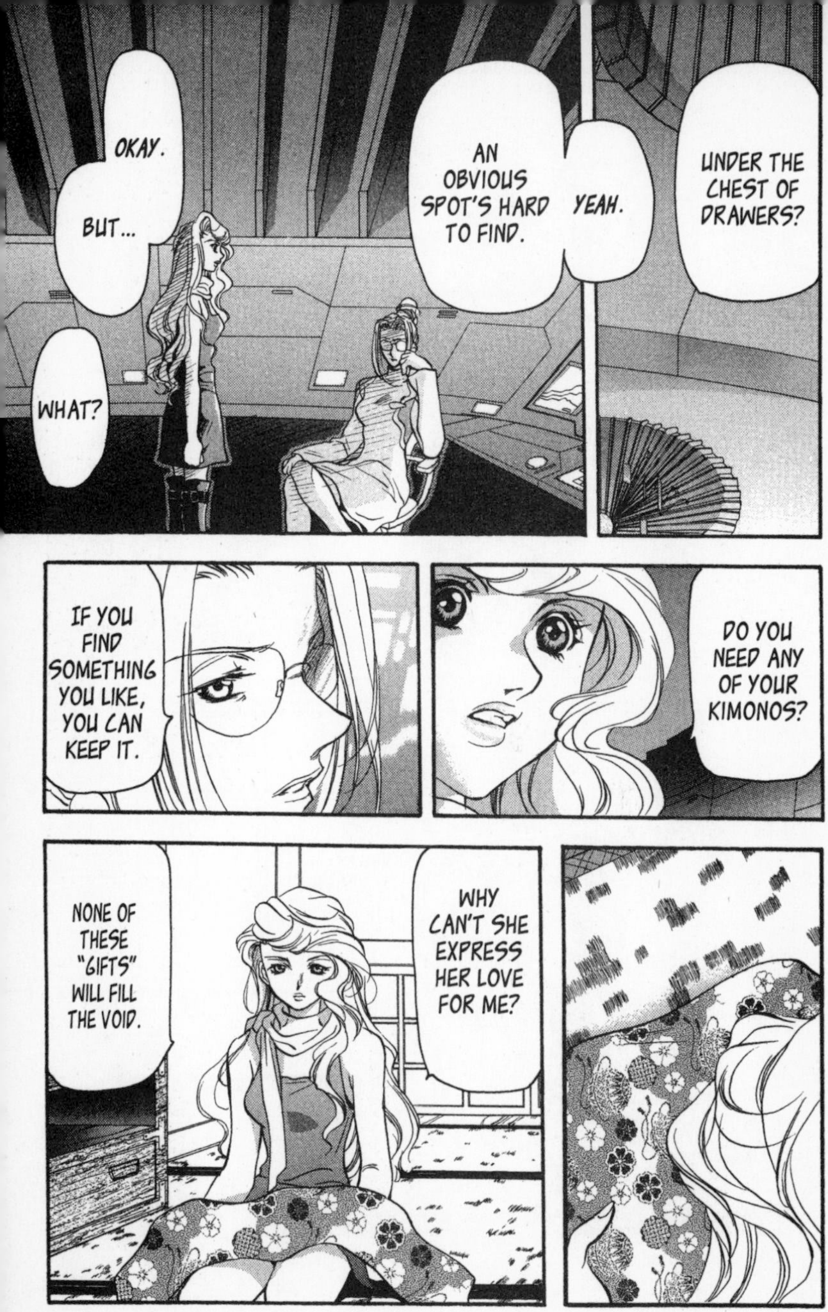
UNDER THE CHEST OF DRAWERS?
YEAH.
AN OBVIOUS SPOT'S HARD TO FIND.
OKAY.
BUT...
WHAT?
DO YOU NEED ANY OF YOUR KIMONOS?
IF YOU FIND SOMETHING YOU LIKE, YOU CAN KEEP IT.
WHY CAN'T SHE EXPRESS HER LOVE FOR ME?
NONE OF THESE "GIFTS" WILL FILL THE VOID.

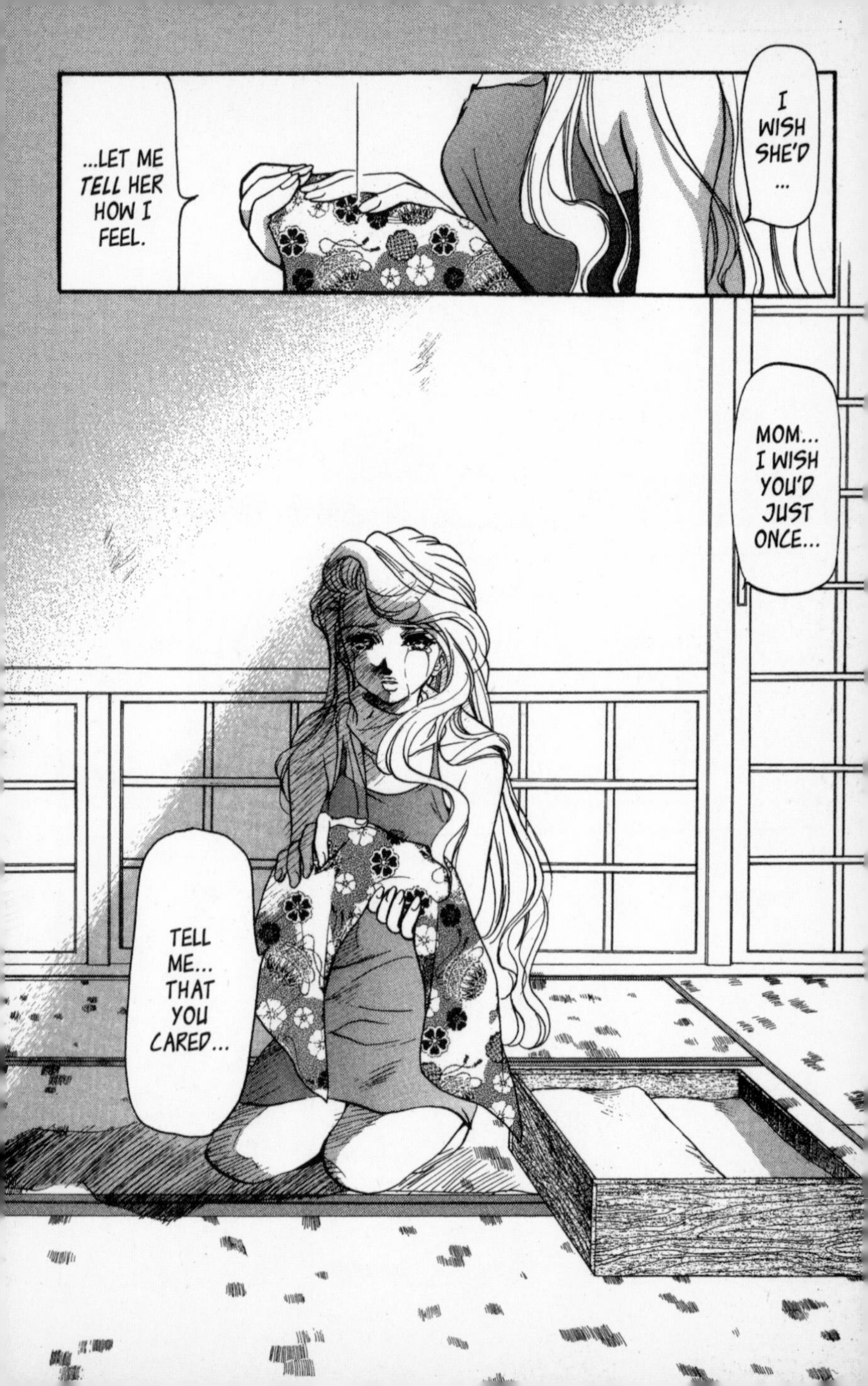
I WISH SHE'D ...
...LET ME TELL HER HOW I FEEL.
MOM... I WISH YOU'D JUST ONCE...
TELL ME... THAT YOU CARED...

REVIVAL 8: RECLAIMER

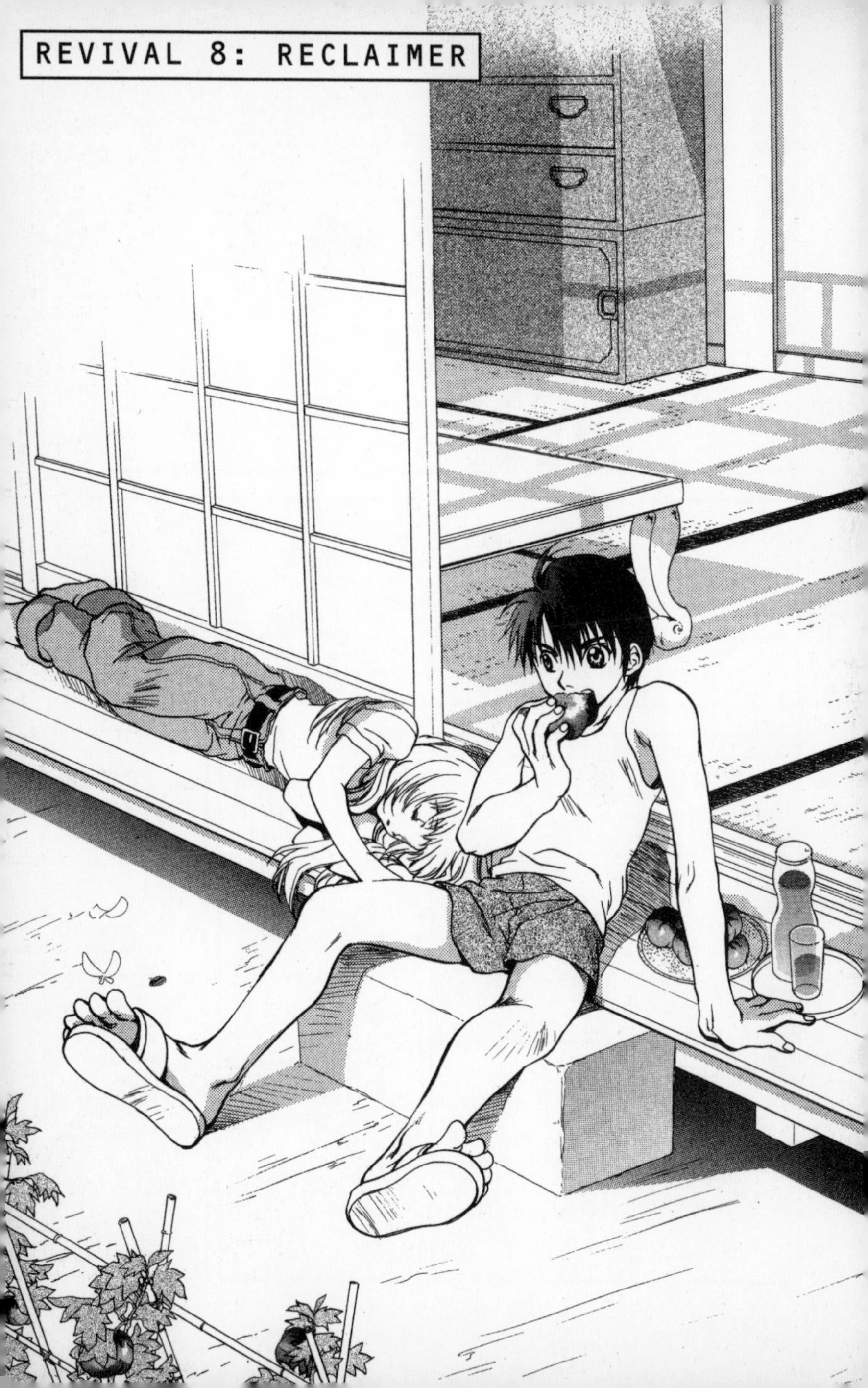

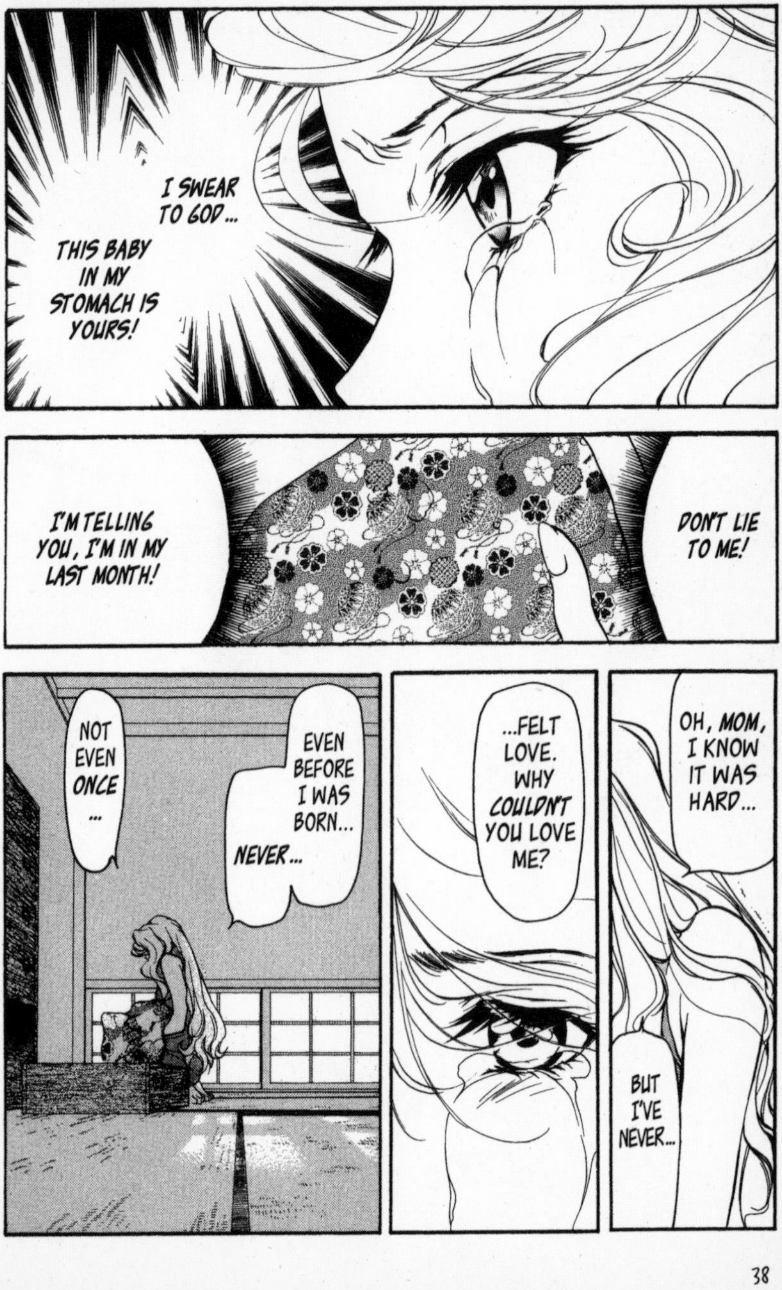
I SWEAR TO GOD...
THIS BABY IN MY STOMACH IS YOURS!
DON'T LIE TO ME!
I'M TELLING YOU, I'M IN MY LAST MONTH!
OH, MOM, I KNOW IT WAS HARD...
BUT I'VE NEVER...
...FELT LOVE. WHY COULDN'T YOU LOVE ME?
EVEN BEFORE I WAS BORN...
NEVER...
NOT EVEN ONCE...

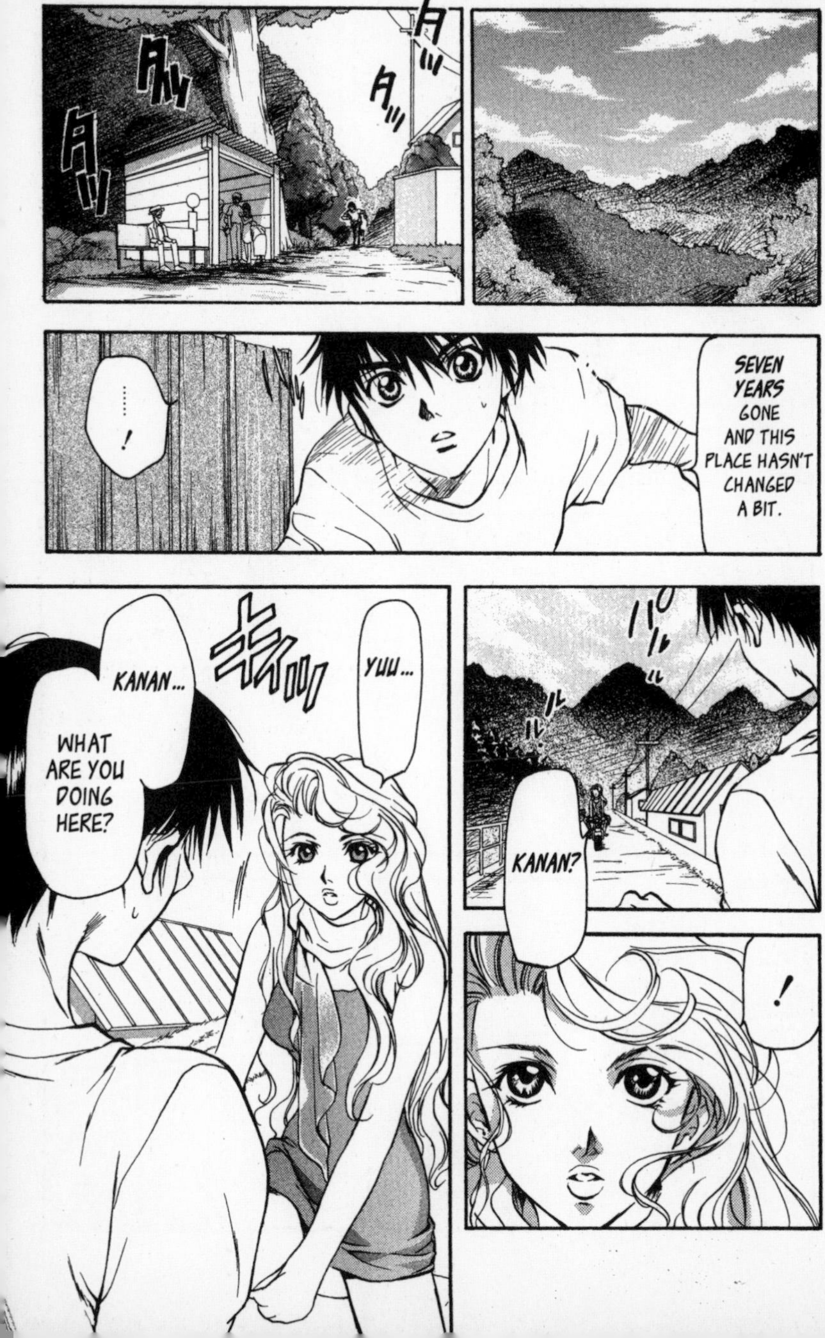
SEVEN YEARS GONE AND THIS PLACE HASN'T CHANGED A BIT.
......!
KANAN?
!
YUU...
KANAN...
WHAT ARE YOU DOING HERE?

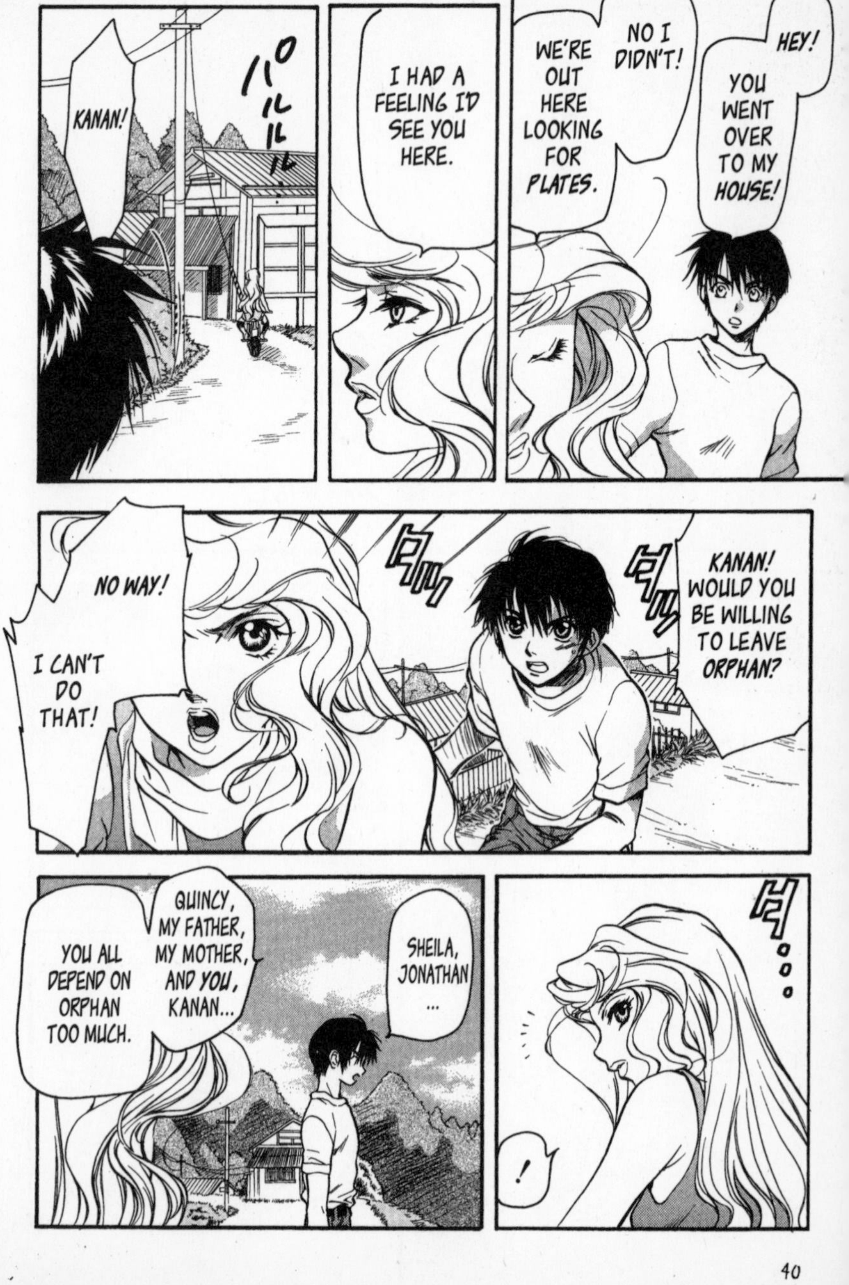
HEY!
YOU WENT OVER TO MY HOUSE!
NO I DIDN'T!
WE'RE OUT HERE LOOKING FOR PLATES.
I HAD A FEELING I'D SEE YOU HERE.
パルルル
KANAN!
KANAN! WOULD YOU BE WILLING TO LEAVE ORPHAN?
NO WAY!
I CAN'T DO THAT!
!
SHEILA, JONATHAN ...
QUINCY, MY FATHER, MY MOTHER, AND YOU, KANAN...
YOU ALL DEPEND ON ORPHAN TOO MUCH.

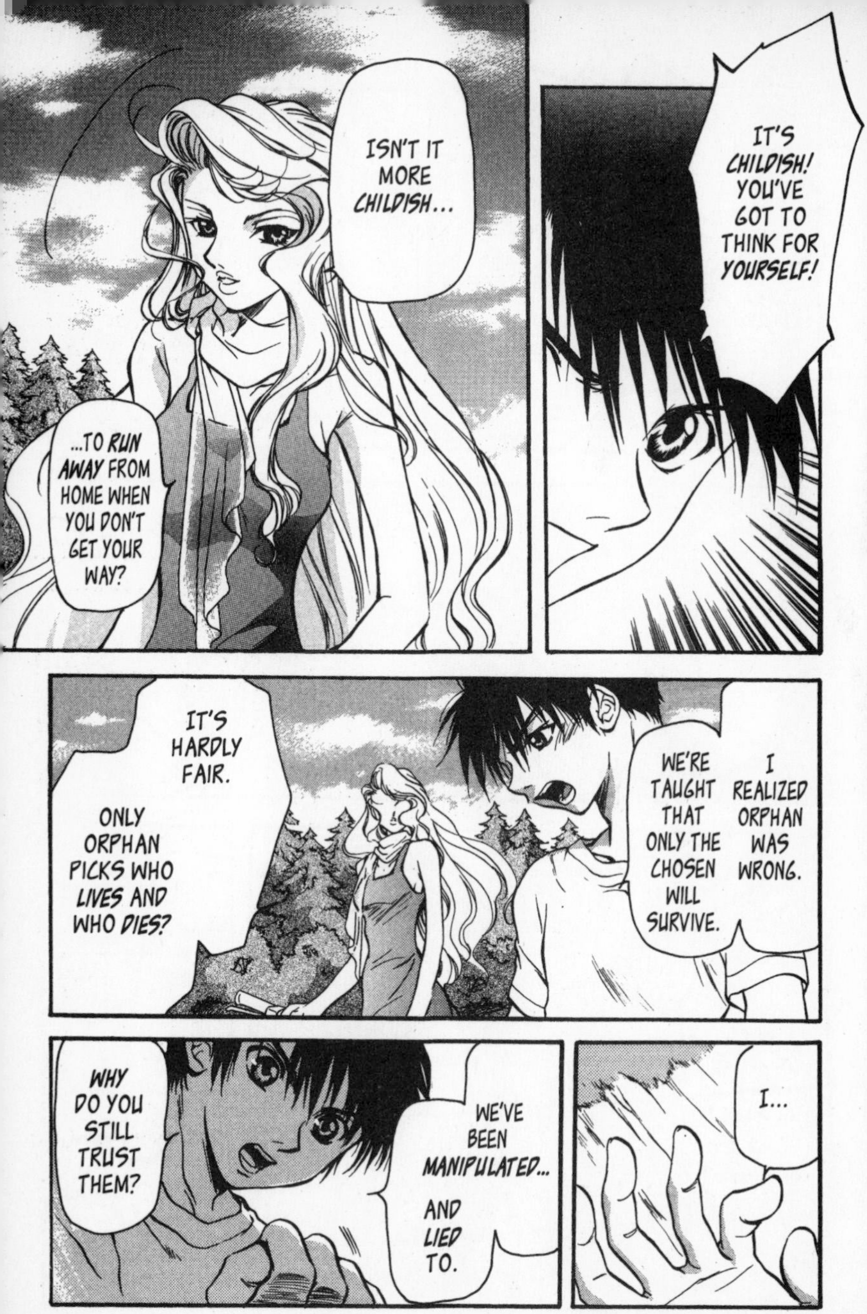
IT'S CHILDISH! YOU'VE GOT TO THINK FOR YOURSELF!
ISN'T IT MORE CHILDISH...
...TO RUN AWAY FROM HOME WHEN YOU DON'T GET YOUR WAY?
I REALIZED ORPHAN WAS WRONG.
WE'RE TAUGHT THAT ONLY THE CHOSEN WILL SURVIVE.
IT'S HARDLY FAIR.
ONLY ORPHAN PICKS WHO LIVES AND WHO DIES?
I...
WE'VE BEEN MANIPULATED...
AND LIED TO.
WHY DO YOU STILL TRUST THEM?

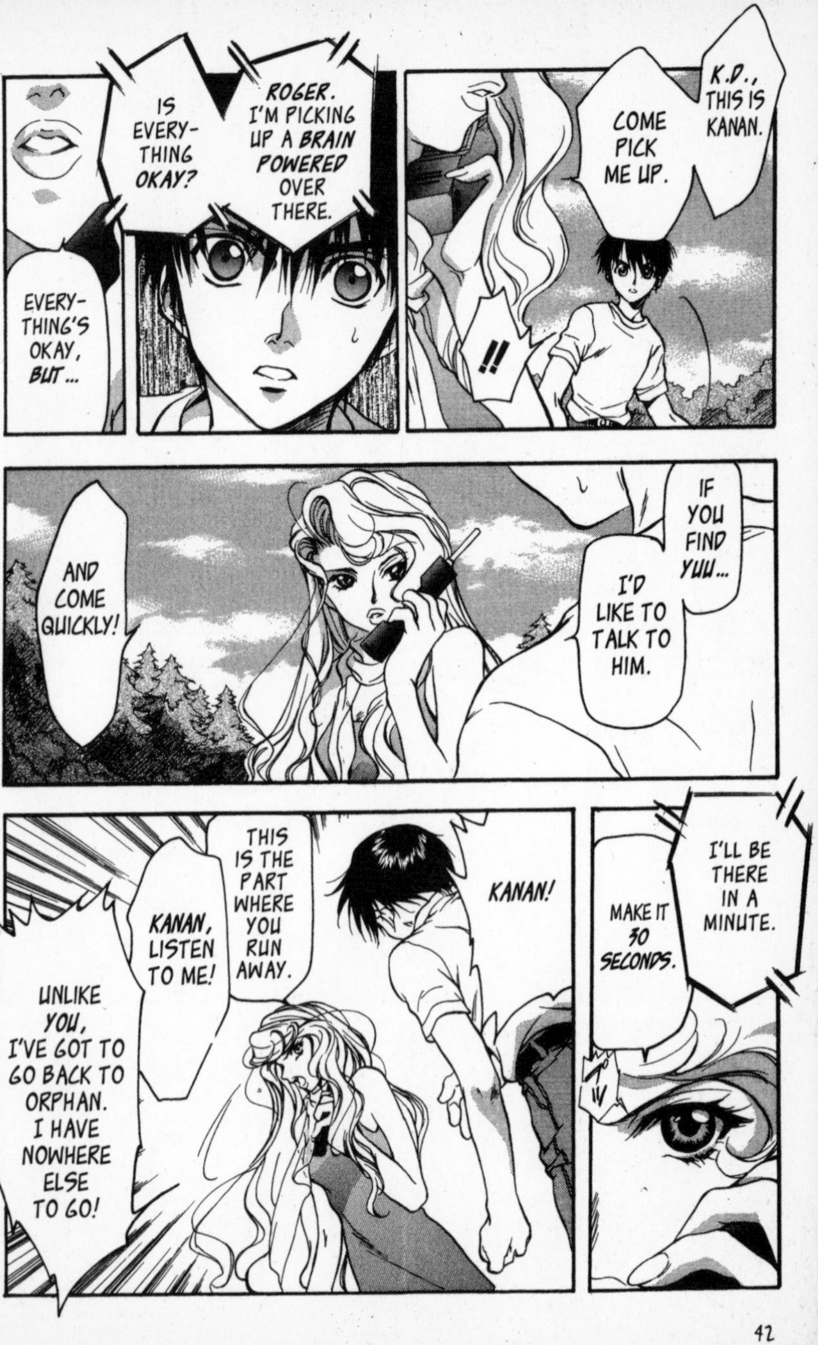
K.D., THIS IS KANAN.
COME PICK ME UP.
!!
ROGER. I'M PICKING UP A *BRAIN POWERED* OVER THERE.
IS EVERYTHING *OKAY?*
EVERYTHING'S OKAY, *BUT...*
IF YOU FIND *YUU...*
I'D LIKE TO TALK TO HIM.
AND COME QUICKLY!
I'LL BE THERE IN A MINUTE.
MAKE IT *30 SECONDS.*
KANAN!
THIS IS THE PART WHERE YOU RUN AWAY.
KANAN, LISTEN TO ME!
UNLIKE *YOU,* I'VE GOT TO GO BACK TO ORPHAN. I HAVE NOWHERE ELSE TO GO!

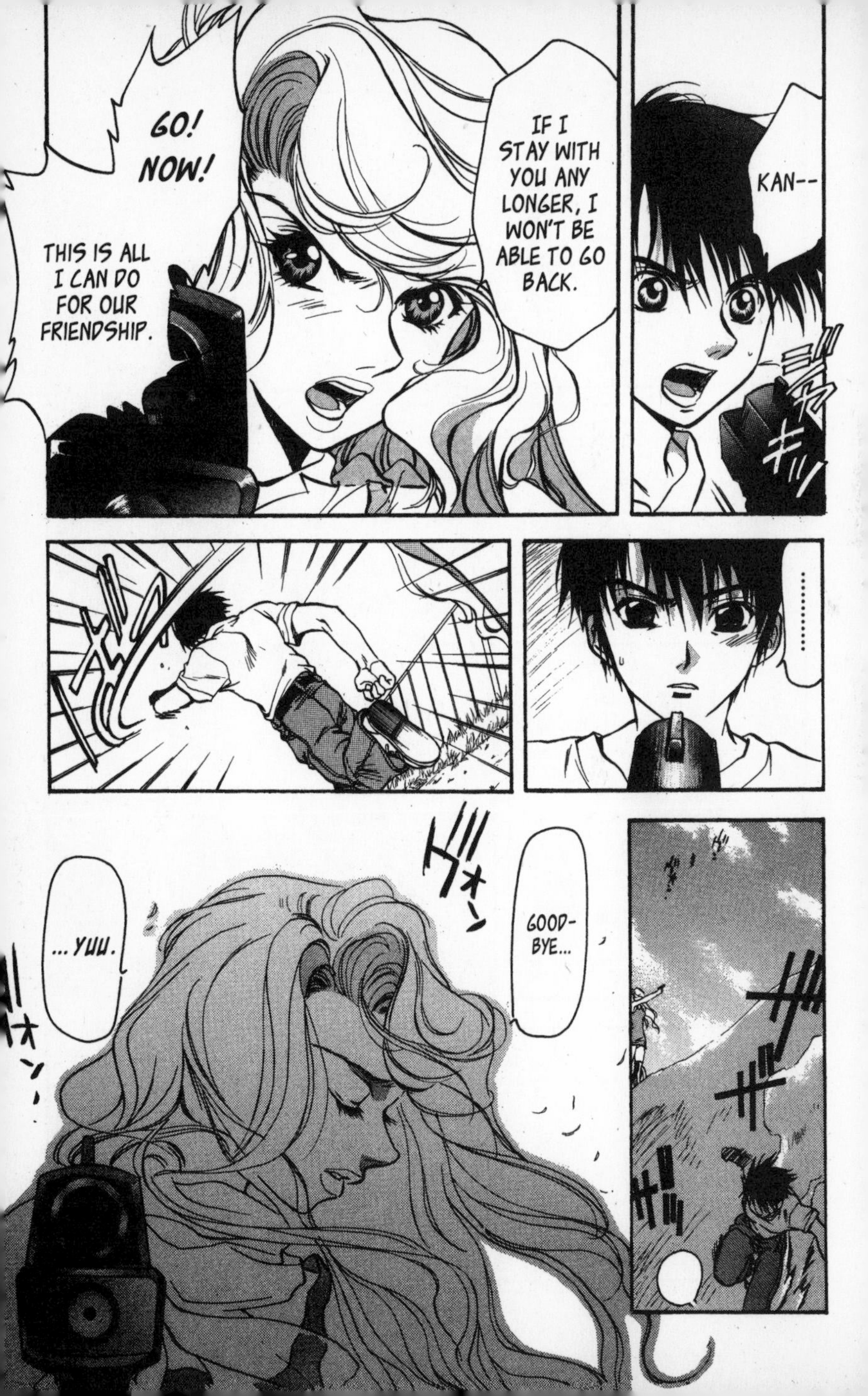
KAN--
IF I STAY WITH YOU ANY LONGER, I WON'T BE ABLE TO GO BACK.
GO! NOW!
THIS IS ALL I CAN DO FOR OUR FRIENDSHIP.
......
GOOD-BYE...
...YUU.

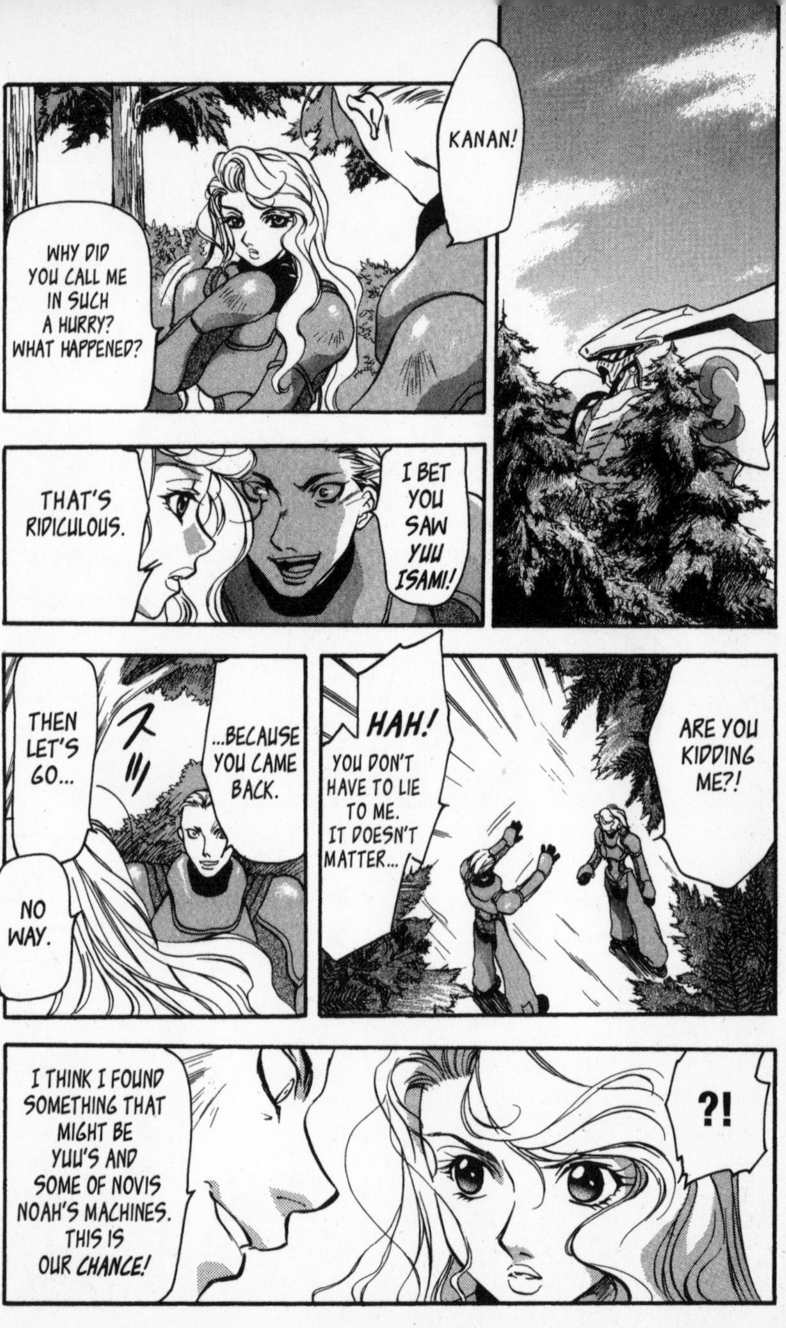
KANAN!
WHY DID YOU CALL ME IN SUCH A HURRY? WHAT HAPPENED?
I BET YOU SAW YUU ISAMI!
THAT'S RIDICULOUS.
ARE YOU KIDDING ME?!
HAH! YOU DON'T HAVE TO LIE TO ME. IT DOESN'T MATTER...
...BECAUSE YOU CAME BACK.
THEN LET'S GO...
NO WAY.
?!
I THINK I FOUND SOMETHING THAT MIGHT BE YUU'S AND SOME OF NOVIS NOAH'S MACHINES. THIS IS OUR *CHANCE!*

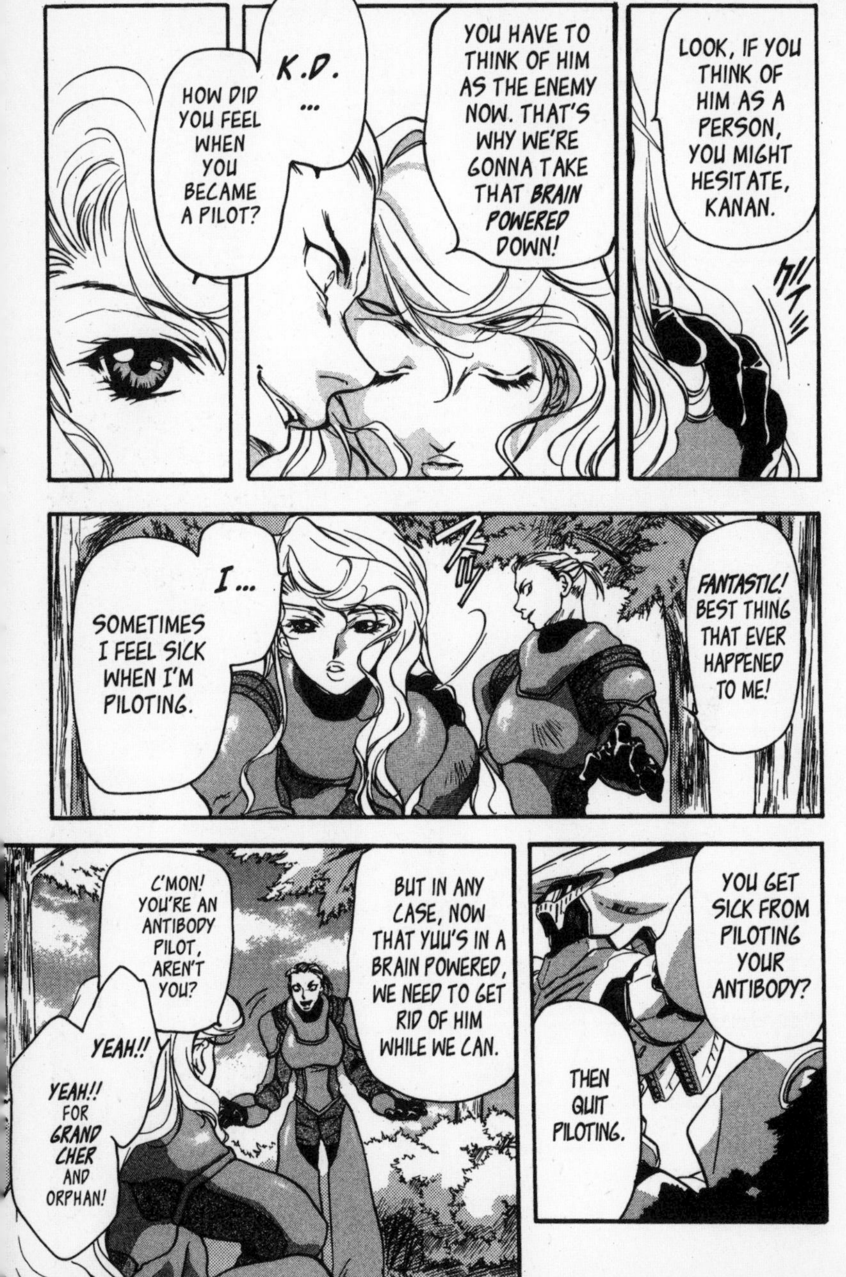
LOOK, IF YOU THINK OF HIM AS A PERSON, YOU MIGHT HESITATE, KANAN.
YOU HAVE TO THINK OF HIM AS THE ENEMY NOW. THAT'S WHY WE'RE GONNA TAKE THAT *BRAIN POWERED* DOWN!
K.D. ...
HOW DID YOU FEEL WHEN YOU BECAME A PILOT?
FANTASTIC! BEST THING THAT EVER HAPPENED TO ME!
I...
SOMETIMES I FEEL SICK WHEN I'M PILOTING.
YOU GET SICK FROM PILOTING YOUR ANTIBODY?
THEN QUIT PILOTING.
BUT IN ANY CASE, NOW THAT YUU'S IN A BRAIN POWERED, WE NEED TO GET RID OF HIM WHILE WE CAN.
C'MON! YOU'RE AN ANTIBODY PILOT, AREN'T YOU?
YEAH!!
YEAH!! FOR *GRAND CHER* AND ORPHAN!

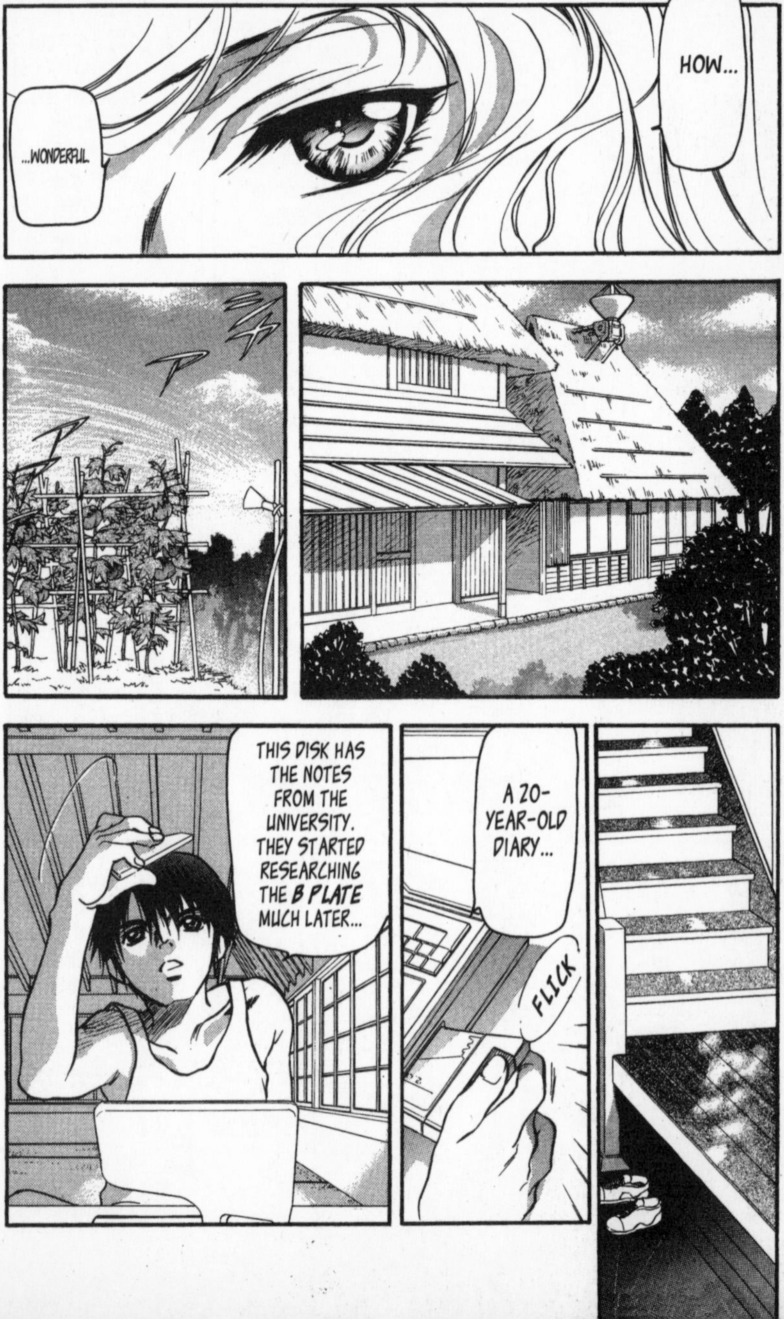
HOW...
...WONDERFUL.
A 20-YEAR-OLD DIARY...
FLICK
THIS DISK HAS THE NOTES FROM THE UNIVERSITY. THEY STARTED RESEARCHING THE B PLATE MUCH LATER...

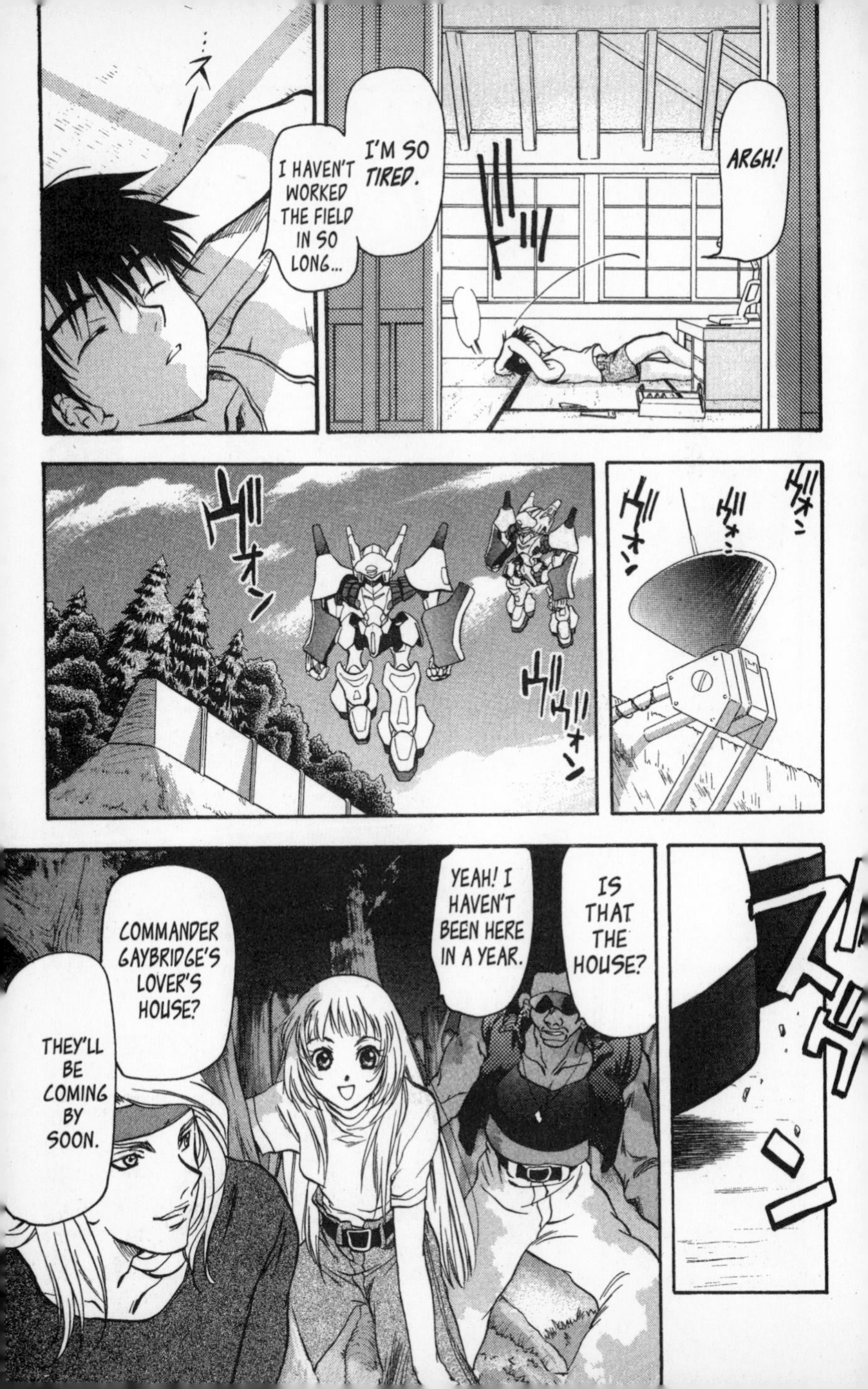
ARGH!
I'M SO TIRED.
I HAVEN'T WORKED THE FIELD IN SO LONG...
IS THAT THE HOUSE?
YEAH! I HAVEN'T BEEN HERE IN A YEAR.
COMMANDER GAYBRIDGE'S LOVER'S HOUSE?
THEY'LL BE COMING BY SOON.

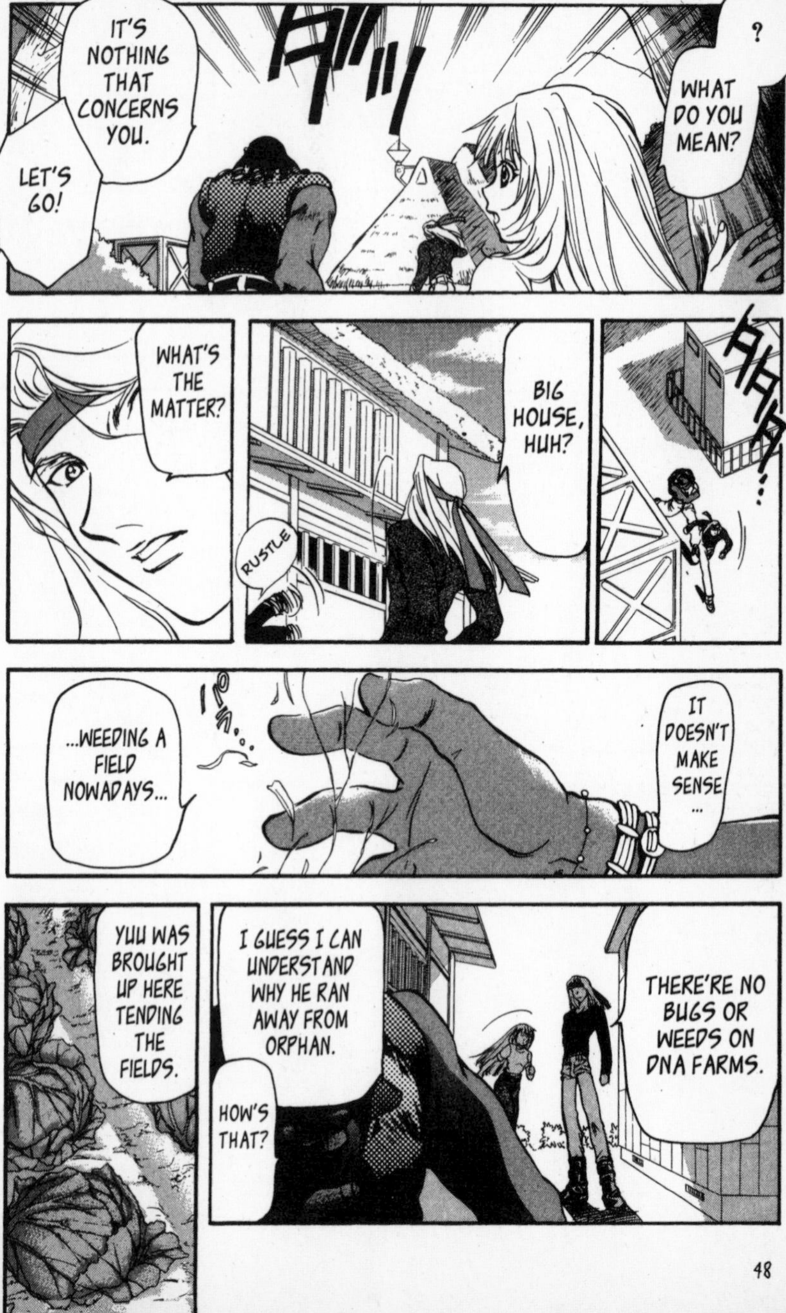
?
WHAT DO YOU MEAN?
IT'S NOTHING THAT CONCERNS YOU.
LET'S GO!
BIG HOUSE, HUH?
RUSTLE
WHAT'S THE MATTER?
IT DOESN'T MAKE SENSE...
...WEEDING A FIELD NOWADAYS...
THERE'RE NO BUGS OR WEEDS ON DNA FARMS.
I GUESS I CAN UNDERSTAND WHY HE RAN AWAY FROM ORPHAN.
HOW'S THAT?
YUU WAS BROUGHT UP HERE TENDING THE FIELDS.

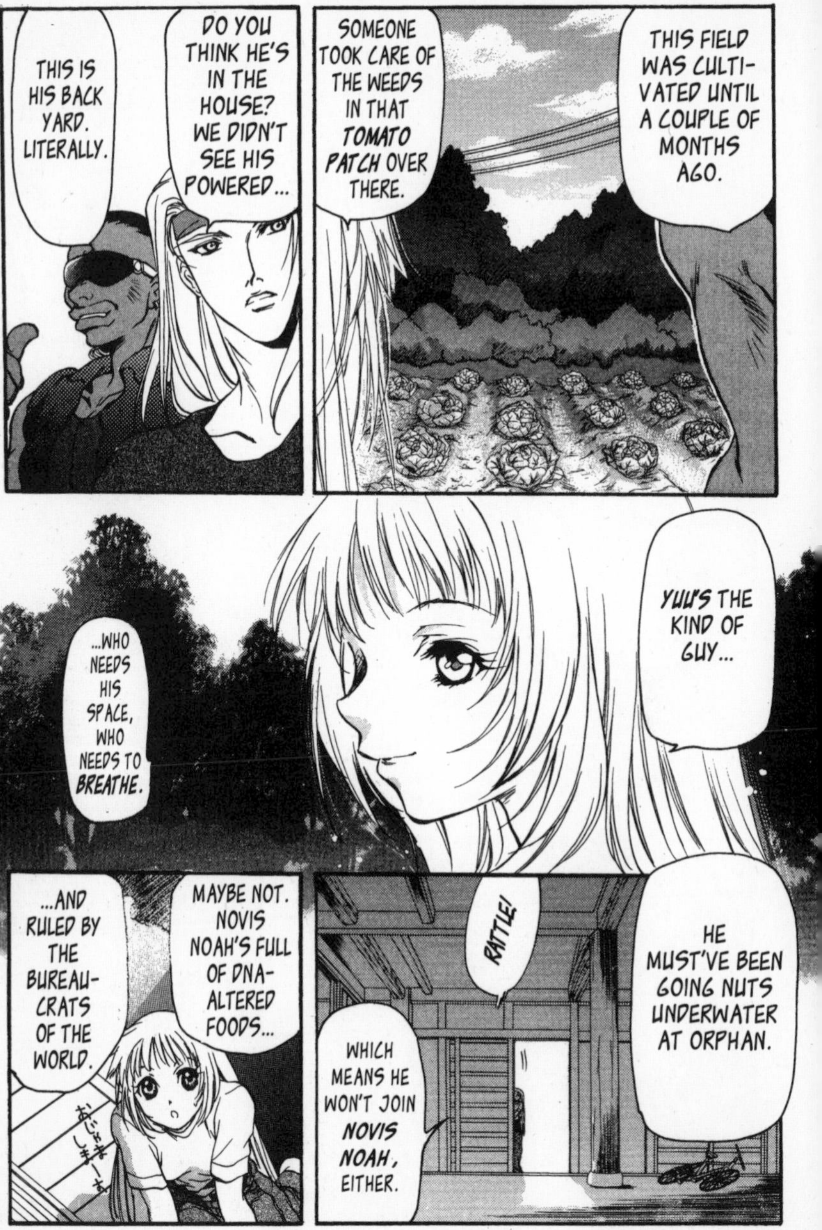
THIS FIELD WAS CULTIVATED UNTIL A COUPLE OF MONTHS AGO.
SOMEONE TOOK CARE OF THE WEEDS IN THAT TOMATO PATCH OVER THERE.
DO YOU THINK HE'S IN THE HOUSE? WE DIDN'T SEE HIS POWERED...
THIS IS HIS BACK YARD. LITERALLY.
YUU'S THE KIND OF GUY...
...WHO NEEDS HIS SPACE, WHO NEEDS TO BREATHE.
HE MUST'VE BEEN GOING NUTS UNDERWATER AT ORPHAN.
RATTLE!
WHICH MEANS HE WON'T JOIN NOVIS NOAH, EITHER.
MAYBE NOT. NOVIS NOAH'S FULL OF DNA-ALTERED FOODS...
...AND RULED BY THE BUREAUCRATS OF THE WORLD.
おじゃましまーす

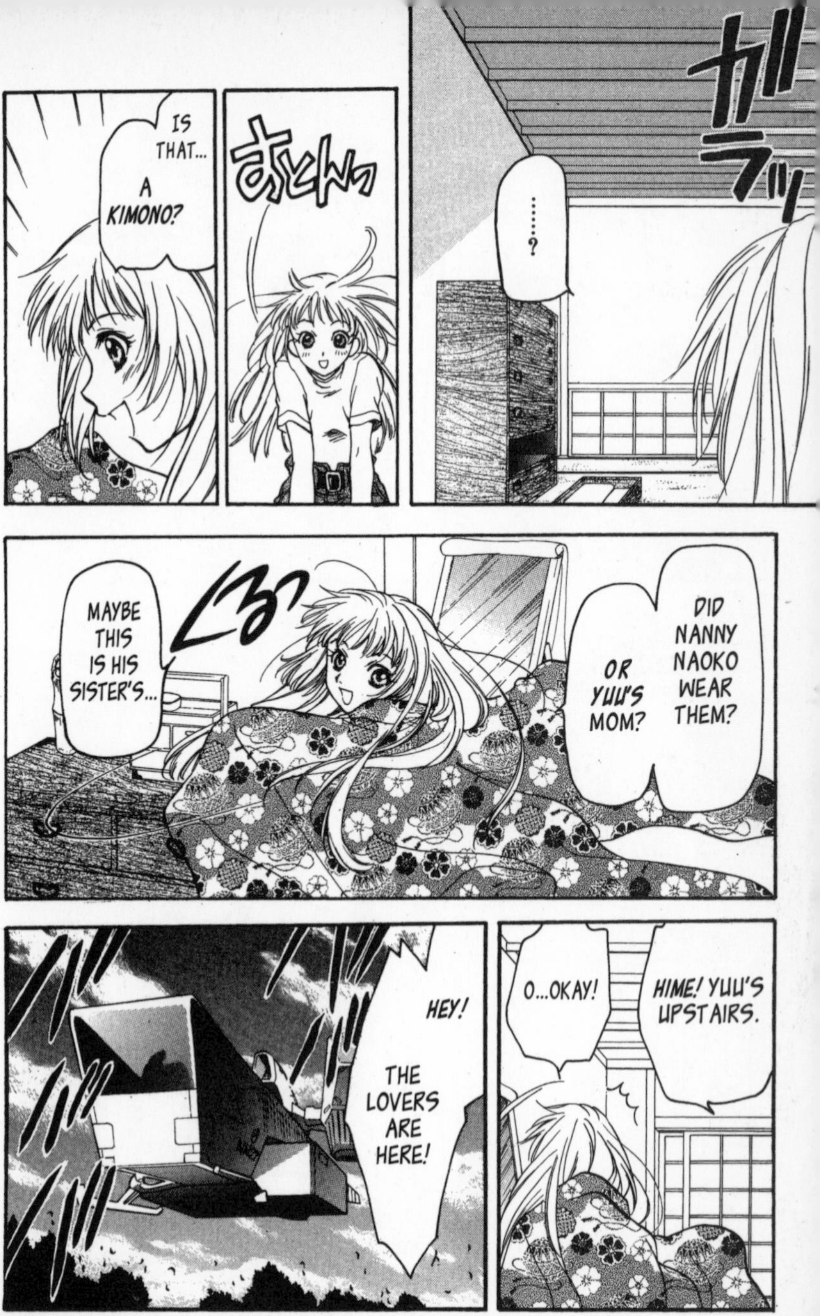
ガラッ
......?
IS THAT... A KIMONO?
DID NANNY NAOKO WEAR THEM?
OR YUU'S MOM?
MAYBE THIS IS HIS SISTER'S...
HIME! YUU'S UPSTAIRS.
O...OKAY!
HEY!
THE LOVERS ARE HERE!

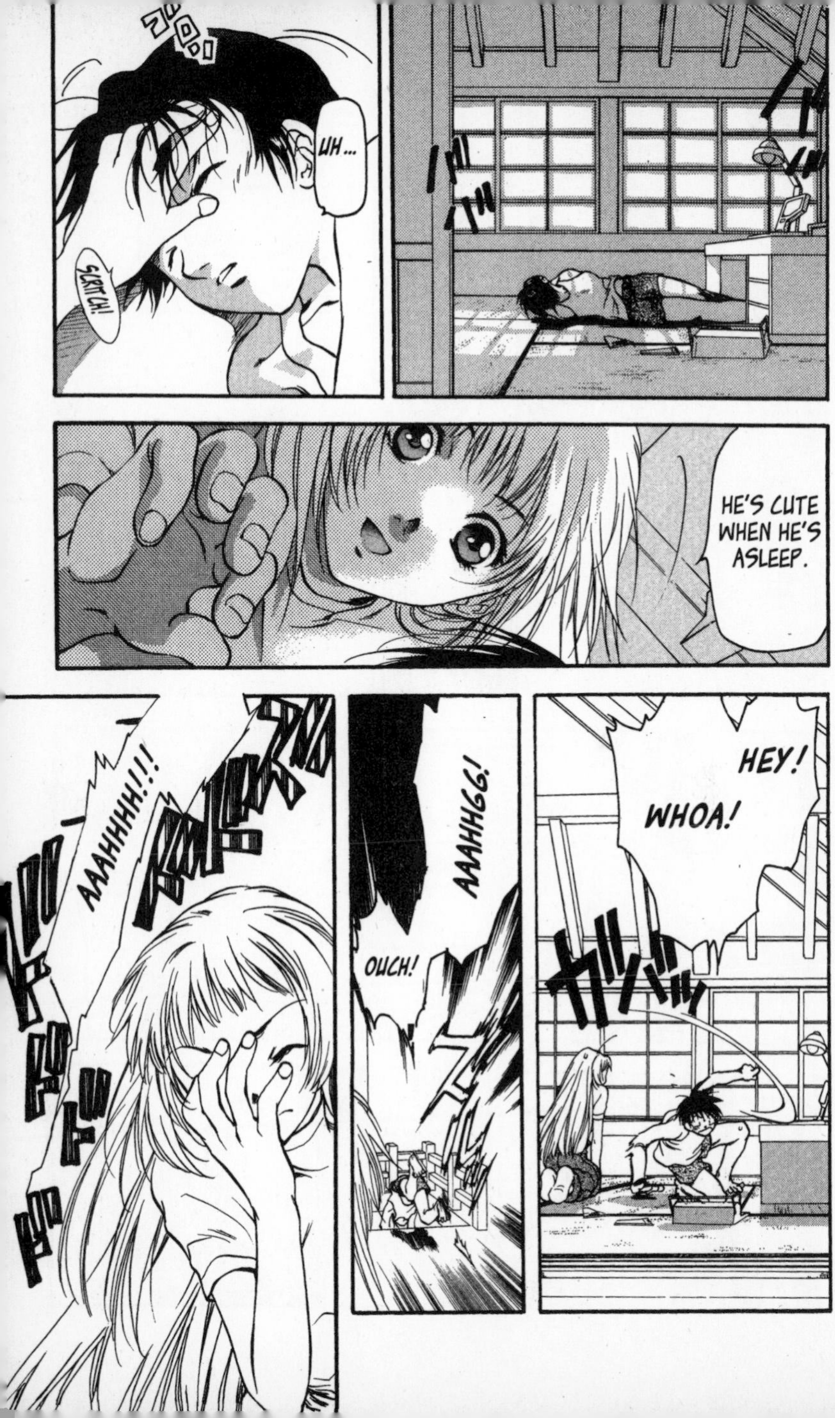
UH...
SCRITCH!
HE'S CUTE WHEN HE'S ASLEEP.
HEY!
WHOA!
AAAAHHGG!
OUCH!
AAAHHHH!!!

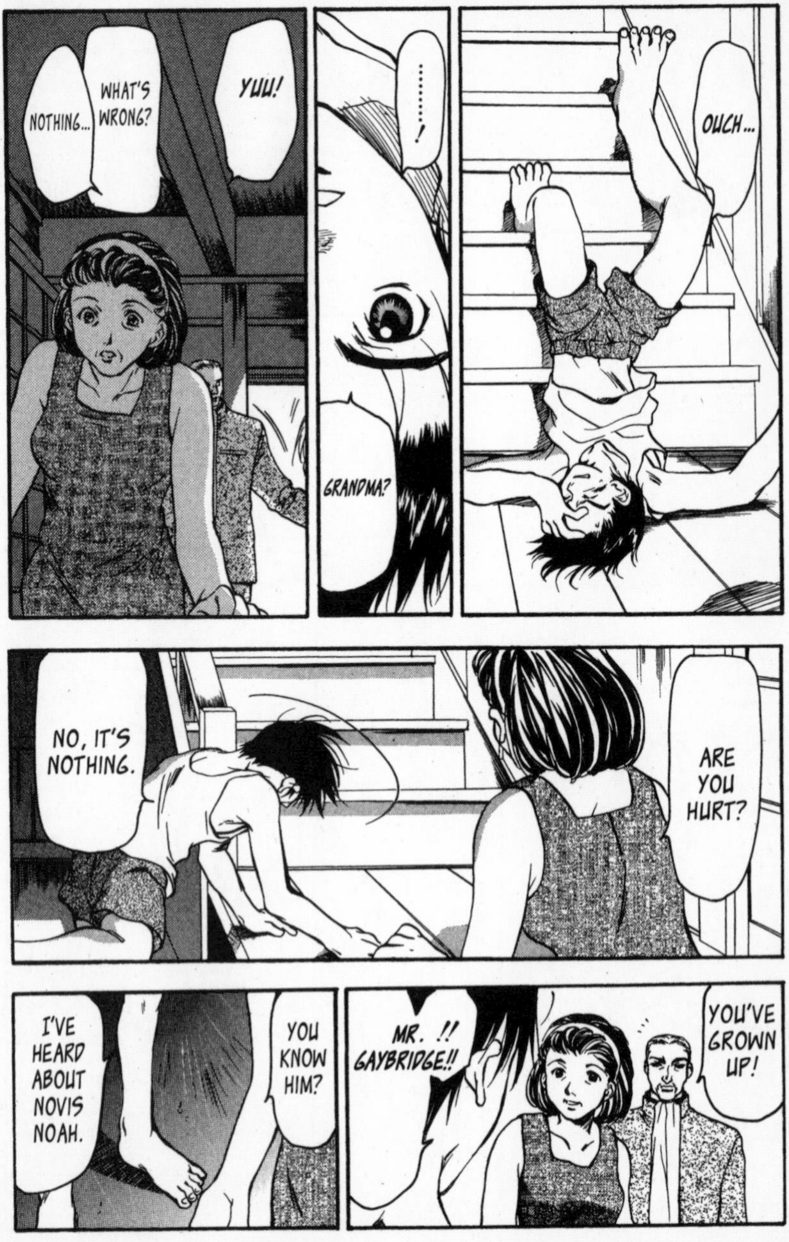
OUCH...
......!
GRANDMA?
YUU!
WHAT'S WRONG?
NOTHING...
ARE YOU HURT?
NO, IT'S NOTHING.
YOU'VE GROWN UP!
MR. !! GAYBRIDGE!!
YOU KNOW HIM?
I'VE HEARD ABOUT NOVIS NOAH.

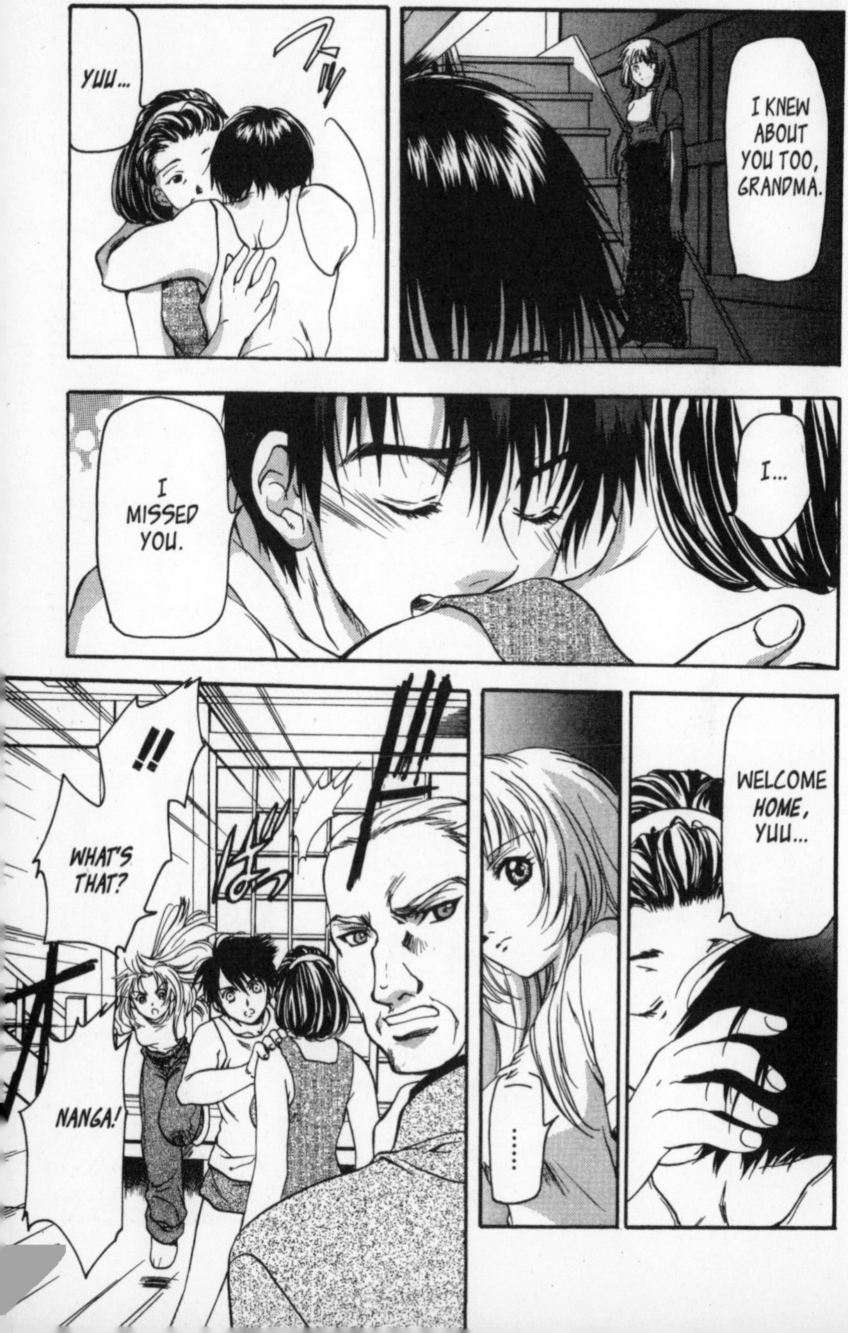
I KNEW ABOUT YOU TOO, GRANDMA.
YUU...
I...
I MISSED YOU.
WELCOME HOME, YUU...
......
!!
WHAT'S THAT?
NANGA!

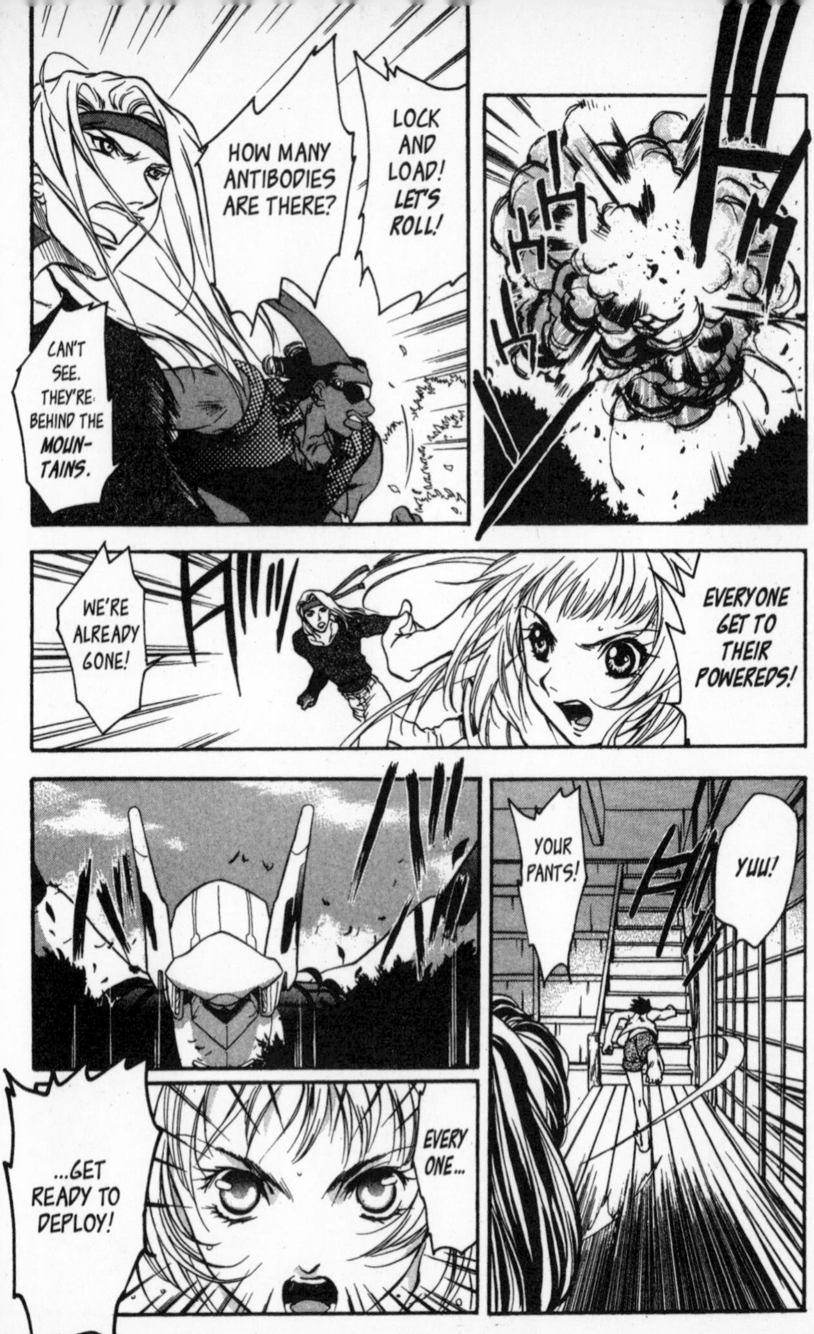
LOCK AND LOAD! LET'S ROLL!
HOW MANY ANTIBODIES ARE THERE?
CAN'T SEE. THEY'RE BEHIND THE MOUN-TAINS.
EVERYONE GET TO THEIR POWEREDS!
WE'RE ALREADY GONE!
YUU!
YOUR PANTS!
EVERY ONE...
...GET READY TO DEPLOY!

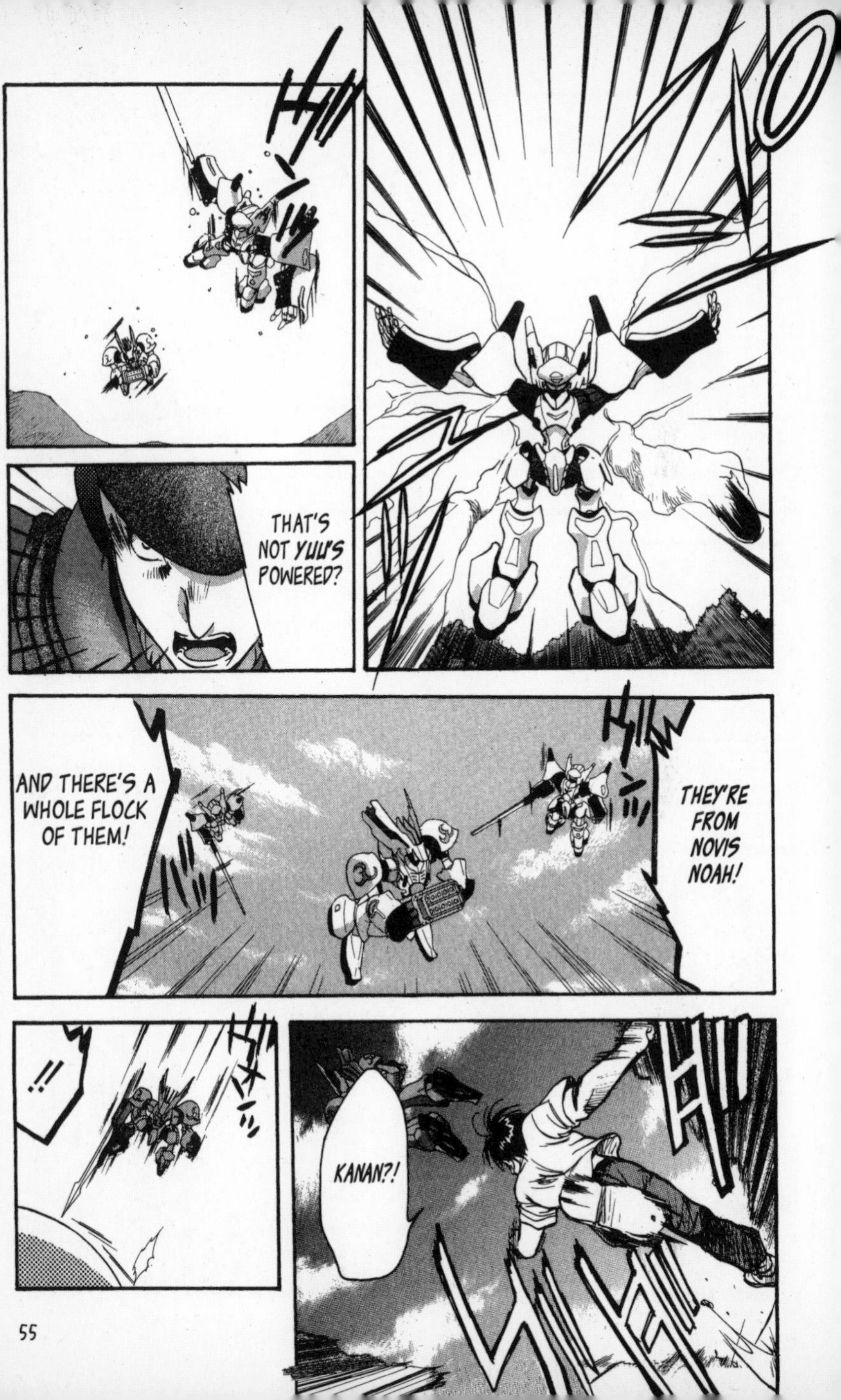
THAT'S NOT *YUU'S* POWERED?
THEY'RE FROM NOVIS NOAH!
AND THERE'S A WHOLE FLOCK OF THEM!
KANAN?!
!!

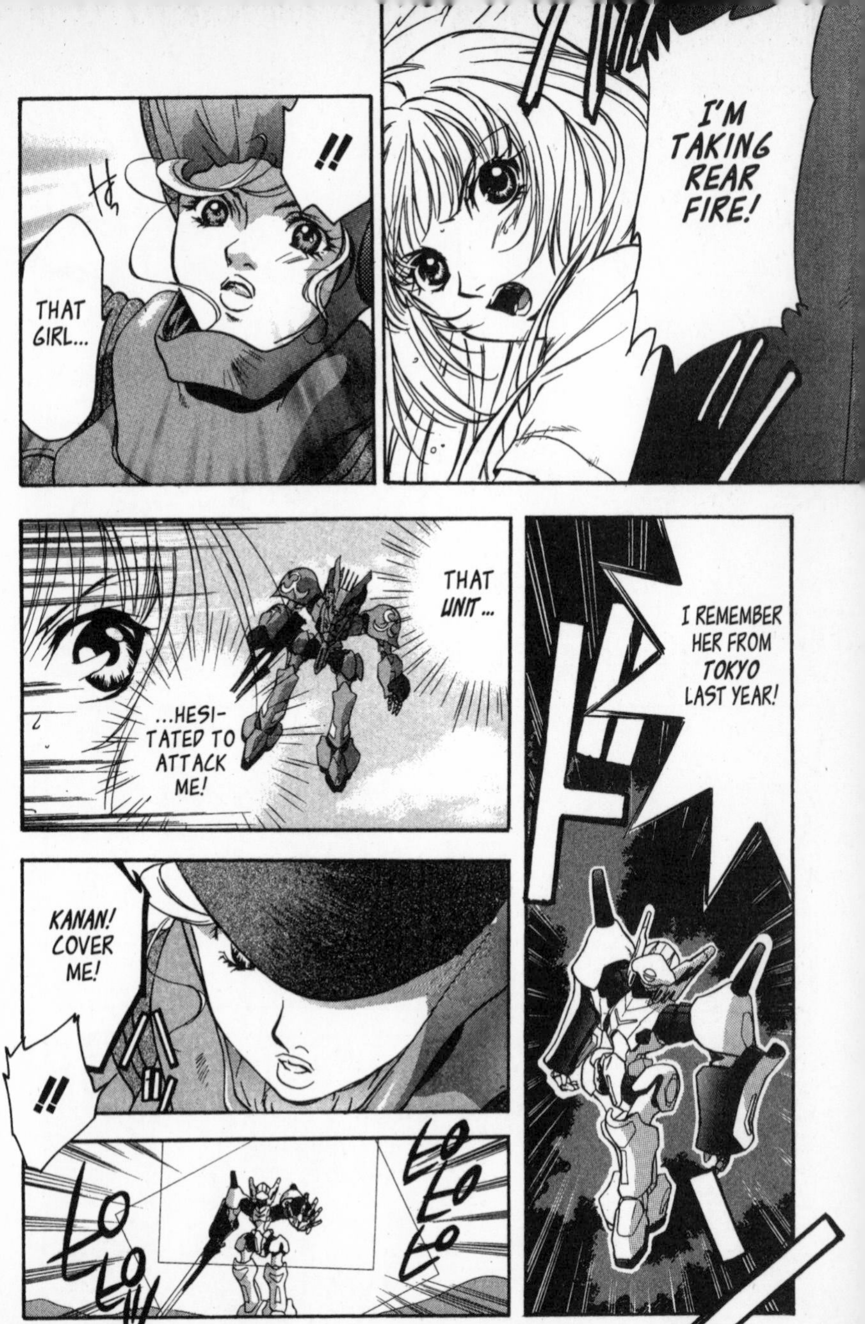
I'M TAKING REAR FIRE!
!!
THAT GIRL...
I REMEMBER HER FROM TOKYO LAST YEAR!
THAT UNIT...
...HESI-TATED TO ATTACK ME!
KANAN! COVER ME!
!!

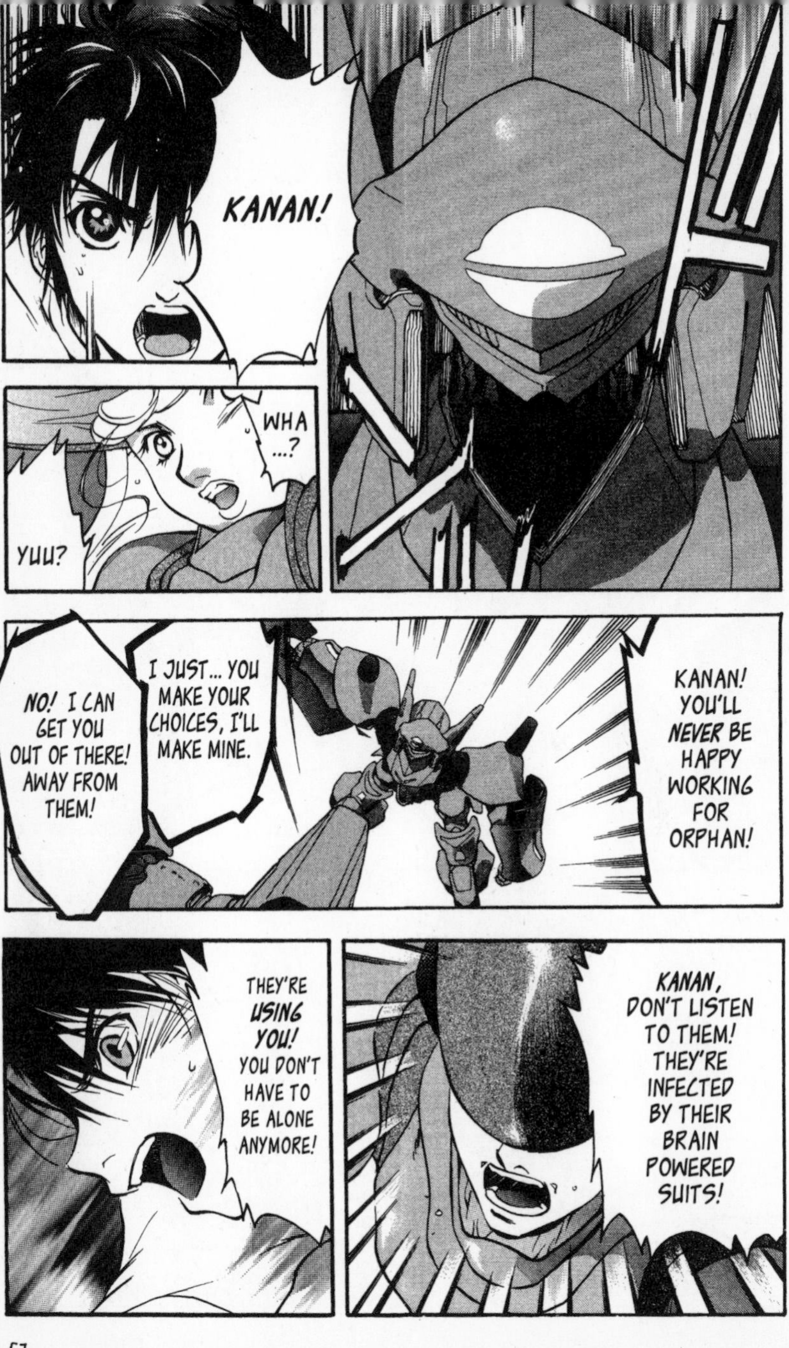
KANAN!
WHA ...?
YUU?
KANAN! YOU'LL *NEVER* BE HAPPY WORKING FOR ORPHAN!
I JUST... YOU MAKE YOUR CHOICES, I'LL MAKE MINE.
NO! I CAN GET YOU OUT OF THERE! AWAY FROM THEM!
KANAN, DON'T LISTEN TO THEM! THEY'RE INFECTED BY THEIR BRAIN POWERED SUITS!
THEY'RE *USING YOU!* YOU DON'T HAVE TO BE ALONE ANYMORE!

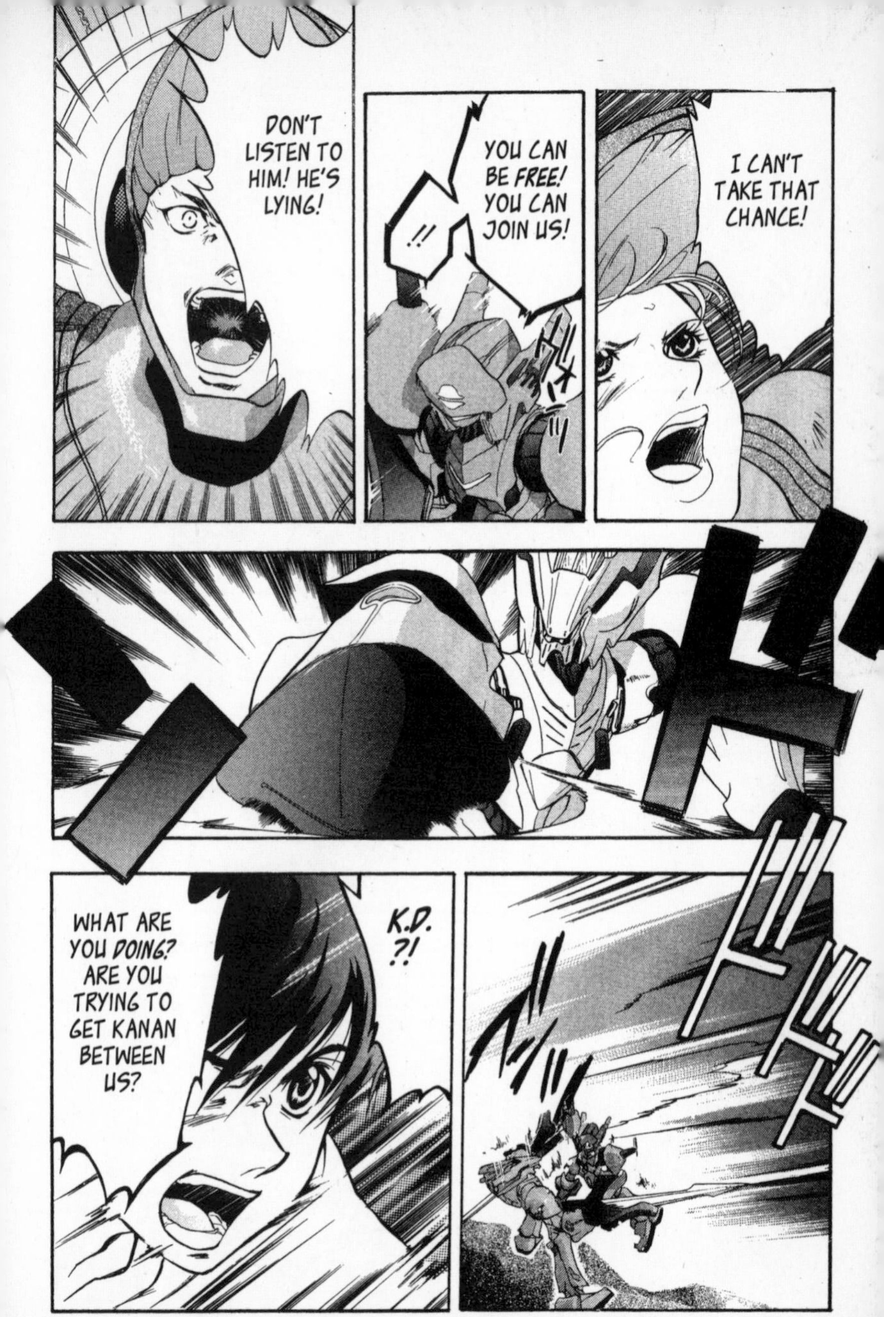
I CAN'T TAKE THAT CHANCE!
YOU CAN BE FREE! YOU CAN JOIN US!
!!
DON'T LISTEN TO HIM! HE'S LYING!
K.D. ?!
WHAT ARE YOU DOING? ARE YOU TRYING TO GET KANAN BETWEEN US?

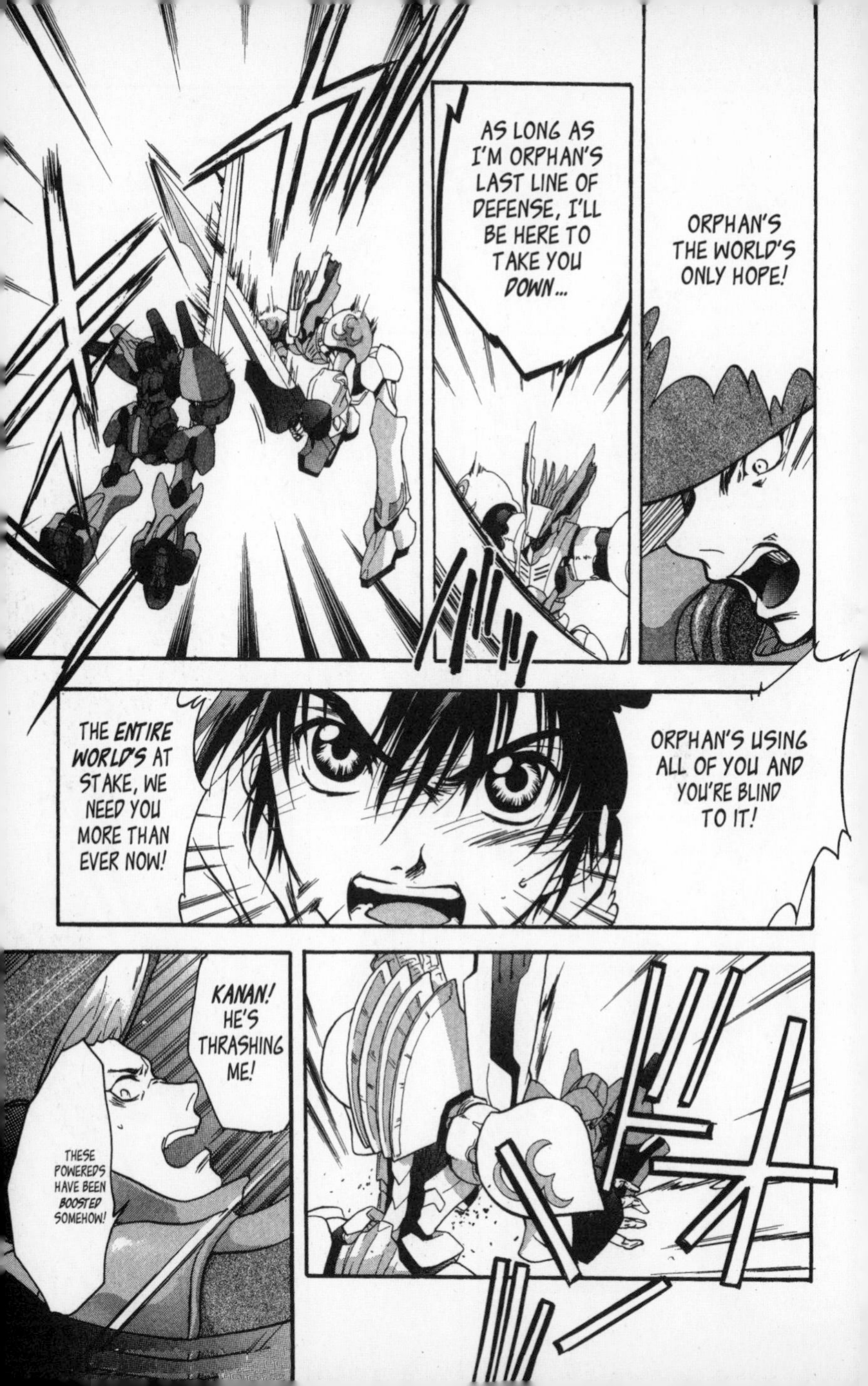
ORPHAN'S THE WORLD'S ONLY HOPE!
AS LONG AS I'M ORPHAN'S LAST LINE OF DEFENSE, I'LL BE HERE TO TAKE YOU DOWN...
ORPHAN'S USING ALL OF YOU AND YOU'RE BLIND TO IT!
THE ENTIRE WORLD'S AT STAKE, WE NEED YOU MORE THAN EVER NOW!
KANAN! HE'S THRASHING ME!
THESE POWEREDS HAVE BEEN BOOSTED SOMEHOW!

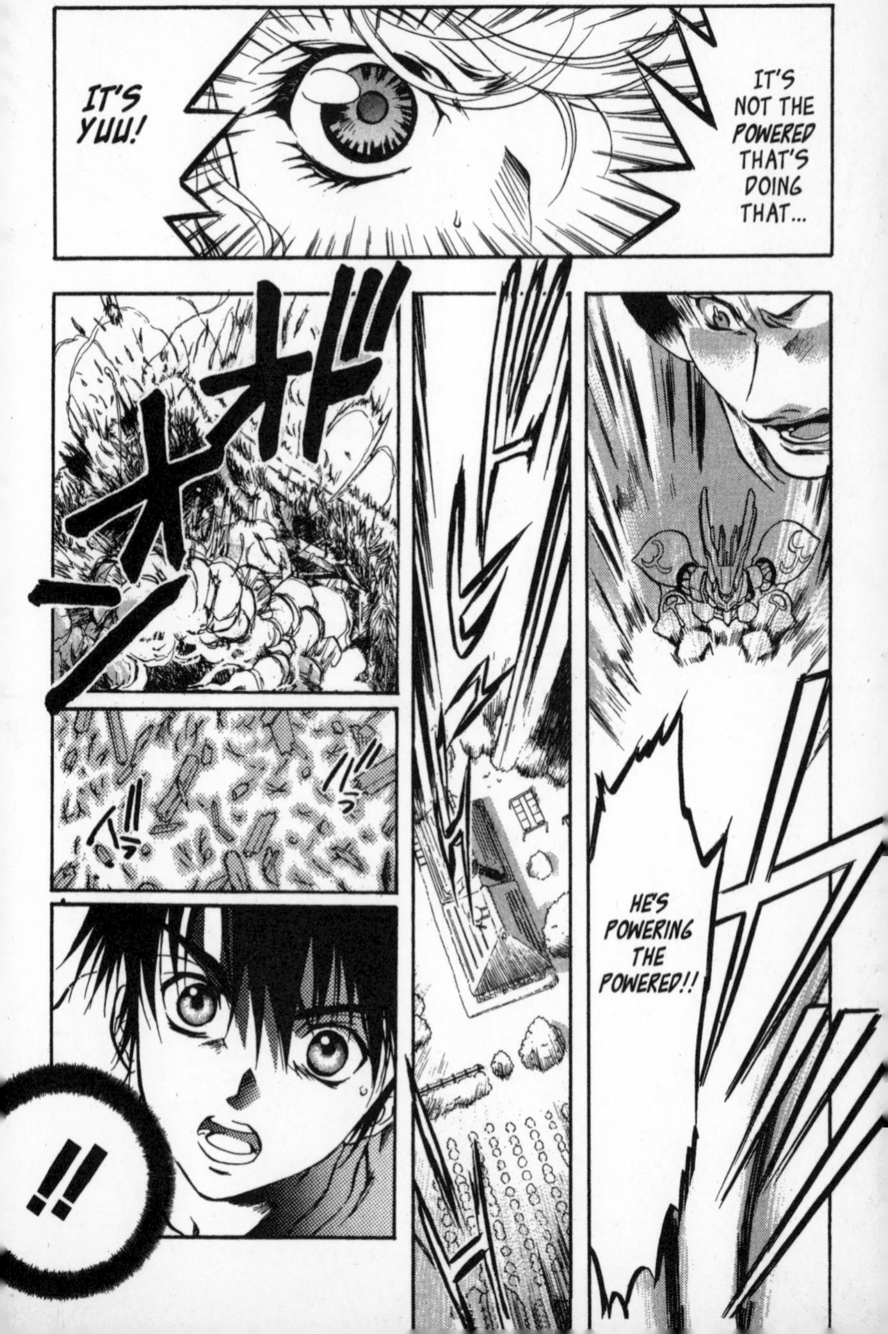

IT'S NOT THE POWERED THAT'S DOING THAT...
IT'S YUU!
HE'S POWERING THE POWERED!!
!!

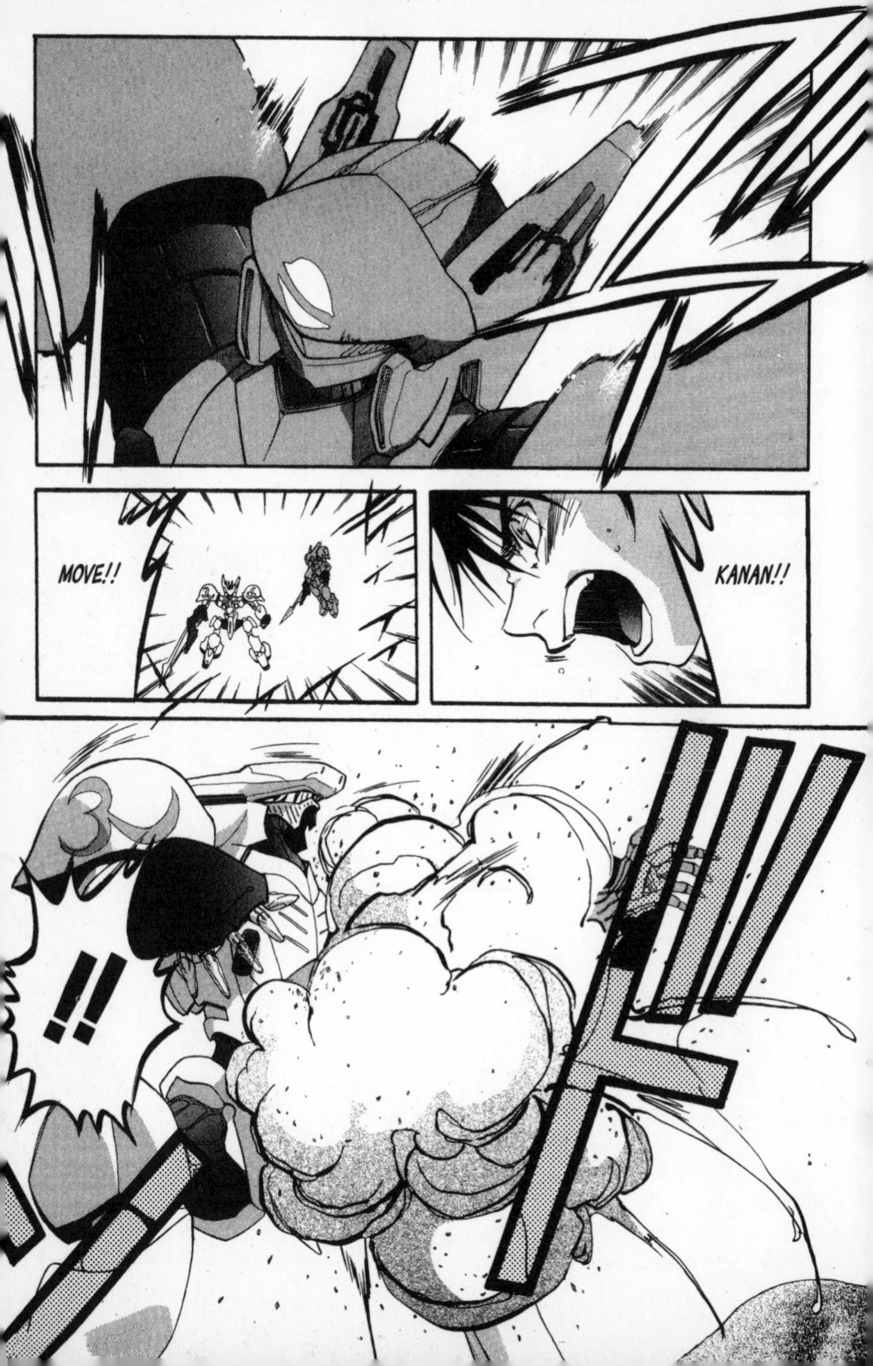
KANAN!!
MOVE!!
!!

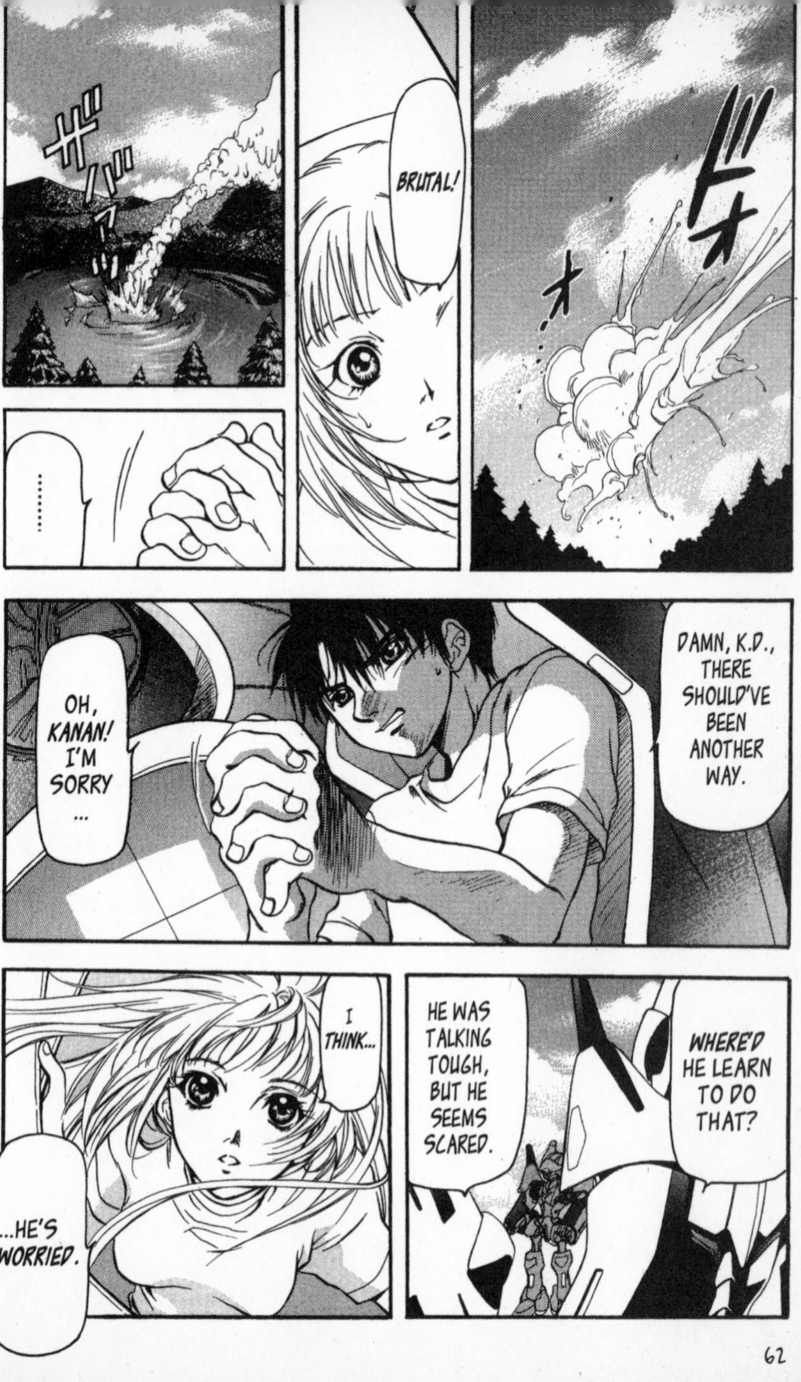
BRUTAL!
......
DAMN, K.D., THERE SHOULD'VE BEEN ANOTHER WAY.
OH, KANAN! I'M SORRY ...
WHERE'D HE LEARN TO DO THAT?
HE WAS TALKING TOUGH, BUT HE SEEMS SCARED.
I THINK...
...HE'S WORRIED.

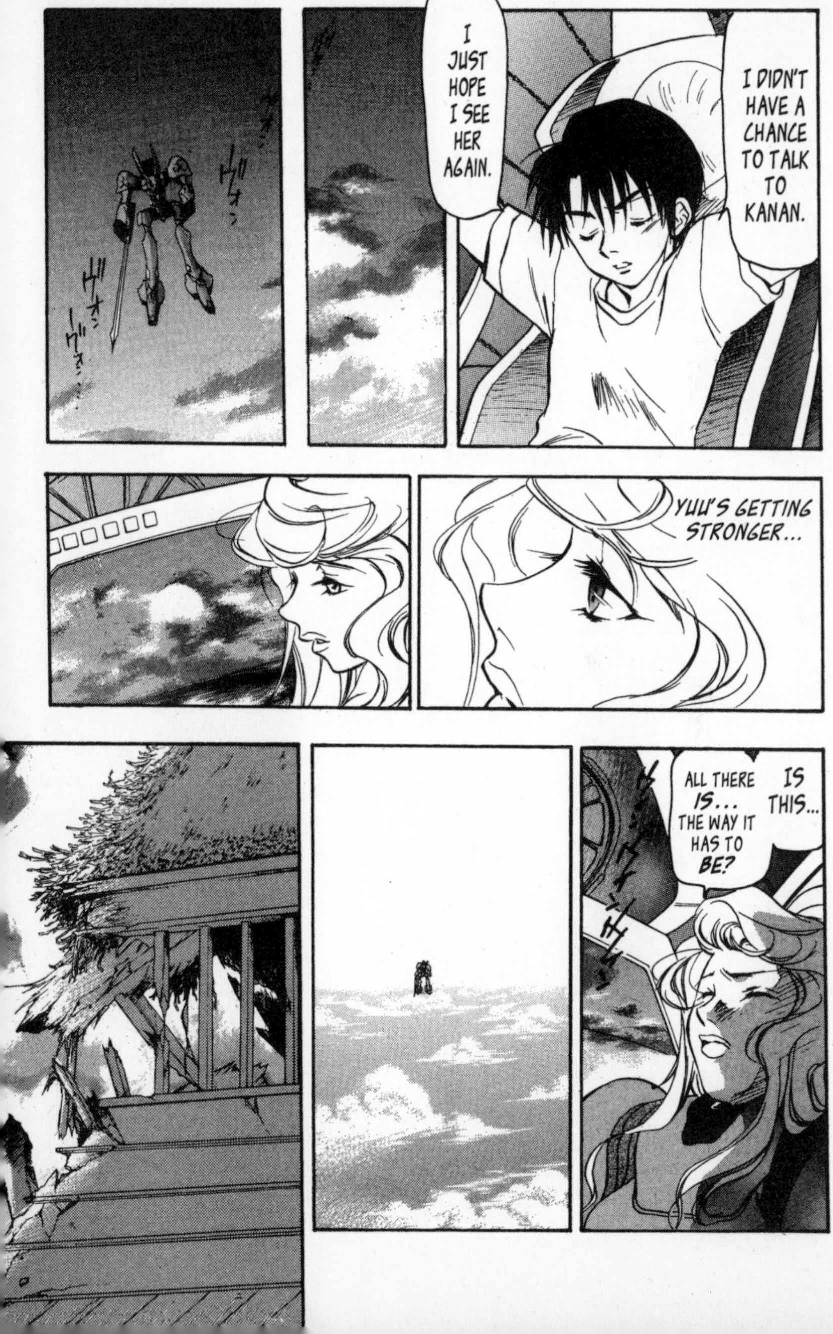
I DIDN'T HAVE A CHANCE TO TALK TO KANAN.
I JUST HOPE I SEE HER AGAIN.
YUU'S GETTING STRONGER...
IS THIS...
ALL THERE *IS*... THE WAY IT HAS TO *BE?*

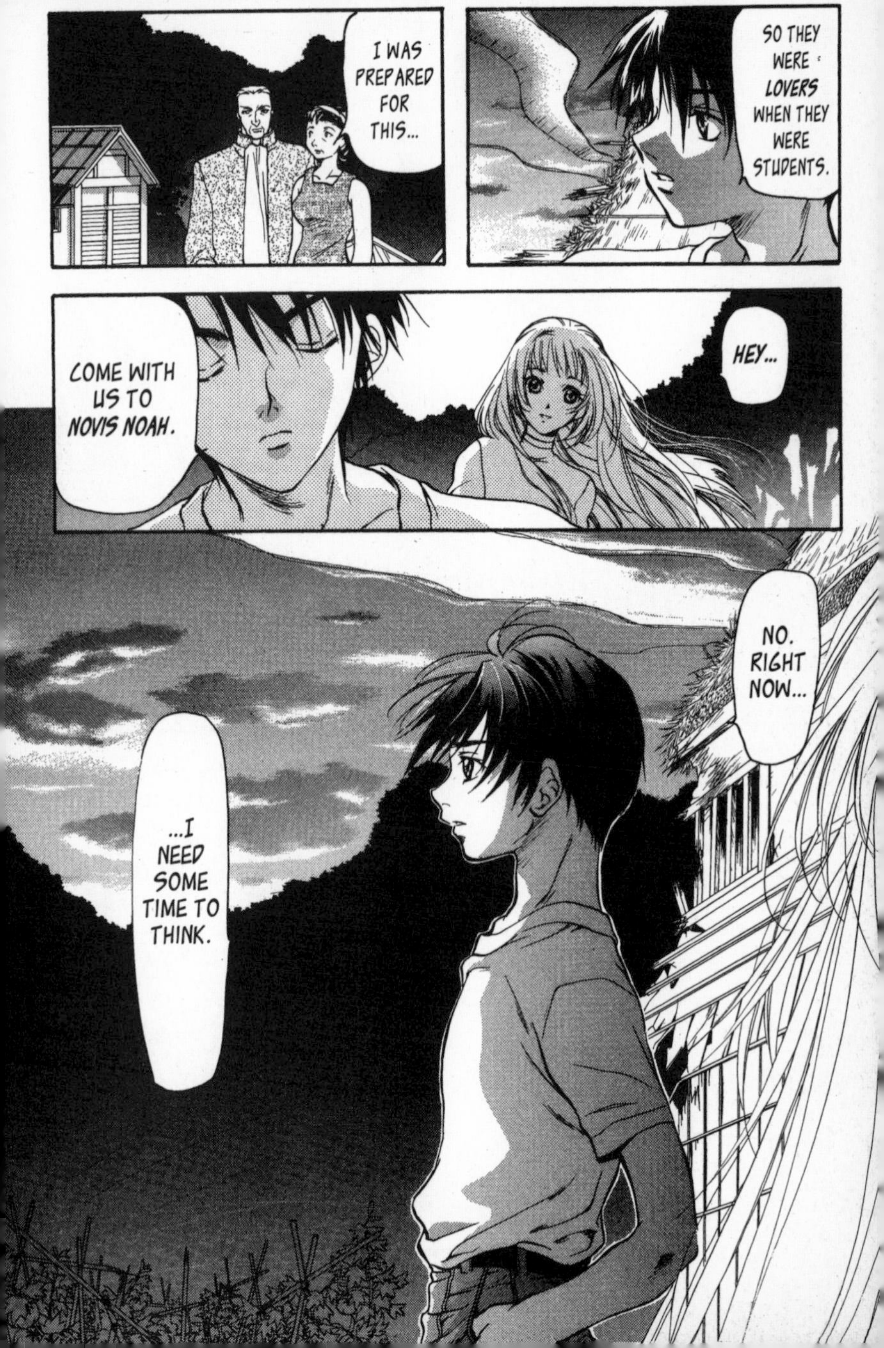
SO THEY WERE LOVERS WHEN THEY WERE STUDENTS.
I WAS PREPARED FOR THIS...
HEY...
COME WITH US TO NOVIS NOAH.
NO. RIGHT NOW...
...I NEED SOME TIME TO THINK.

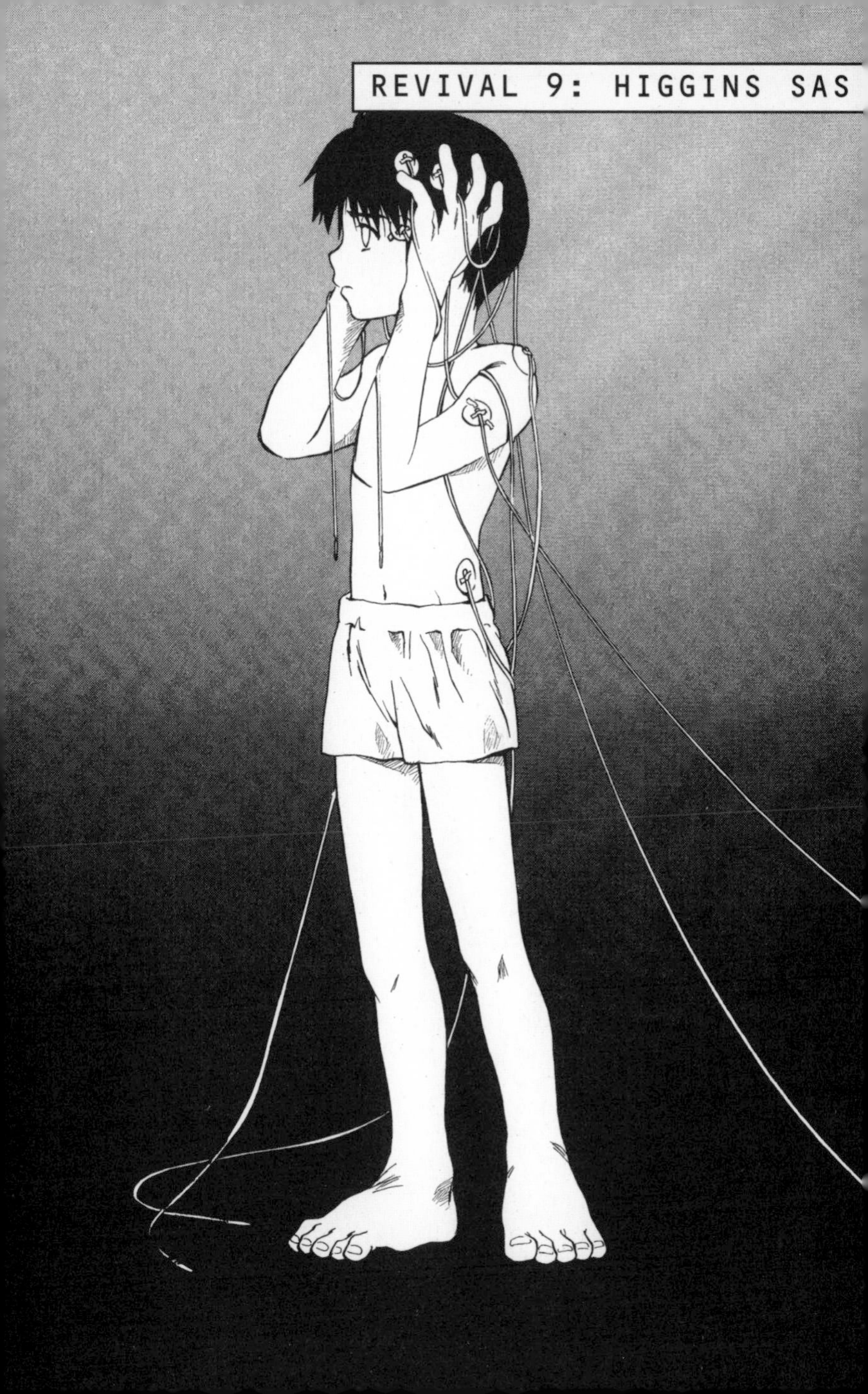
REVIVAL 9: HIGGINS SAS

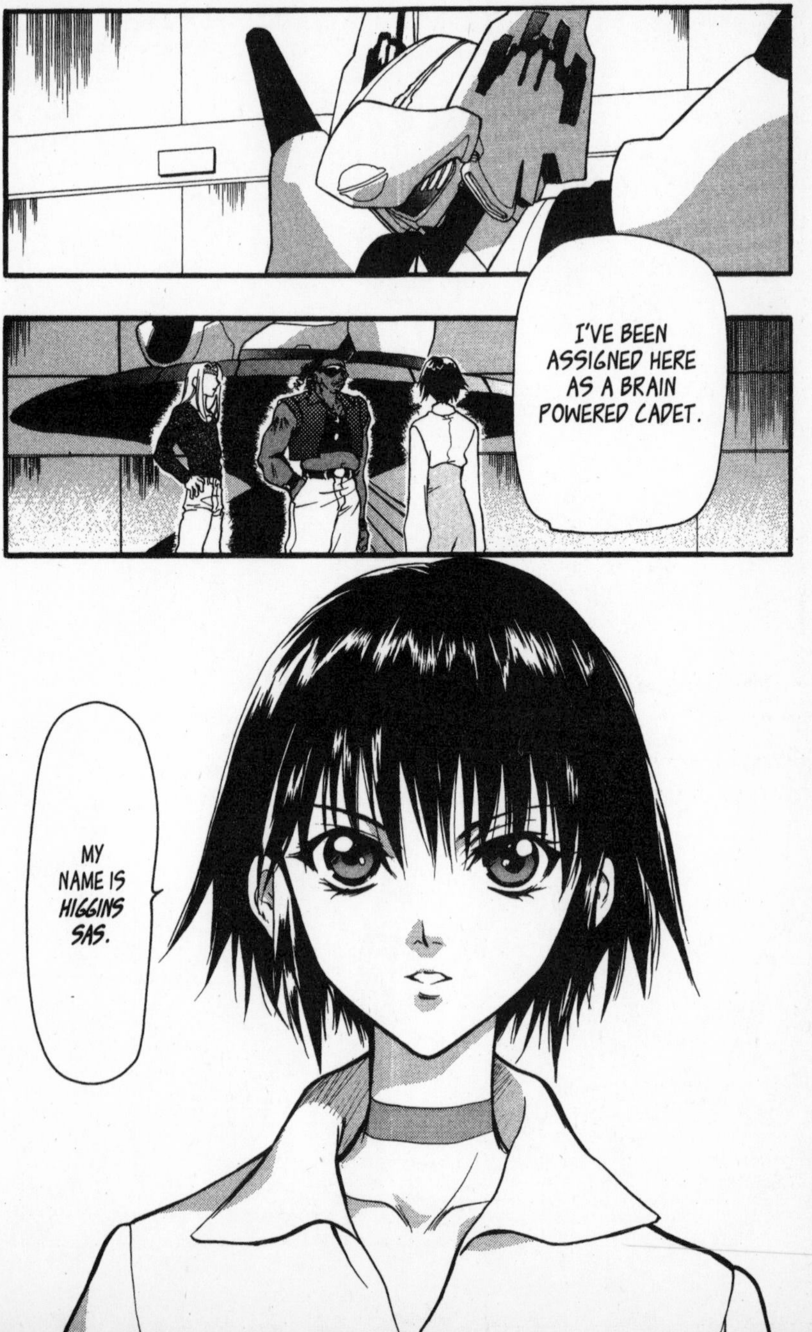
I'VE BEEN ASSIGNED HERE AS A BRAIN POWERED CADET.
MY NAME IS HIGGINS SAS.

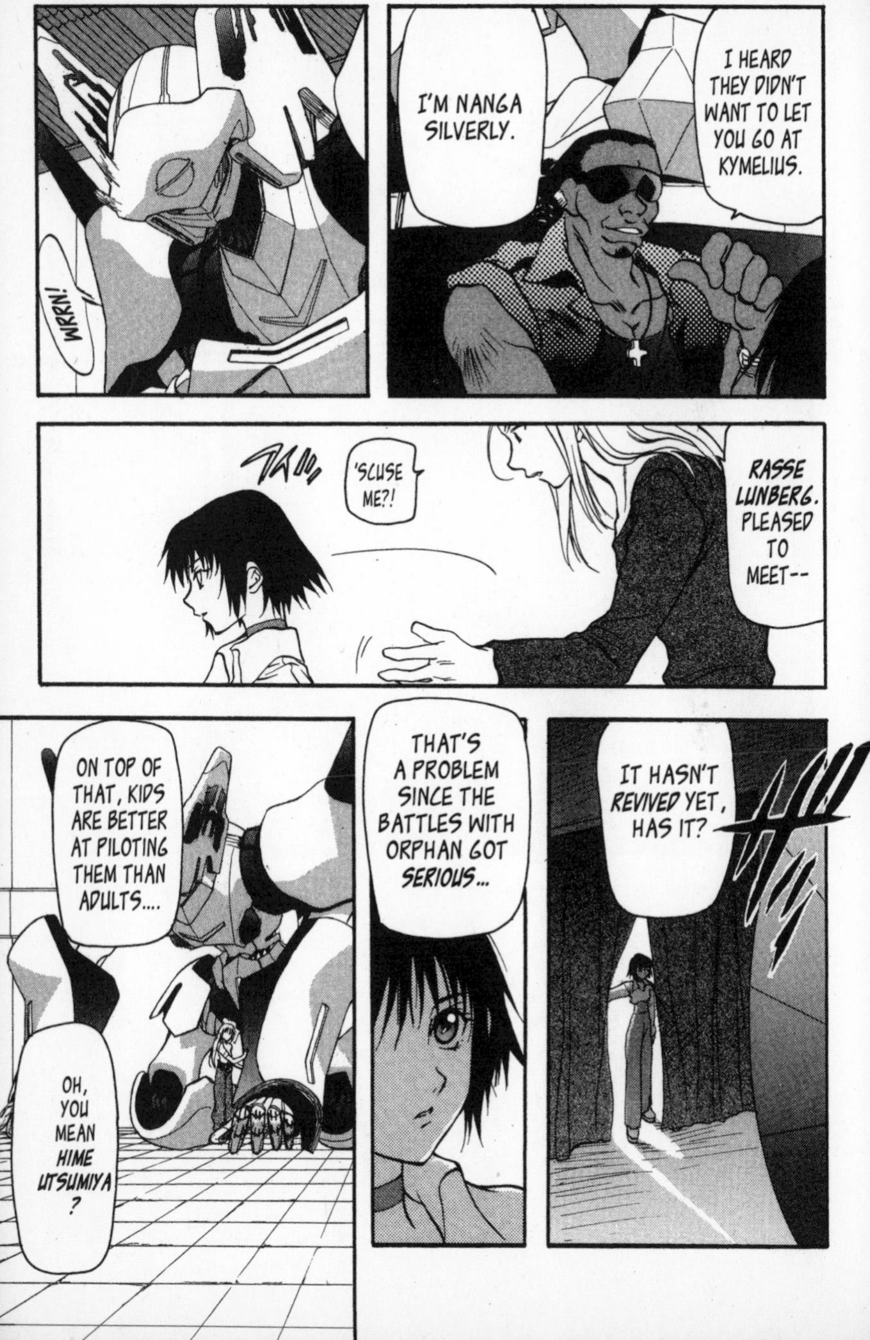
I HEARD THEY DIDN'T WANT TO LET YOU GO AT KYMELIUS.
I'M NANGA SILVERLY.
WRRN!
RASSE LUNBERG. PLEASED TO MEET--
'SCUSE ME?!
IT HASN'T REVIVED YET, HAS IT?
THAT'S A PROBLEM SINCE THE BATTLES WITH ORPHAN GOT SERIOUS...
ON TOP OF THAT, KIDS ARE BETTER AT PILOTING THEM THAN ADULTS....
OH, YOU MEAN HIME UTSUMIYA?

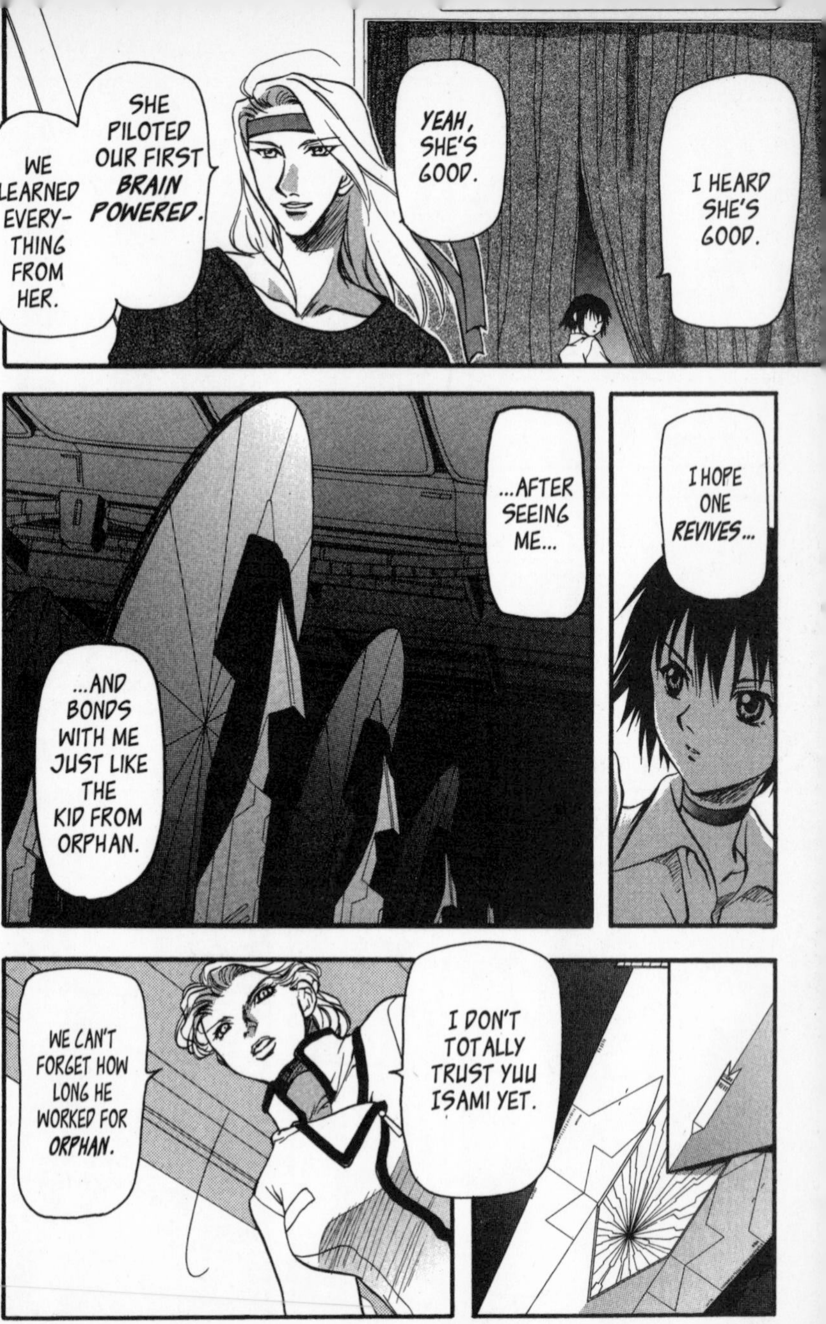
I HEARD SHE'S GOOD.
YEAH, SHE'S GOOD.
SHE PILOTED OUR FIRST *BRAIN POWERED*.
WE LEARNED EVERYTHING FROM HER.
I HOPE ONE *REVIVES*...
...AFTER SEEING ME...
...AND BONDS WITH ME JUST LIKE THE KID FROM ORPHAN.
I DON'T TOTALLY TRUST YUU ISAMI YET.
WE CAN'T FORGET HOW LONG HE WORKED FOR *ORPHAN*.

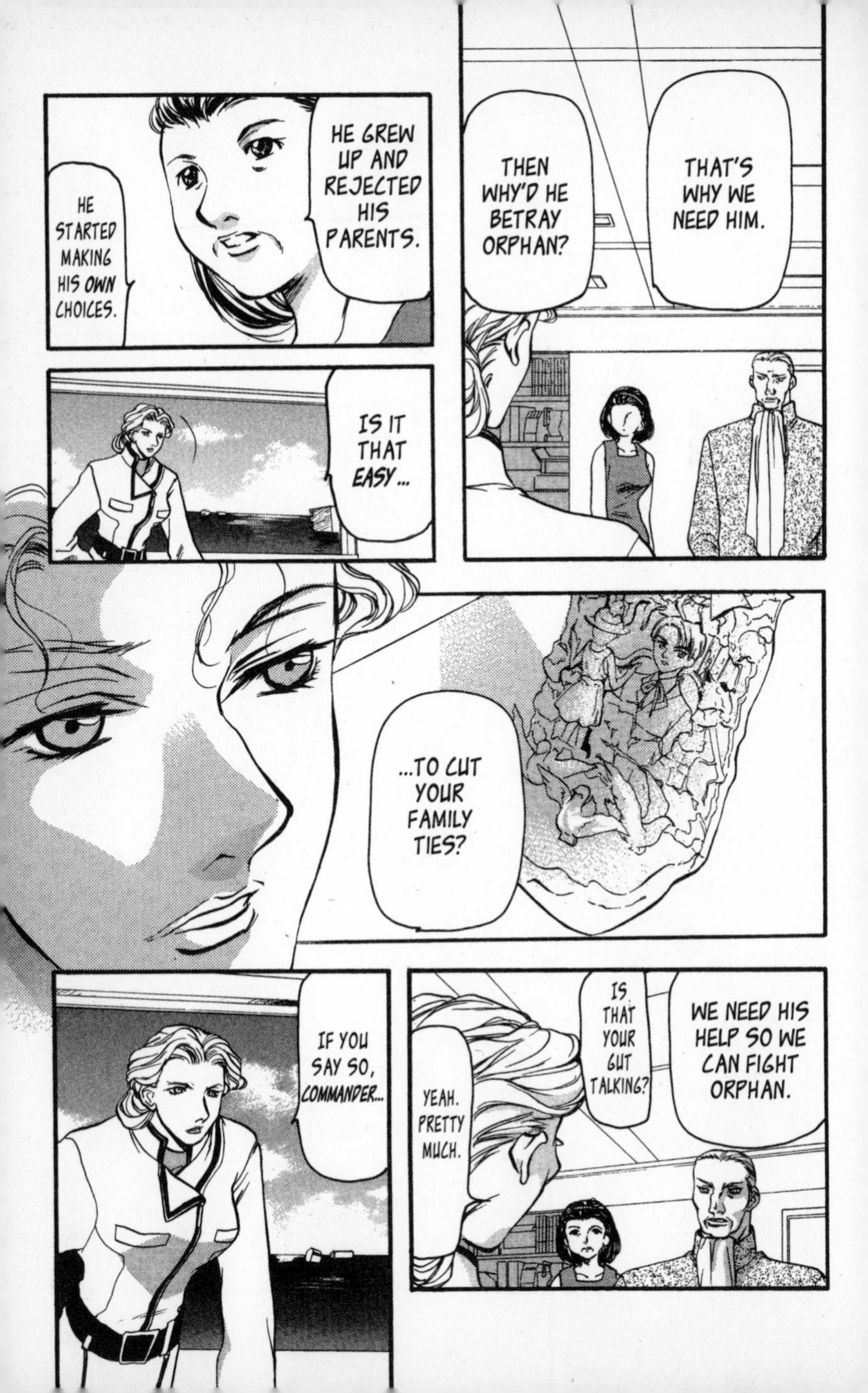
THAT'S WHY WE NEED HIM.
THEN WHY'D HE BETRAY ORPHAN?
HE GREW UP AND REJECTED HIS PARENTS.
HE STARTED MAKING HIS *OWN* CHOICES.
IS IT THAT *EASY*...
...TO CUT YOUR FAMILY TIES?
WE NEED HIS HELP SO WE CAN FIGHT ORPHAN.
IS THAT YOUR GUT TALKING?
YEAH. PRETTY MUCH.
IF YOU SAY SO, *COMMANDER*...

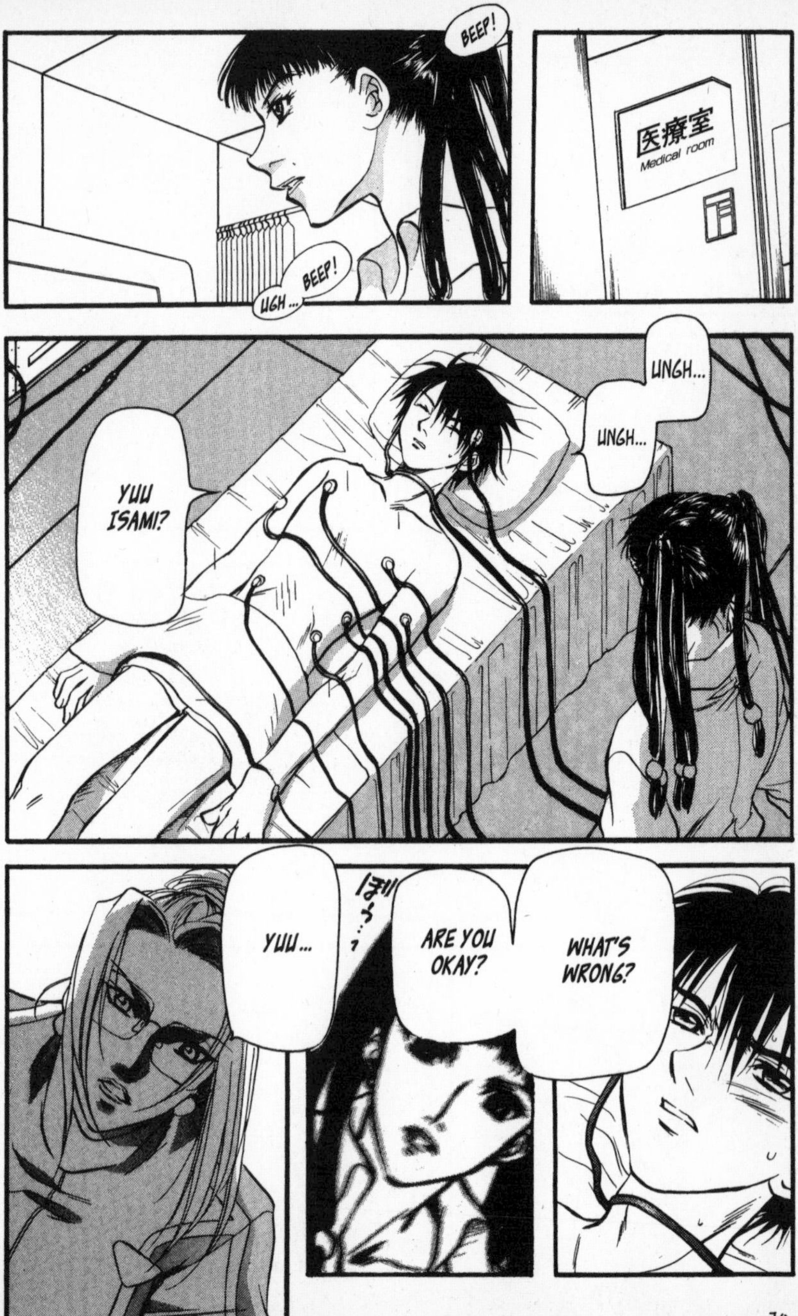
医療室
Medical room
BEEP!
BEEP!
UGH...
UNGH...
UNGH...
YUU ISAMI?
WHAT'S WRONG?
ARE YOU OKAY?
YUU...

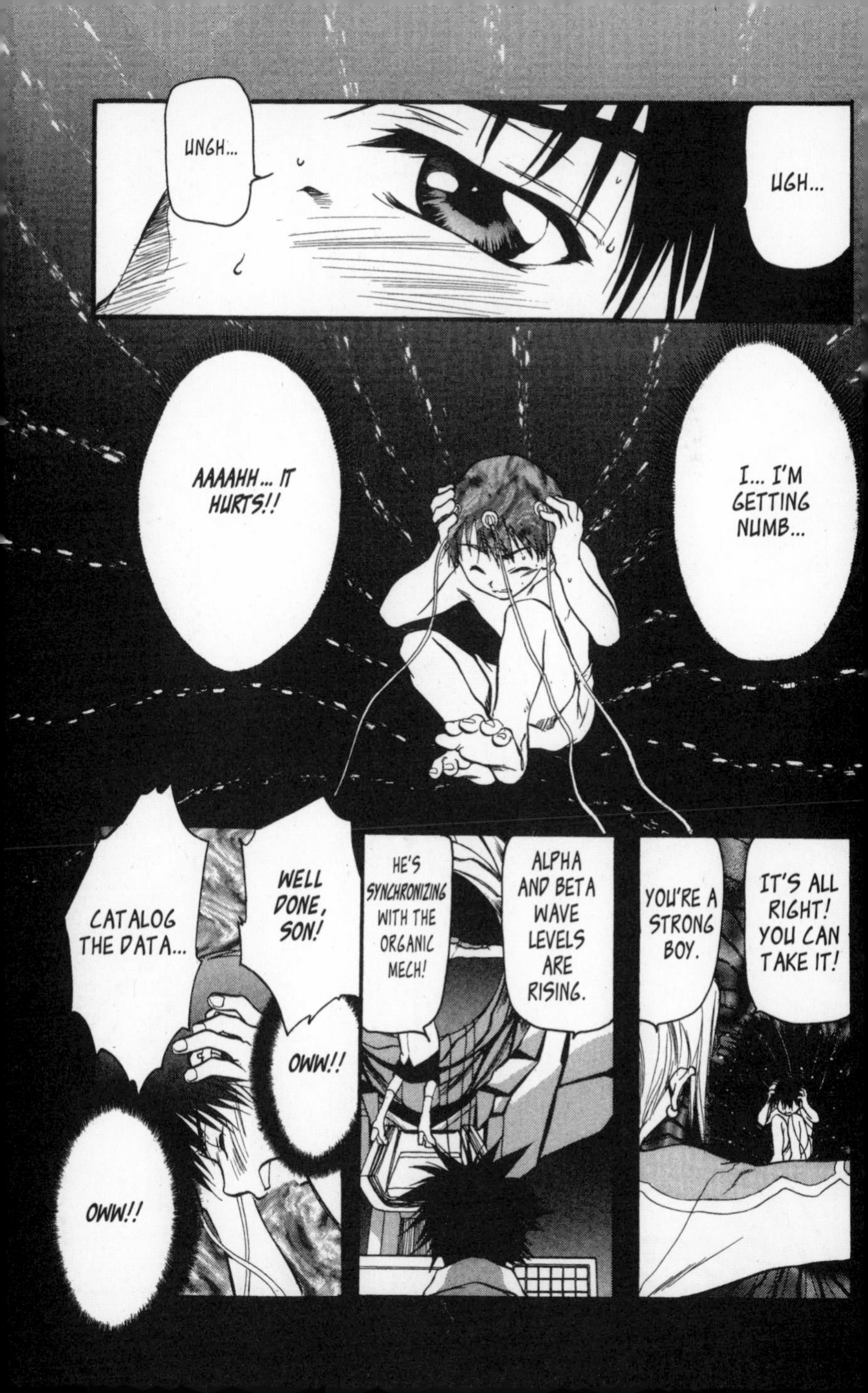
UGH...
UNGH...
I... I'M GETTING NUMB...
AAAAHH... IT HURTS!!
IT'S ALL RIGHT! YOU CAN TAKE IT!
YOU'RE A STRONG BOY.
ALPHA AND BETA WAVE LEVELS ARE RISING.
HE'S SYNCHRONIZING WITH THE ORGANIC MECH!
WELL DONE, SON!
CATALOG THE DATA...
OWW!!
OWW!!

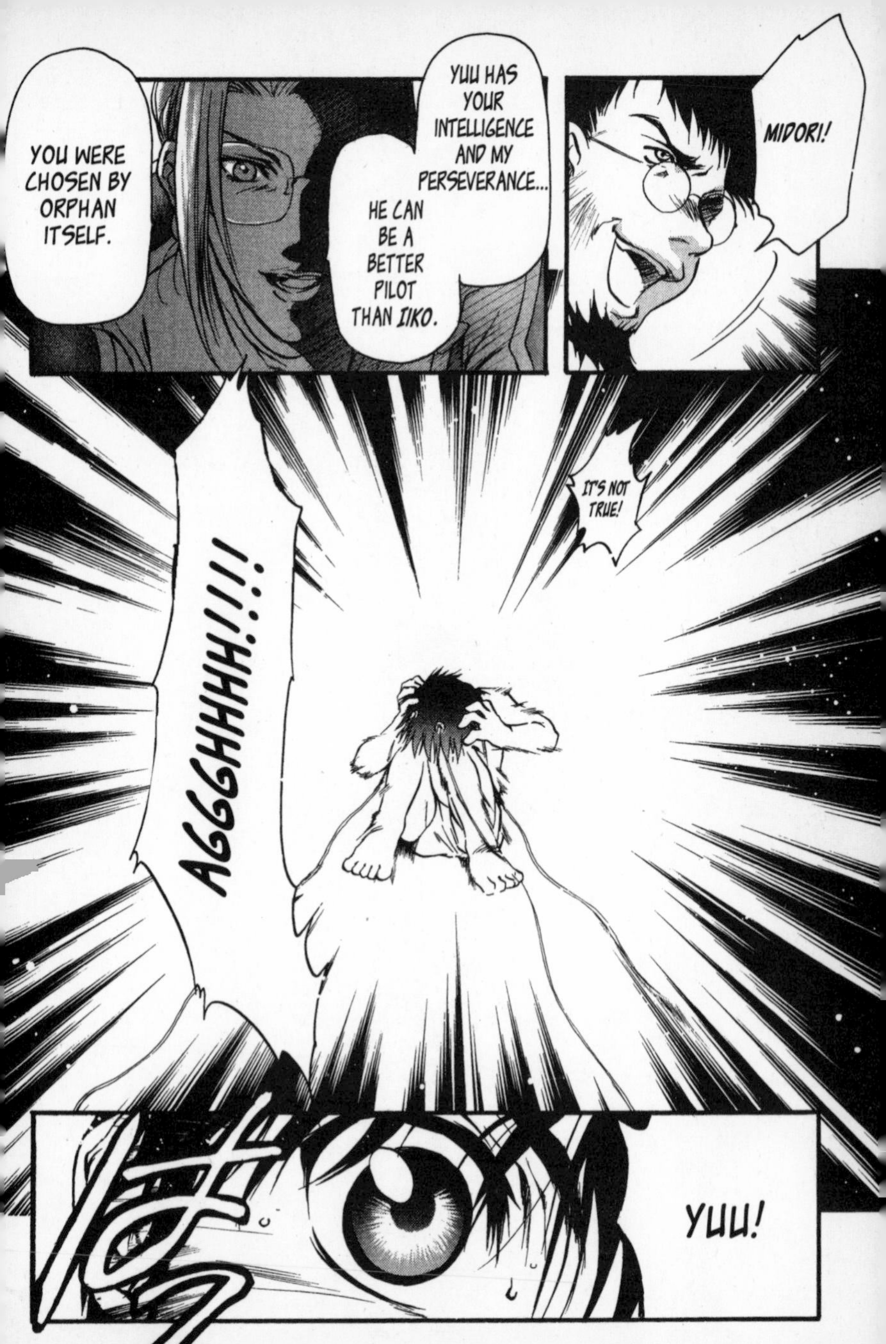
MIDORI!
YUU HAS YOUR INTELLIGENCE AND MY PERSEVERANCE...
HE CAN BE A BETTER PILOT THAN IIKO.
YOU WERE CHOSEN BY ORPHAN ITSELF.
IT'S NOT TRUE!
AGGGHHHHH!!!!!
YUU!

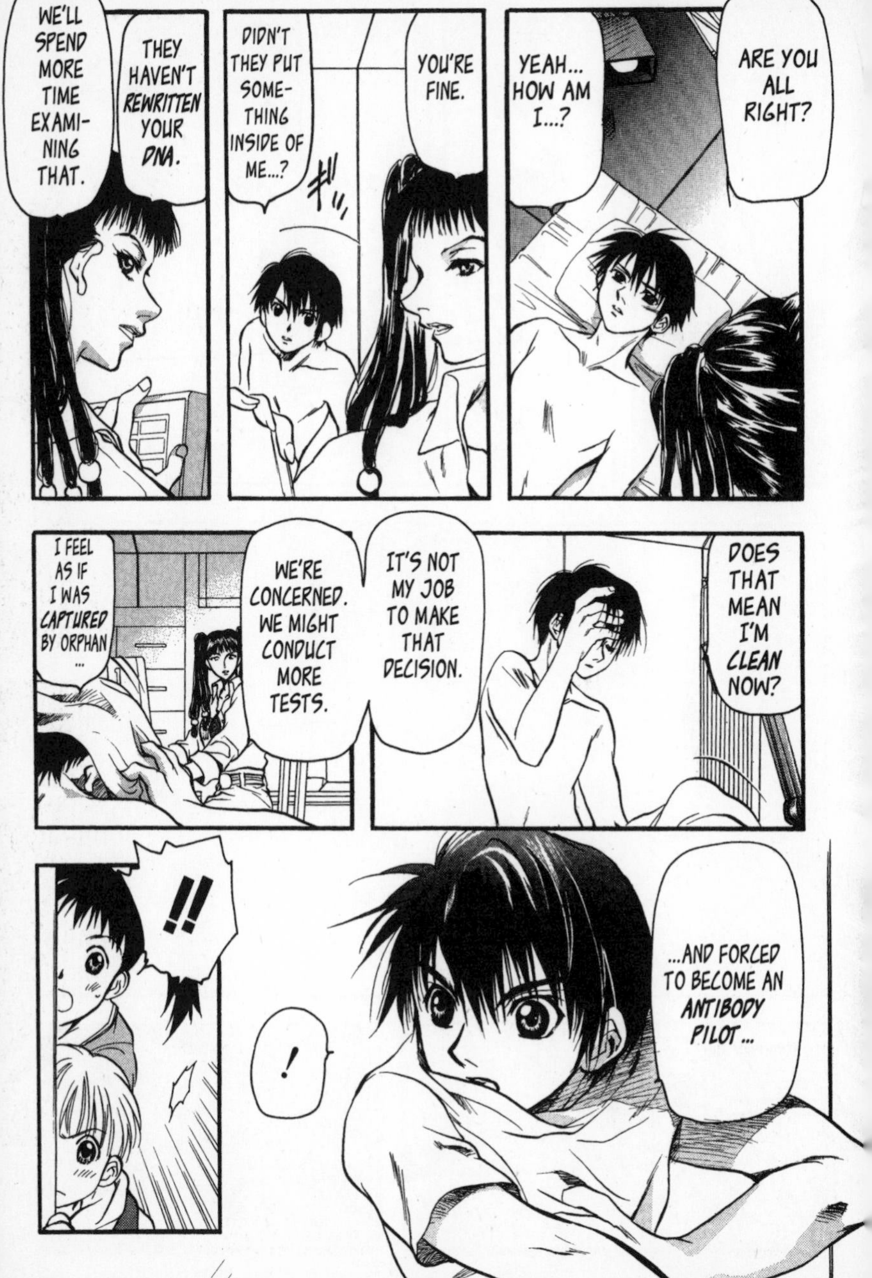
ARE YOU ALL RIGHT?
YEAH... HOW AM I...?
YOU'RE FINE.
DIDN'T THEY PUT SOME-THING INSIDE OF ME...?
THEY HAVEN'T REWRITTEN YOUR DNA.
WE'LL SPEND MORE TIME EXAMI-NING THAT.
DOES THAT MEAN I'M CLEAN NOW?
IT'S NOT MY JOB TO MAKE THAT DECISION.
WE'RE CONCERNED. WE MIGHT CONDUCT MORE TESTS.
I FEEL AS IF I WAS CAPTURED BY ORPHAN ...
...AND FORCED TO BECOME AN ANTIBODY PILOT...
!
!!

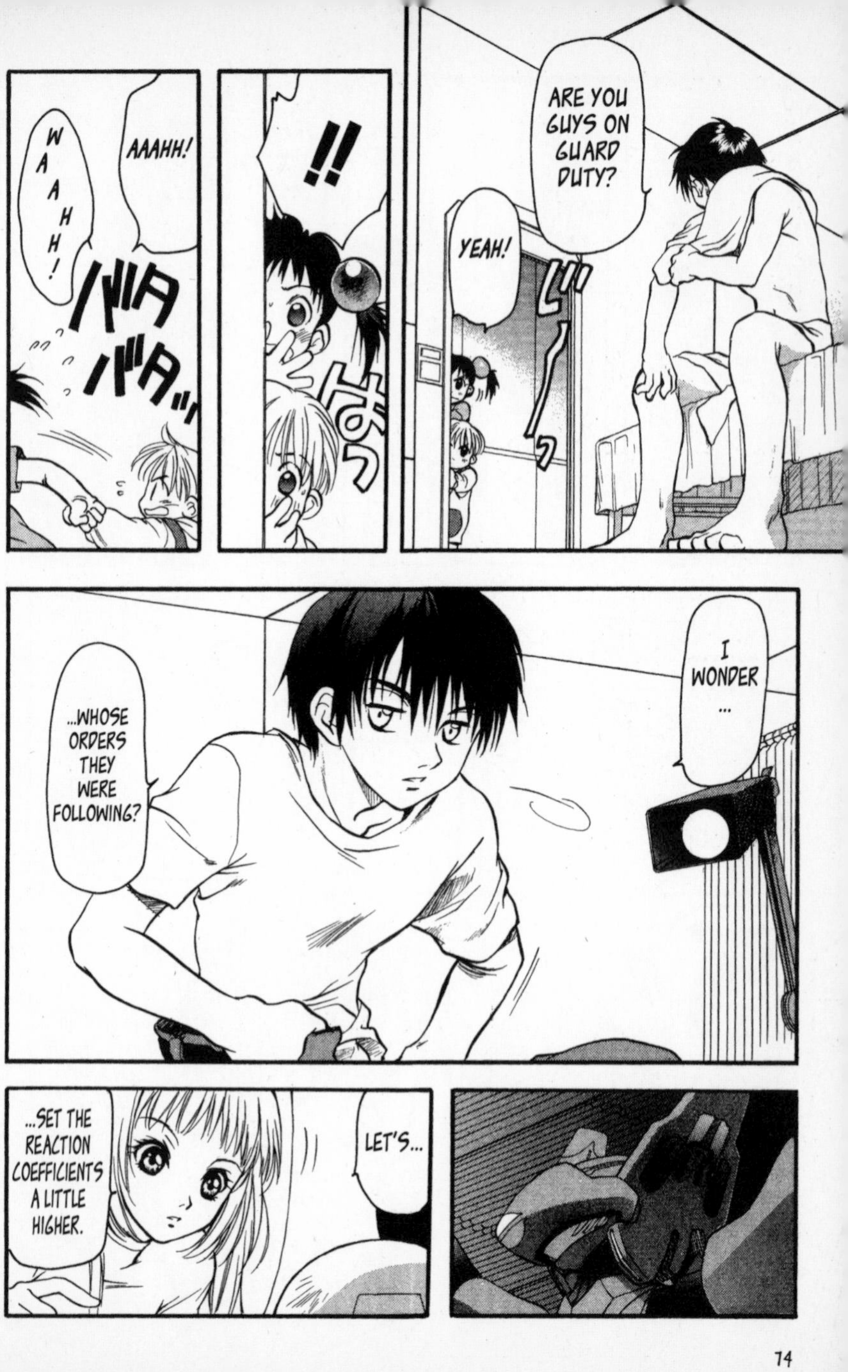
ARE YOU GUYS ON GUARD DUTY?
YEAH!
!!
はっ
AAAHH!
WAAHH!
バタバタッ
I WONDER...
...WHOSE ORDERS THEY WERE FOLLOWING?
LET'S...
...SET THE REACTION COEFFICIENTS A LITTLE HIGHER.

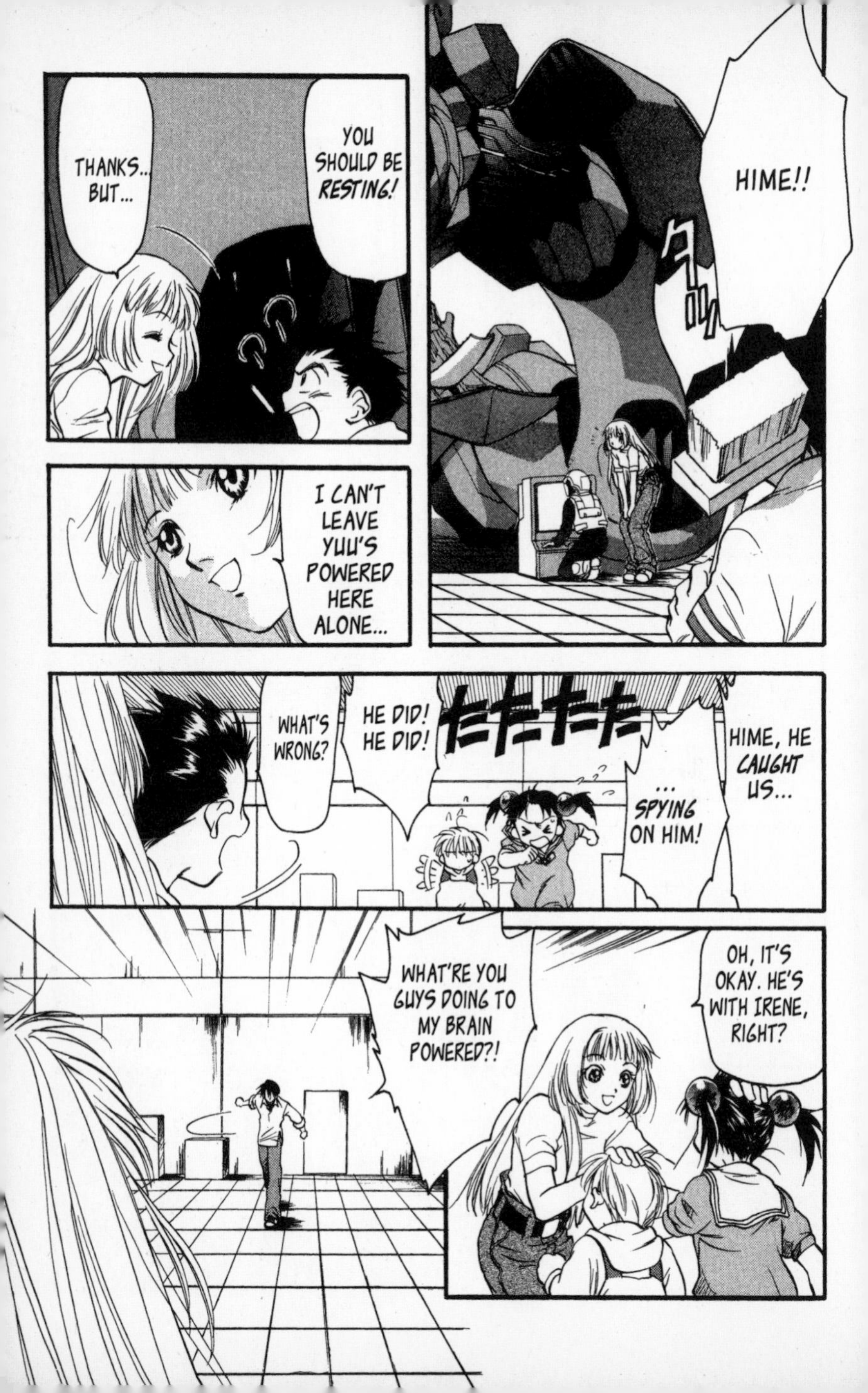
HIME!!
YOU SHOULD BE RESTING!
THANKS... BUT...
I CAN'T LEAVE YUU'S POWERED HERE ALONE...
HIME, HE CAUGHT US...
... SPYING ON HIM!
HE DID! HE DID!
WHAT'S WRONG?
OH, IT'S OKAY. HE'S WITH IRENE, RIGHT?
WHAT'RE YOU GUYS DOING TO MY BRAIN POWERED?!

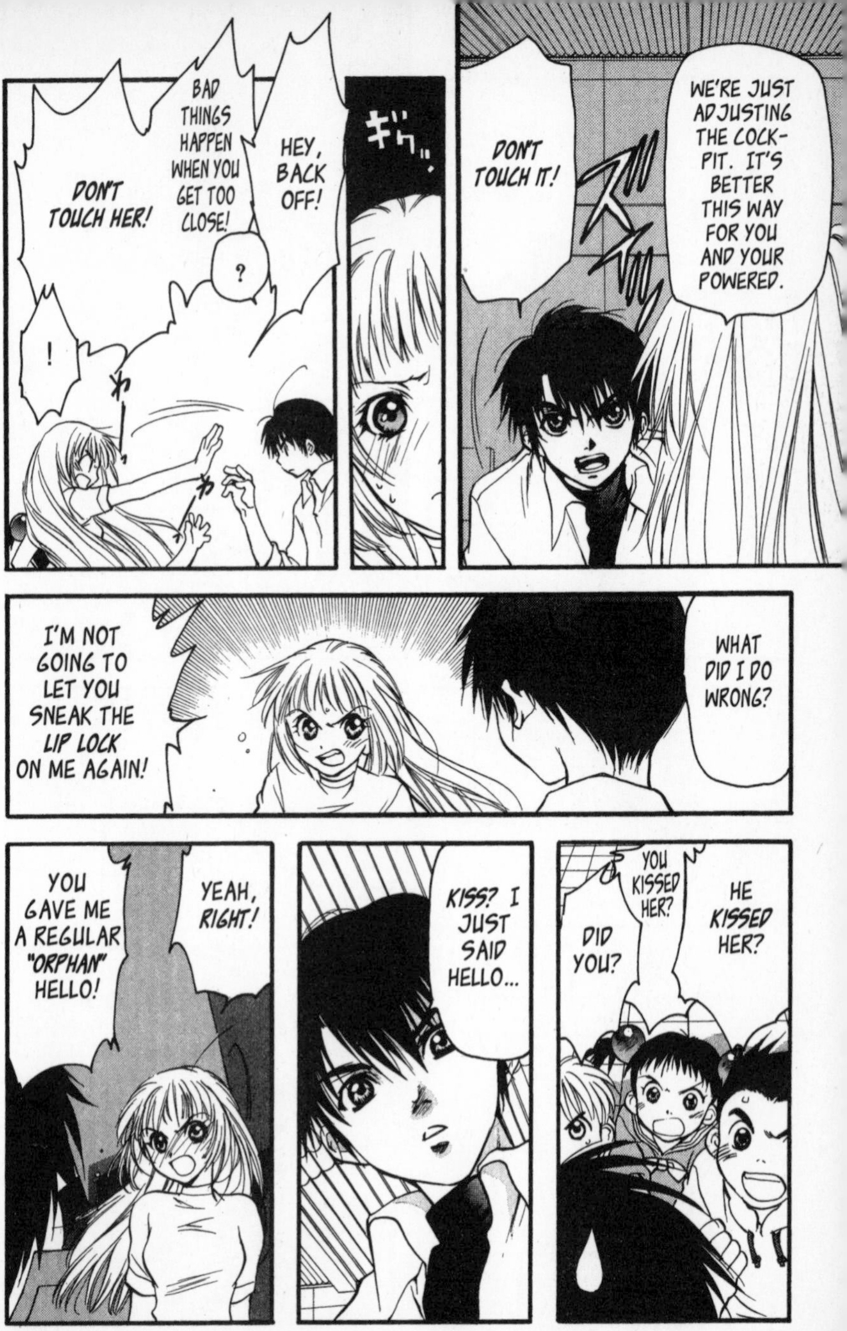
WE'RE JUST ADJUSTING THE COCK-PIT. IT'S BETTER THIS WAY FOR YOU AND YOUR POWERED.
DON'T TOUCH IT!
HEY, BACK OFF!
BAD THINGS HAPPEN WHEN YOU GET TOO CLOSE!
DON'T TOUCH HER!
?
!
WHAT DID I DO WRONG?
I'M NOT GOING TO LET YOU SNEAK THE LIP LOCK ON ME AGAIN!
HE KISSED HER?
YOU KISSED HER?
DID YOU?
KISS? I JUST SAID HELLO...
YEAH, RIGHT!
YOU GAVE ME A REGULAR "ORPHAN" HELLO!

?

MAYBE I WAS...

...I'M SORRY.

HEY *MISTER*, YOU'RE MESSING WITH MY GIRL!

·········

THIS POWERED SURE SEEMS TO LIKE HIM...

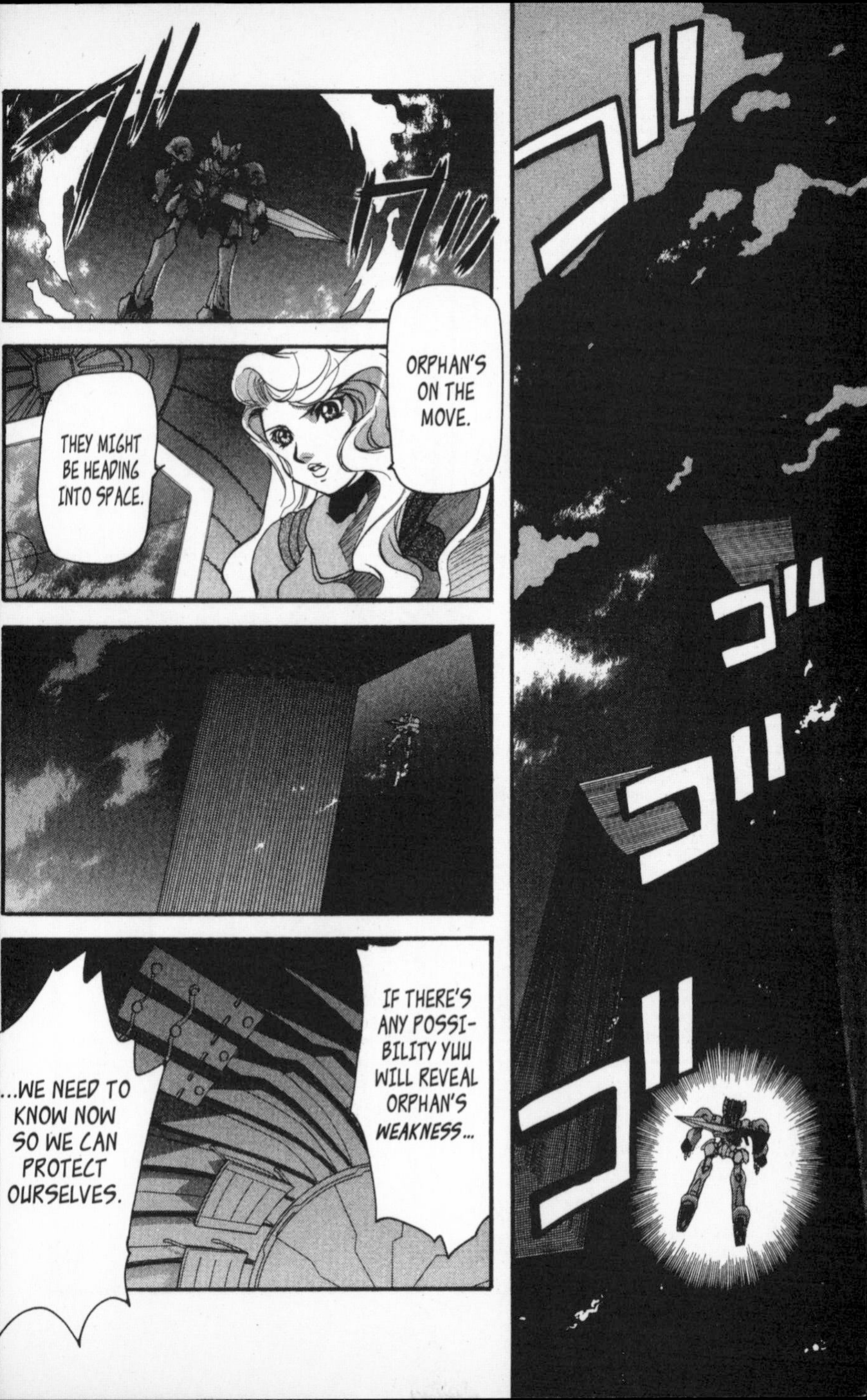
ORPHAN'S ON THE MOVE.
THEY MIGHT BE HEADING INTO SPACE.
IF THERE'S ANY POSSI-BILITY YUU WILL REVEAL ORPHAN'S *WEAKNESS*...
...WE NEED TO KNOW NOW SO WE CAN PROTECT OURSELVES.

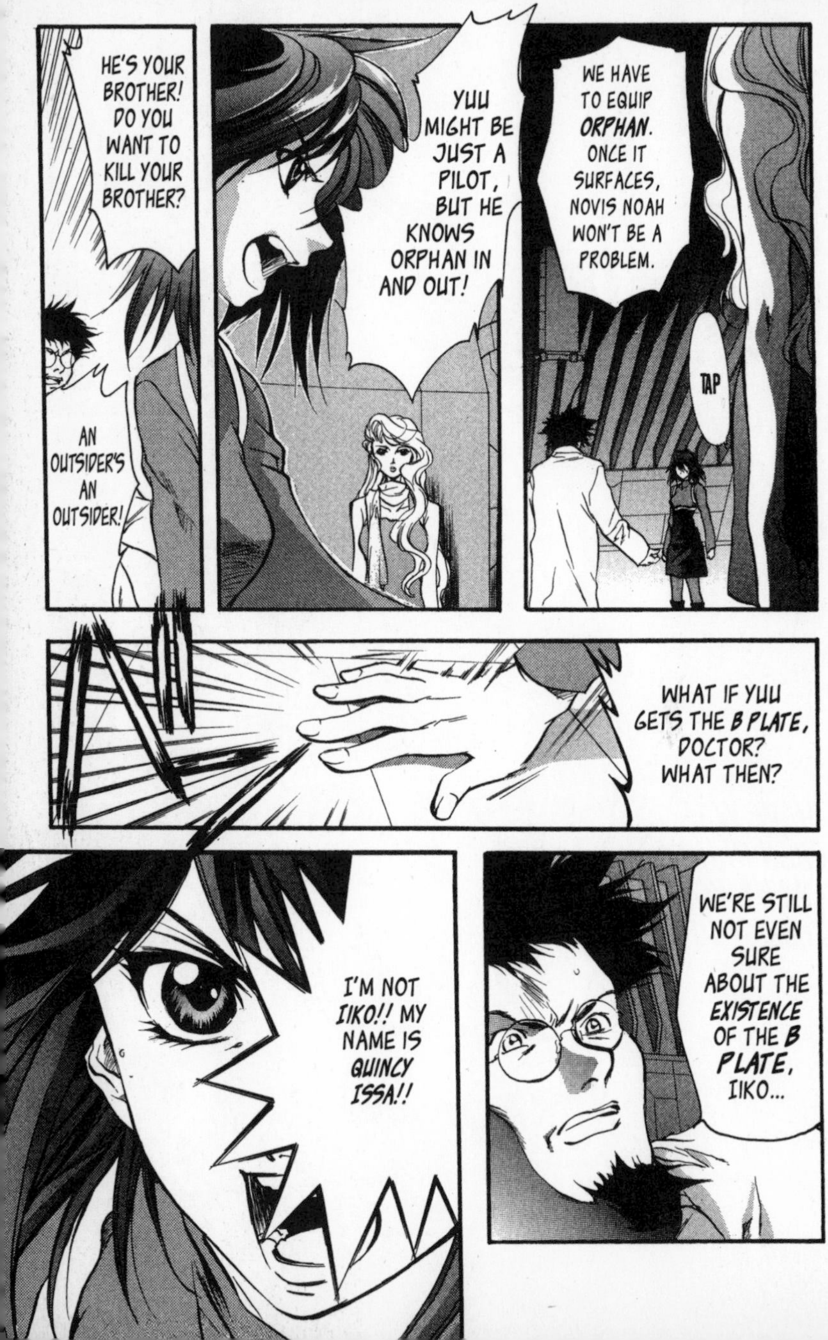
WE HAVE TO EQUIP *ORPHAN*. ONCE IT SURFACES, NOVIS NOAH WON'T BE A PROBLEM.
TAP
YUU MIGHT BE JUST A PILOT, BUT HE KNOWS ORPHAN IN AND OUT!
HE'S YOUR BROTHER! DO YOU WANT TO KILL YOUR BROTHER?
AN OUTSIDER'S AN OUTSIDER!
WHAT IF YUU GETS THE *B PLATE*, DOCTOR? WHAT THEN?
WE'RE STILL NOT EVEN SURE ABOUT THE *EXISTENCE* OF THE *B PLATE*, IIKO...
I'M NOT *IIKO!!* MY NAME IS *QUINCY ISSA!!*

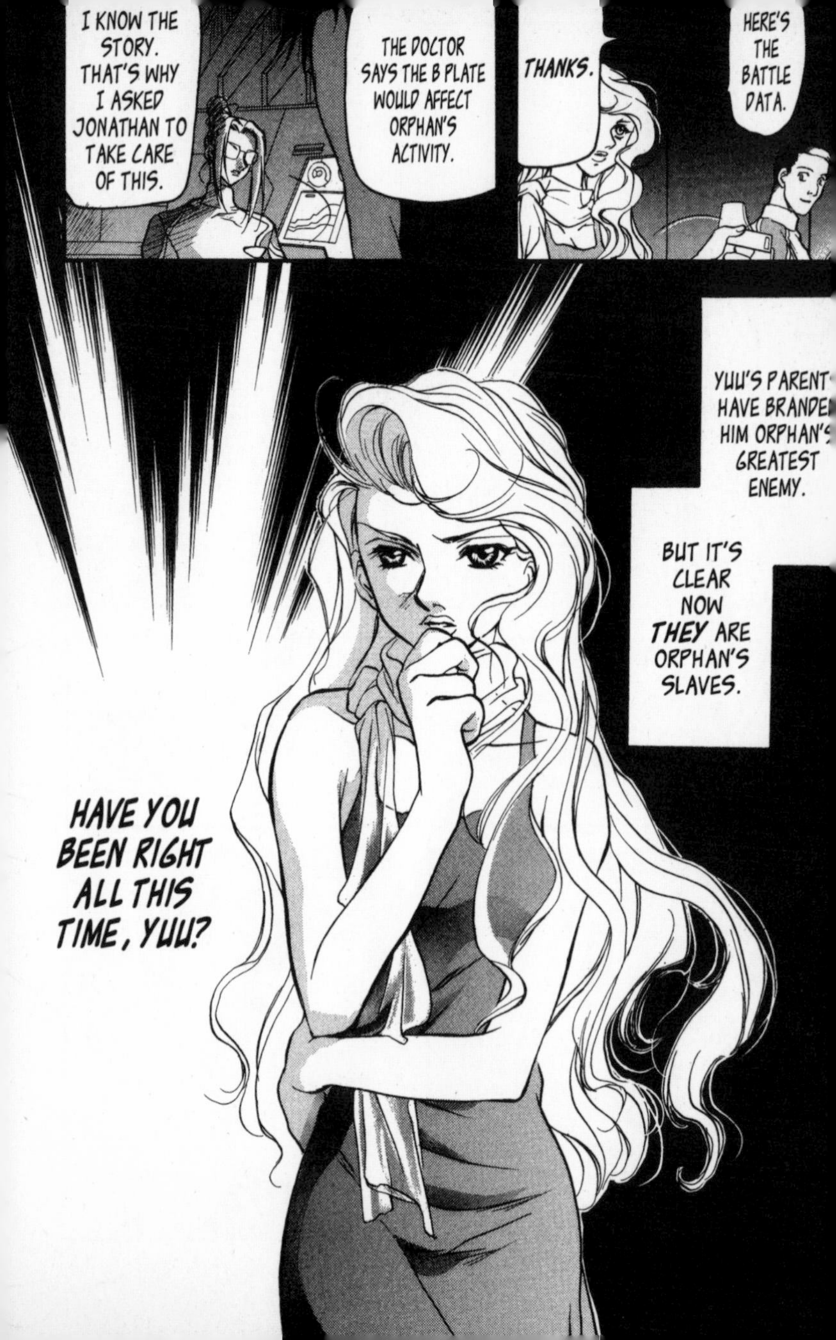
HERE'S THE BATTLE DATA.
THANKS.
THE DOCTOR SAYS THE B PLATE WOULD AFFECT ORPHAN'S ACTIVITY.
I KNOW THE STORY. THAT'S WHY I ASKED JONATHAN TO TAKE CARE OF THIS.
YUU'S PARENTS HAVE BRANDED HIM ORPHAN'S GREATEST ENEMY.
BUT IT'S CLEAR NOW THEY ARE ORPHAN'S SLAVES.
HAVE YOU BEEN RIGHT ALL THIS TIME, YUU?

REVIVAL 10: COMODO MAHAMA

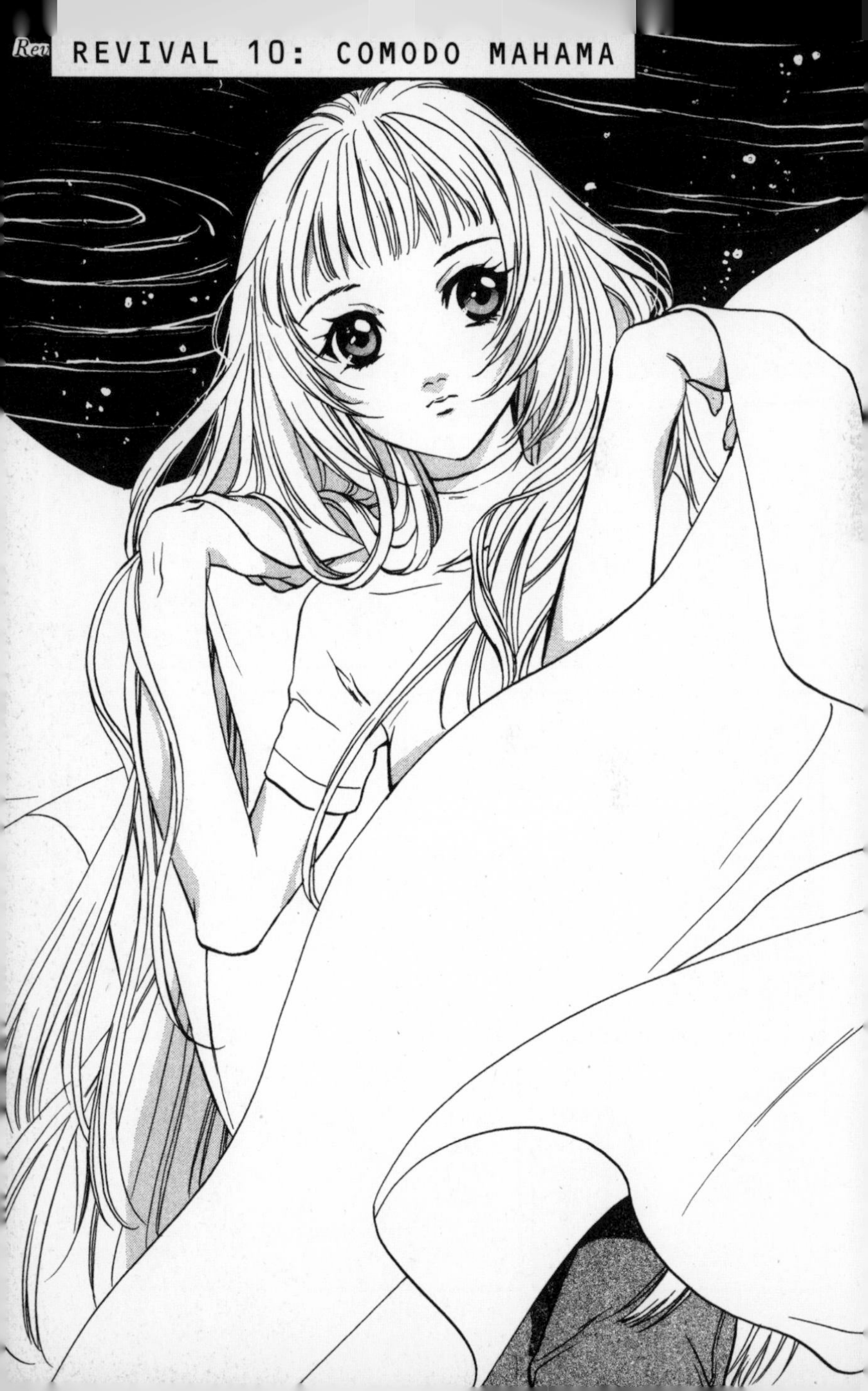

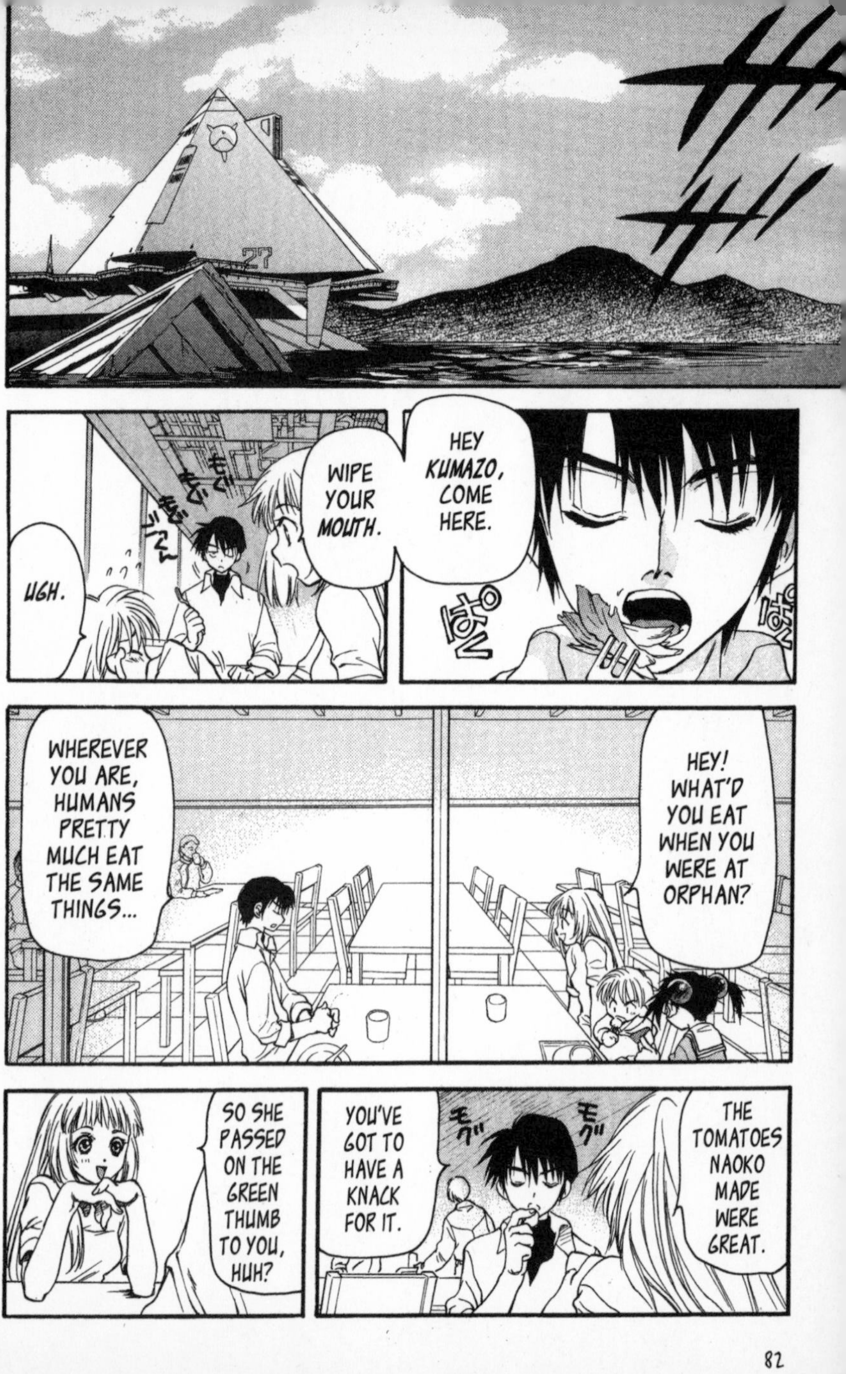
HEY KUMAZO, COME HERE.
WIPE YOUR MOUTH.
UGH.
HEY! WHAT'D YOU EAT WHEN YOU WERE AT ORPHAN?
WHEREVER YOU ARE, HUMANS PRETTY MUCH EAT THE SAME THINGS...
THE TOMATOES NAOKO MADE WERE GREAT.
モグ
モグ
YOU'VE GOT TO HAVE A KNACK FOR IT.
SO SHE PASSED ON THE GREEN THUMB TO YOU, HUH?

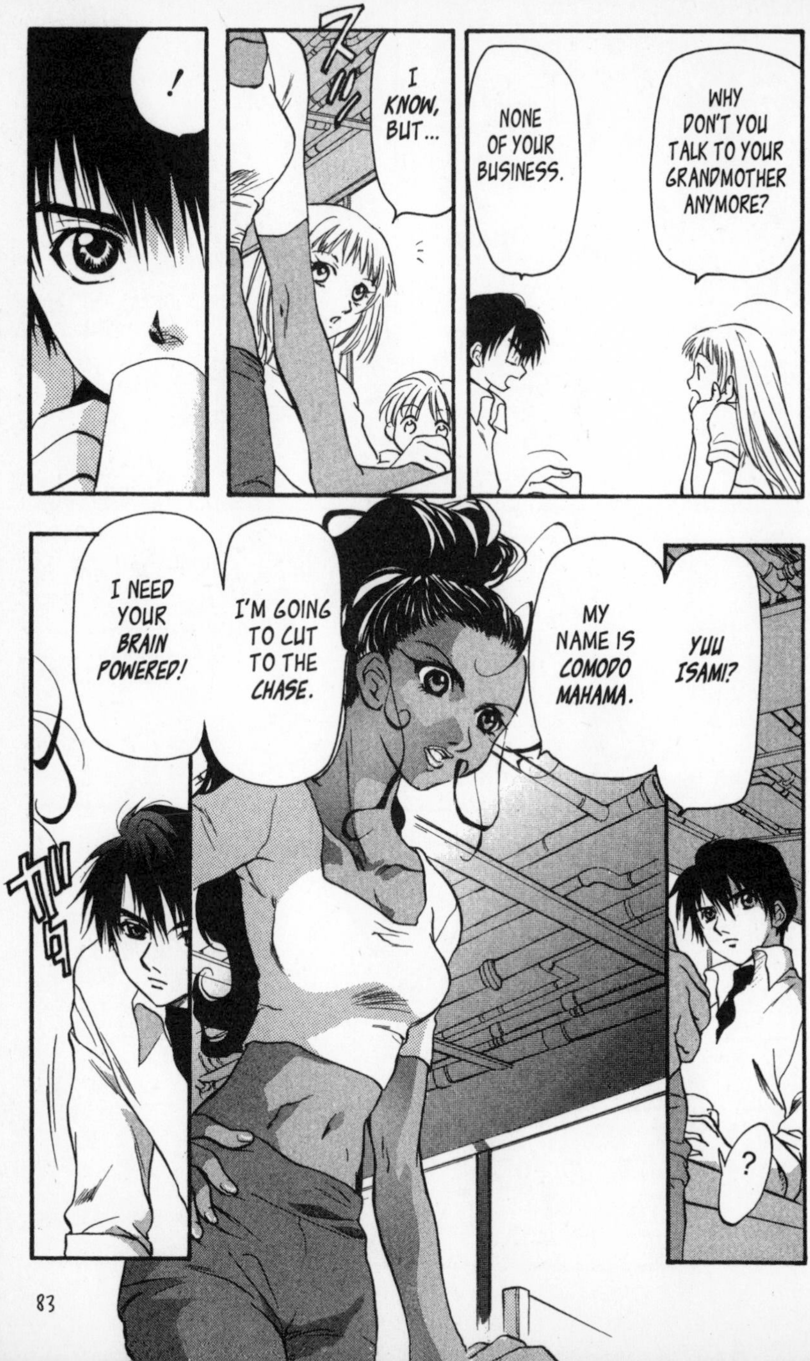

WHY DON'T YOU TALK TO YOUR GRANDMOTHER ANYMORE?
NONE OF YOUR BUSINESS.
I KNOW, BUT...
!
YUU ISAMI?
?
MY NAME IS COMODO MAHAMA.
I'M GOING TO CUT TO THE CHASE.
I NEED YOUR BRAIN POWERED!

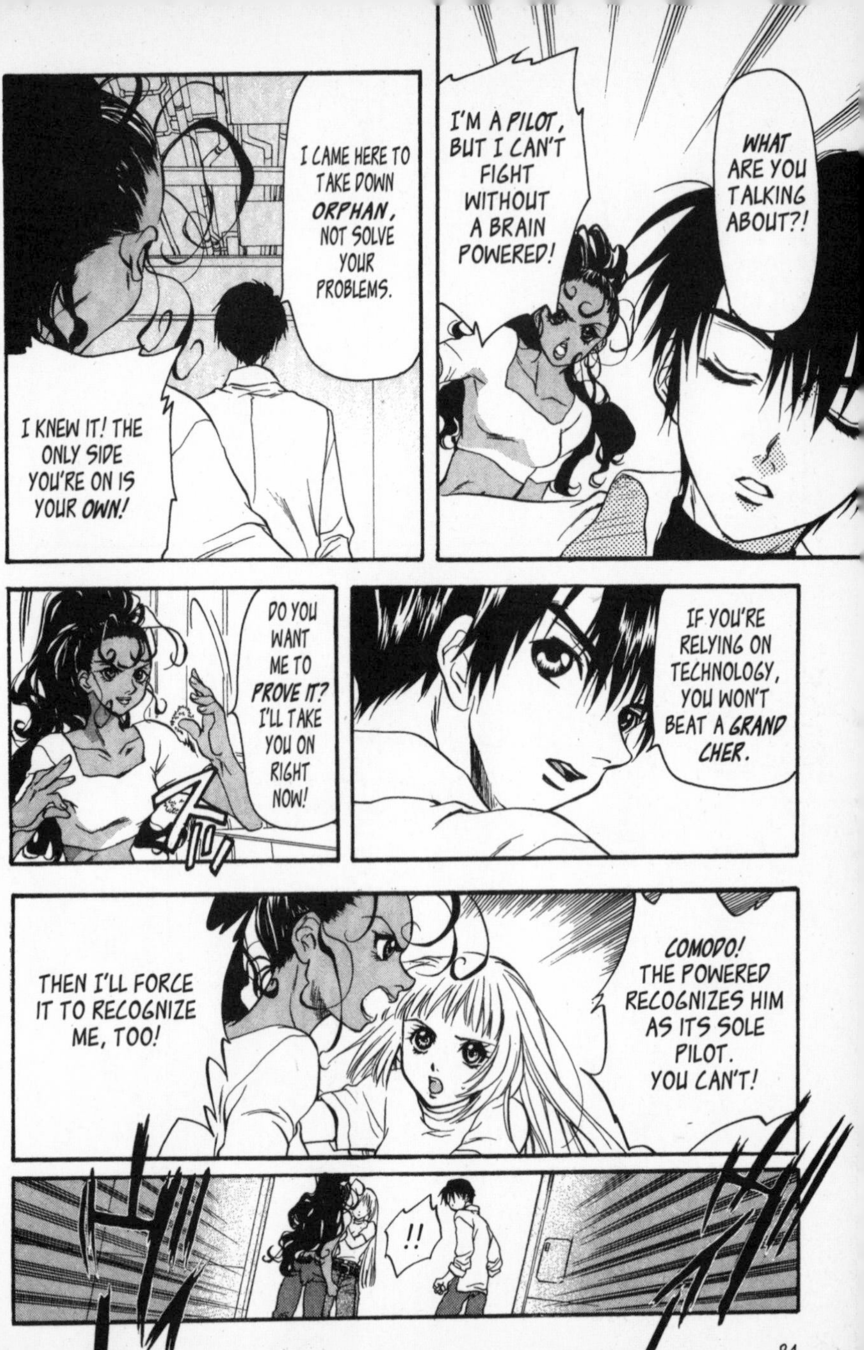
WHAT ARE YOU TALKING ABOUT?!
I'M A PILOT, BUT I CAN'T FIGHT WITHOUT A BRAIN POWERED!
I CAME HERE TO TAKE DOWN ORPHAN, NOT SOLVE YOUR PROBLEMS.
I KNEW IT! THE ONLY SIDE YOU'RE ON IS YOUR OWN!
IF YOU'RE RELYING ON TECHNOLOGY, YOU WON'T BEAT A GRAND CHER.
DO YOU WANT ME TO PROVE IT? I'LL TAKE YOU ON RIGHT NOW!
COMODO! THE POWERED RECOGNIZES HIM AS ITS SOLE PILOT. YOU CAN'T!
THEN I'LL FORCE IT TO RECOGNIZE ME, TOO!
!!

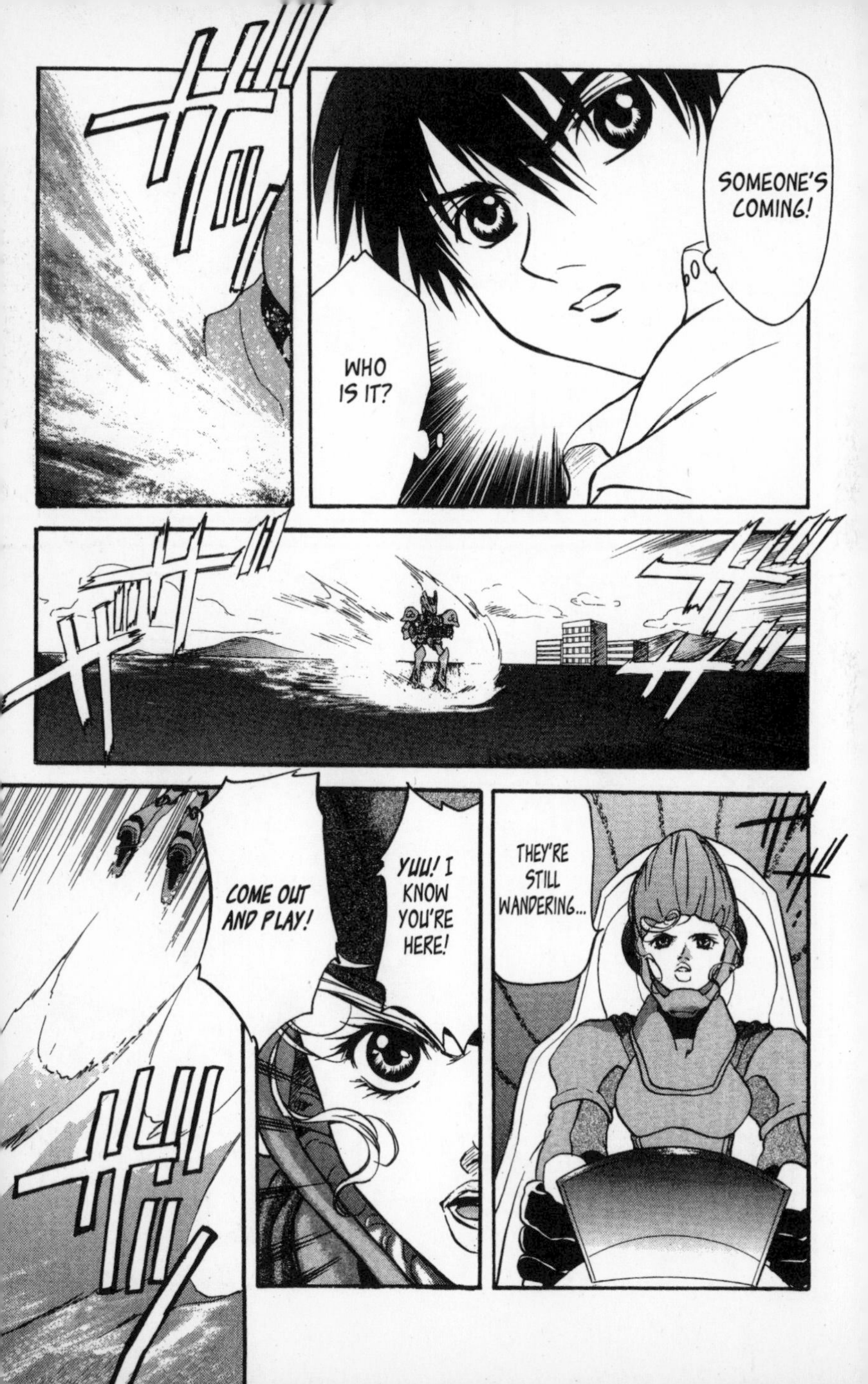
SOMEONE'S COMING!
WHO IS IT?
THEY'RE STILL WANDERING...
YUU! I KNOW YOU'RE HERE!
COME OUT AND PLAY!

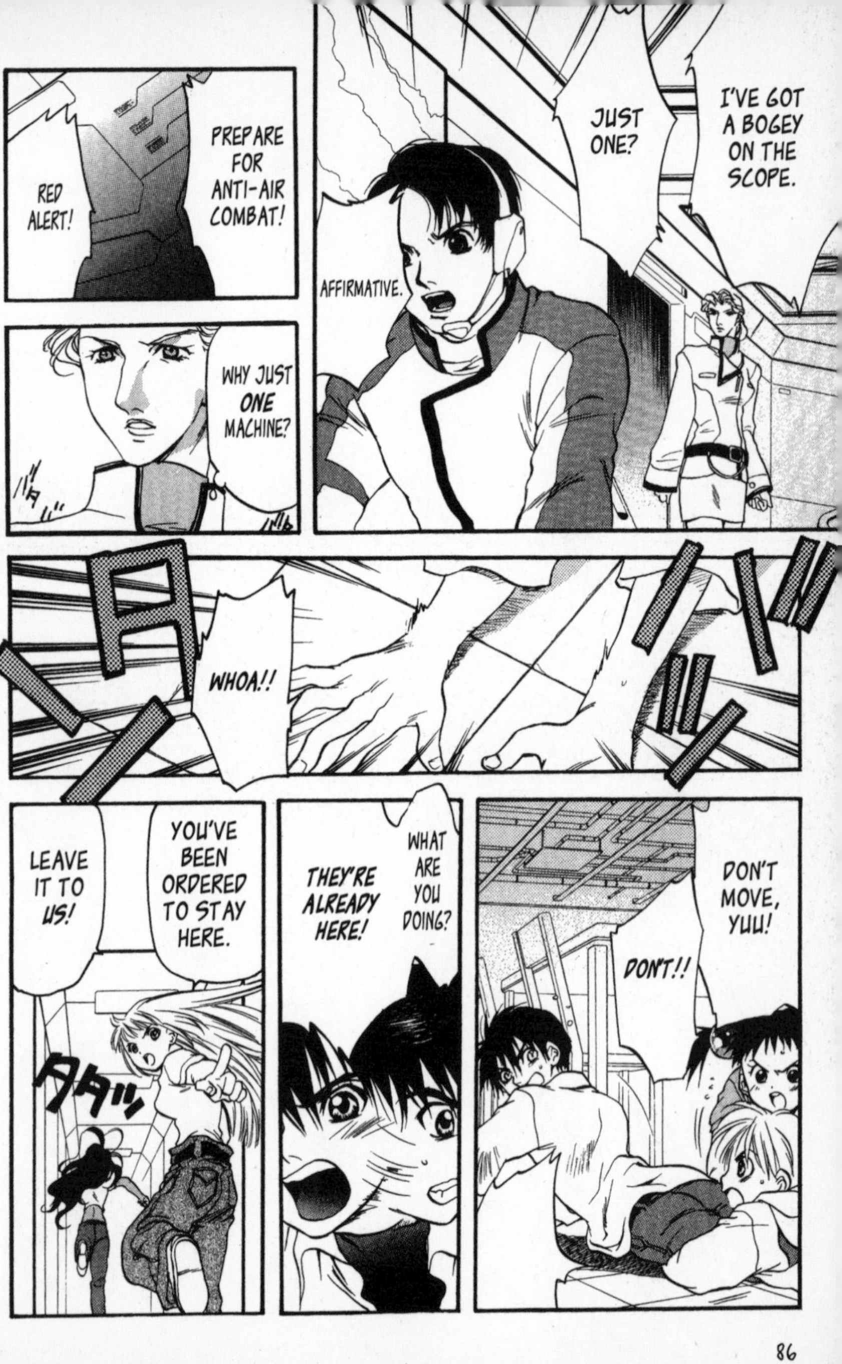
I'VE GOT A BOGEY ON THE SCOPE.
JUST ONE?
AFFIRMATIVE.
PREPARE FOR ANTI-AIR COMBAT!
RED ALERT!
WHY JUST *ONE* MACHINE?
WHOA!!
DON'T MOVE, YUU!
DON'T!!
WHAT ARE YOU DOING?
THEY'RE ALREADY HERE!
YOU'VE BEEN ORDERED TO STAY HERE.
LEAVE IT TO *US!*

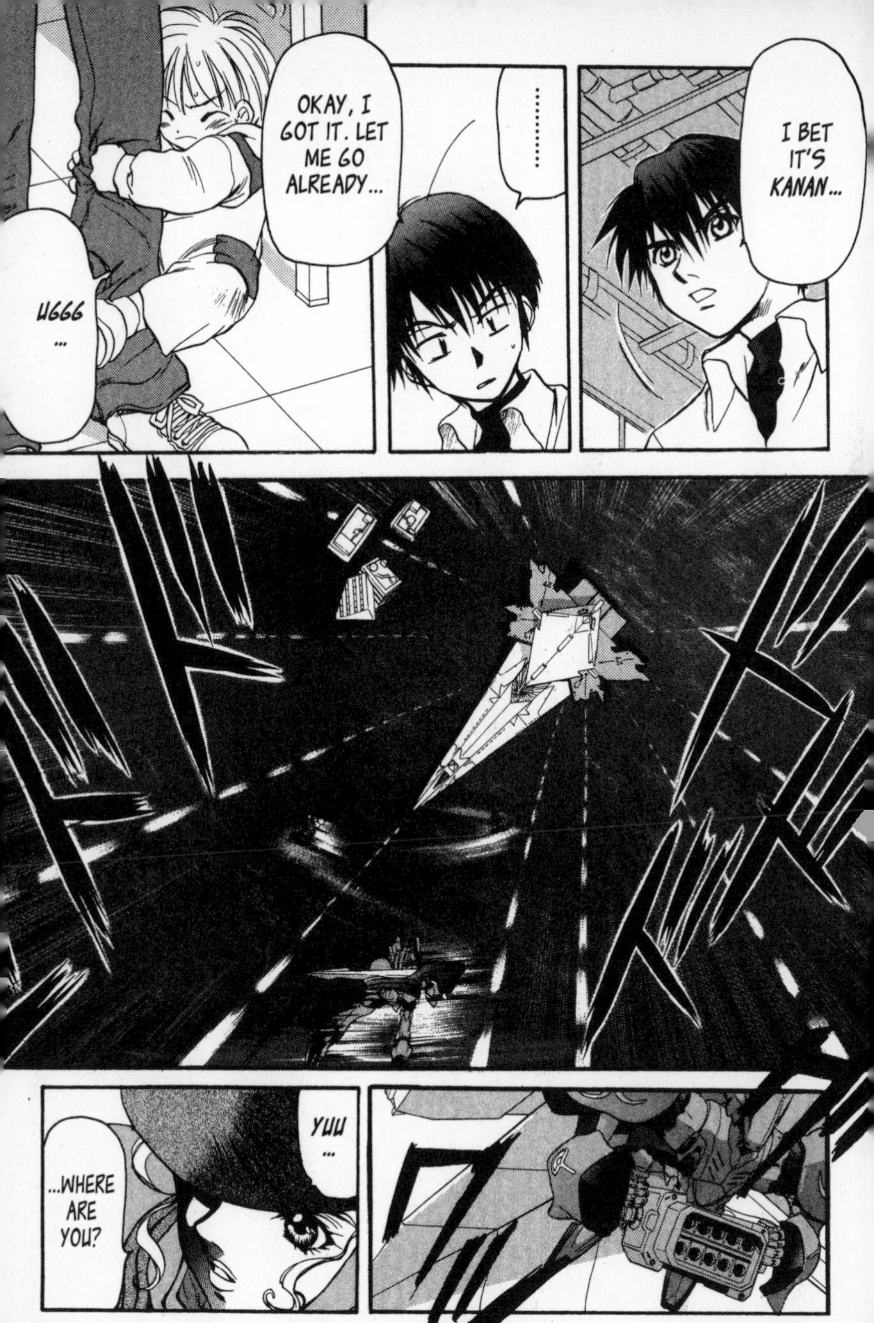
I BET IT'S KANAN...
....
OKAY, I GOT IT. LET ME GO ALREADY...
UGGG...
YUU...
...WHERE ARE YOU?

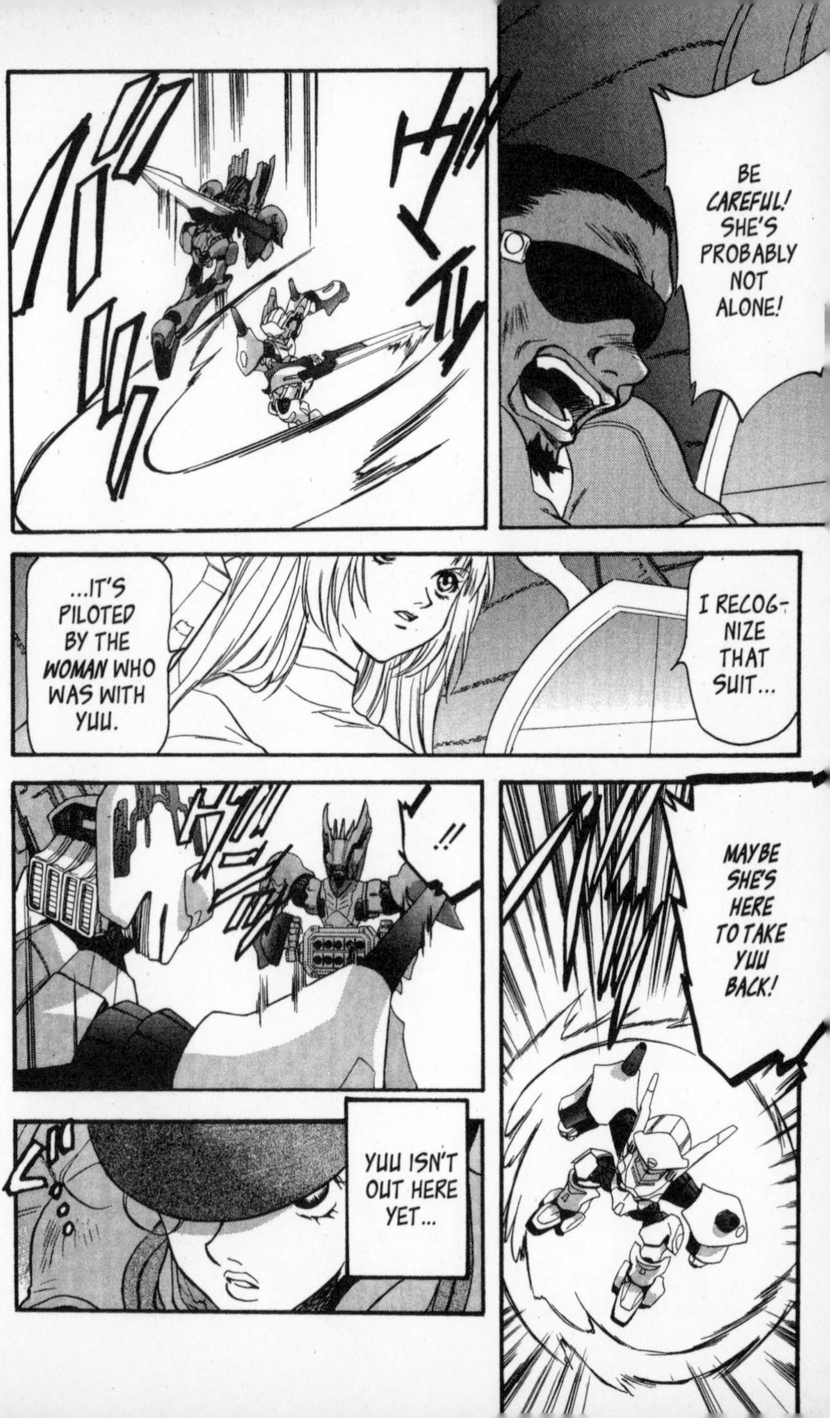
BE CAREFUL! SHE'S PROBABLY NOT ALONE!
I RECOG-NIZE THAT SUIT...
...IT'S PILOTED BY THE WOMAN WHO WAS WITH YUU.
MAYBE SHE'S HERE TO TAKE YUU BACK!
!!
YUU ISN'T OUT HERE YET...

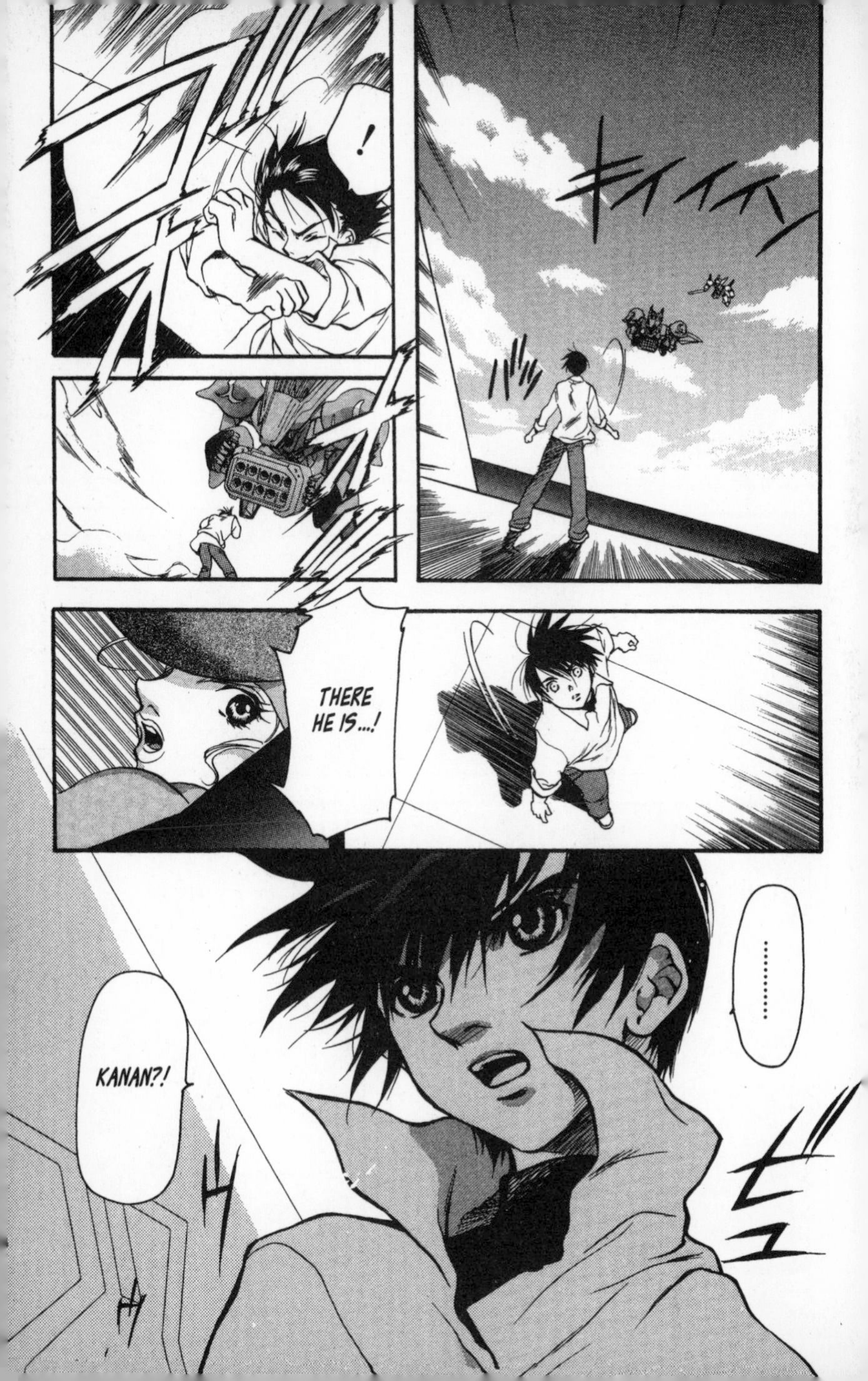
!
THERE HE IS...!
....
KANAN?!

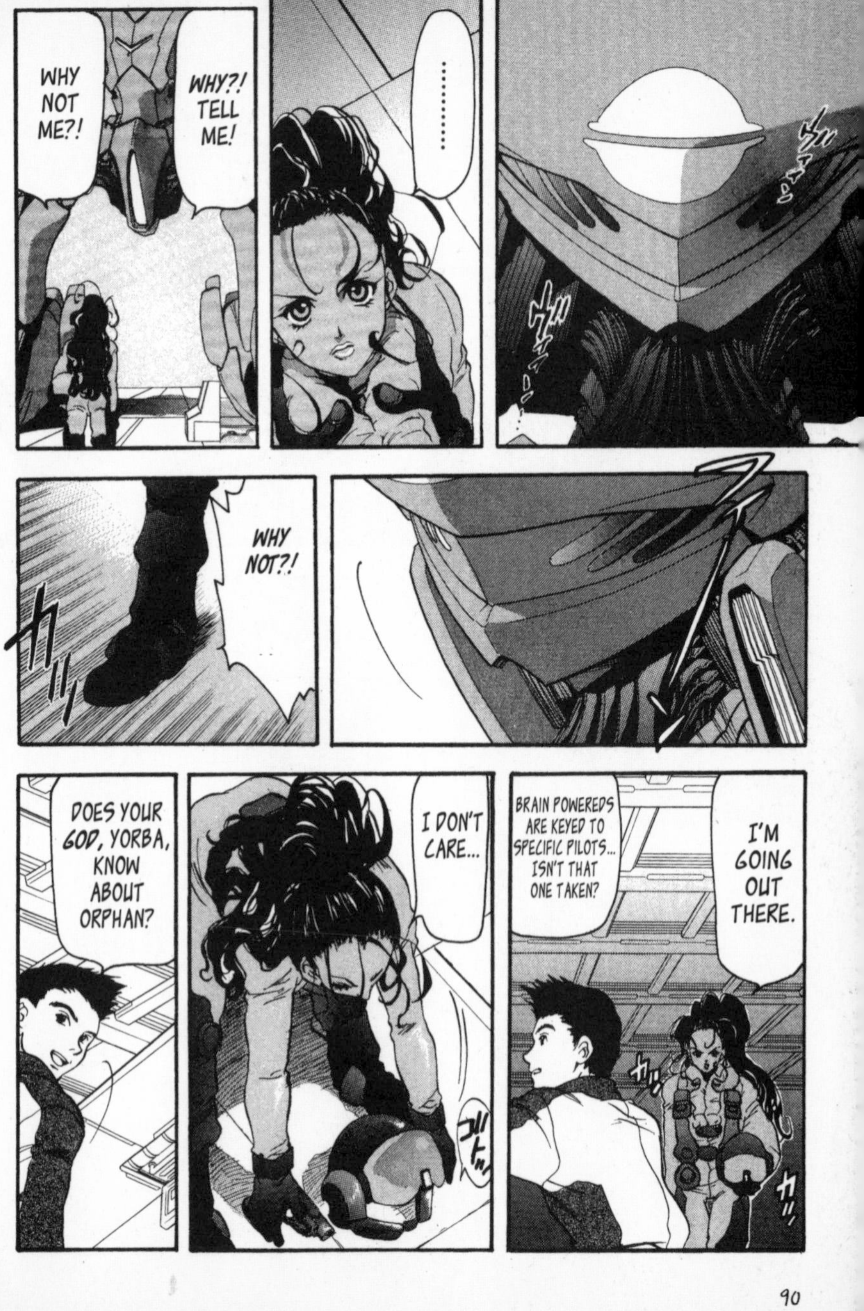
……
WHY?! TELL ME!
WHY NOT ME?!
WHY NOT?!
I'M GOING OUT THERE.
BRAIN POWEREDS ARE KEYED TO SPECIFIC PILOTS... ISN'T THAT ONE TAKEN?
I DON'T CARE...
DOES YOUR GOD, YORBA, KNOW ABOUT ORPHAN?

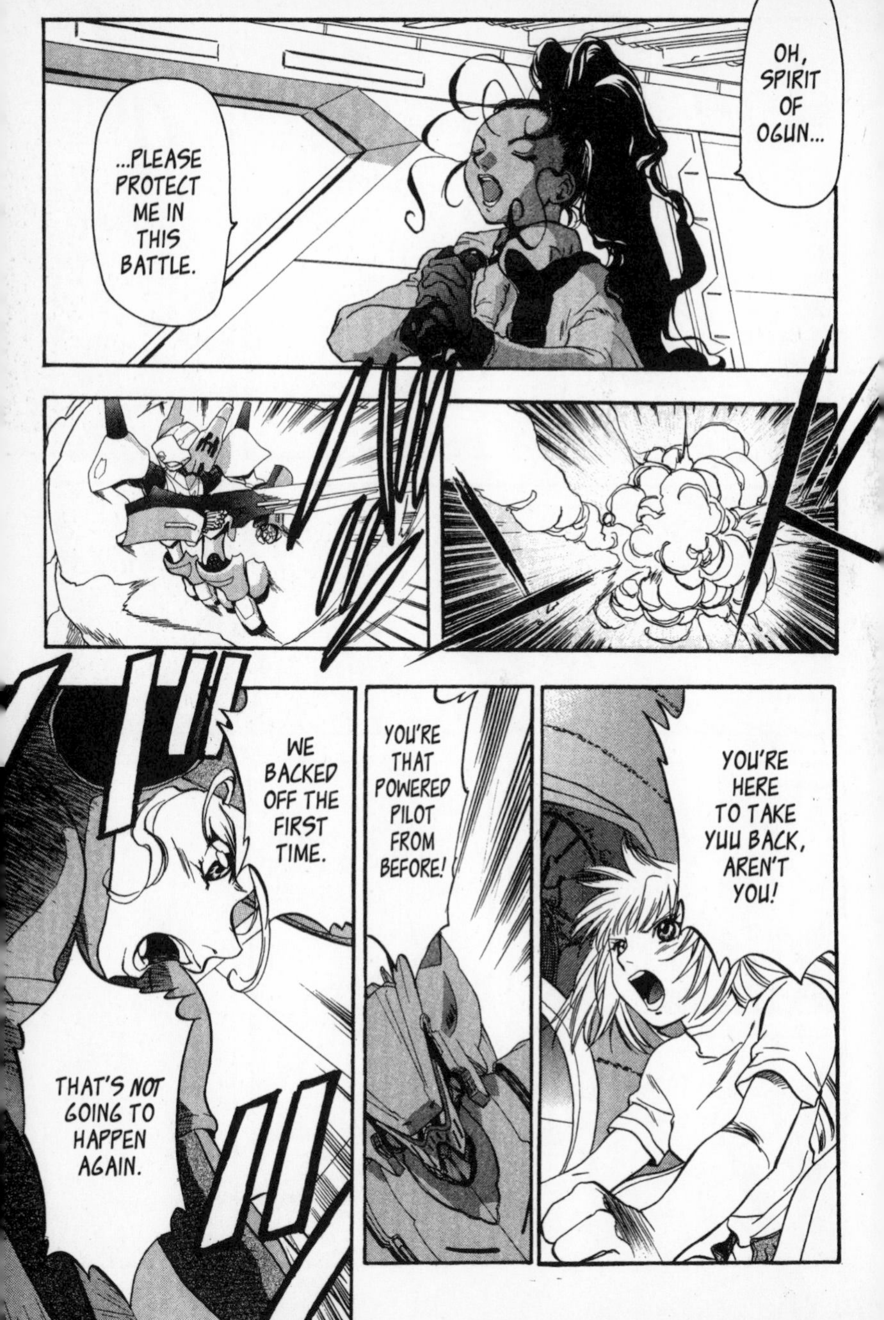
OH, SPIRIT OF OGUN...
...PLEASE PROTECT ME IN THIS BATTLE.
YOU'RE HERE TO TAKE YUU BACK, AREN'T YOU!
YOU'RE THAT POWERED PILOT FROM BEFORE!
WE BACKED OFF THE FIRST TIME.
THAT'S NOT GOING TO HAPPEN AGAIN.

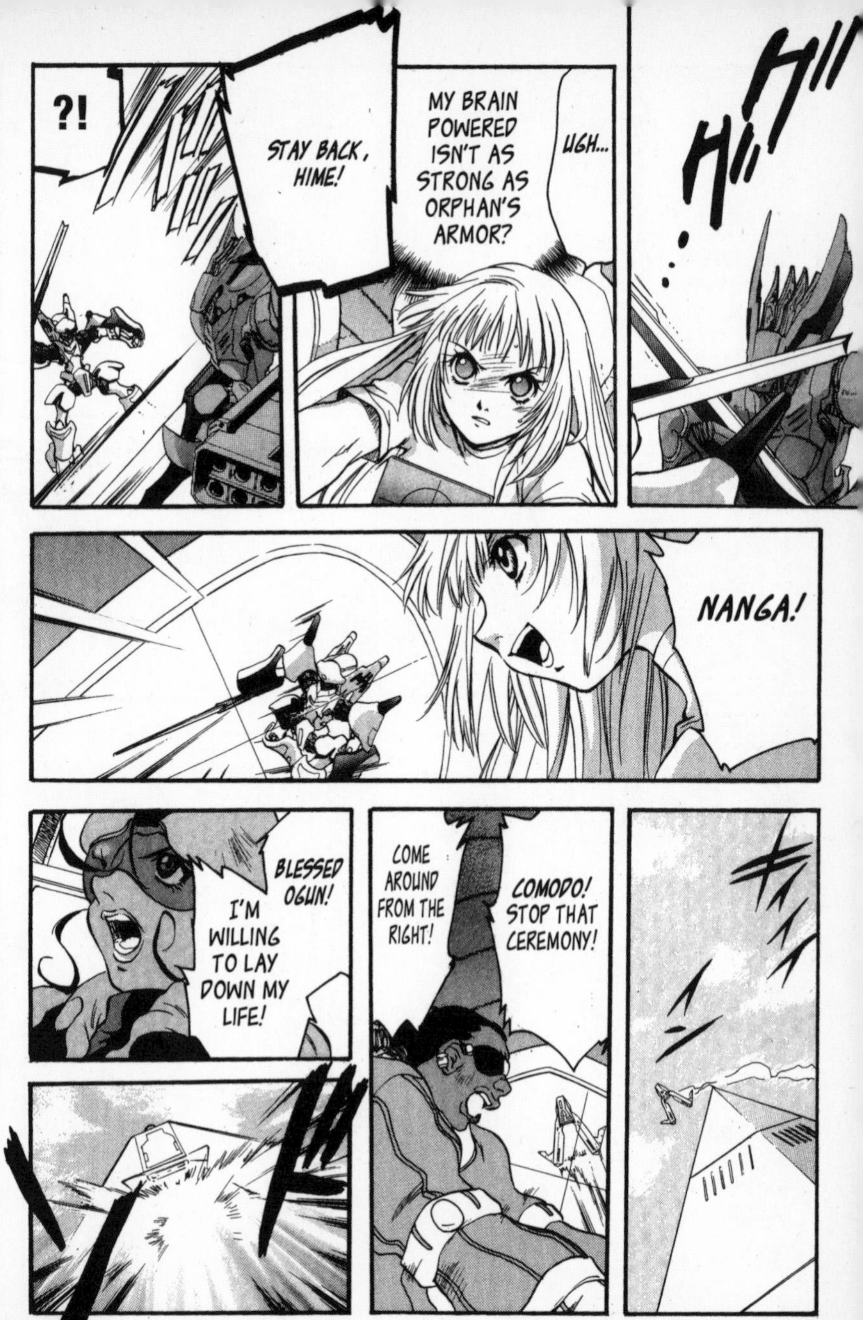
UGH...
MY BRAIN POWERED ISN'T AS STRONG AS ORPHAN'S ARMOR?
STAY BACK, HIME!
?!
NANGA!
COMODO! STOP THAT CEREMONY!
COME AROUND FROM THE RIGHT!
BLESSED OGUN!
I'M WILLING TO LAY DOWN MY LIFE!

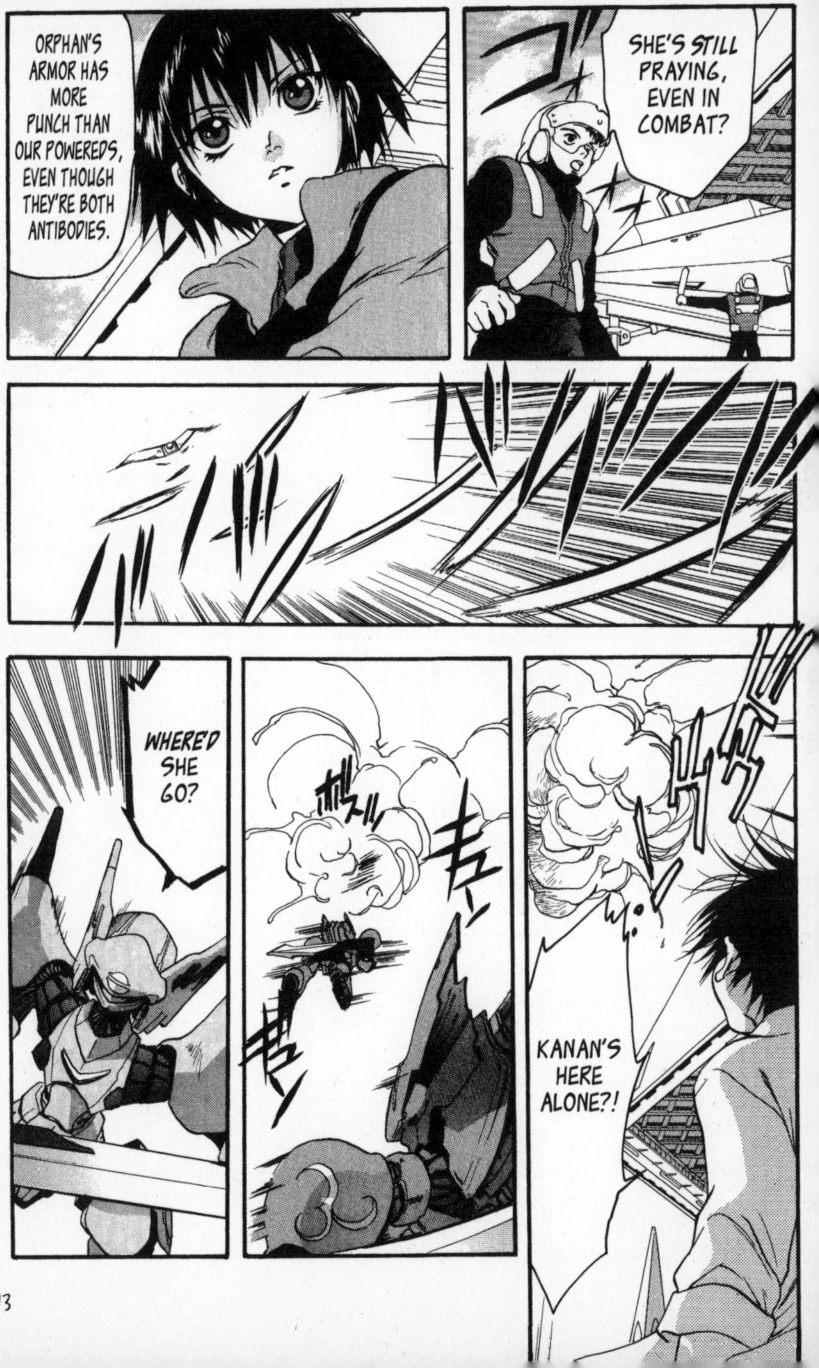
SHE'S STILL PRAYING, EVEN IN COMBAT?
ORPHAN'S ARMOR HAS MORE PUNCH THAN OUR POWEREDS, EVEN THOUGH THEY'RE BOTH ANTIBODIES.
KANAN'S HERE ALONE?!
WHERE'D SHE GO?

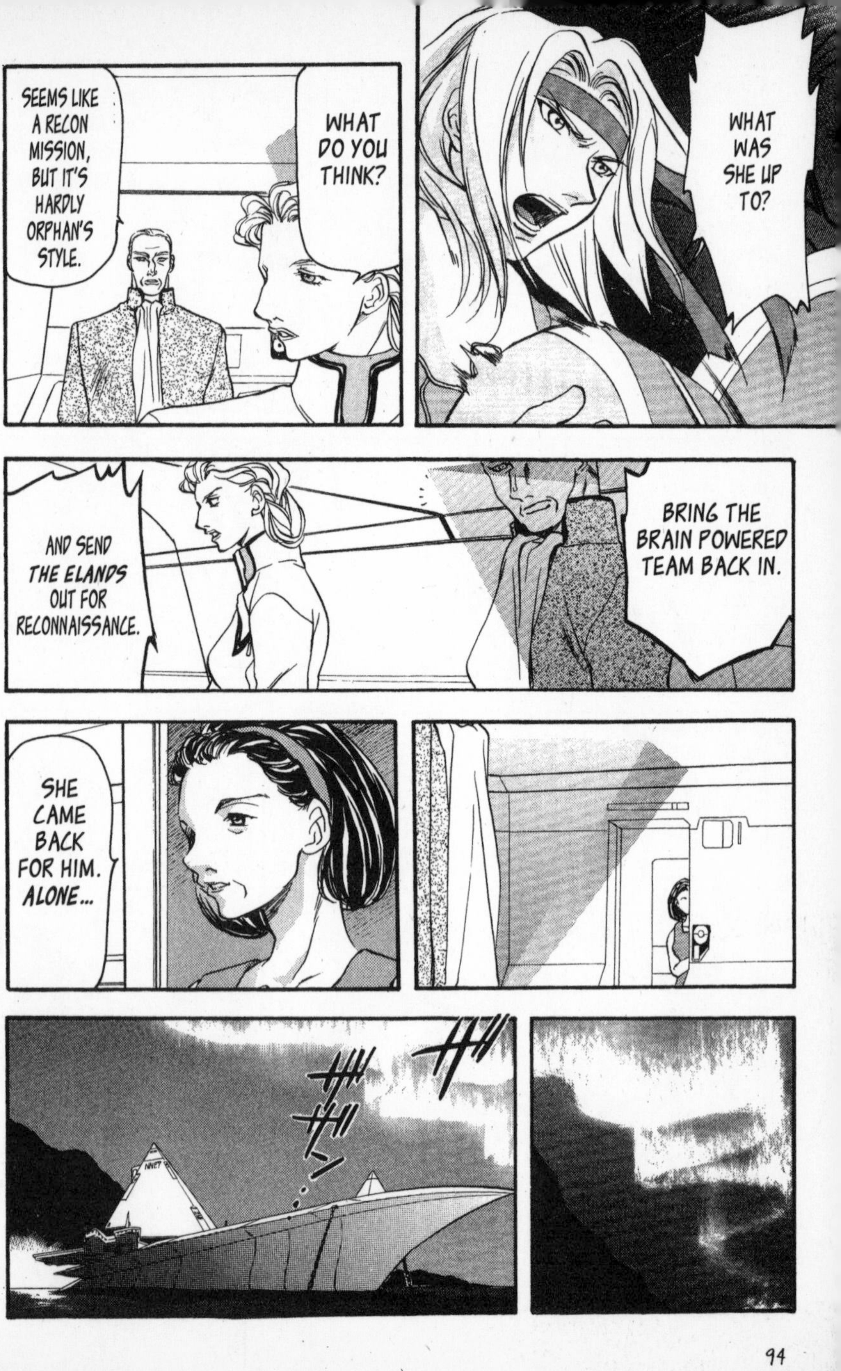
WHAT WAS SHE UP TO?
WHAT DO YOU THINK?
SEEMS LIKE A RECON MISSION, BUT IT'S HARDLY ORPHAN'S STYLE.
BRING THE BRAIN POWERED TEAM BACK IN.
AND SEND *THE ELANDS* OUT FOR RECONNAISSANCE.
SHE CAME BACK FOR HIM. *ALONE...*

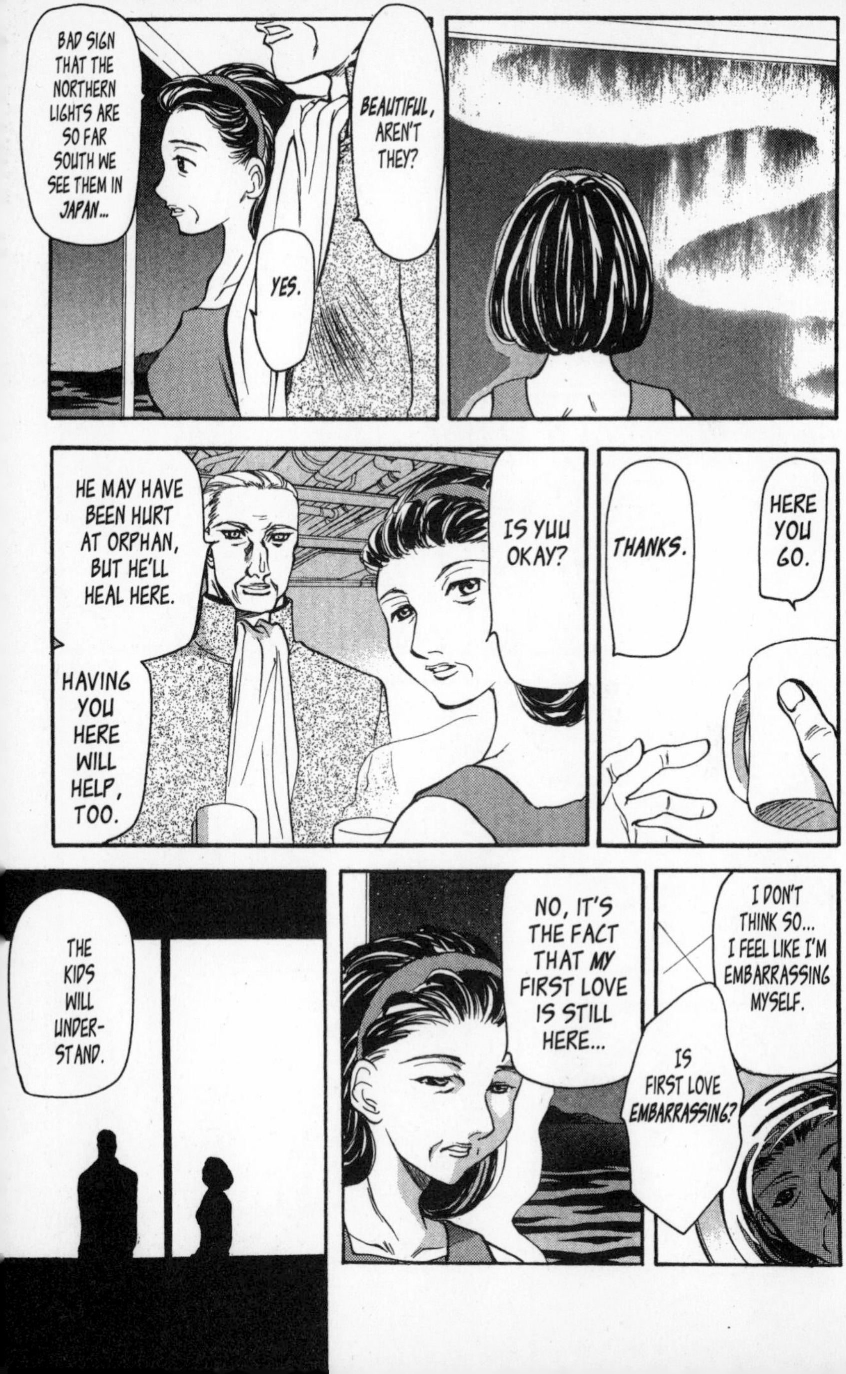

BEAUTIFUL, AREN'T THEY?
YES.
BAD SIGN THAT THE NORTHERN LIGHTS ARE SO FAR SOUTH WE SEE THEM IN JAPAN...
HERE YOU GO.
THANKS.
IS YUU OKAY?
HE MAY HAVE BEEN HURT AT ORPHAN, BUT HE'LL HEAL HERE.
HAVING YOU HERE WILL HELP, TOO.
I DON'T THINK SO... I FEEL LIKE I'M EMBARRASSING MYSELF.
IS FIRST LOVE EMBARRASSING?
NO, IT'S THE FACT THAT *MY* FIRST LOVE IS STILL HERE...
THE KIDS WILL UNDER-STAND.

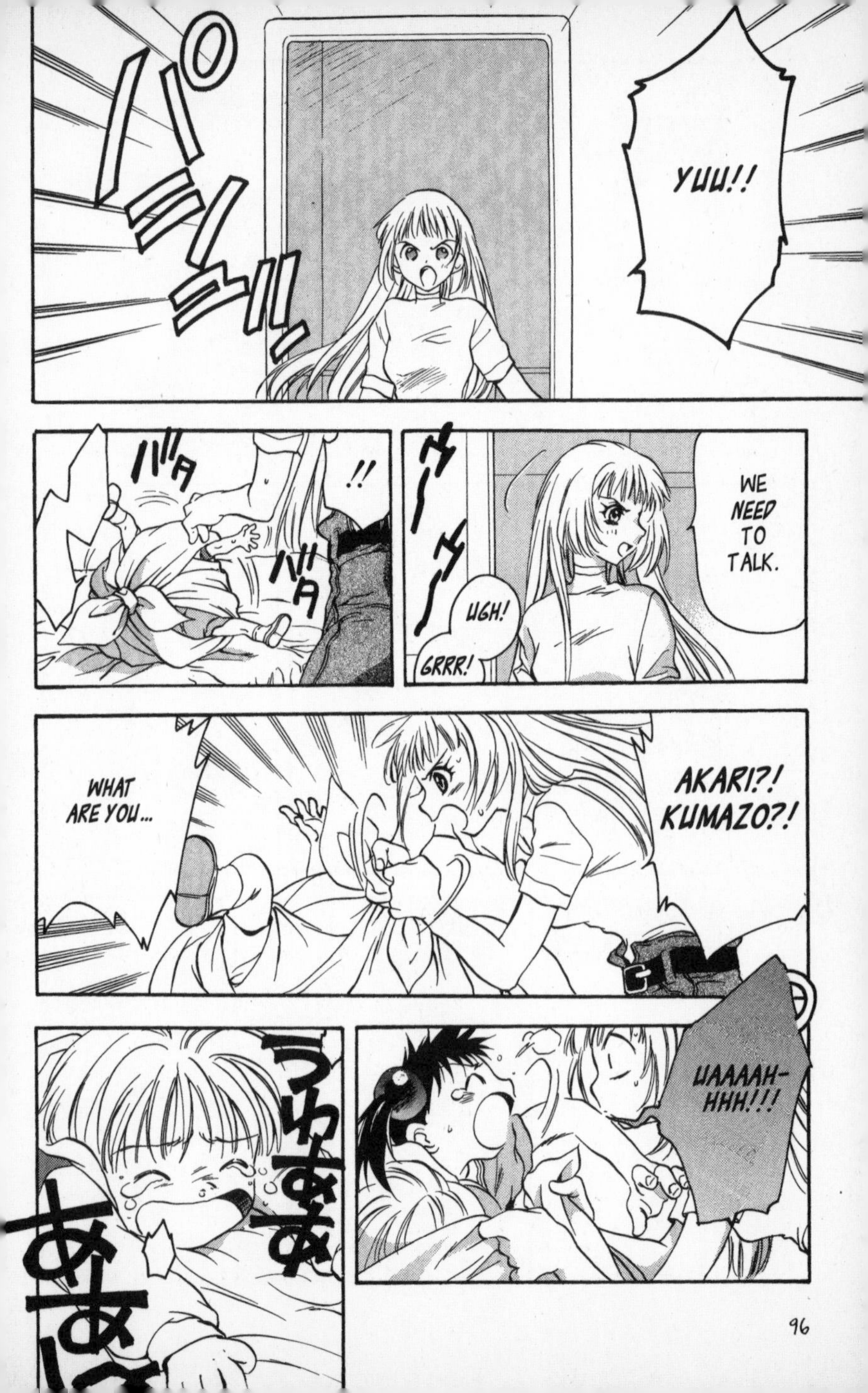
YUU!!
WE NEED TO TALK.
UGH!
GRRR!
!!
AKARI?! KUMAZO?!
WHAT ARE YOU...
UAAAAH-HHH!!!

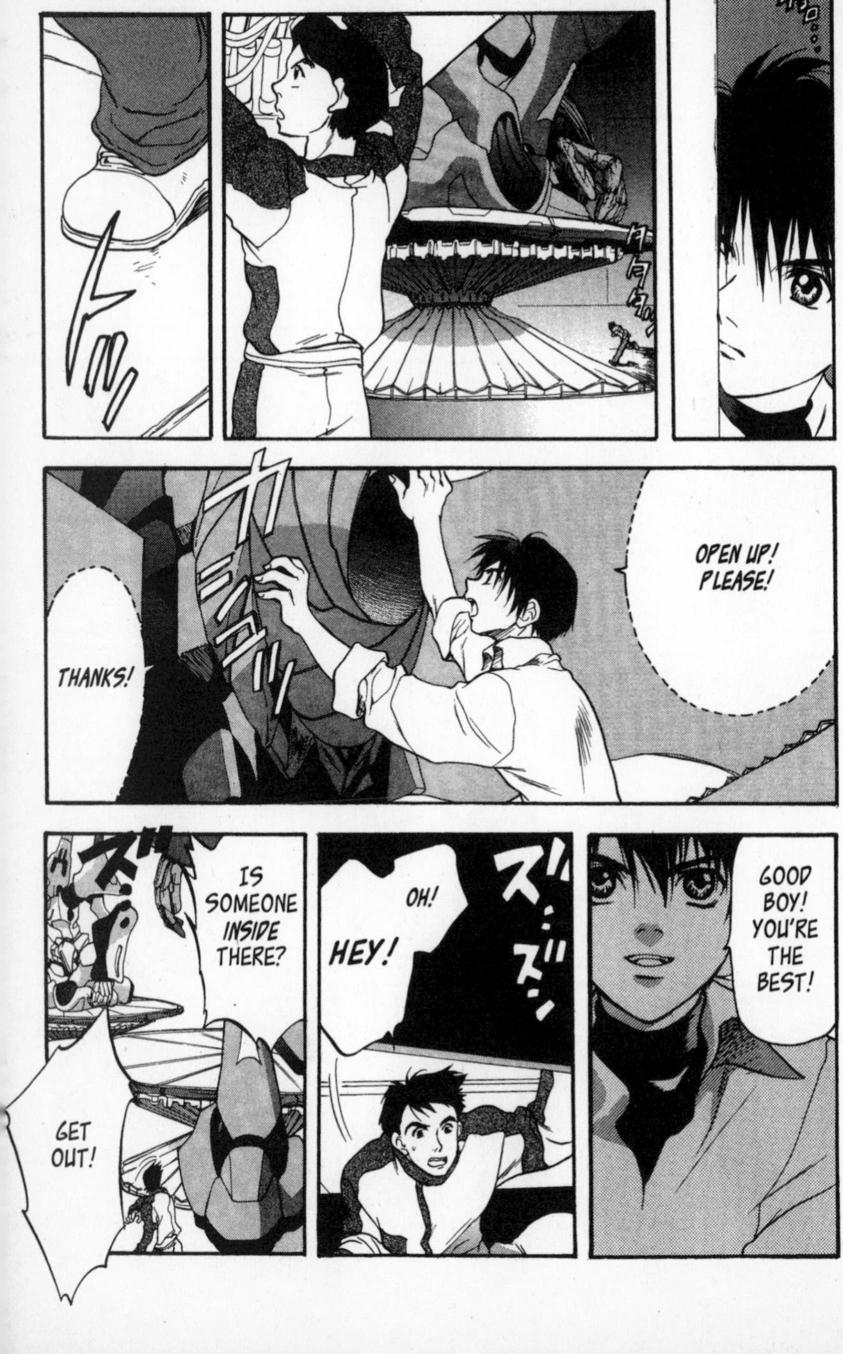
OPEN UP! PLEASE!
THANKS!
GOOD BOY! YOU'RE THE BEST!
OH!
HEY!
IS SOMEONE INSIDE THERE?
GET OUT!

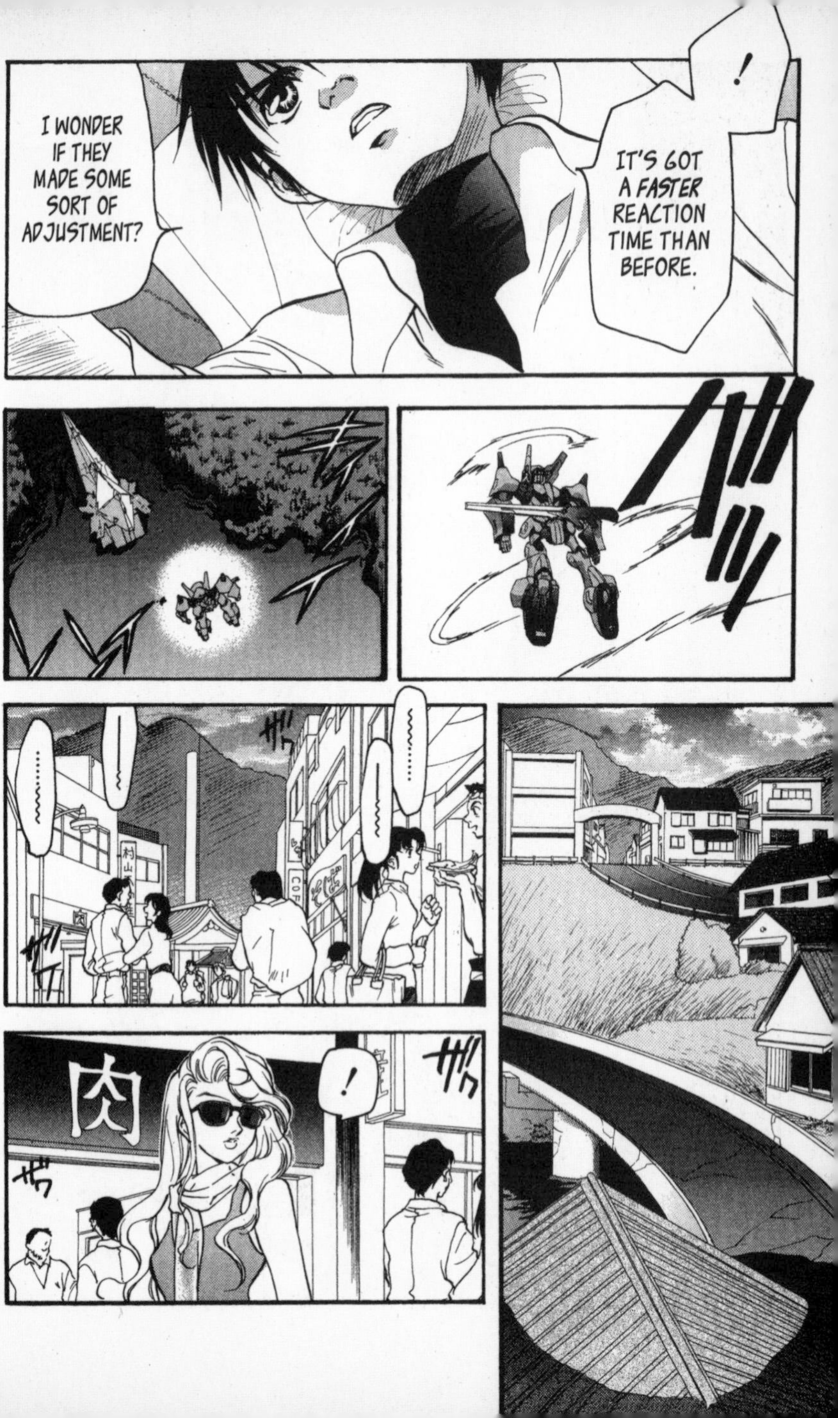
!
IT'S GOT A FASTER REACTION TIME THAN BEFORE.
I WONDER IF THEY MADE SOME SORT OF ADJUSTMENT?
ババッ
ザワ
そば
COF
村山
ザワ
肉
!
ザワ

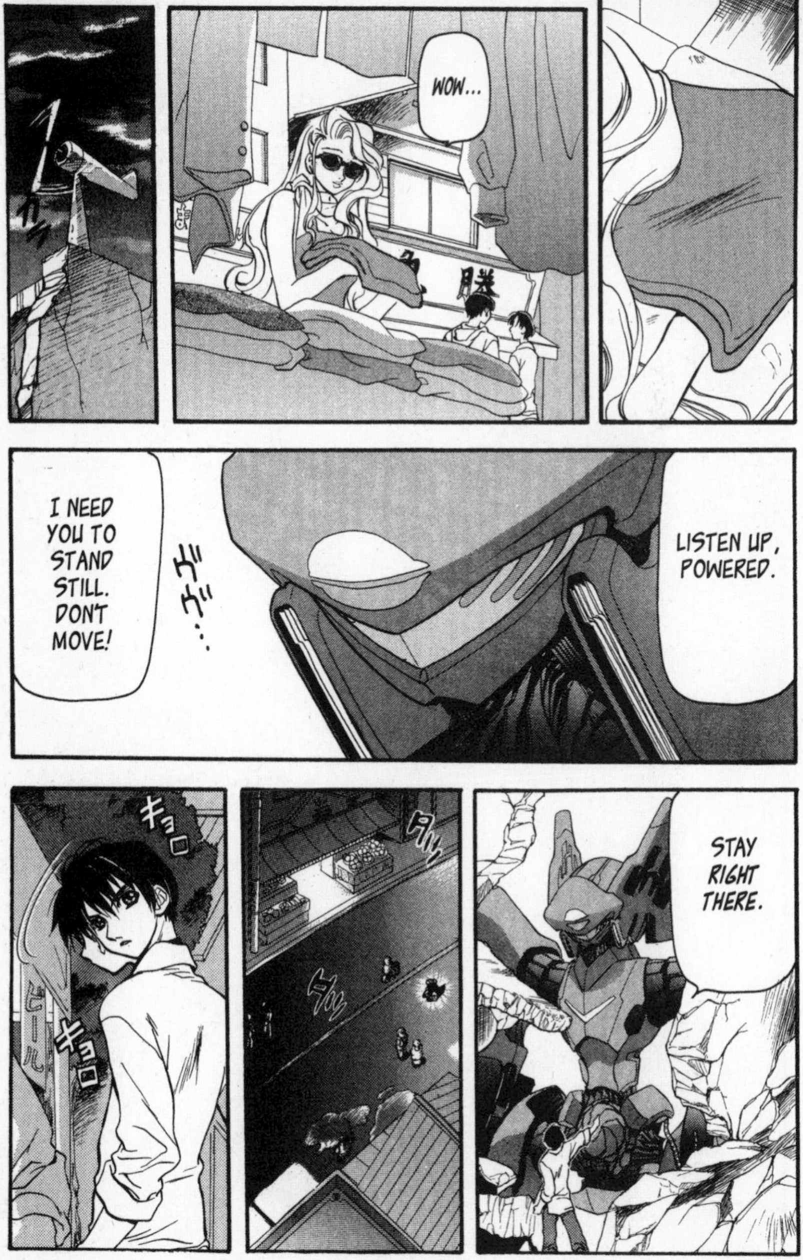
WOW...
LISTEN UP, POWERED.
I NEED YOU TO STAND STILL. DON'T MOVE!
STAY RIGHT THERE.

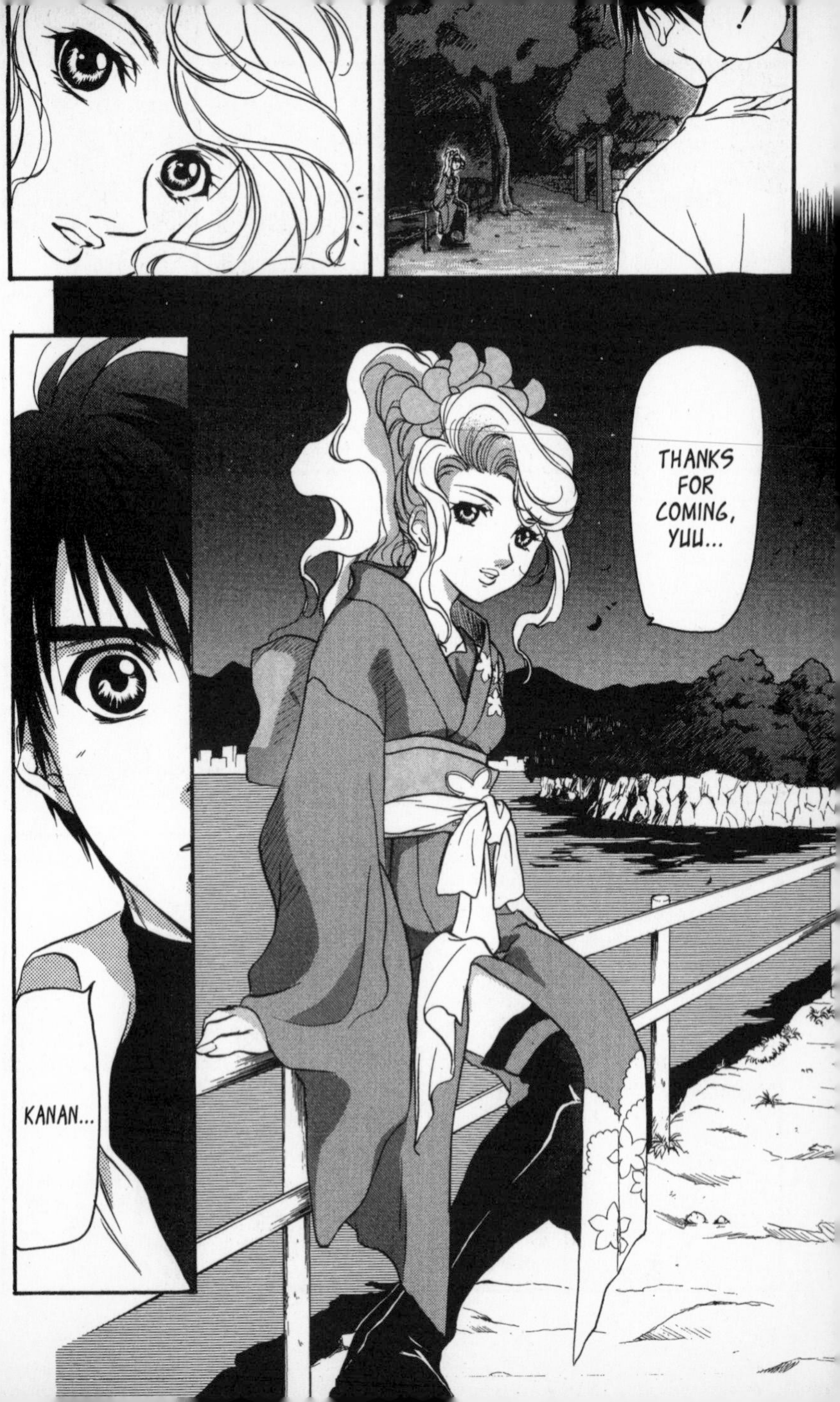
!
THANKS FOR COMING, YUU...
KANAN...

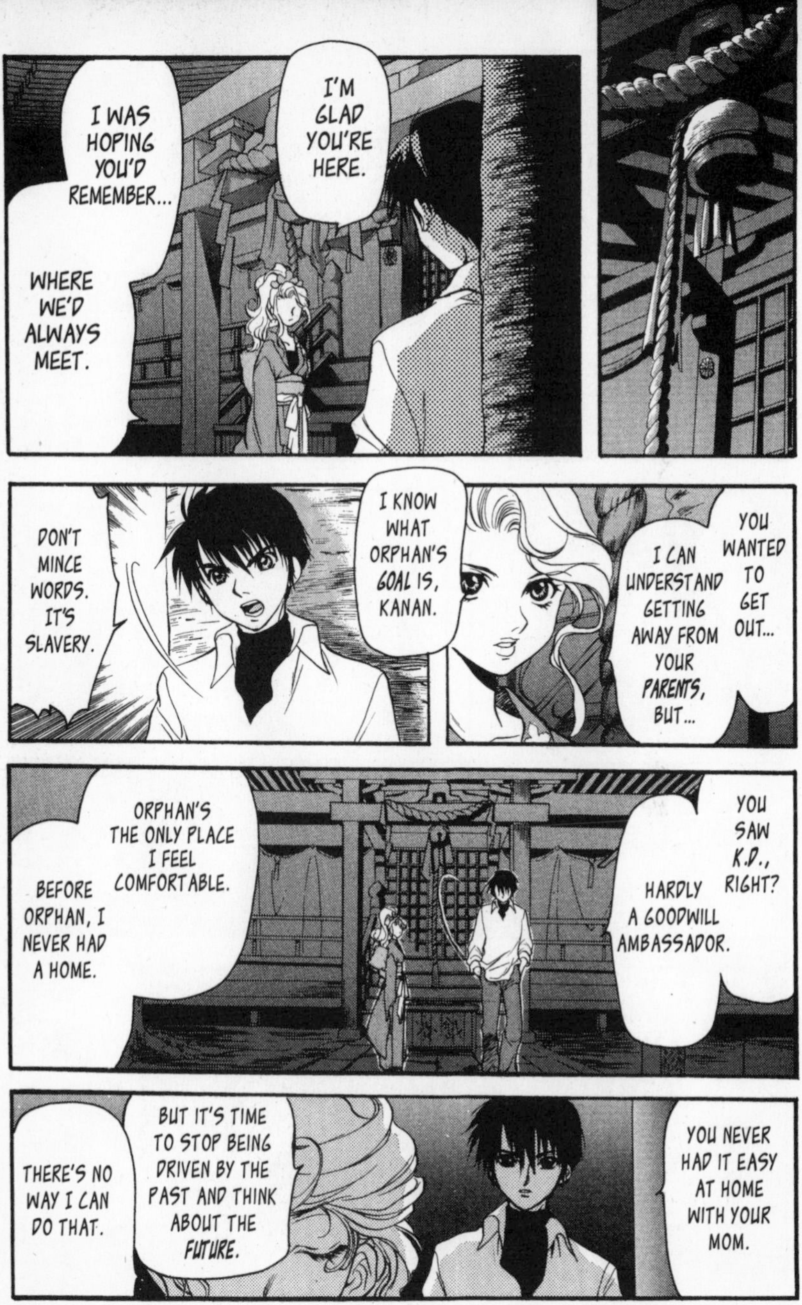
I'M GLAD YOU'RE HERE.
I WAS HOPING YOU'D REMEMBER...
WHERE WE'D ALWAYS MEET.
YOU WANTED TO GET OUT...
I CAN UNDERSTAND GETTING AWAY FROM YOUR PARENTS, BUT...
I KNOW WHAT ORPHAN'S GOAL IS, KANAN.
DON'T MINCE WORDS. IT'S SLAVERY.
YOU SAW K.D., RIGHT?
HARDLY A GOODWILL AMBASSADOR.
ORPHAN'S THE ONLY PLACE I FEEL COMFORTABLE.
BEFORE ORPHAN, I NEVER HAD A HOME.
YOU NEVER HAD IT EASY AT HOME WITH YOUR MOM.
BUT IT'S TIME TO STOP BEING DRIVEN BY THE PAST AND THINK ABOUT THE FUTURE.
THERE'S NO WAY I CAN DO THAT.

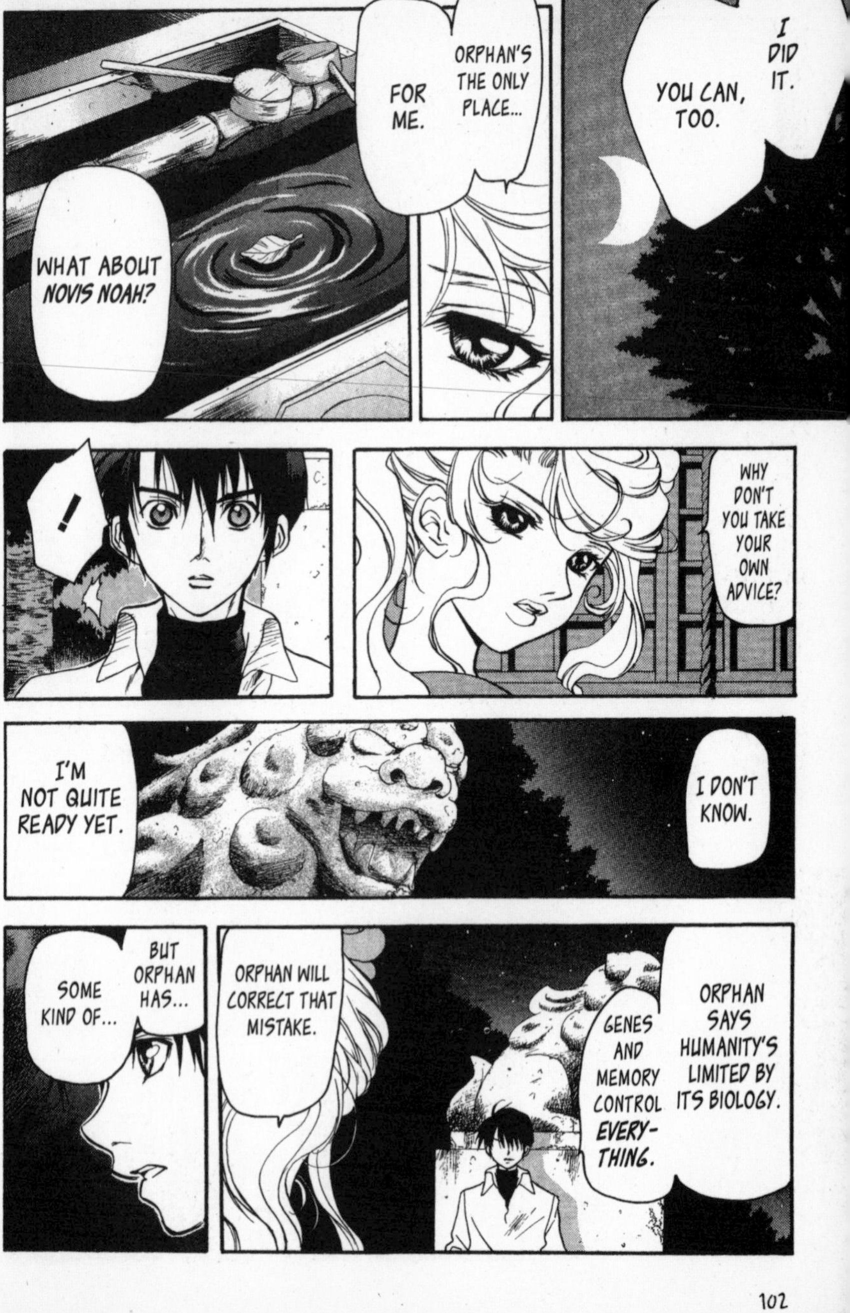
I DID IT.
YOU CAN, TOO.
ORPHAN'S THE ONLY PLACE...
FOR ME.
WHAT ABOUT *NOVIS NOAH?*
WHY DON'T YOU TAKE YOUR OWN ADVICE?
!
I DON'T KNOW.
I'M NOT QUITE READY YET.
ORPHAN SAYS HUMANITY'S LIMITED BY ITS BIOLOGY.
GENES AND MEMORY CONTROL *EVERYTHING.*
ORPHAN WILL CORRECT THAT MISTAKE.
BUT ORPHAN HAS...
SOME KIND OF...

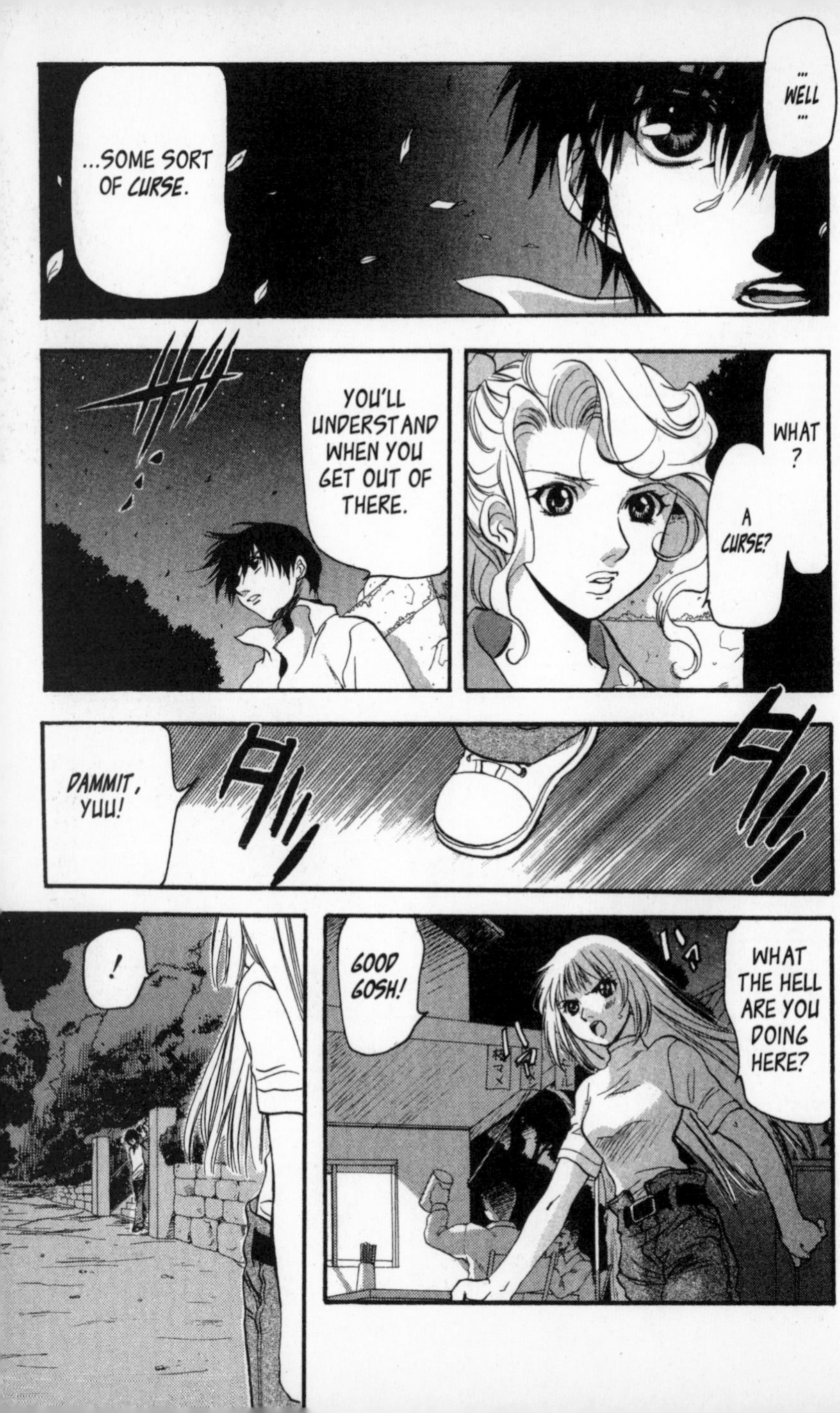
...WELL...
...SOME SORT OF CURSE.
WHAT? A CURSE?
YOU'LL UNDERSTAND WHEN YOU GET OUT OF THERE.
DAMMIT, YUU!
WHAT THE HELL ARE YOU DOING HERE?
GOOD GOSH!
!

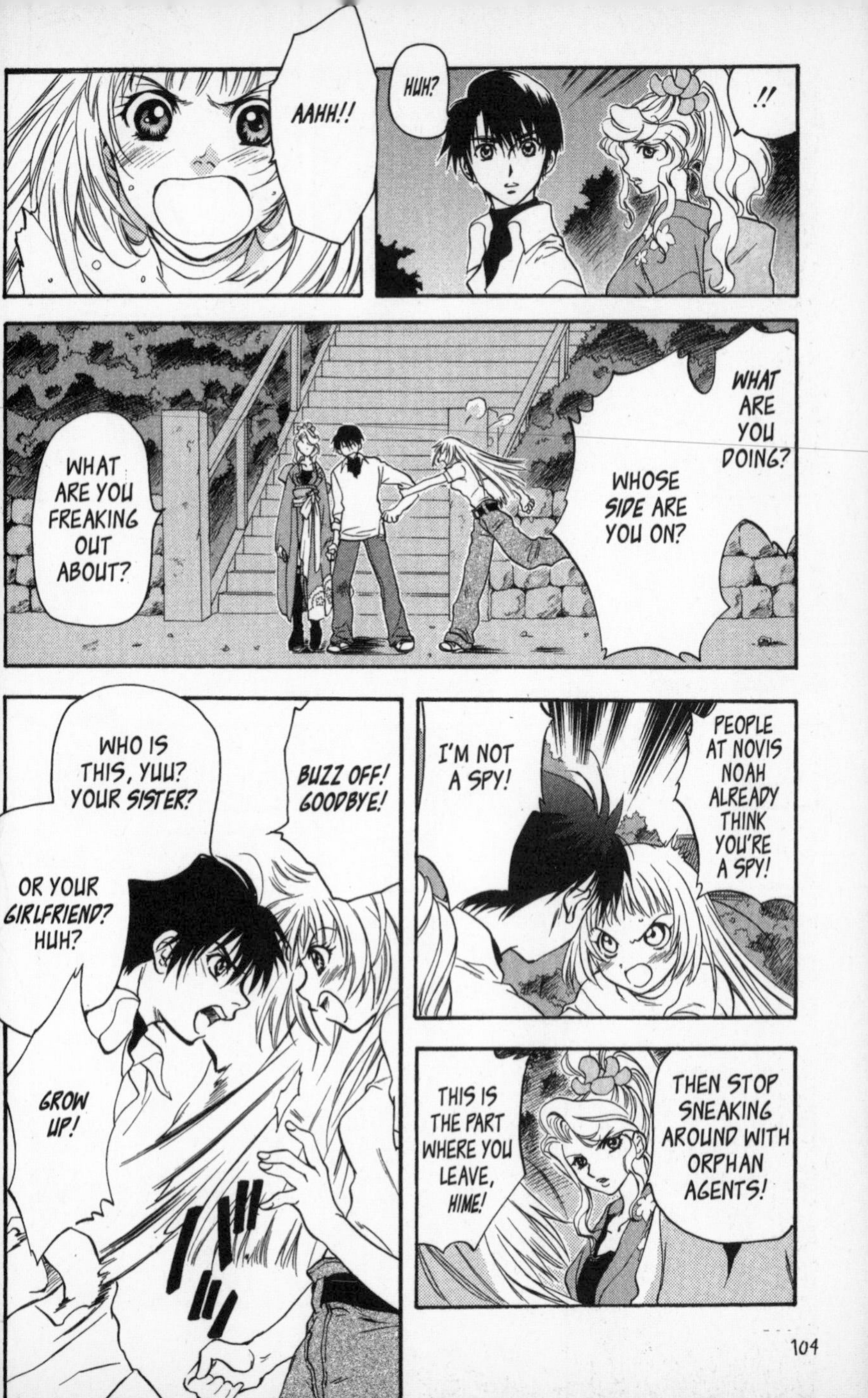
!!
HUH?
AAHH!!
WHAT ARE YOU DOING?
WHOSE SIDE ARE YOU ON?
WHAT ARE YOU FREAKING OUT ABOUT?
PEOPLE AT NOVIS NOAH ALREADY THINK YOU'RE A SPY!
I'M NOT A SPY!
THEN STOP SNEAKING AROUND WITH ORPHAN AGENTS!
THIS IS THE PART WHERE YOU LEAVE, HIME!
BUZZ OFF! GOODBYE!
WHO IS THIS, YUU? YOUR SISTER?
OR YOUR GIRLFRIEND? HUH?
GROW UP!

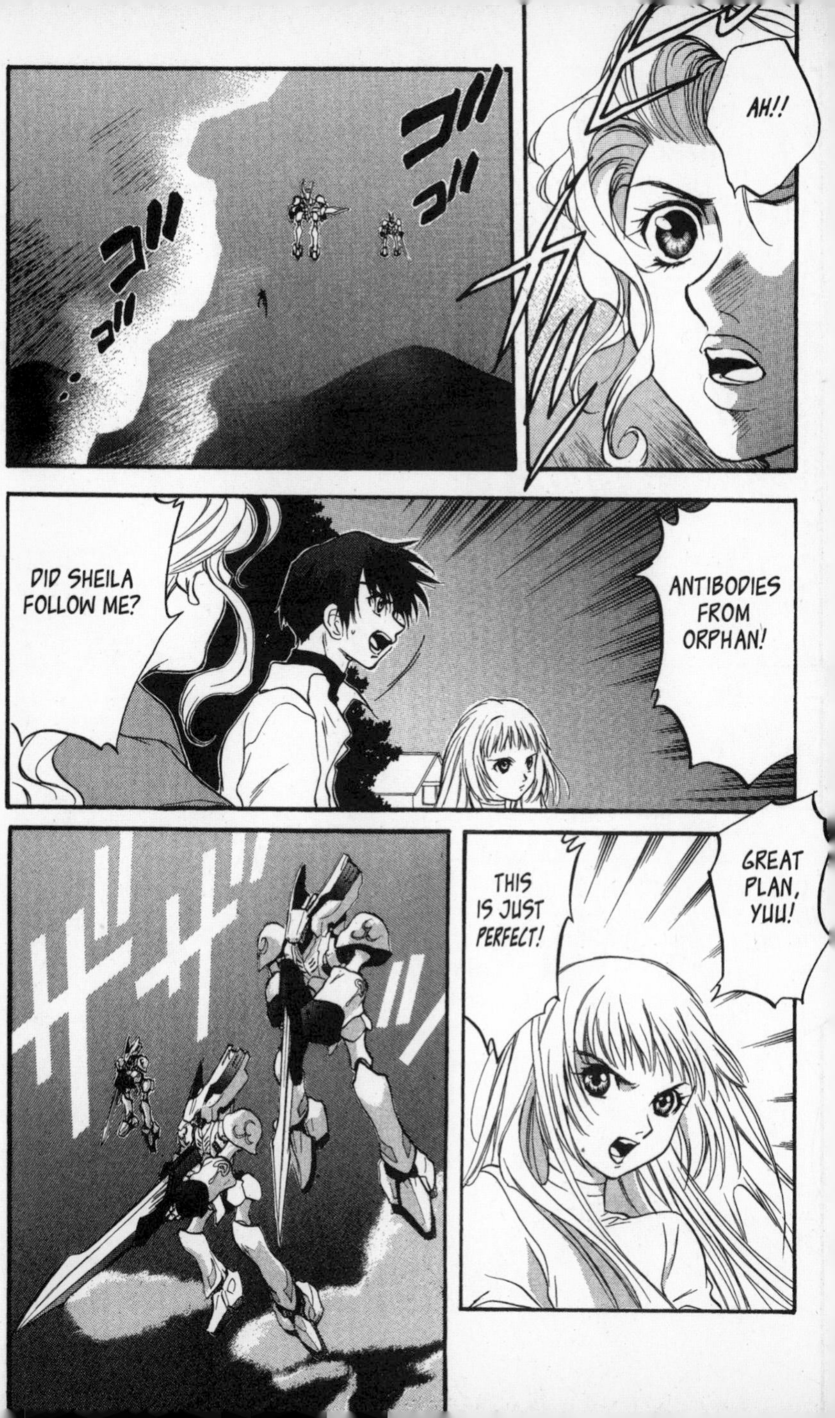
AH!!
ANTIBODIES FROM ORPHAN!
DID SHEILA FOLLOW ME?
GREAT PLAN, YUU!
THIS IS JUST PERFECT!

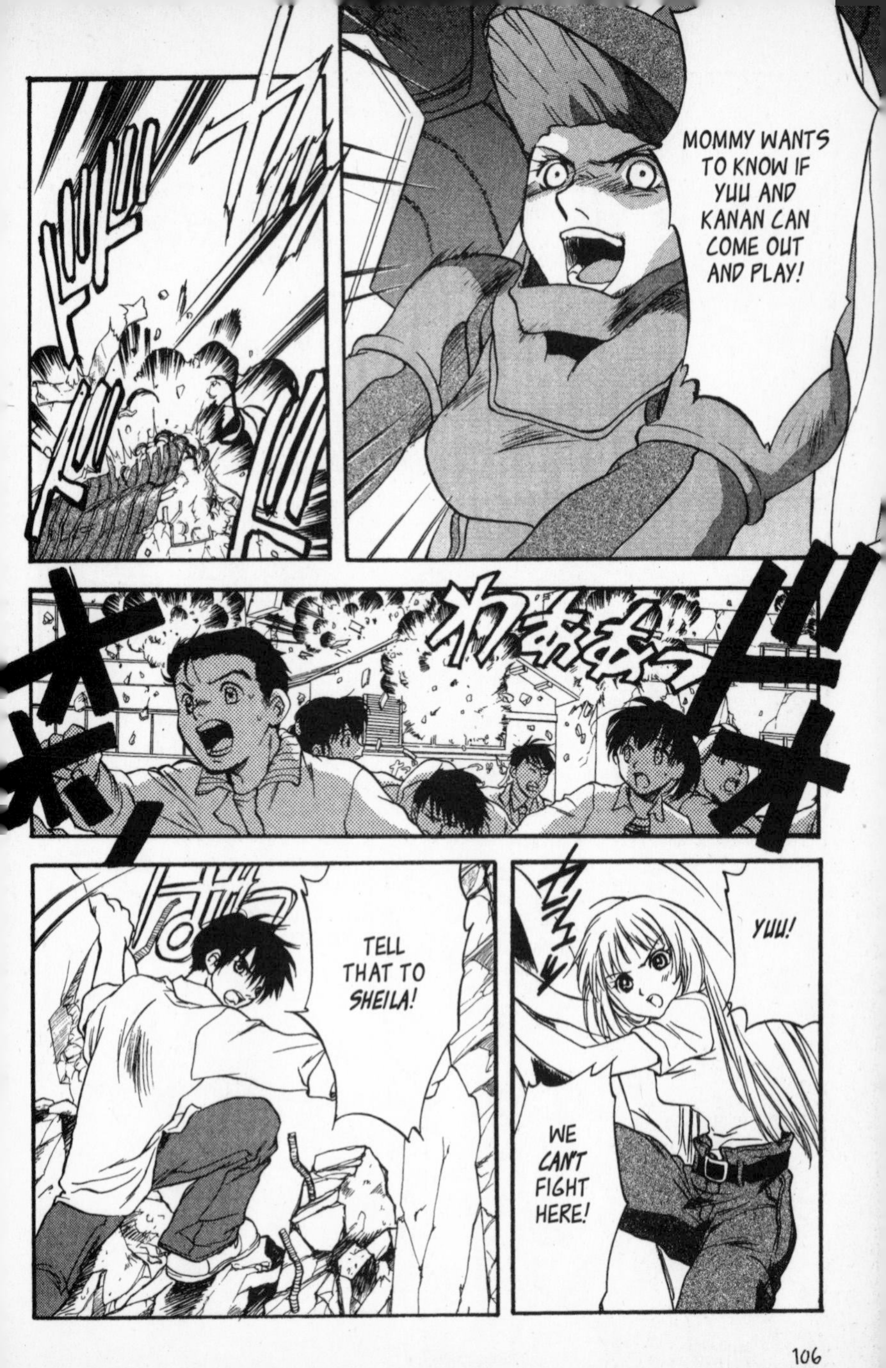
MOMMY WANTS TO KNOW IF YUU AND KANAN CAN COME OUT AND PLAY!
YUU!
WE CAN'T FIGHT HERE!
TELL THAT TO SHEILA!

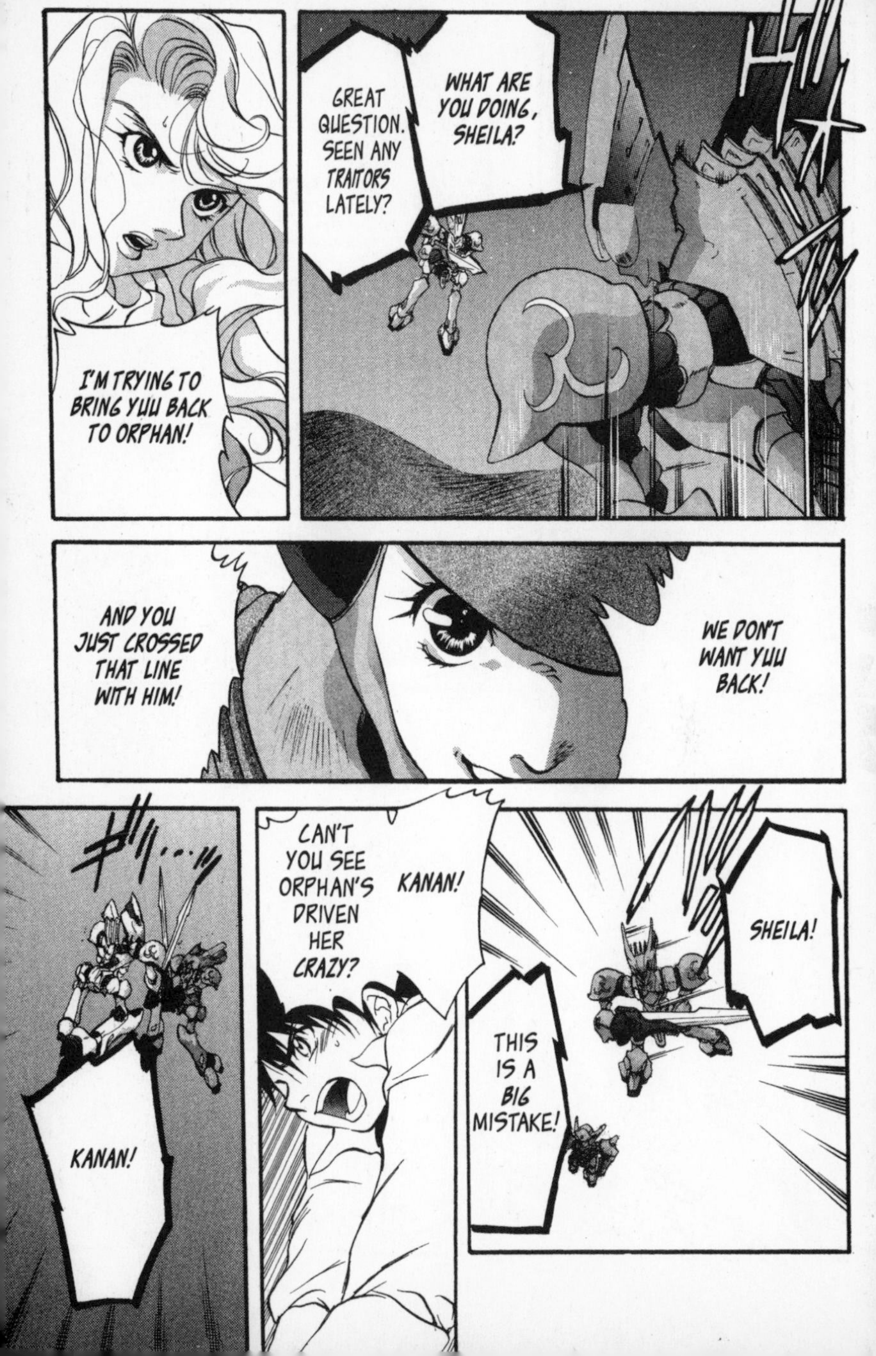
WHAT ARE YOU DOING, SHEILA?
GREAT QUESTION. SEEN ANY TRAITORS LATELY?
I'M TRYING TO BRING YUU BACK TO ORPHAN!
WE DON'T WANT YUU BACK!
AND YOU JUST CROSSED THAT LINE WITH HIM!
SHEILA!
THIS IS A BIG MISTAKE!
KANAN!
CAN'T YOU SEE ORPHAN'S DRIVEN HER CRAZY?
KANAN!

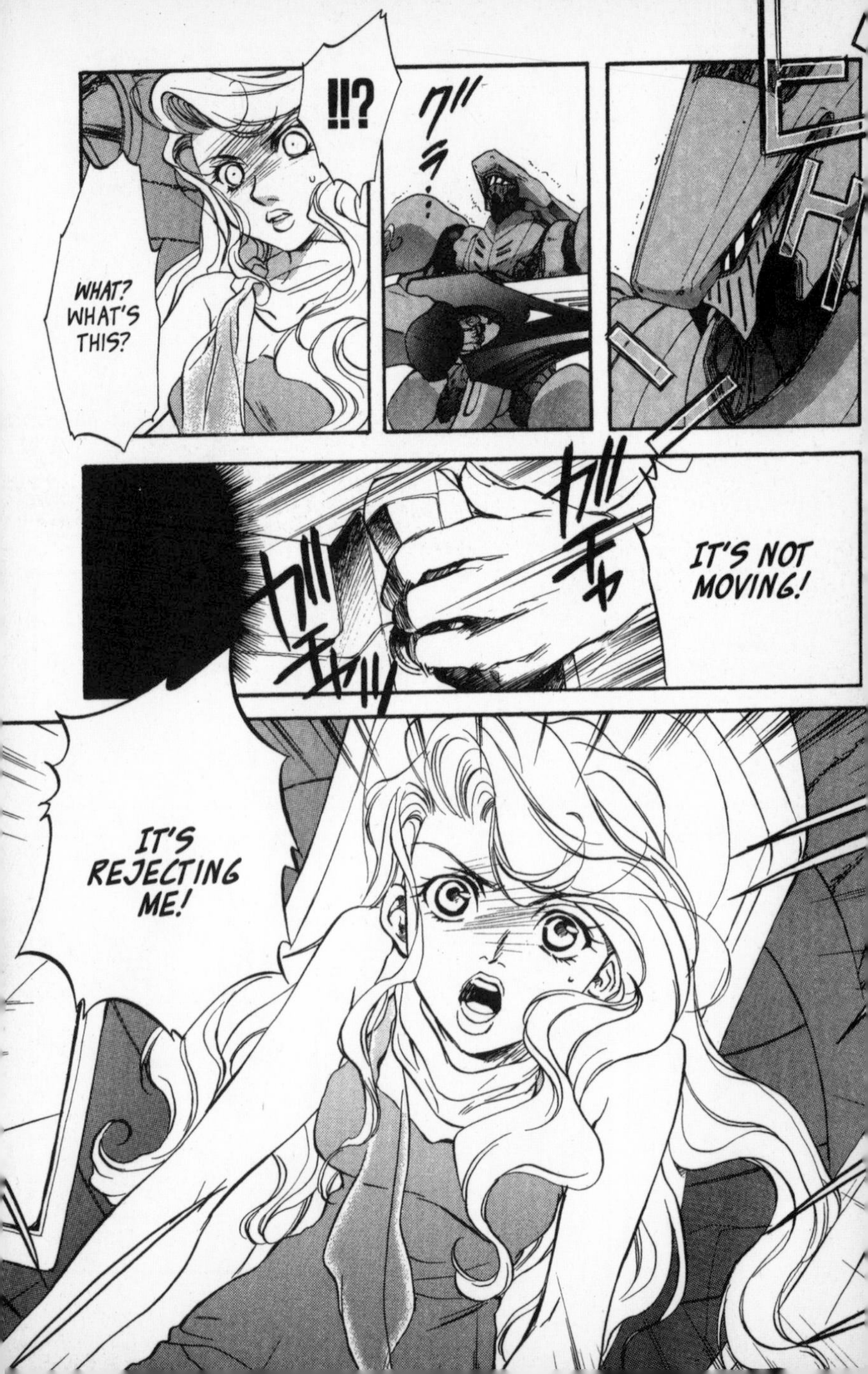

グラ…
!!?
WHAT? WHAT'S THIS?
ガチャ
ガチャッ
IT'S NOT MOVING!
IT'S REJECTING ME!

REVIVAL 11: VITAL GLOBE

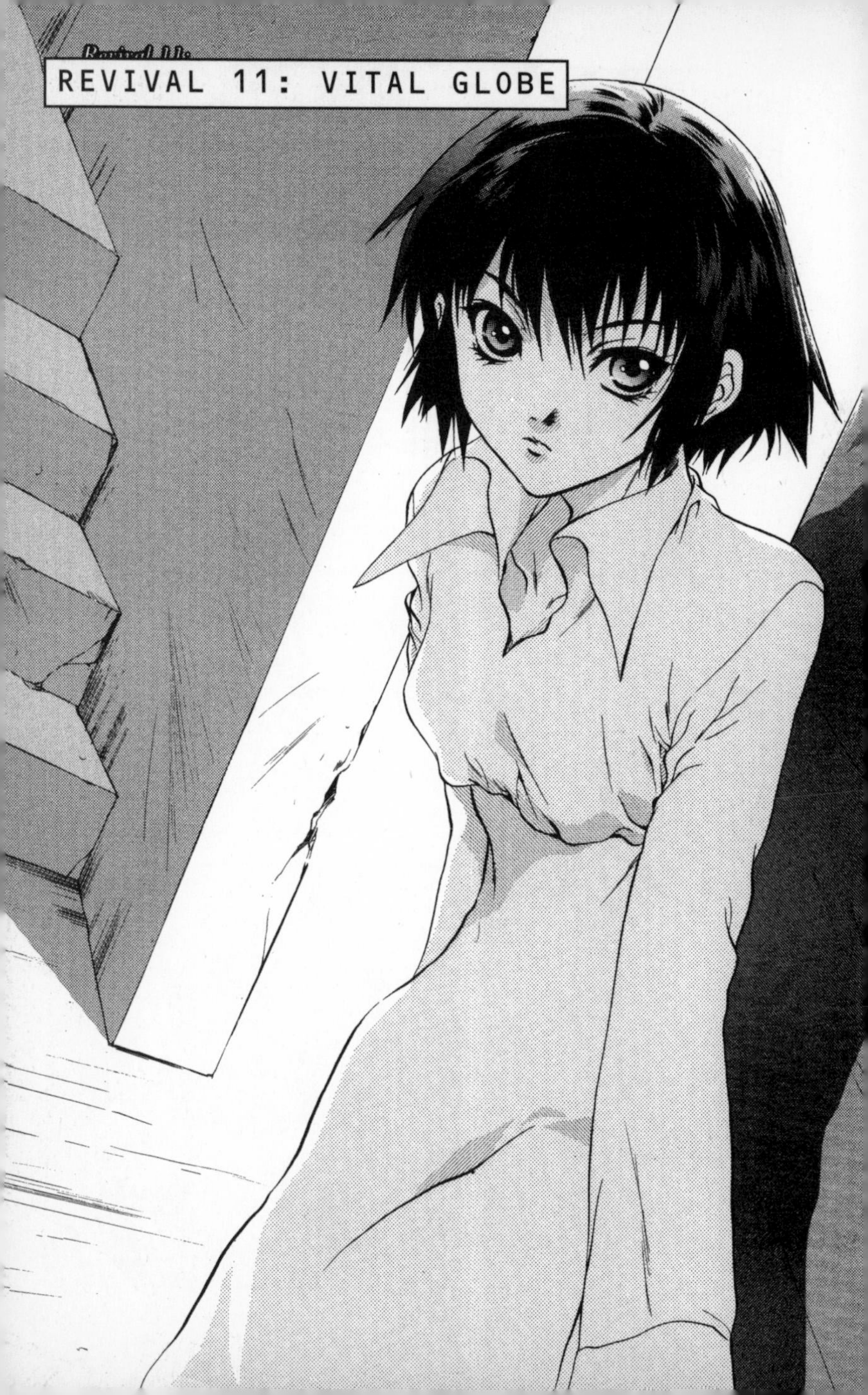

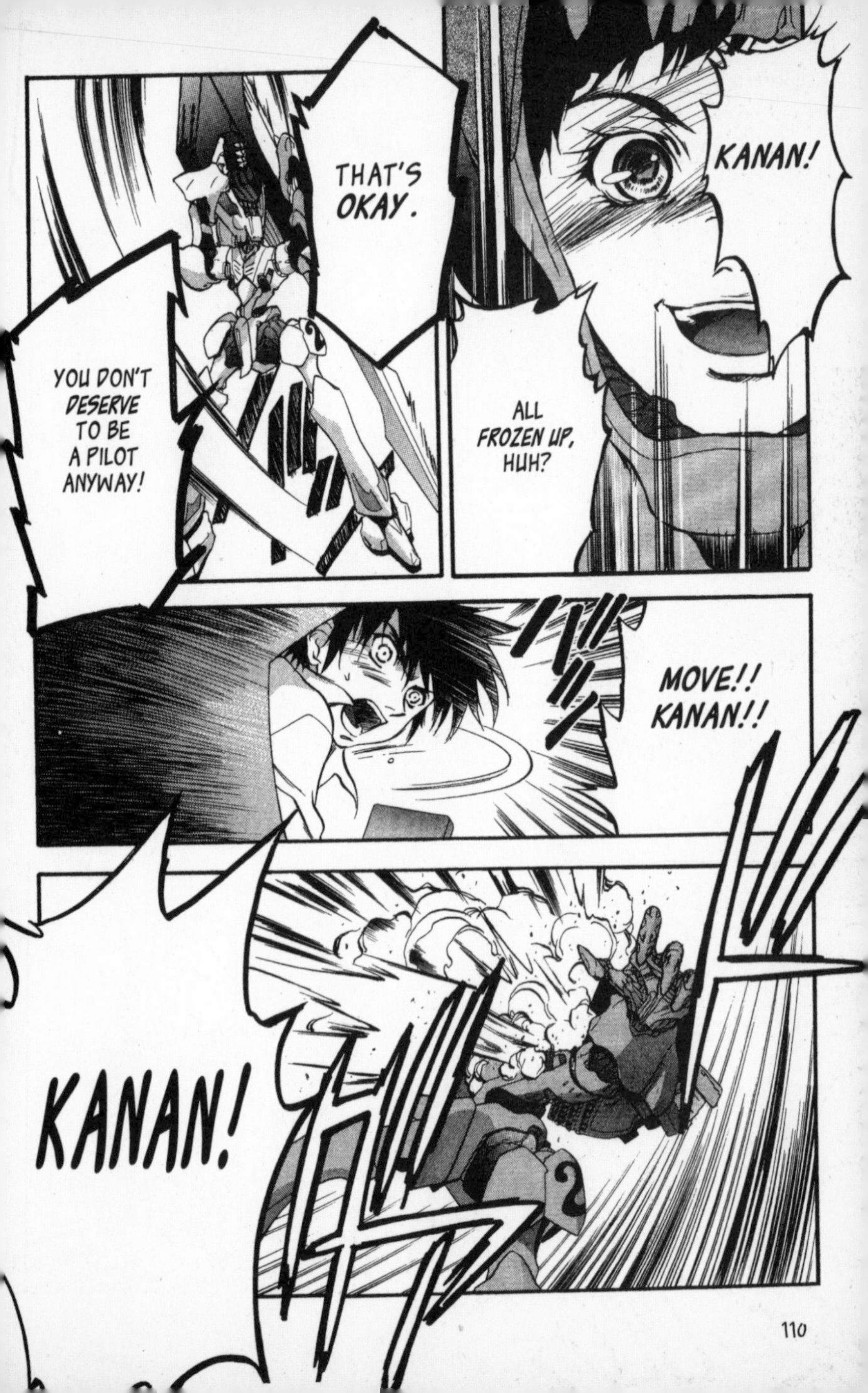

KANAN!
ALL FROZEN UP, HUH?
THAT'S OKAY.
YOU DON'T DESERVE TO BE A PILOT ANYWAY!
MOVE!! KANAN!!
KANAN!

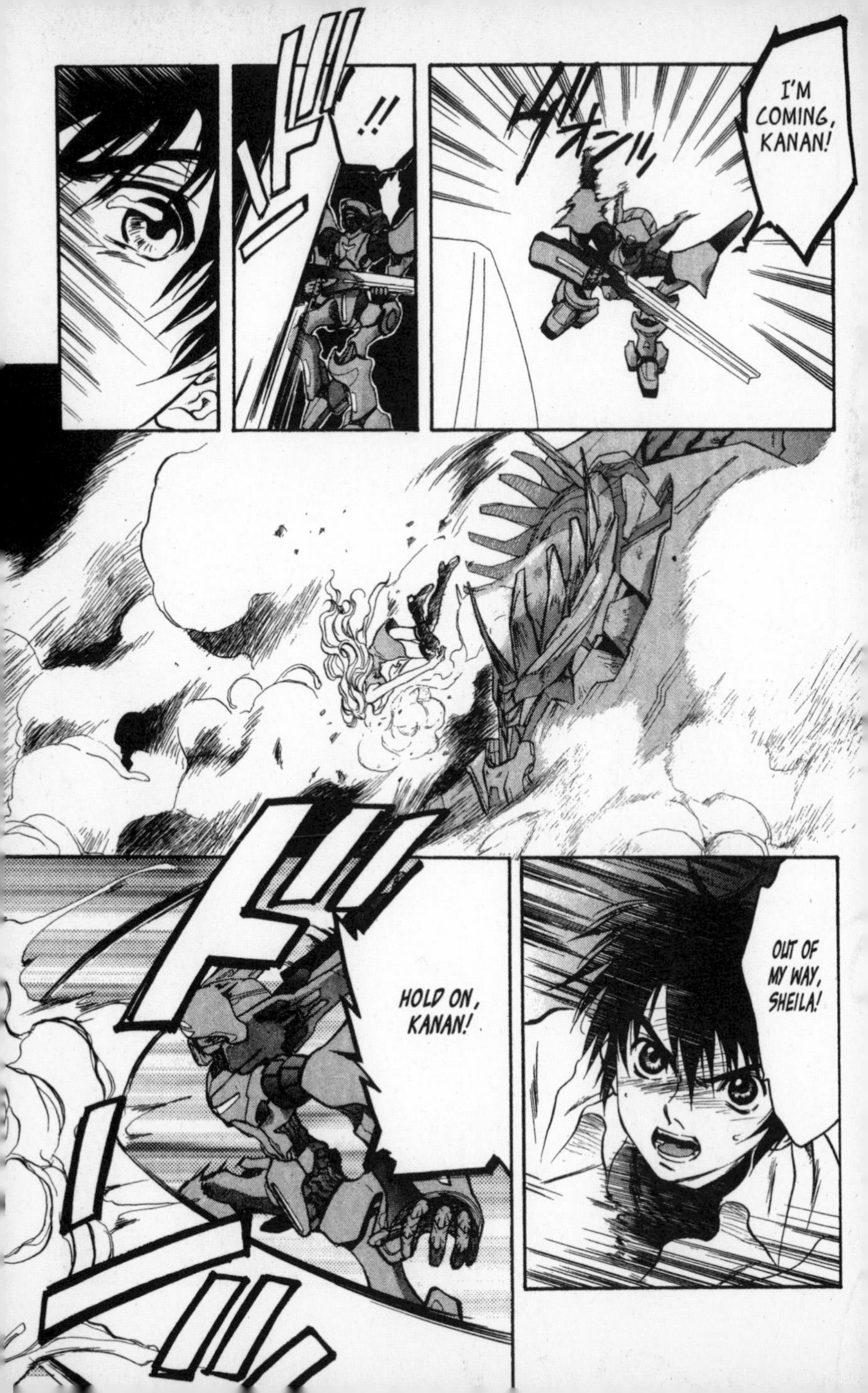
I'M COMING, KANAN!
!!
OUT OF MY WAY, SHEILA!
HOLD ON, KANAN!

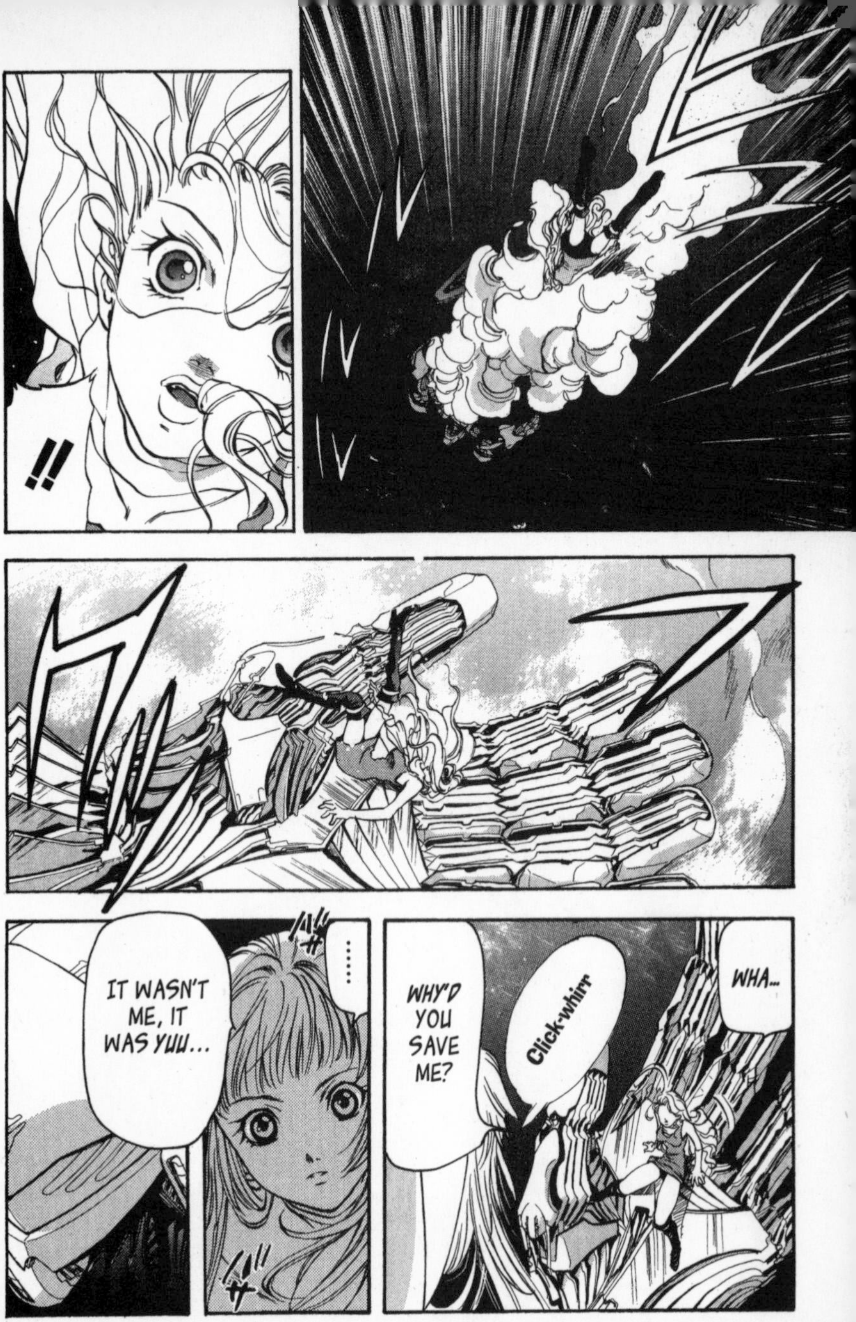
!!
WHA...
Click-whirr
WHY'D YOU SAVE ME?
......
IT WASN'T ME, IT WAS YUU...

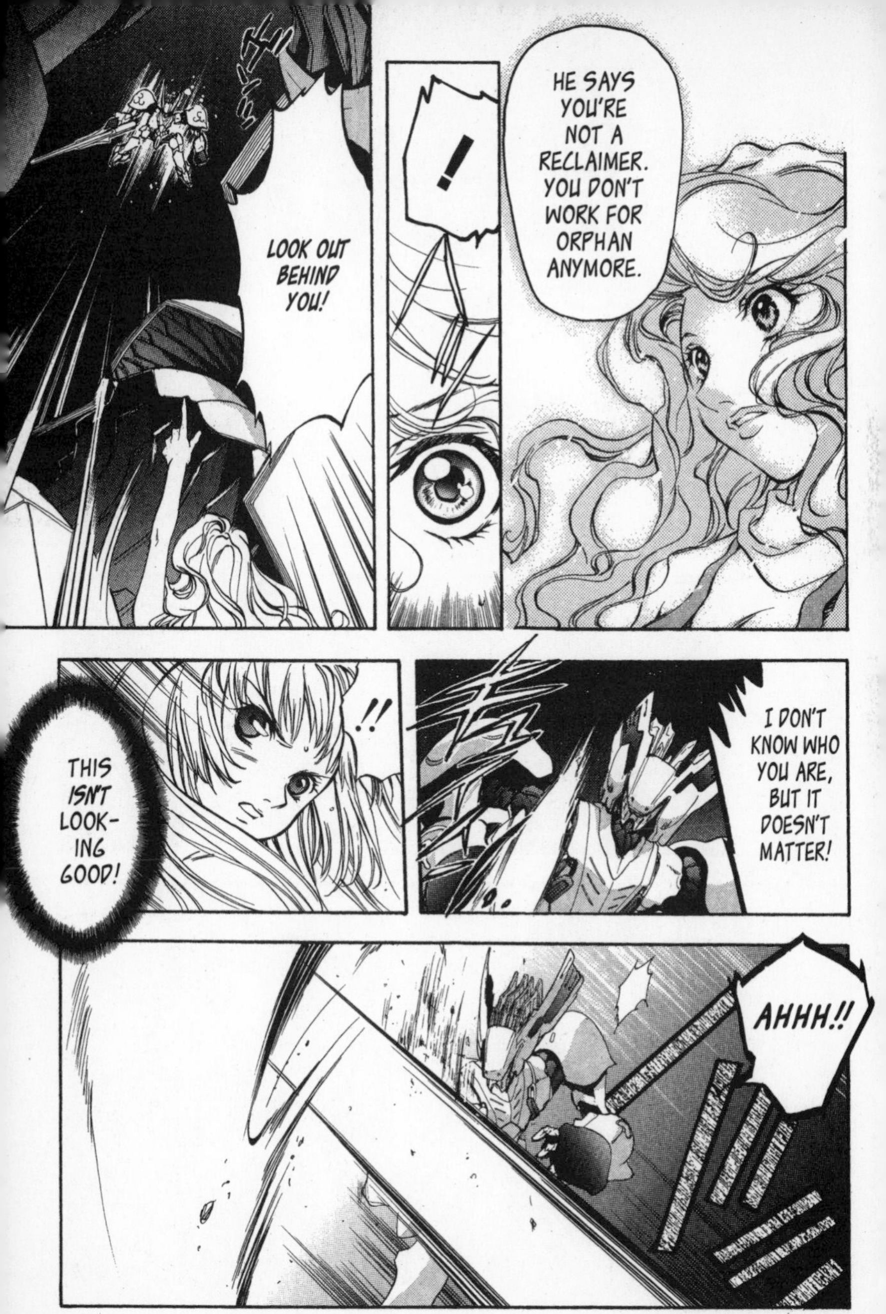
HE SAYS YOU'RE NOT A RECLAIMER. YOU DON'T WORK FOR ORPHAN ANYMORE.
!
LOOK OUT BEHIND YOU!
I DON'T KNOW WHO YOU ARE, BUT IT DOESN'T MATTER!
!!
THIS ISN'T LOOKING GOOD!
AHHH!!

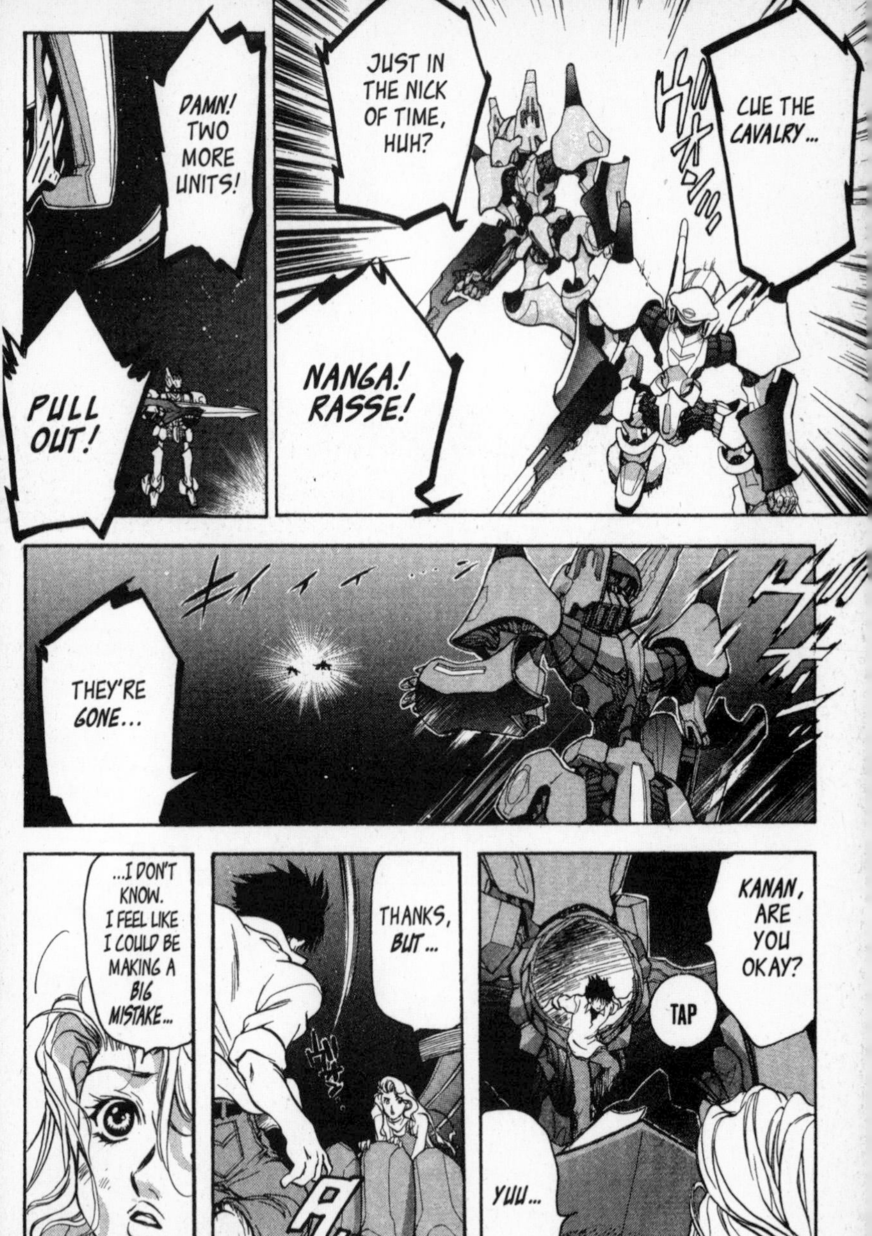
CUE THE CAVALRY...
JUST IN THE NICK OF TIME, HUH?
NANGA! RASSE!
DAMN! TWO MORE UNITS!
PULL OUT!
THEY'RE GONE...
KANAN, ARE YOU OKAY?
TAP
YUU...
THANKS, BUT...
...I DON'T KNOW. I FEEL LIKE I COULD BE MAKING A BIG MISTAKE...

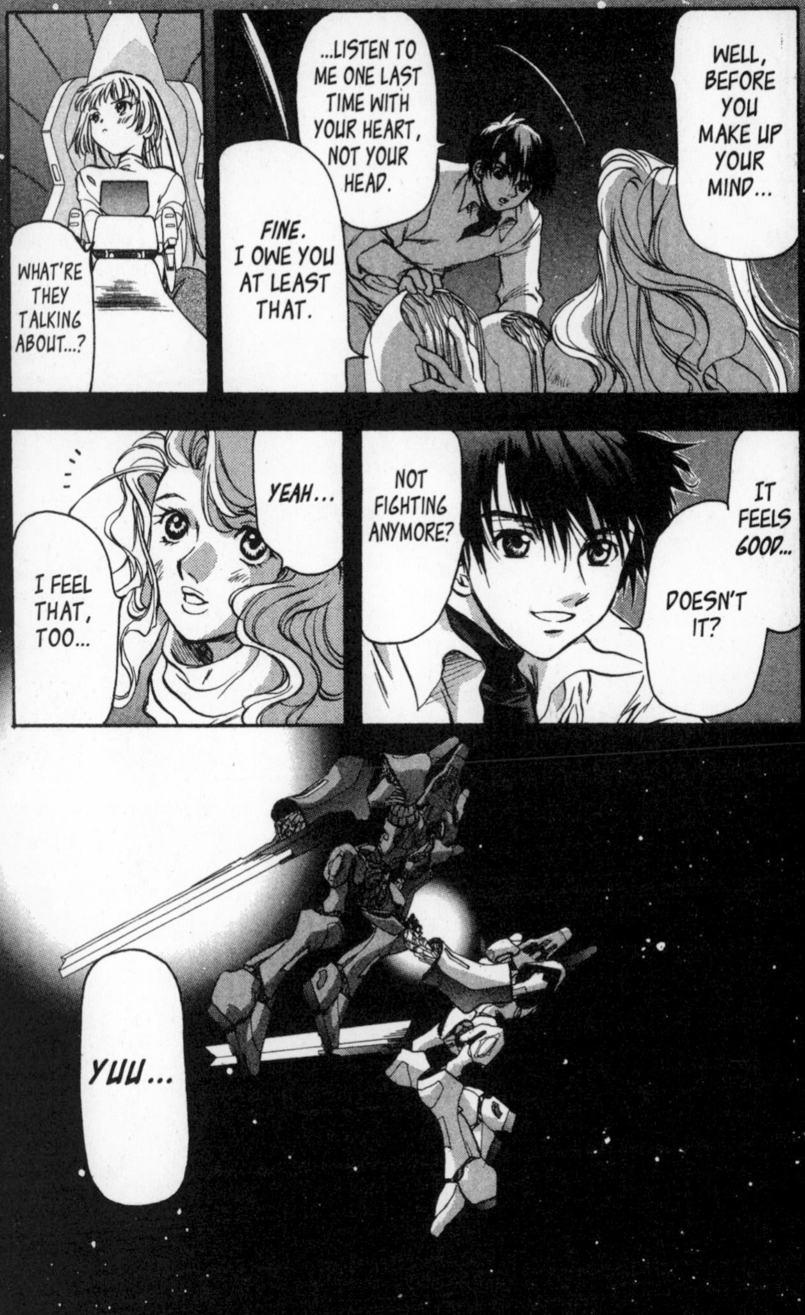
WELL, BEFORE YOU MAKE UP YOUR MIND...
...LISTEN TO ME ONE LAST TIME WITH YOUR HEART, NOT YOUR HEAD.
FINE. I OWE YOU AT LEAST THAT.
WHAT'RE THEY TALKING ABOUT...?
IT FEELS GOOD...
DOESN'T IT?
NOT FIGHTING ANYMORE?
YEAH...
I FEEL THAT, TOO...
YUU...

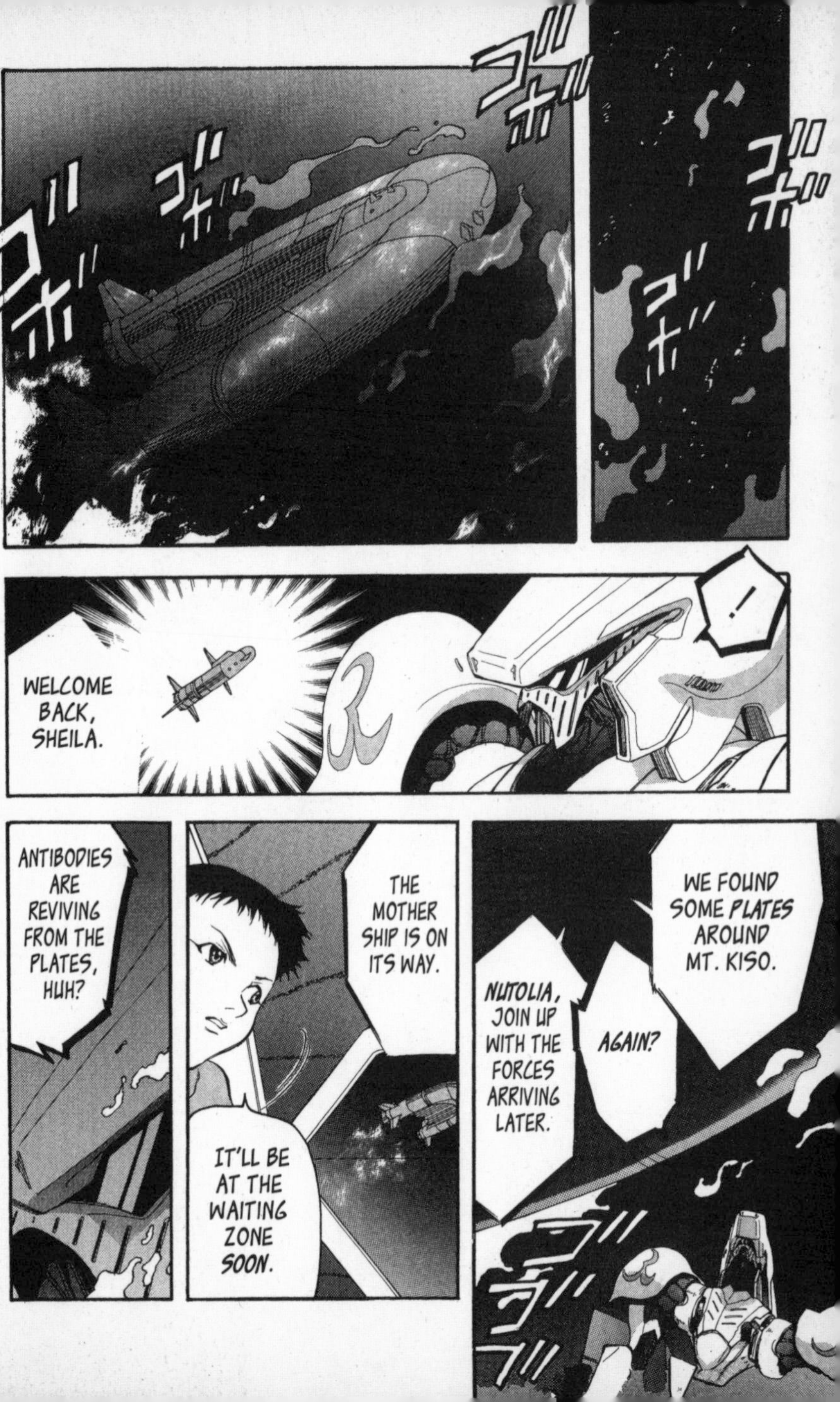
ゴボ
ゴボ
ゴボ
ゴボ
ゴボ
!
WELCOME BACK, SHEILA.
WE FOUND SOME *PLATES* AROUND MT. KISO.
AGAIN?
NUTOLIA, JOIN UP WITH THE FORCES ARRIVING LATER.
THE MOTHER SHIP IS ON ITS WAY.
IT'LL BE AT THE WAITING ZONE *SOON*.
ANTIBODIES ARE REVIVING FROM THE PLATES, HUH?

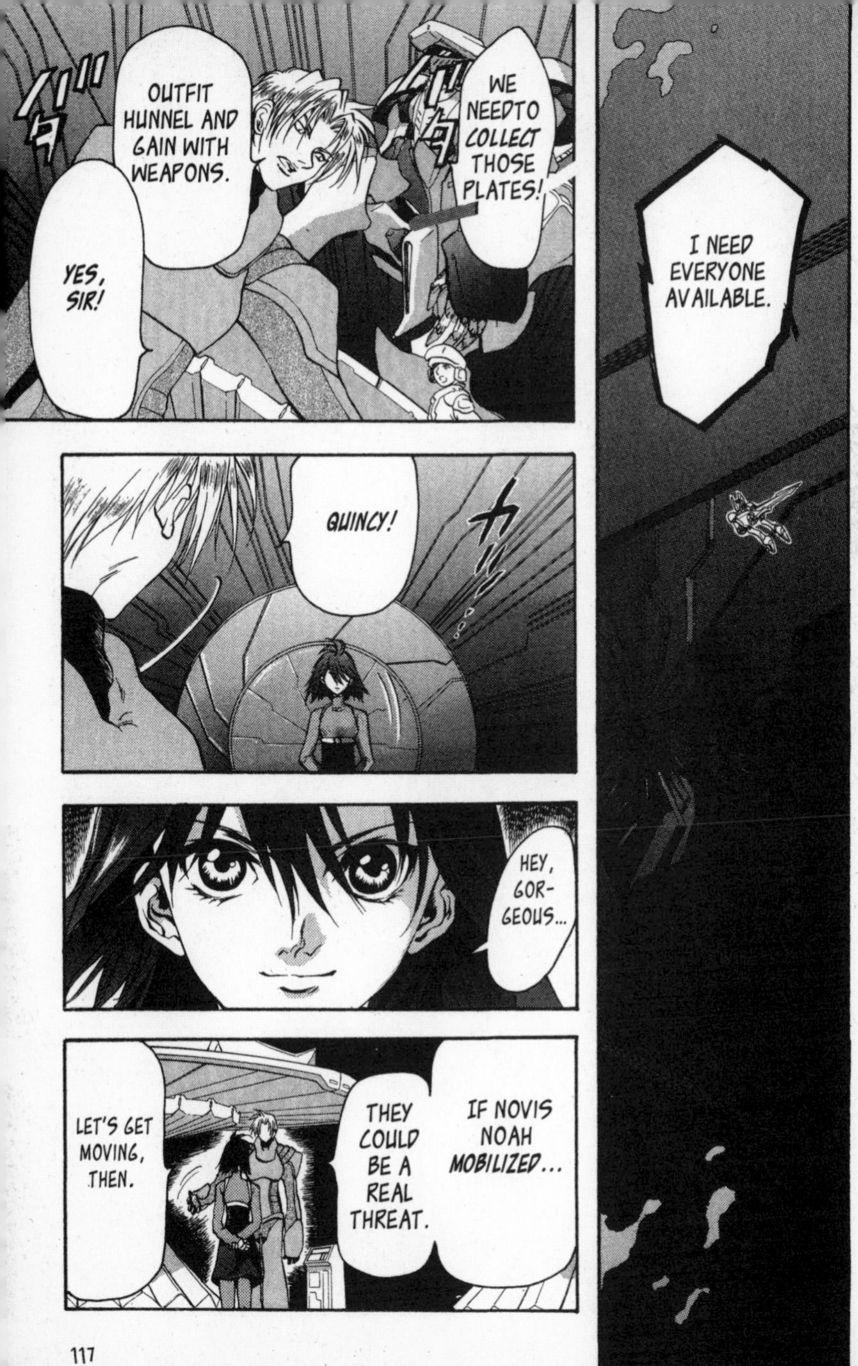
I NEED EVERYONE AVAILABLE.
WE NEEDTO COLLECT THOSE PLATES!
OUTFIT HUNNEL AND GAIN WITH WEAPONS.
YES, SIR!
QUINCY!
HEY, GOR-GEOUS...
IF NOVIS NOAH MOBILIZED...
THEY COULD BE A REAL THREAT.
LET'S GET MOVING, THEN.

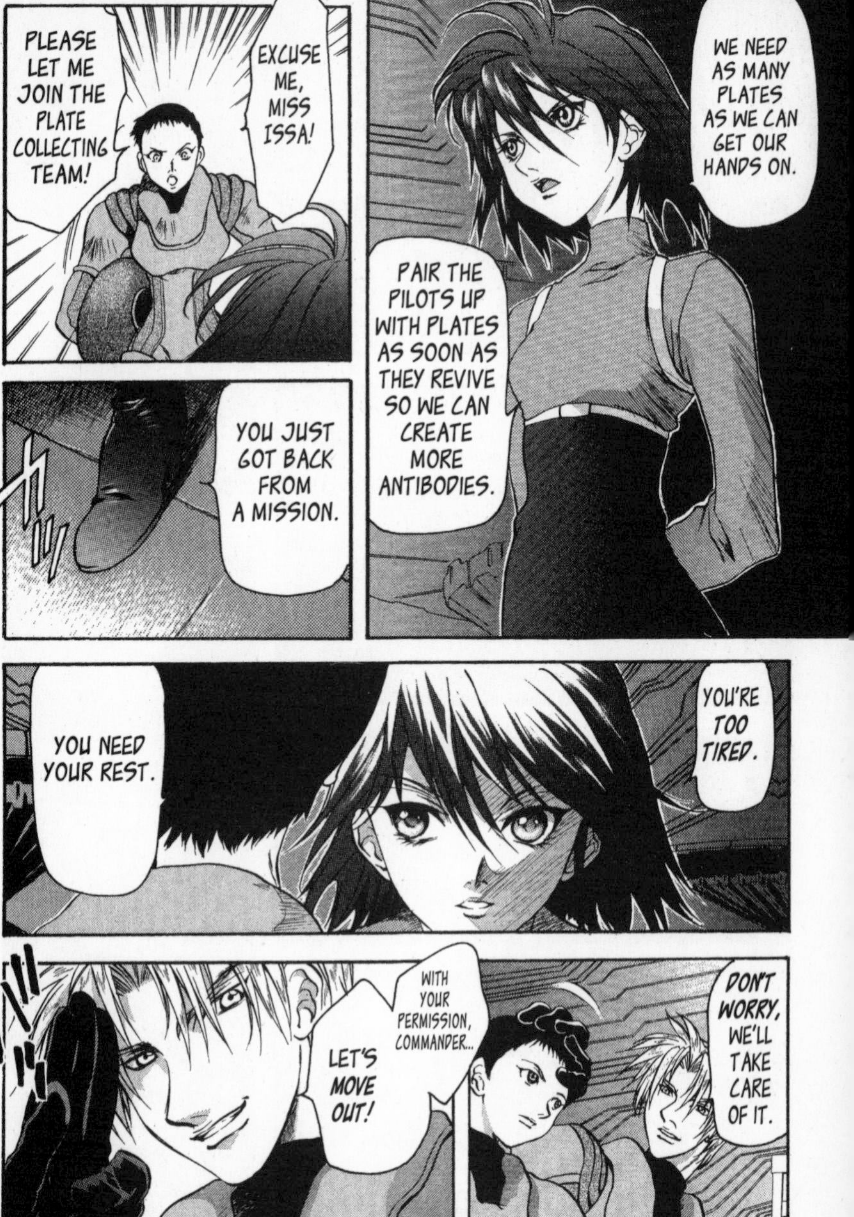
WE NEED AS MANY PLATES AS WE CAN GET OUR HANDS ON.
PAIR THE PILOTS UP WITH PLATES AS SOON AS THEY REVIVE SO WE CAN CREATE MORE ANTIBODIES.
EXCUSE ME, MISS ISSA!
PLEASE LET ME JOIN THE PLATE COLLECTING TEAM!
YOU JUST GOT BACK FROM A MISSION.
YOU'RE TOO TIRED.
YOU NEED YOUR REST.
DON'T WORRY, WE'LL TAKE CARE OF IT.
WITH YOUR PERMISSION, COMMANDER...
LET'S MOVE OUT!

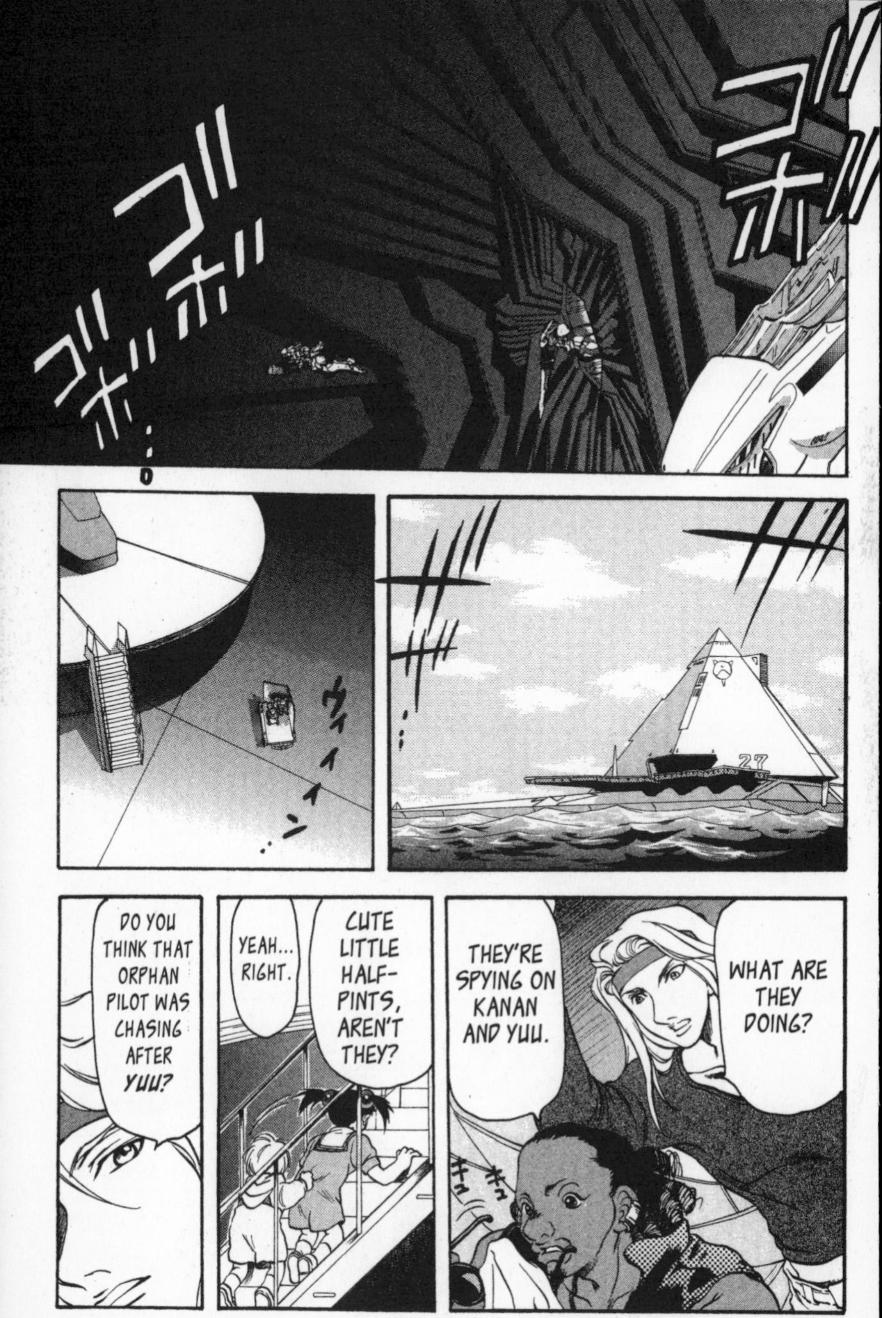
ヴィイイン…
WHAT ARE THEY DOING?
THEY'RE SPYING ON KANAN AND YUU.
CUTE LITTLE HALF-PINTS, AREN'T THEY?
YEAH... RIGHT.
DO YOU THINK THAT ORPHAN PILOT WAS CHASING AFTER *YUU*?

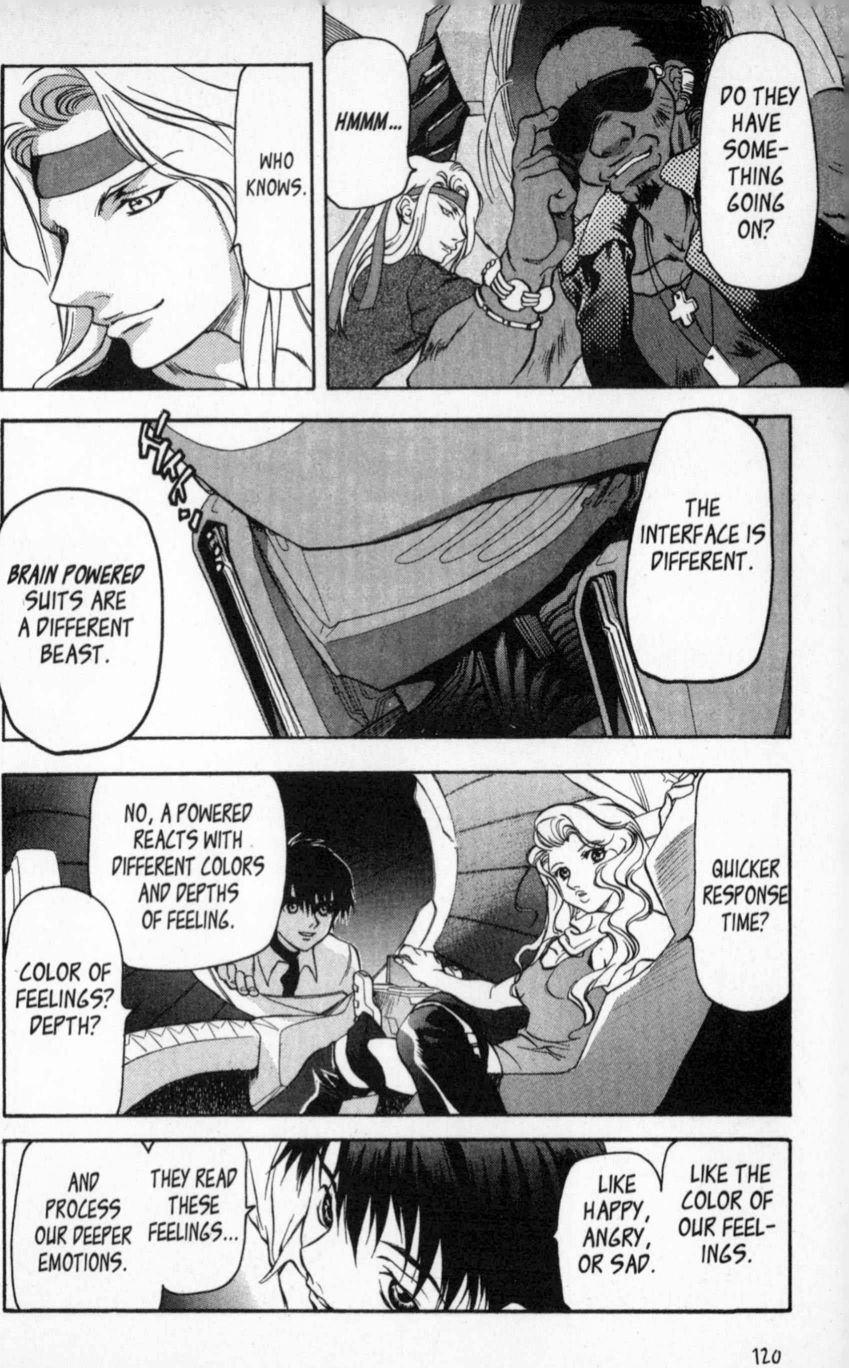
DO THEY HAVE SOME-THING GOING ON?
HMMM...
WHO KNOWS.
THE INTERFACE IS DIFFERENT.
BRAIN POWERED SUITS ARE A DIFFERENT BEAST.
QUICKER RESPONSE TIME?
NO, A POWERED REACTS WITH DIFFERENT COLORS AND DEPTHS OF FEELING.
COLOR OF FEELINGS? DEPTH?
LIKE THE COLOR OF OUR FEEL-INGS.
LIKE HAPPY, ANGRY, OR SAD.
THEY READ THESE FEELINGS...
AND PROCESS OUR DEEPER EMOTIONS.

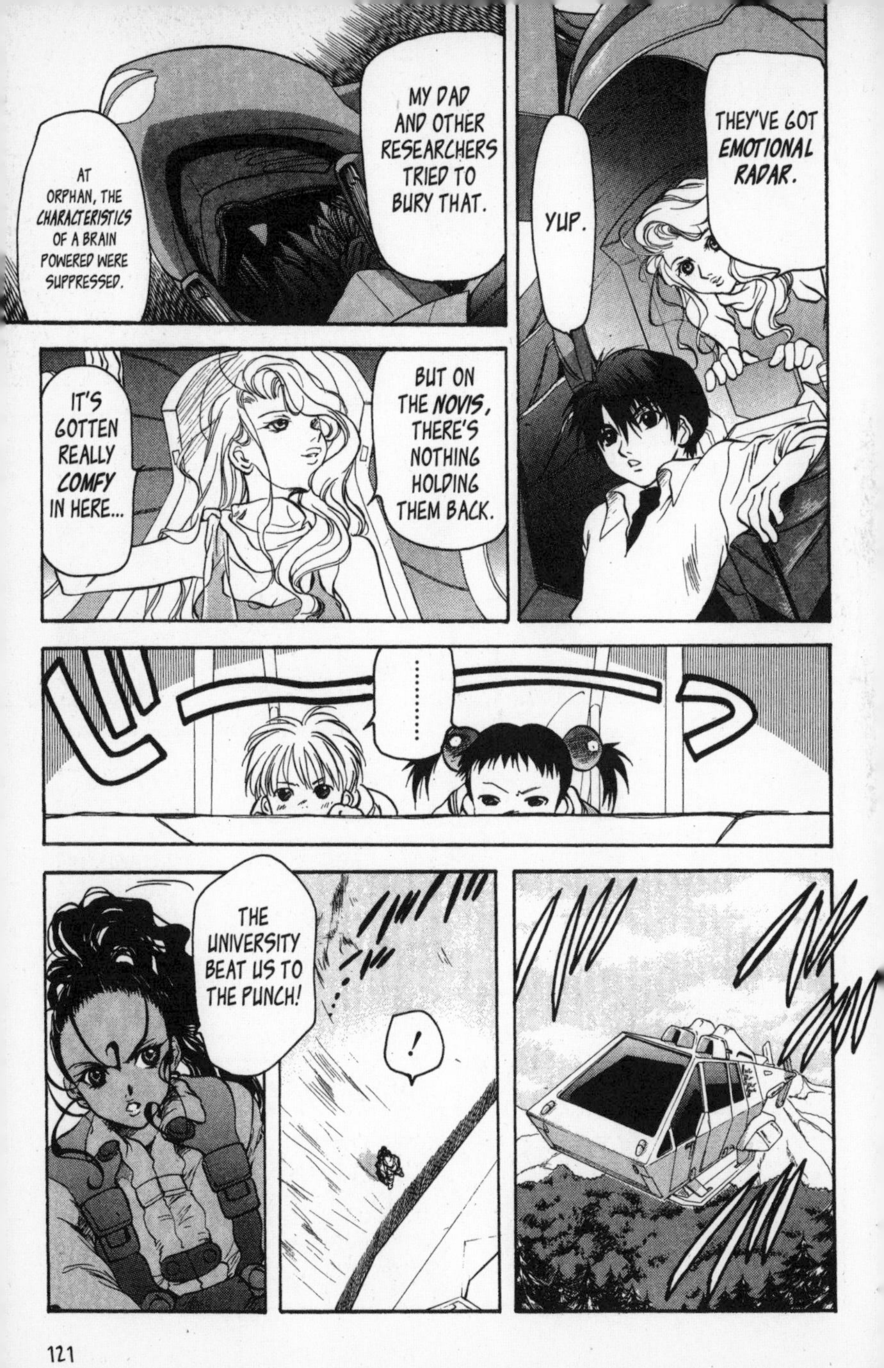
THEY'VE GOT EMOTIONAL RADAR.
YUP.
MY DAD AND OTHER RESEARCHERS TRIED TO BURY THAT.
AT ORPHAN, THE CHARACTERISTICS OF A BRAIN POWERED WERE SUPPRESSED.
BUT ON THE NOVIS, THERE'S NOTHING HOLDING THEM BACK.
IT'S GOTTEN REALLY COMFY IN HERE...
......
!
THE UNIVERSITY BEAT US TO THE PUNCH!

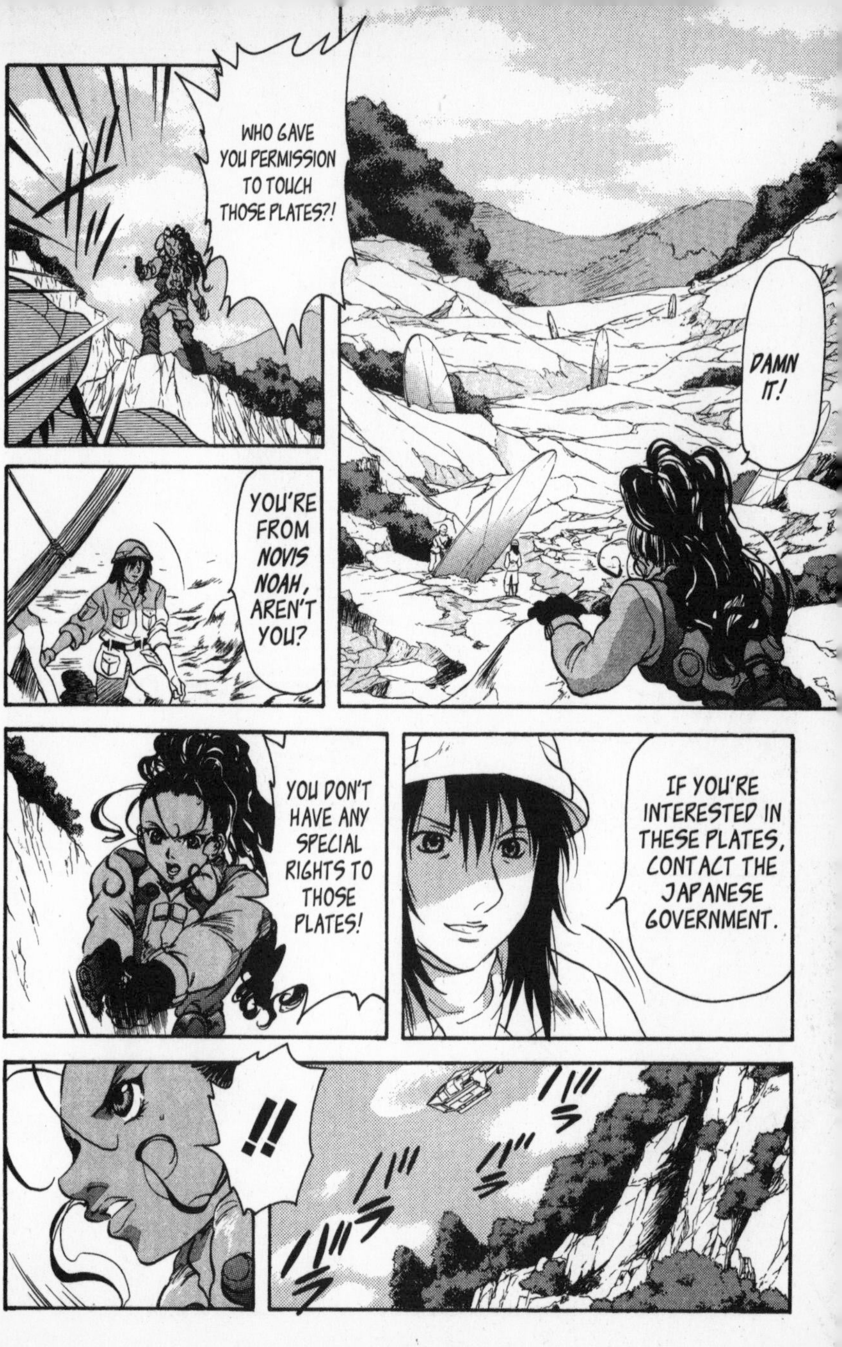
DAMN IT!
WHO GAVE YOU PERMISSION TO TOUCH THOSE PLATES?!
YOU'RE FROM NOVIS NOAH, AREN'T YOU?
IF YOU'RE INTERESTED IN THESE PLATES, CONTACT THE JAPANESE GOVERNMENT.
YOU DON'T HAVE ANY SPECIAL RIGHTS TO THOSE PLATES!
バラ
バラ
バラ
!!

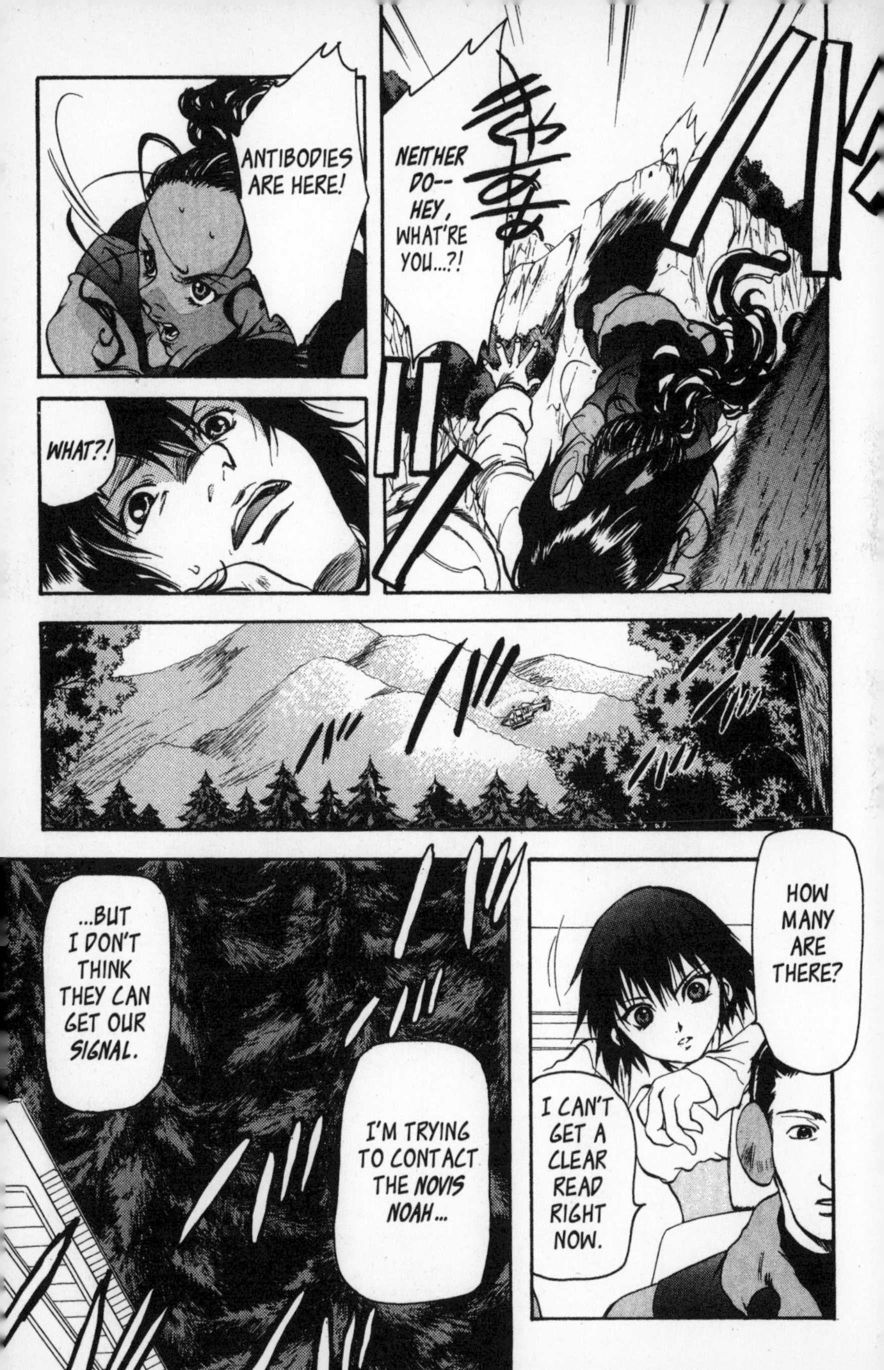
NEITHER DO-- HEY, WHAT'RE YOU...?!
きゃあぁ
ANTIBODIES ARE HERE!
WHAT?!
HOW MANY ARE THERE?
I CAN'T GET A CLEAR READ RIGHT NOW.
I'M TRYING TO CONTACT THE NOVIS NOAH...
...BUT I DON'T THINK THEY CAN GET OUR SIGNAL.

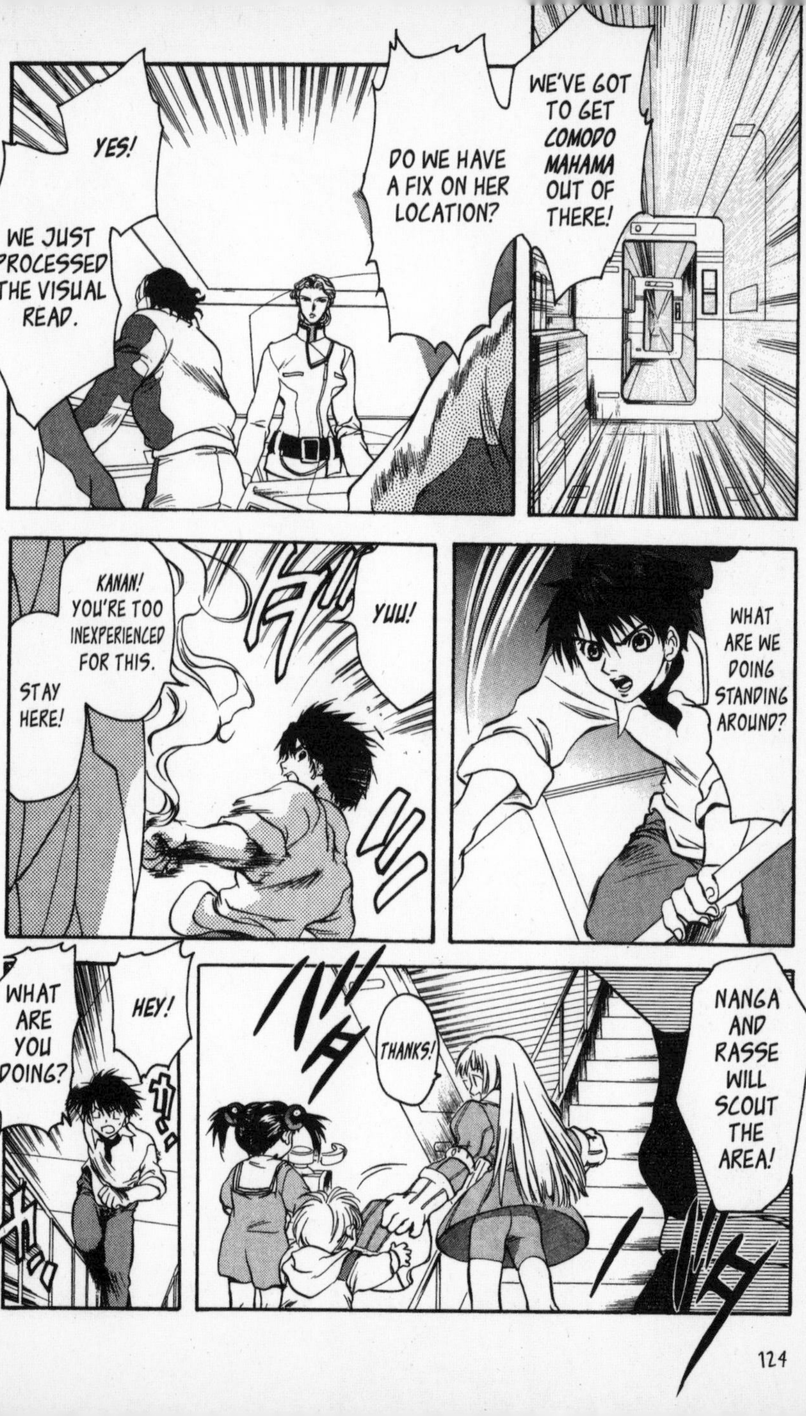
WE'VE GOT TO GET COMODO MAHAMA OUT OF THERE!
DO WE HAVE A FIX ON HER LOCATION?
YES!
WE JUST PROCESSED THE VISUAL READ.
WHAT ARE WE DOING STANDING AROUND?
YUU!
KANAN! YOU'RE TOO INEXPERIENCED FOR THIS.
STAY HERE!
NANGA AND RASSE WILL SCOUT THE AREA!
THANKS!
HEY!
WHAT ARE YOU DOING?

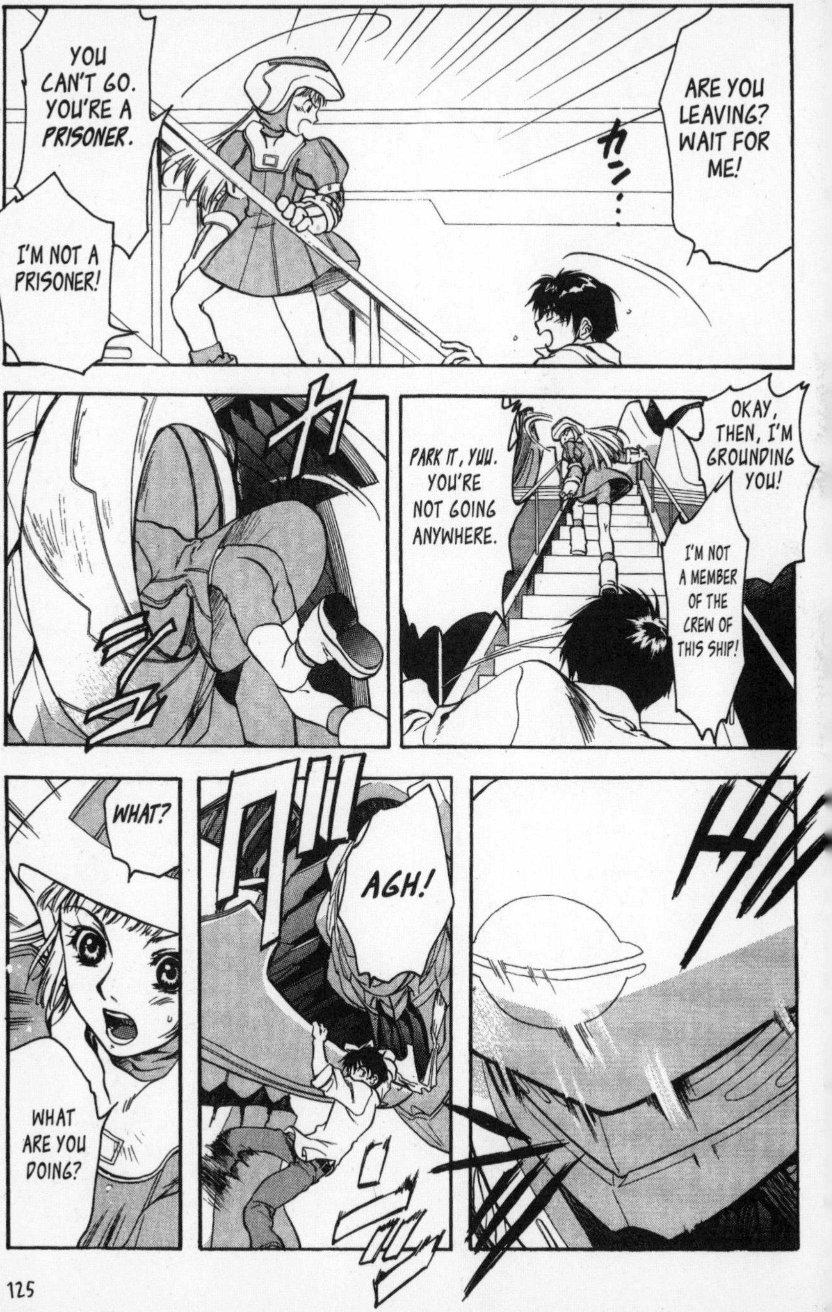
ARE YOU LEAVING? WAIT FOR ME!
カン…
YOU CAN'T GO. YOU'RE A *PRISONER*.
I'M NOT A PRISONER!
OKAY, THEN, I'M GROUNDING YOU!
I'M NOT A MEMBER OF THE CREW OF THIS SHIP!
PARK IT, YUU. YOU'RE NOT GOING ANYWHERE.
AGH!
WHAT?
WHAT ARE YOU DOING?

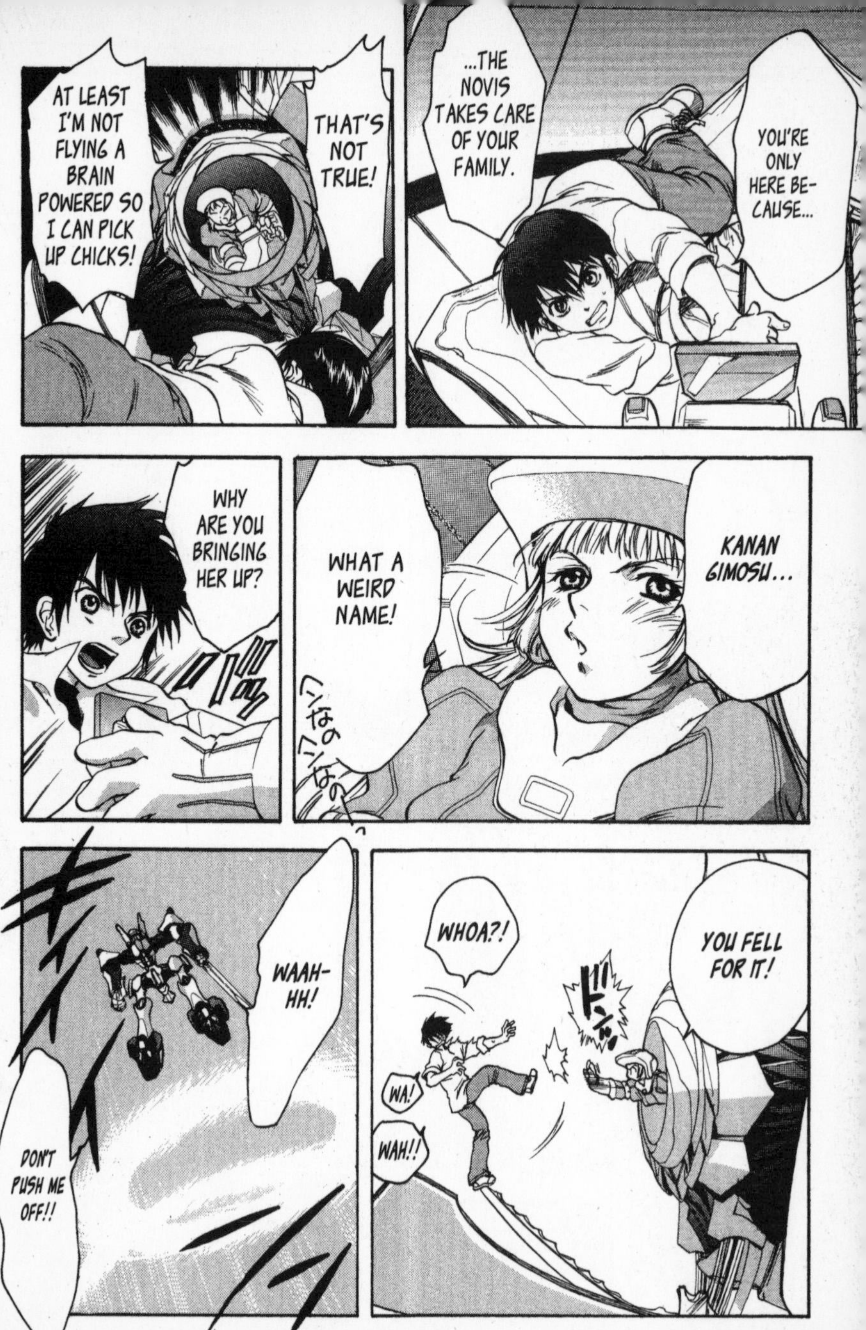
YOU'RE ONLY HERE BE-CAUSE...
...THE NOVIS TAKES CARE OF YOUR FAMILY.
THAT'S NOT TRUE!
AT LEAST I'M NOT FLYING A BRAIN POWERED SO I CAN PICK UP CHICKS!
KANAN GIMOSU...
WHAT A WEIRD NAME!
ヘンなのヘンなの～
WHY ARE YOU BRINGING HER UP?
YOU FELL FOR IT!
WHOA?!
WA!
WAH!!
WAAH-HH!
DON'T PUSH ME OFF!!

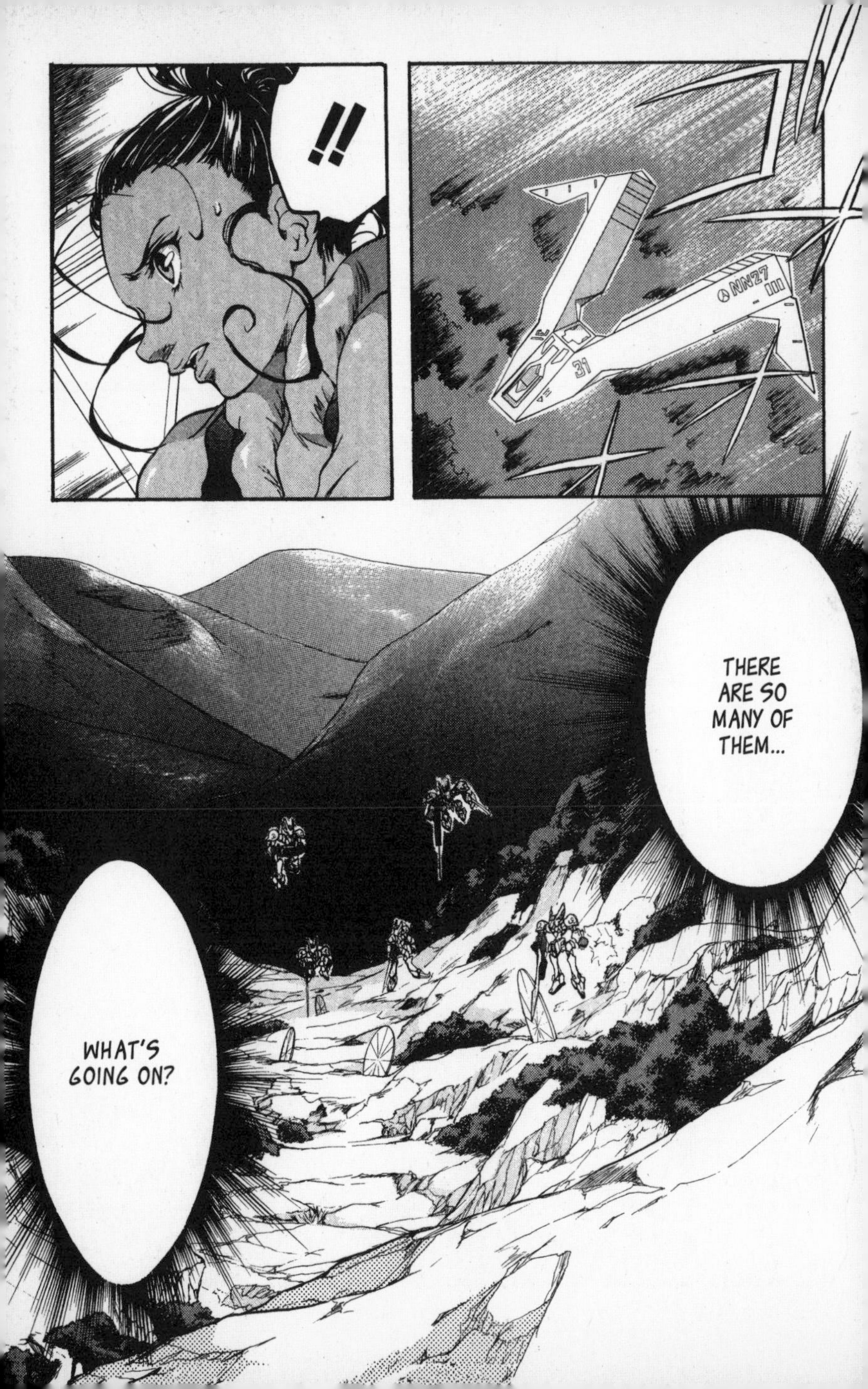
NN27
31
!!
THERE ARE SO MANY OF THEM...
WHAT'S GOING ON?

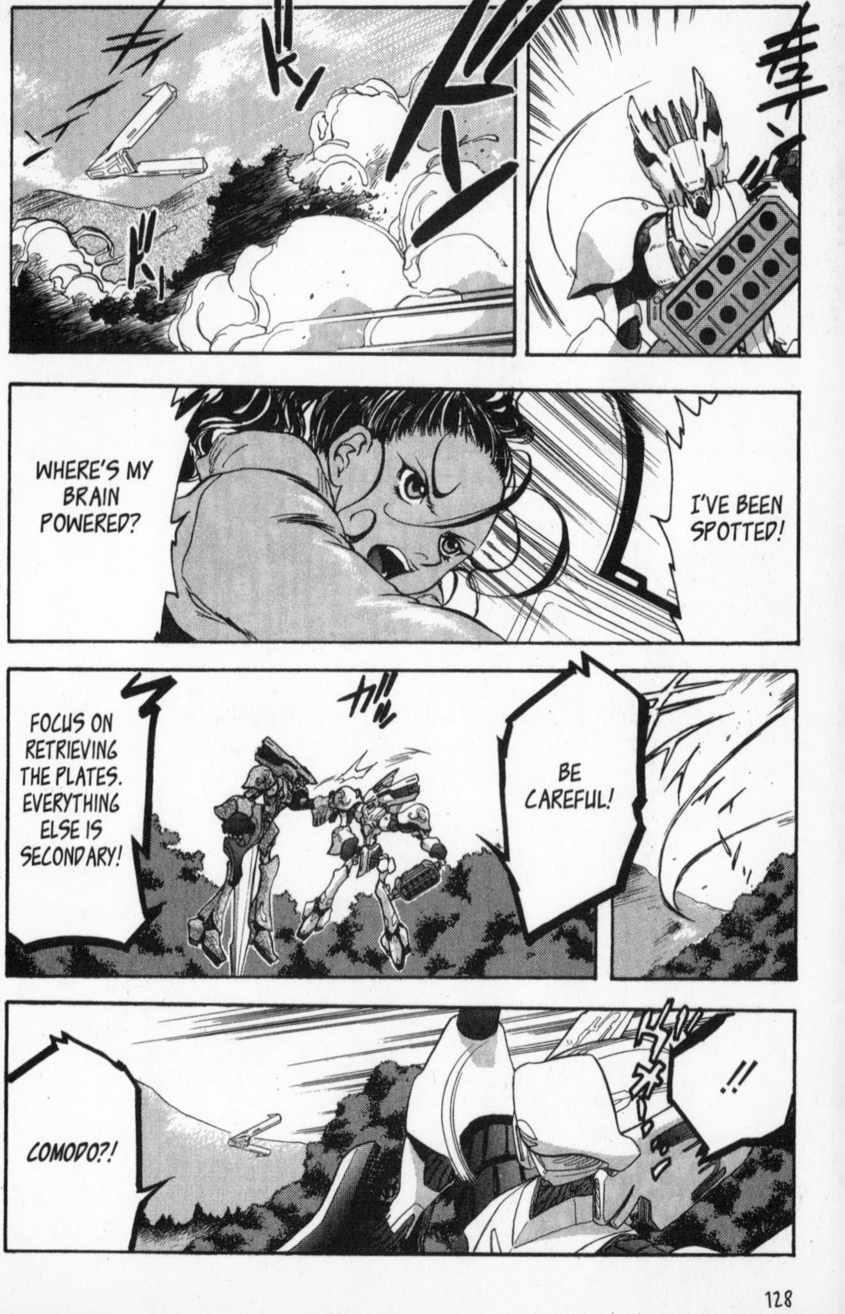

I'VE BEEN SPOTTED!
WHERE'S MY BRAIN POWERED?
BE CAREFUL!
FOCUS ON RETRIEVING THE PLATES. EVERYTHING ELSE IS SECONDARY!
!!
COMODO?!

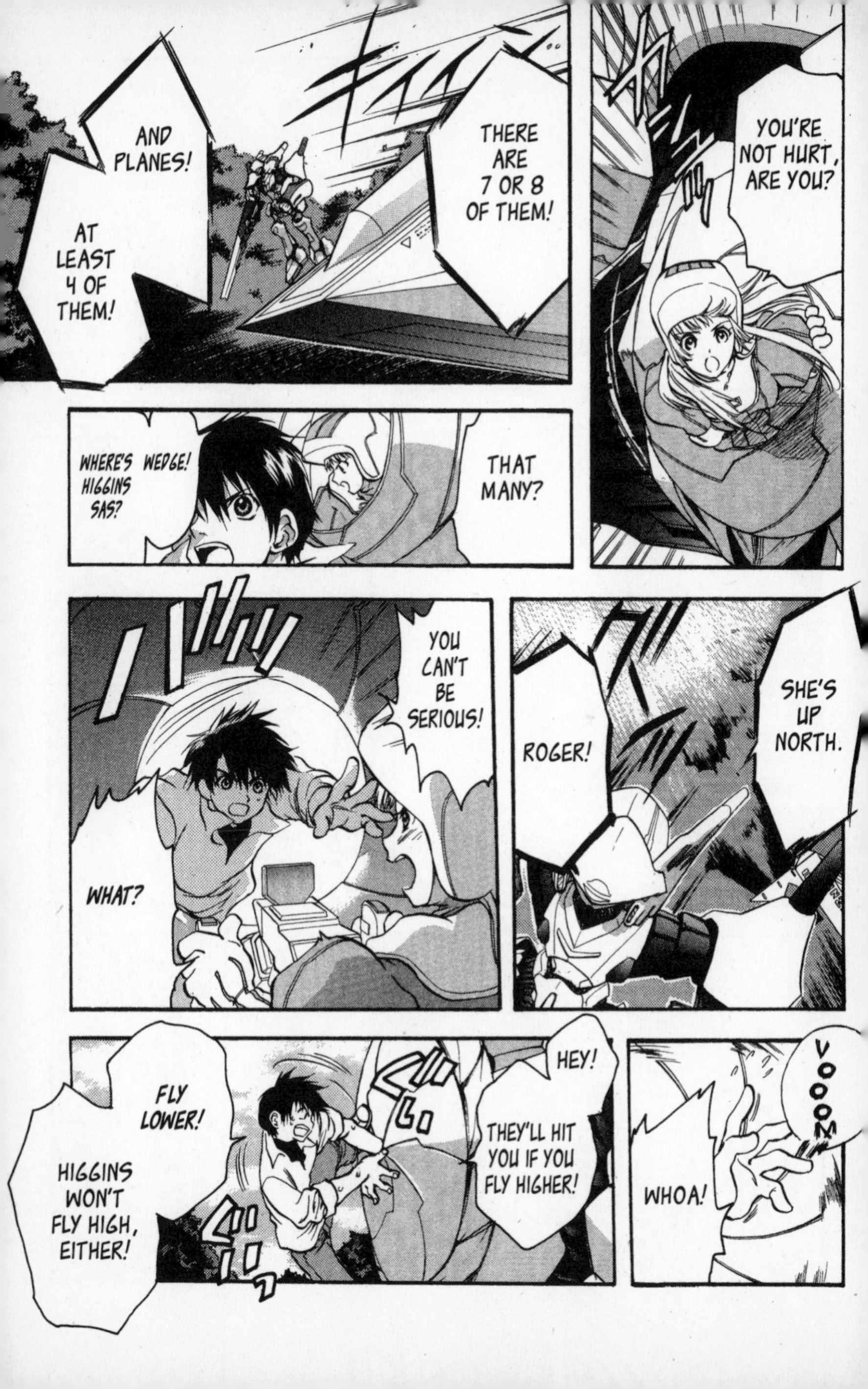
YOU'RE NOT HURT, ARE YOU?
THERE ARE 7 OR 8 OF THEM!
AND PLANES!
AT LEAST 4 OF THEM!
THAT MANY?
WEDGE!
WHERE'S HIGGINS SAS?
SHE'S UP NORTH.
ROGER!
YOU CAN'T BE SERIOUS!
WHAT?
VOOOOM
WHOA!
HEY!
THEY'LL HIT YOU IF YOU FLY HIGHER!
FLY LOWER!
HIGGINS WON'T FLY HIGH, EITHER!

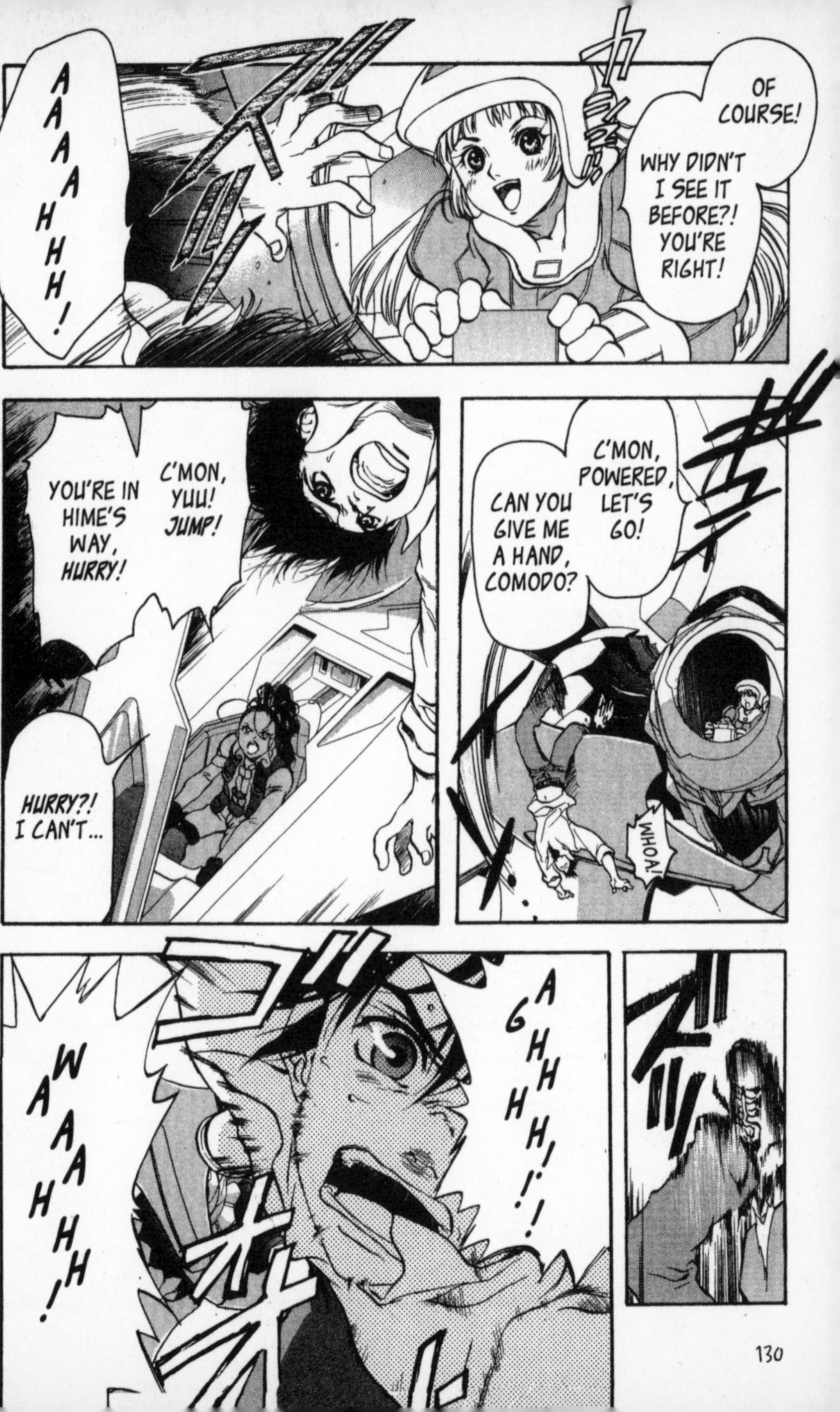
OF COURSE!
WHY DIDN'T I SEE IT BEFORE?! YOU'RE RIGHT!
AAAAAHHH!
C'MON, POWERED, LET'S GO!
CAN YOU GIVE ME A HAND, COMODO?
WHOA!
C'MON, YUU! JUMP!
YOU'RE IN HIME'S WAY, HURRY!
HURRY?! I CAN'T...
AGHHHHH!!!
WAAAAHHHH!

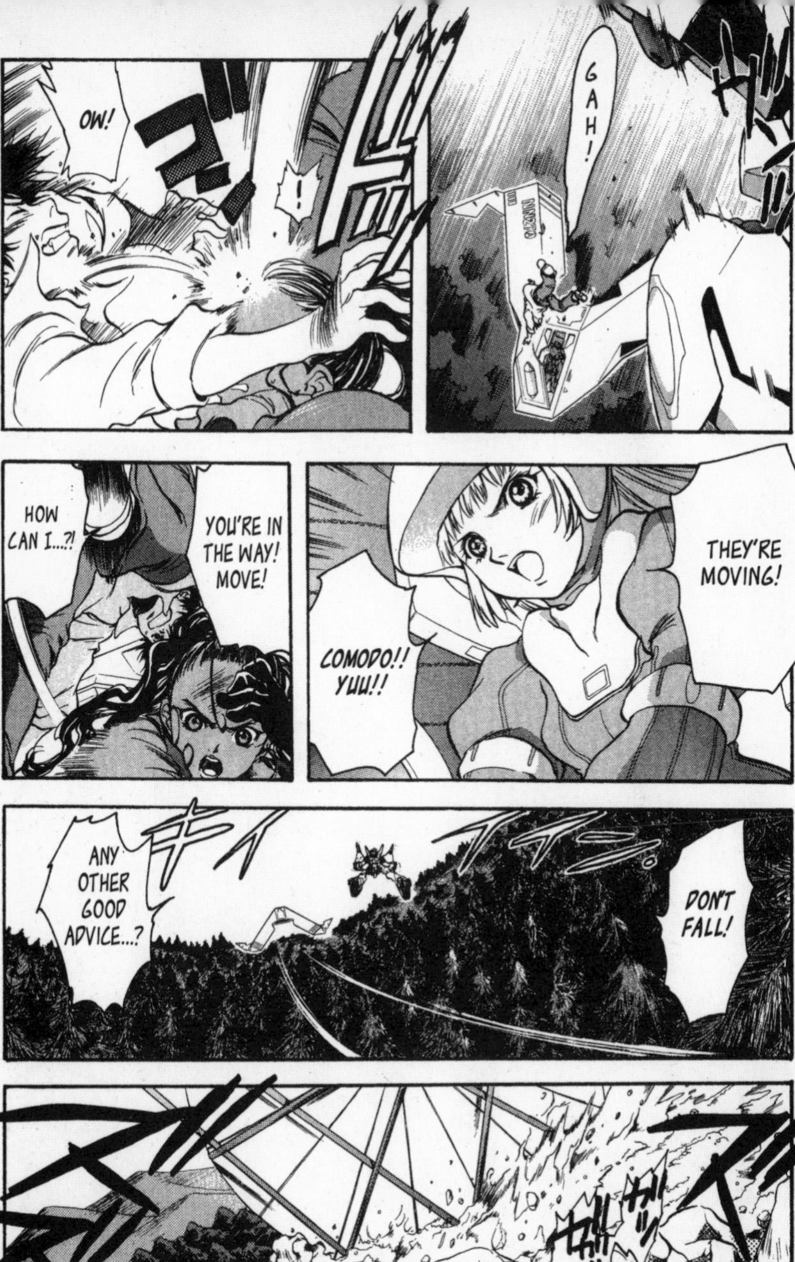
GAH!
OW!
!
THEY'RE MOVING!
COMODO!! YUU!!
YOU'RE IN THE WAY! MOVE!
HOW CAN I...?!
DON'T FALL!
ANY OTHER GOOD ADVICE...?

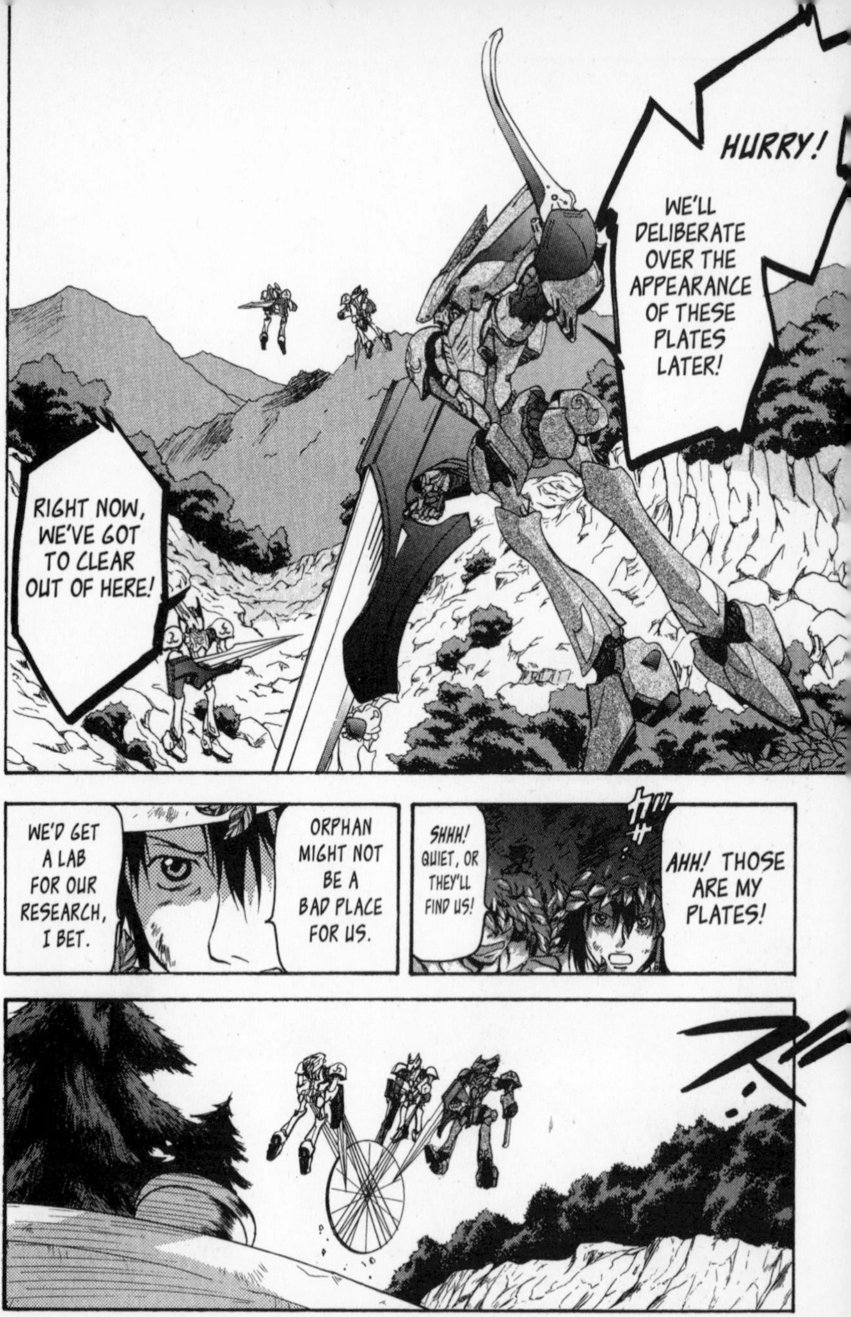
HURRY!
WE'LL DELIBERATE OVER THE APPEARANCE OF THESE PLATES LATER!
RIGHT NOW, WE'VE GOT TO CLEAR OUT OF HERE!
AHH! THOSE ARE MY PLATES!
SHHH! QUIET, OR THEY'LL FIND US!
ORPHAN MIGHT NOT BE A BAD PLACE FOR US.
WE'D GET A LAB FOR OUR RESEARCH, I BET.

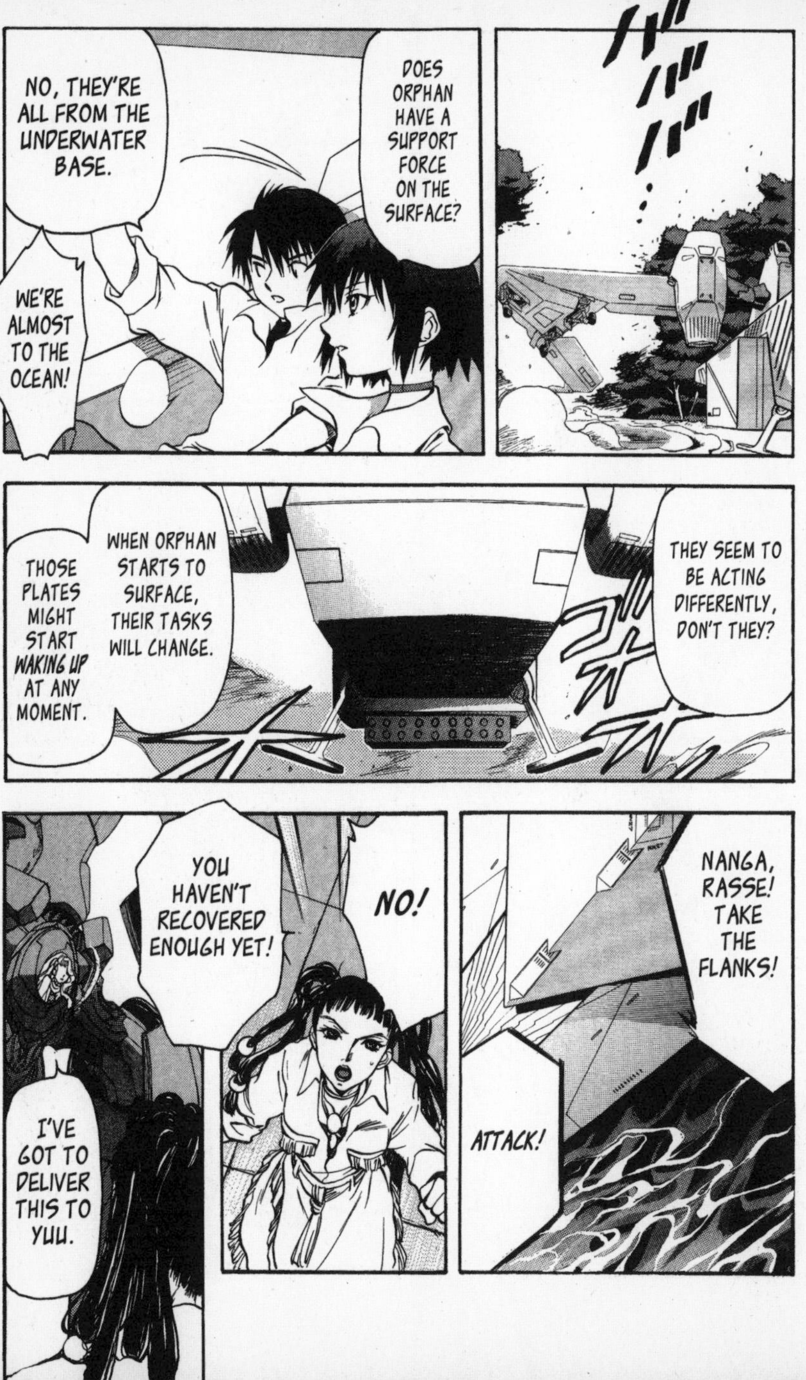
DOES ORPHAN HAVE A SUPPORT FORCE ON THE SURFACE?
NO, THEY'RE ALL FROM THE UNDERWATER BASE.
WE'RE ALMOST TO THE OCEAN!
THEY SEEM TO BE ACTING DIFFERENTLY, DON'T THEY?
WHEN ORPHAN STARTS TO SURFACE, THEIR TASKS WILL CHANGE.
THOSE PLATES MIGHT START *WAKING UP* AT ANY MOMENT.
NANGA, RASSE! TAKE THE FLANKS!
ATTACK!
NO!
YOU HAVEN'T RECOVERED ENOUGH YET!
I'VE GOT TO DELIVER THIS TO YUU.

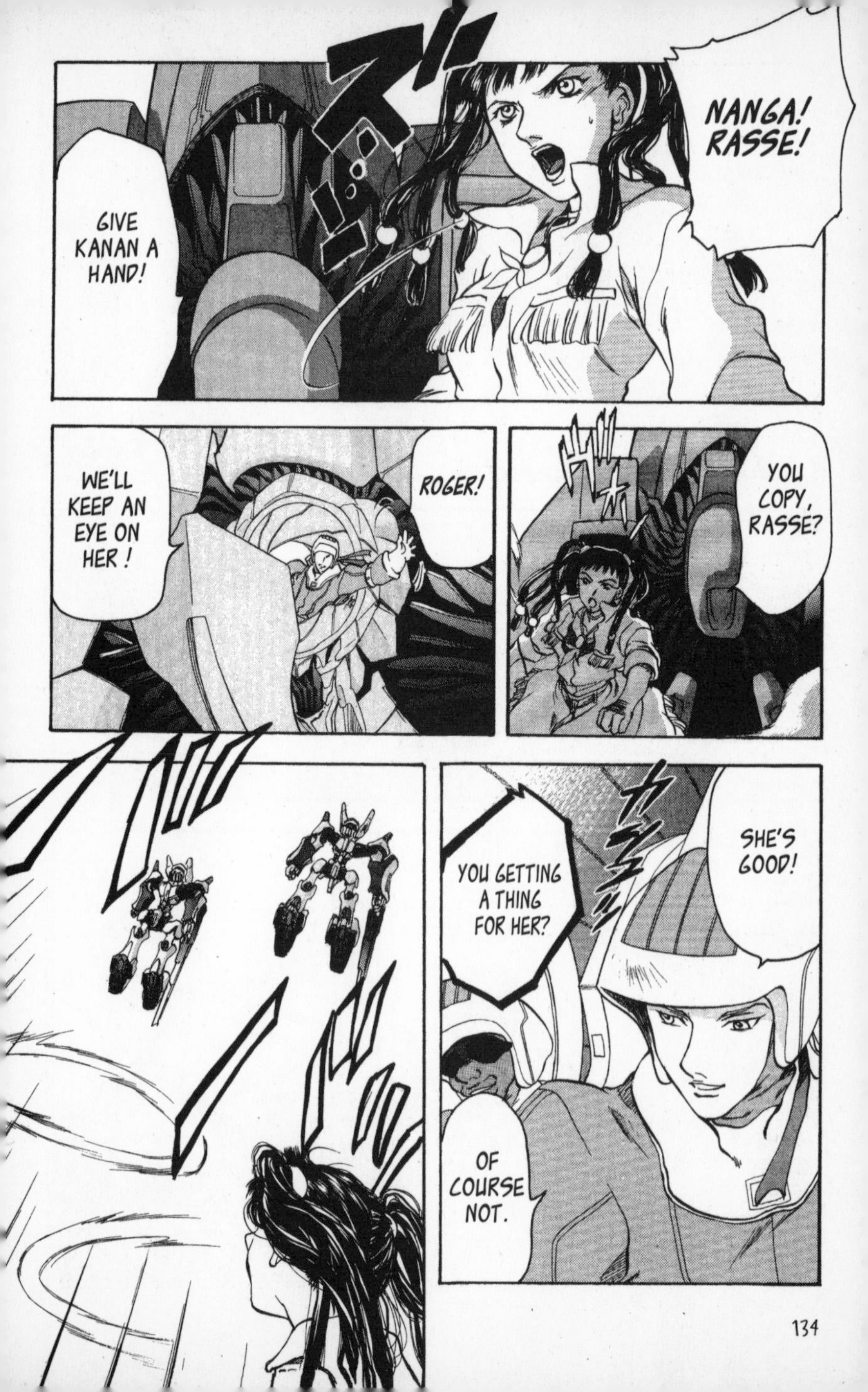
NANGA! RASSE!
GIVE KANAN A HAND!
YOU COPY, RASSE?
ROGER!
WE'LL KEEP AN EYE ON HER!
SHE'S GOOD!
YOU GETTING A THING FOR HER?
OF COURSE NOT.

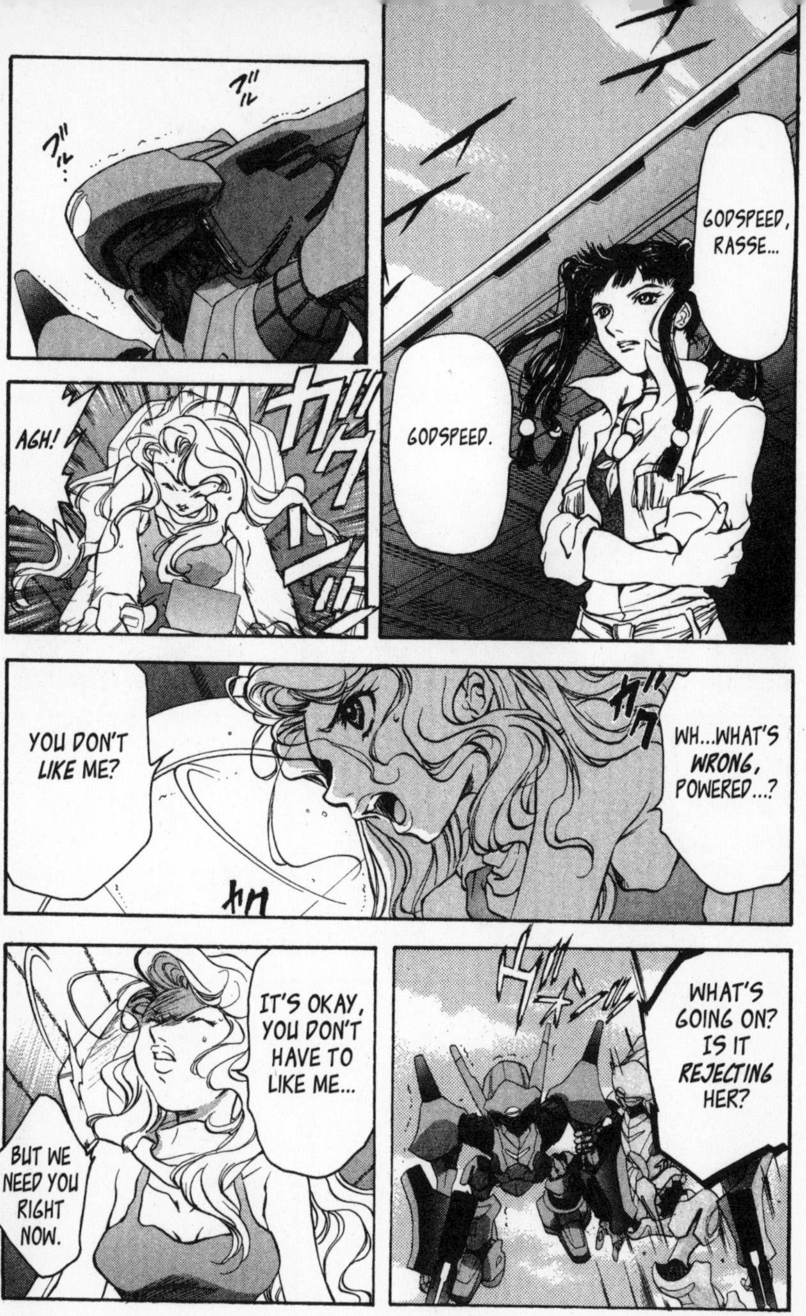
GODSPEED, RASSE...
GODSPEED.
AGH!
WH...WHAT'S WRONG, POWERED...?
YOU DON'T LIKE ME?
WHAT'S GOING ON? IS IT REJECTING HER?
IT'S OKAY, YOU DON'T HAVE TO LIKE ME...
BUT WE NEED YOU RIGHT NOW.

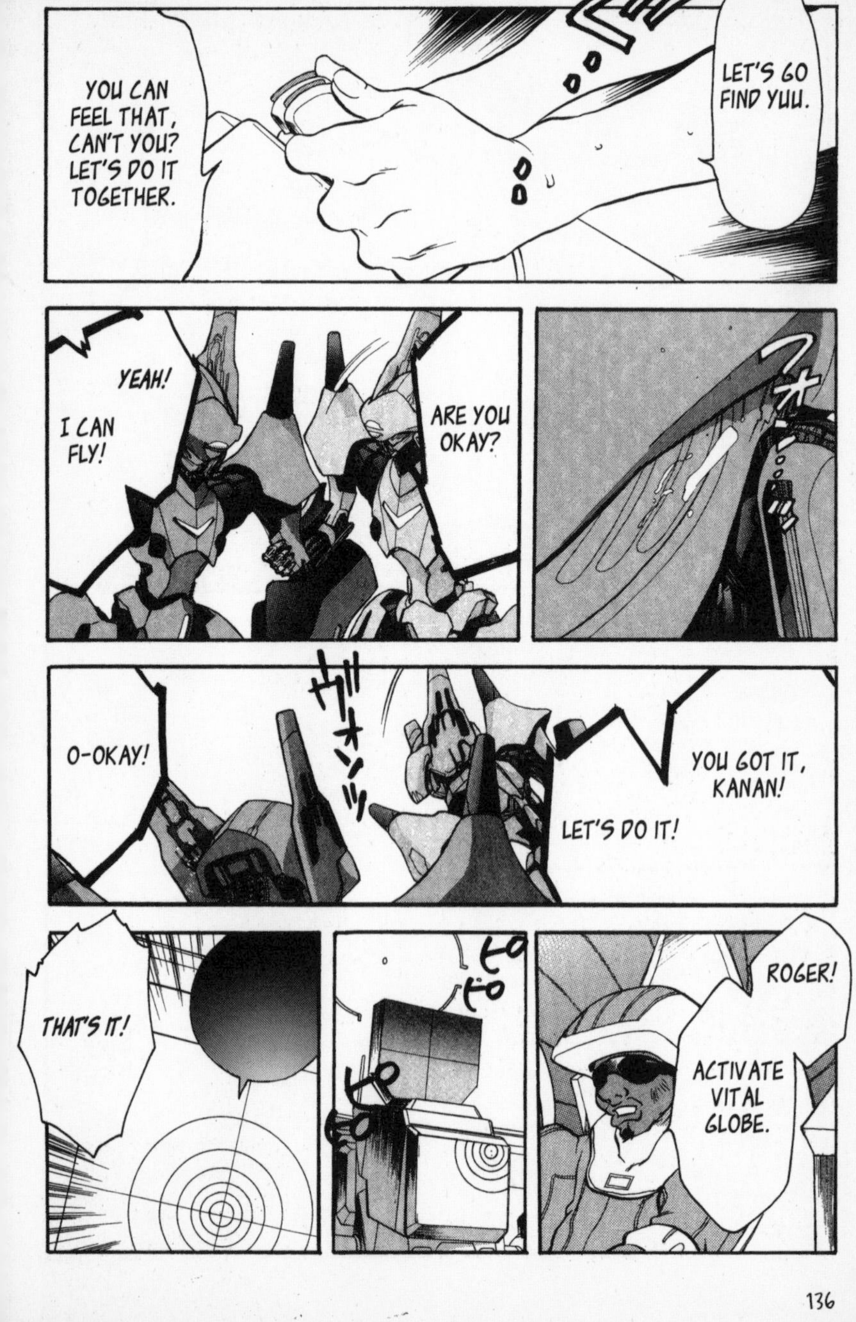
LET'S GO FIND YUU.
YOU CAN FEEL THAT, CAN'T YOU? LET'S DO IT TOGETHER.
ARE YOU OKAY?
YEAH!
I CAN FLY!
YOU GOT IT, KANAN!
LET'S DO IT!
O-OKAY!
ROGER!
ACTIVATE VITAL GLOBE.
THAT'S IT!

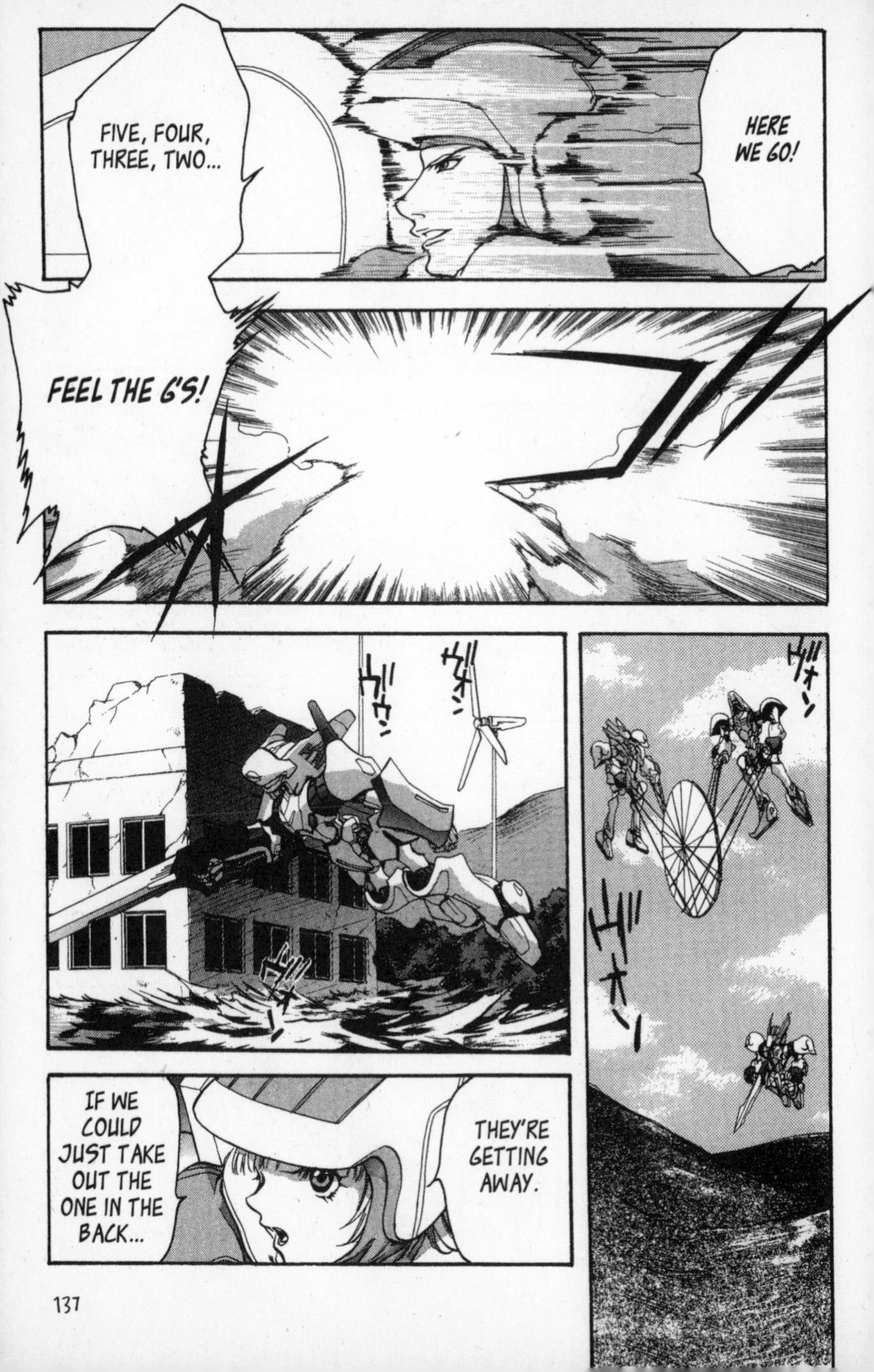
HERE WE GO!
FIVE, FOUR, THREE, TWO...
FEEL THE G'S!
THEY'RE GETTING AWAY.
IF WE COULD JUST TAKE OUT THE ONE IN THE BACK...

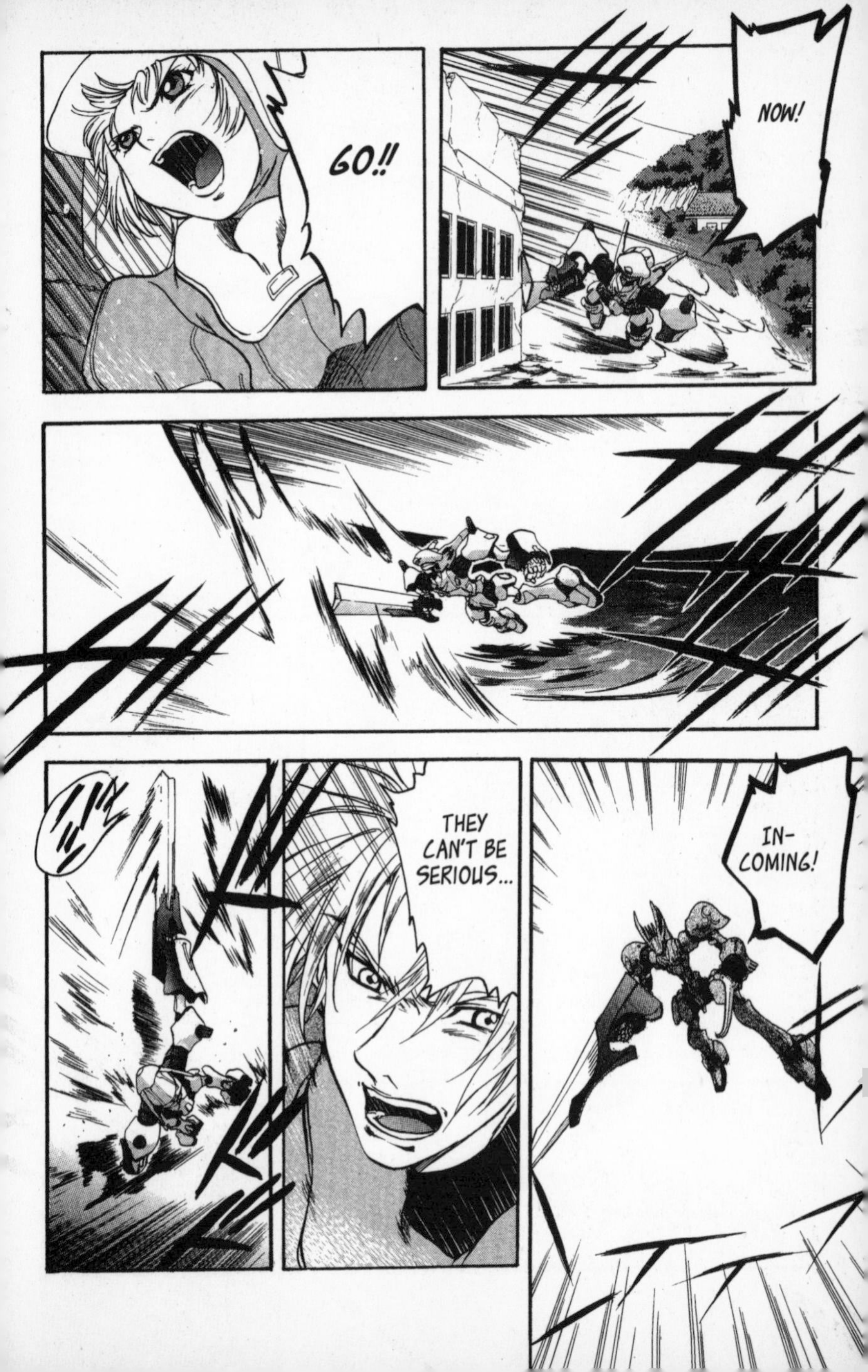
NOW!
GO!!
IN-COMING!
THEY CAN'T BE SERIOUS...

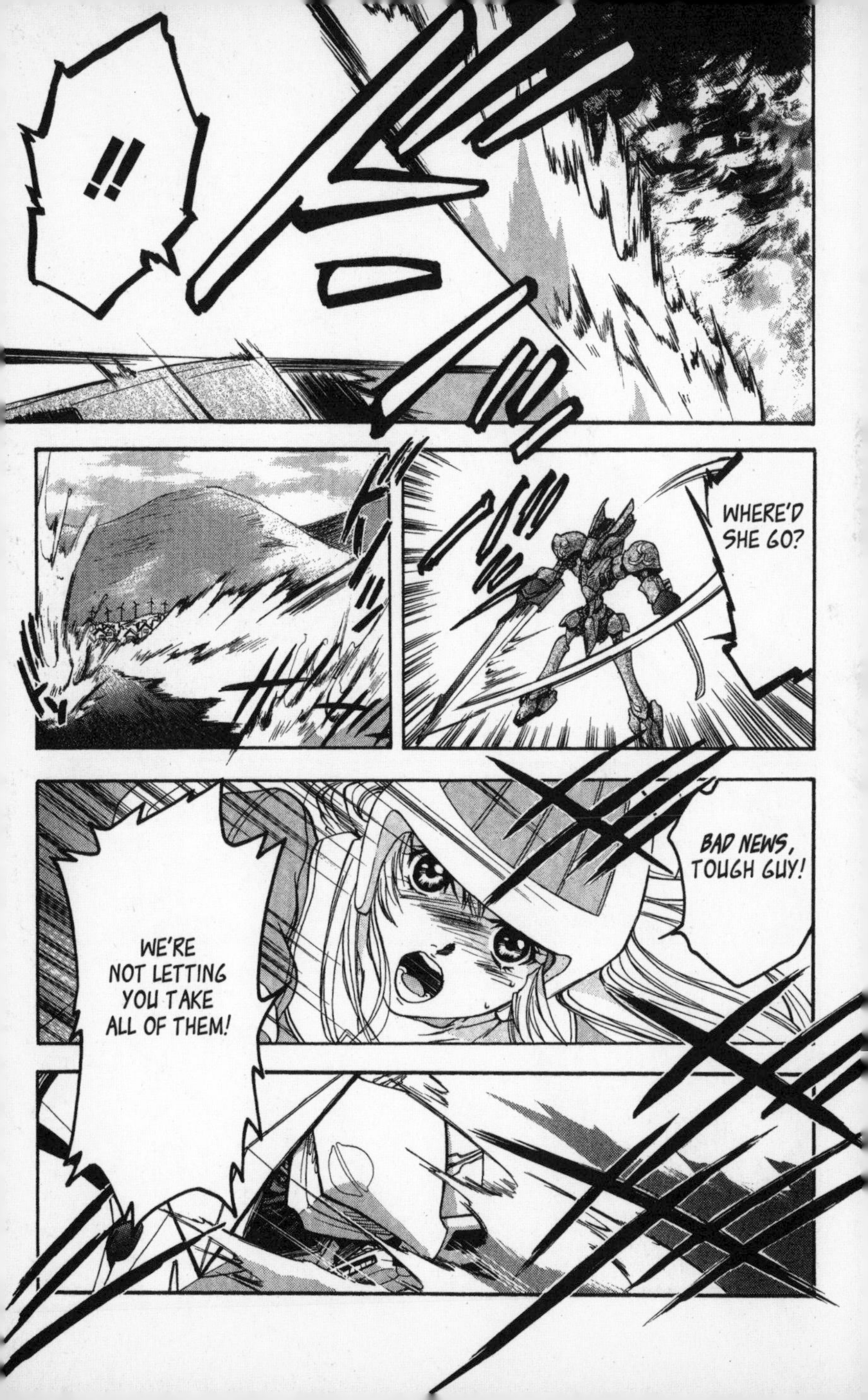
!!
WHERE'D SHE GO?
BAD NEWS, TOUGH GUY!
WE'RE NOT LETTING YOU TAKE ALL OF THEM!

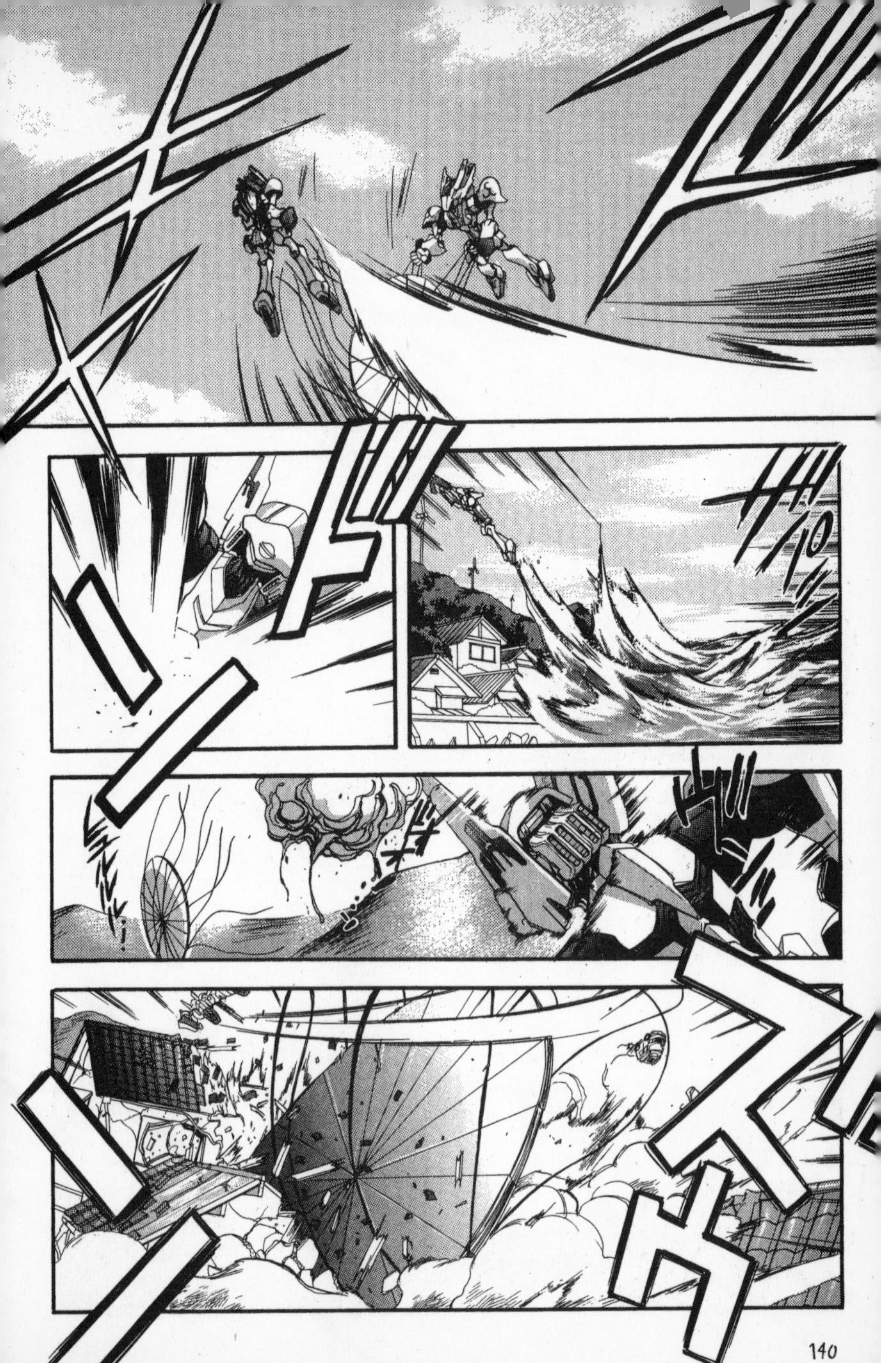

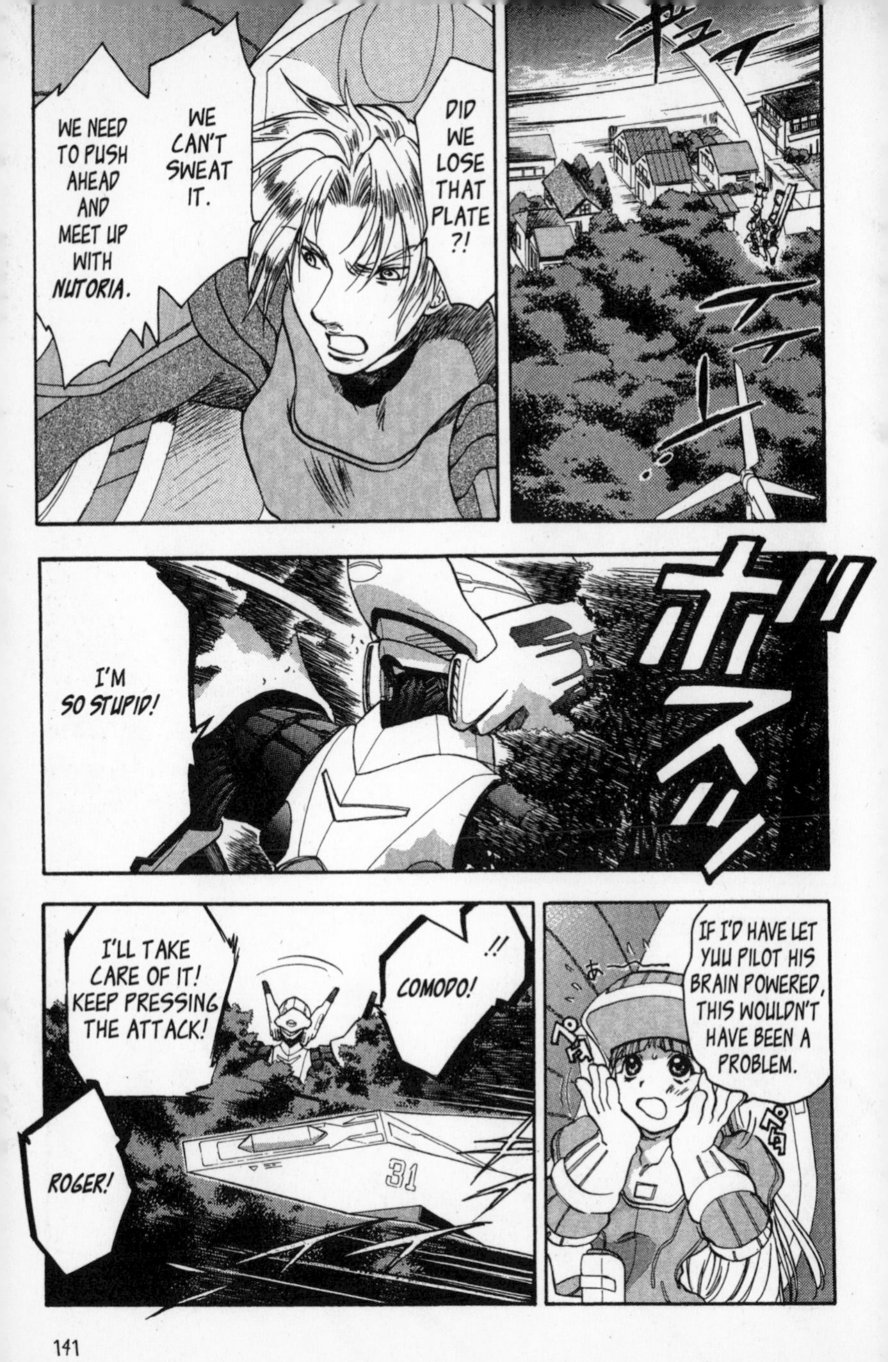
DID WE LOSE THAT PLATE?!
WE CAN'T SWEAT IT.
WE NEED TO PUSH AHEAD AND MEET UP WITH NUTORIA.
I'M SO STUPID!
IF I'D HAVE LET YUU PILOT HIS BRAIN POWERED, THIS WOULDN'T HAVE BEEN A PROBLEM.
!!
COMODO!
I'LL TAKE CARE OF IT! KEEP PRESSING THE ATTACK!
ROGER!

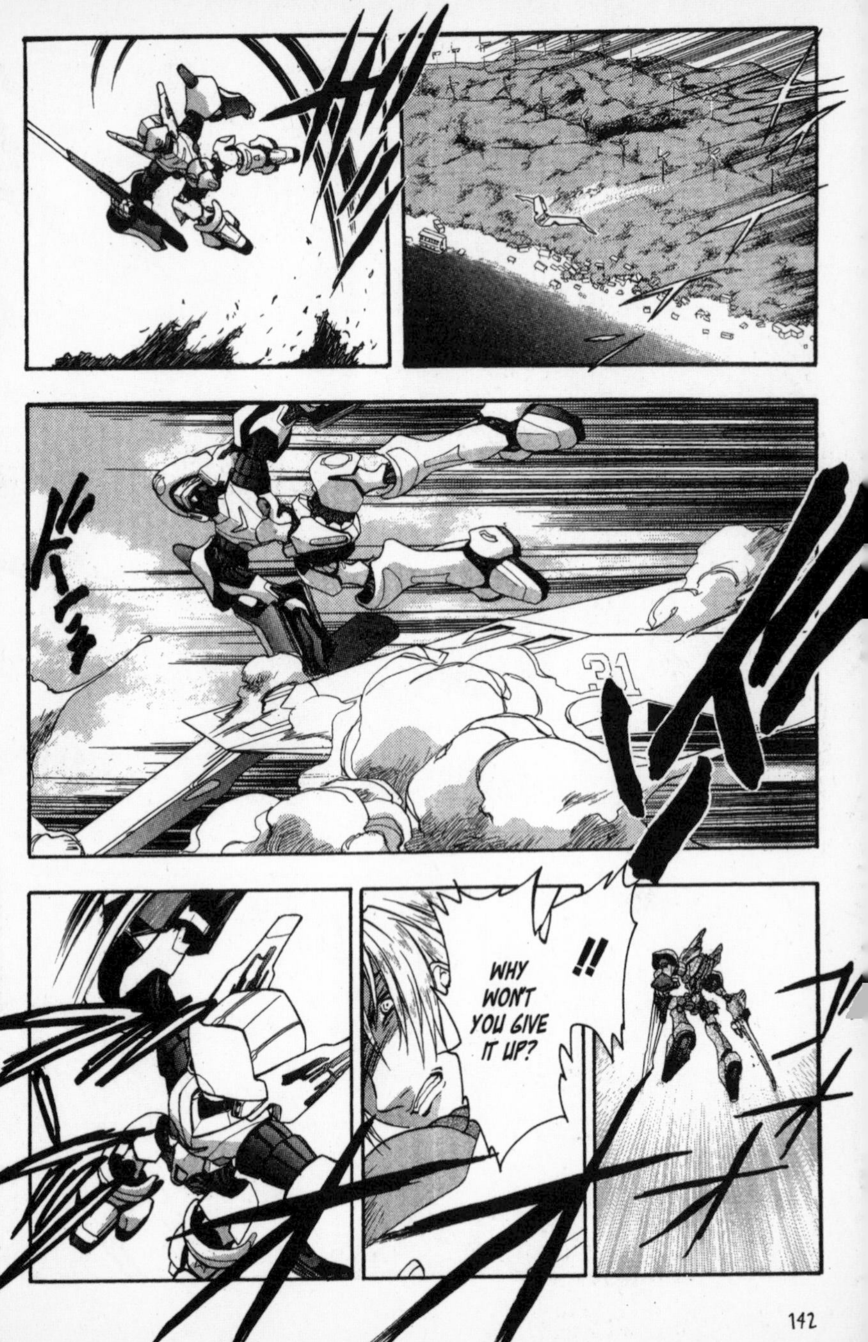
!!
WHY WON'T YOU GIVE IT UP?

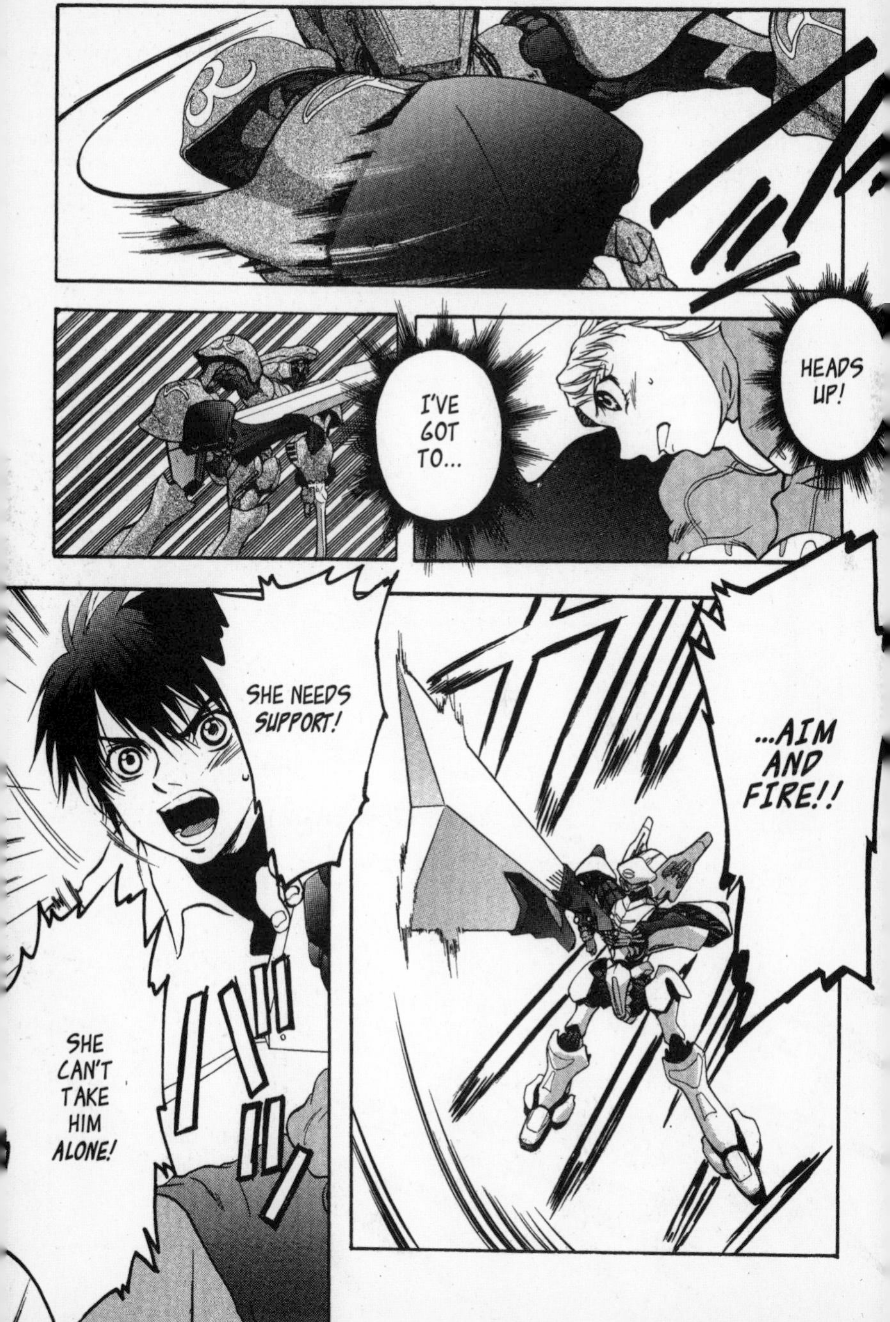
HEADS UP!
I'VE GOT TO...
...AIM AND FIRE!!
SHE NEEDS SUPPORT!
SHE CAN'T TAKE HIM ALONE!

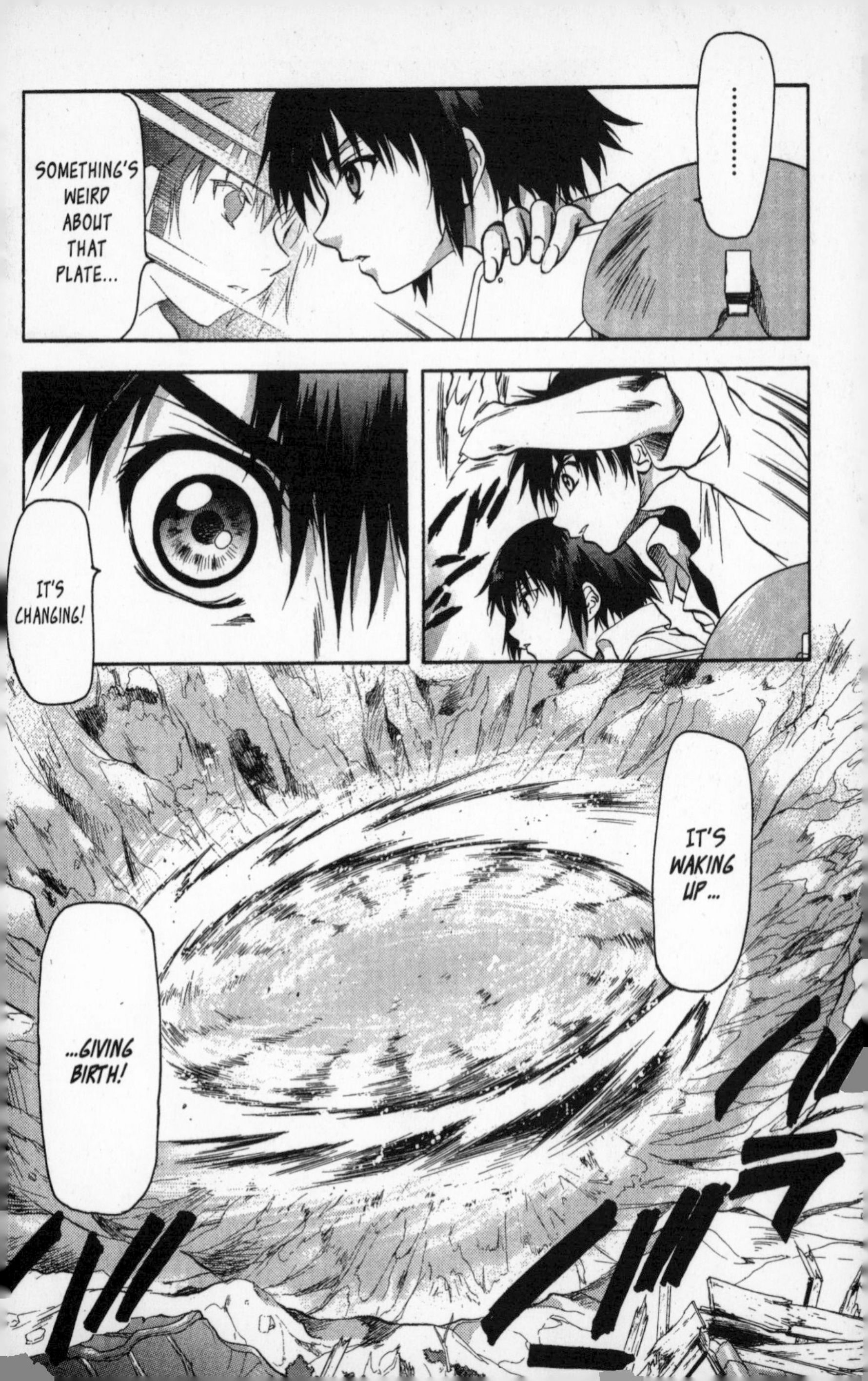
........!
SOMETHING'S WEIRD ABOUT THAT PLATE...
IT'S CHANGING!
IT'S WAKING UP...
...GIVING BIRTH!

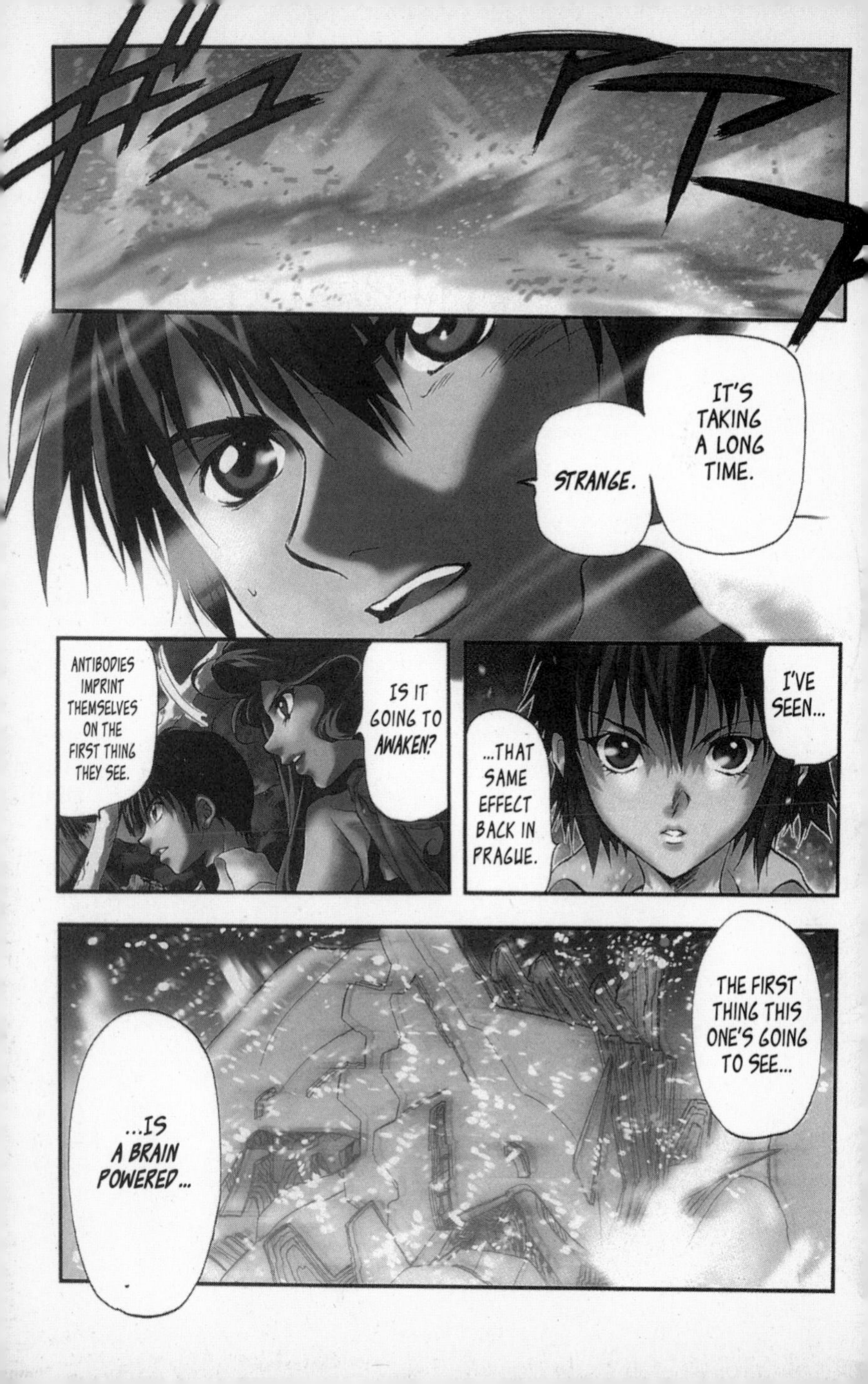

IT'S TAKING A LONG TIME.
STRANGE.
I'VE SEEN...
...THAT SAME EFFECT BACK IN PRAGUE.
IS IT GOING TO AWAKEN?
ANTIBODIES IMPRINT THEMSELVES ON THE FIRST THING THEY SEE.
THE FIRST THING THIS ONE'S GOING TO SEE...
...IS A BRAIN POWERED...

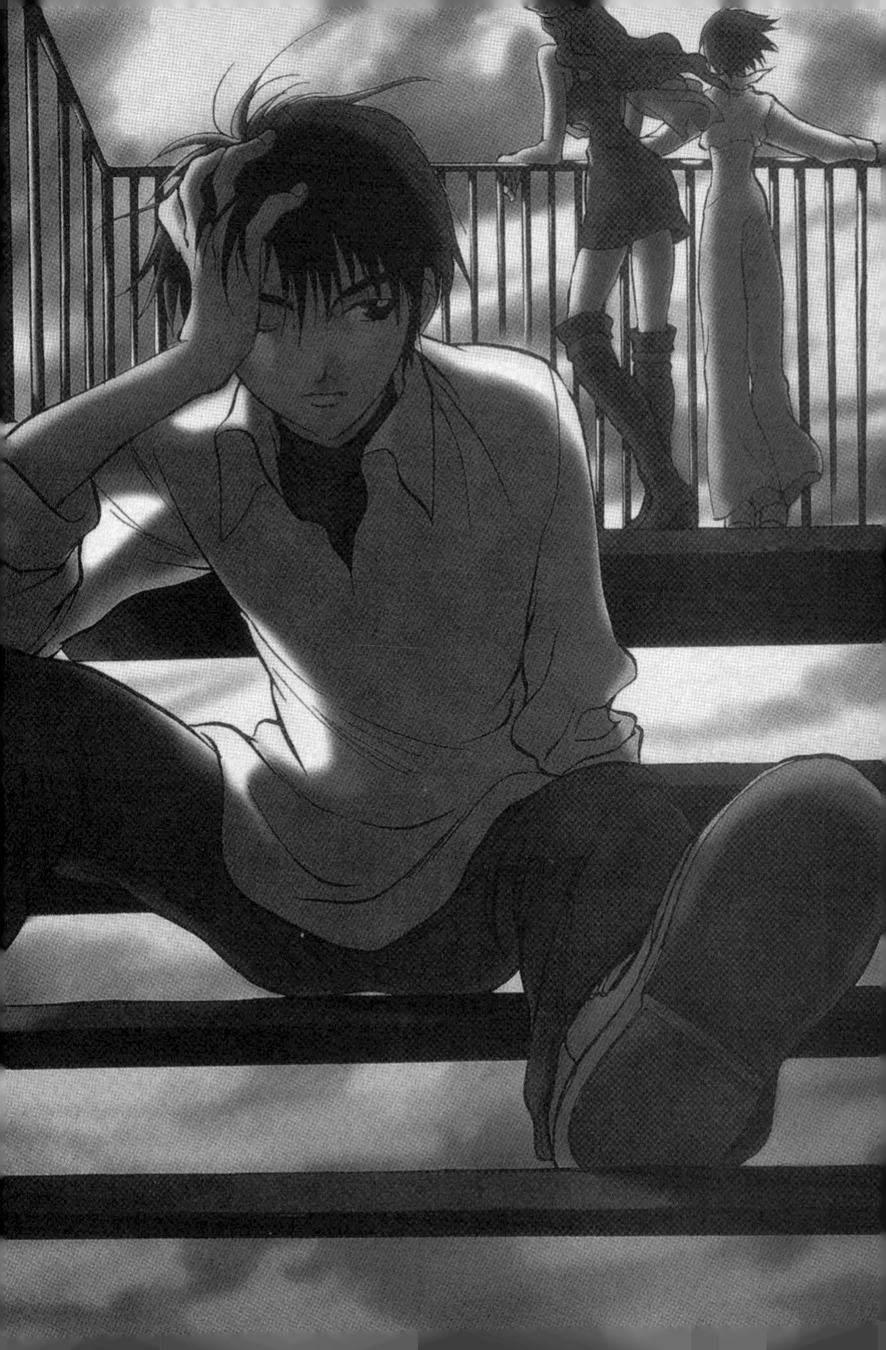

REVIVAL 12: DOUBLE REVIVAL

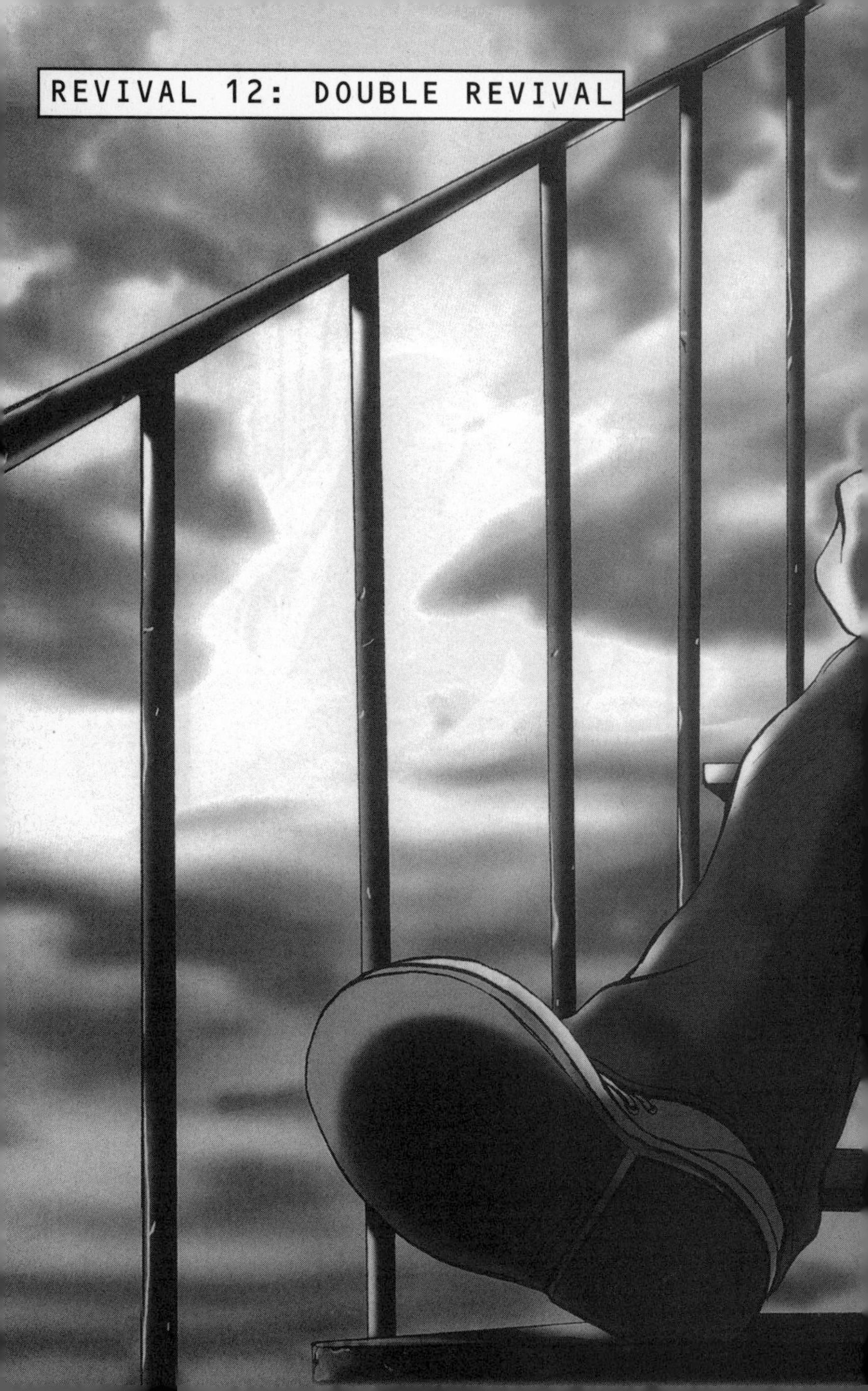

BRAIN POWERED

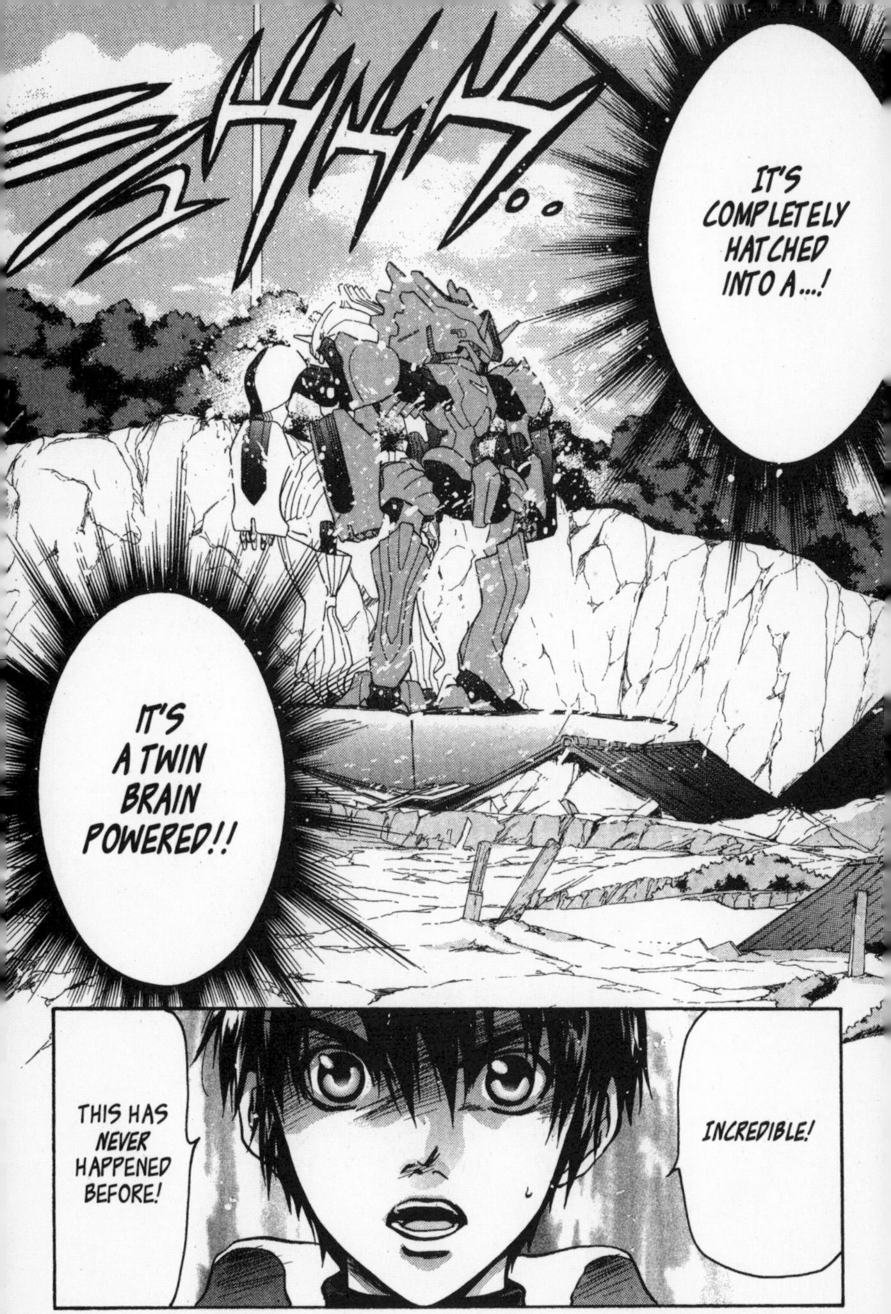
IT'S COMPLETELY HATCHED INTO A...!
IT'S A TWIN BRAIN POWERED!!
INCREDIBLE!
THIS HAS *NEVER* HAPPENED BEFORE!

...WILL YOU...

HEY, POWERED...

HOW DO YOU KNOW IT'S A BRAIN POWERED?

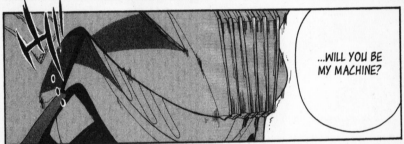

...WILL YOU BE MY MACHINE?

YEAH. SOMEHOW HE DIDN'T CRUSH ME.

ARE YOU OKAY?

WATCH OUT!

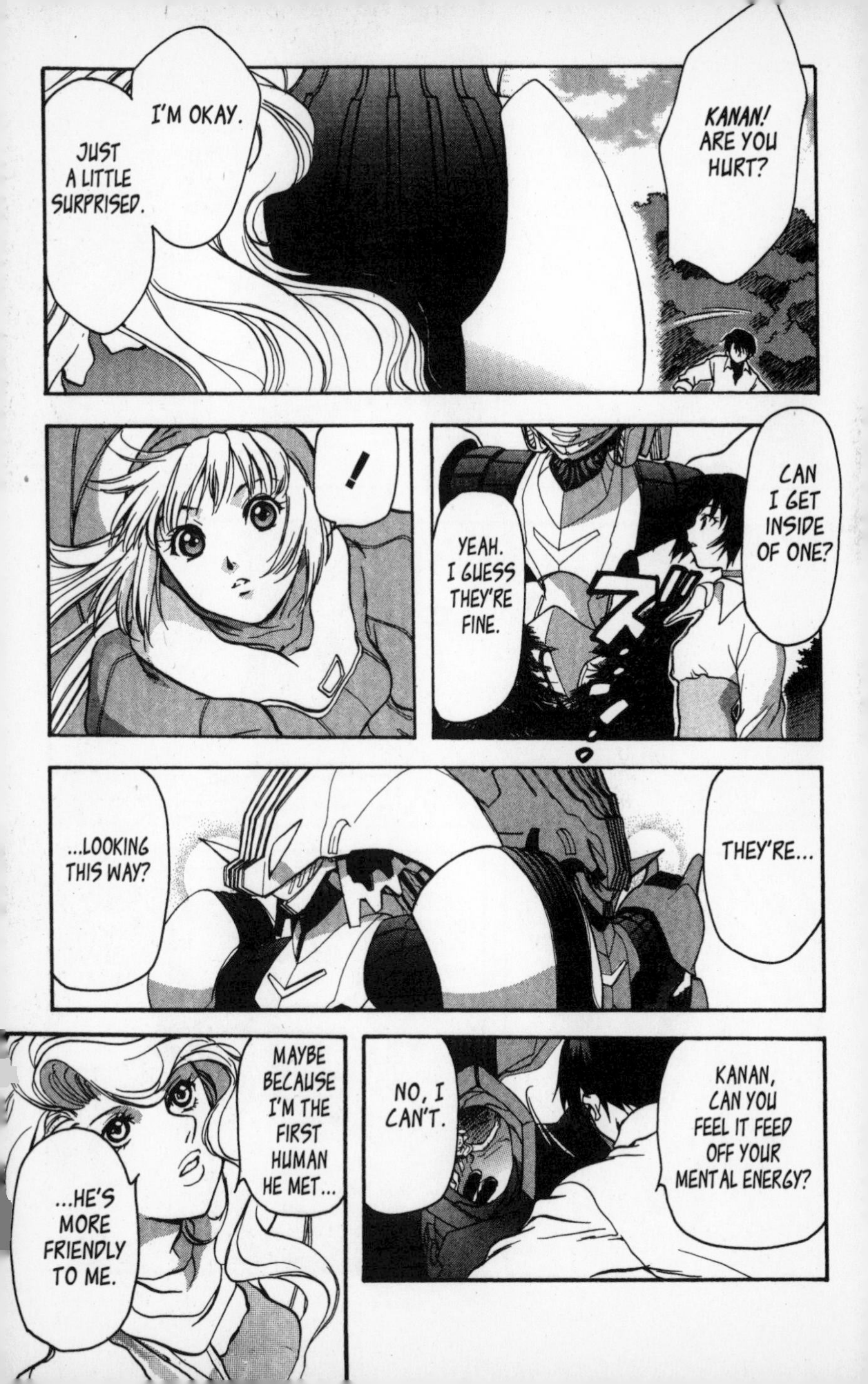
KANAN! ARE YOU HURT?
I'M OKAY.
JUST A LITTLE SURPRISED.
CAN I GET INSIDE OF ONE?
YEAH. I GUESS THEY'RE FINE.
!
THEY'RE...
...LOOKING THIS WAY?
KANAN, CAN YOU FEEL IT FEED OFF YOUR MENTAL ENERGY?
NO, I CAN'T.
MAYBE BECAUSE I'M THE FIRST HUMAN HE MET...
...HE'S MORE FRIENDLY TO ME.

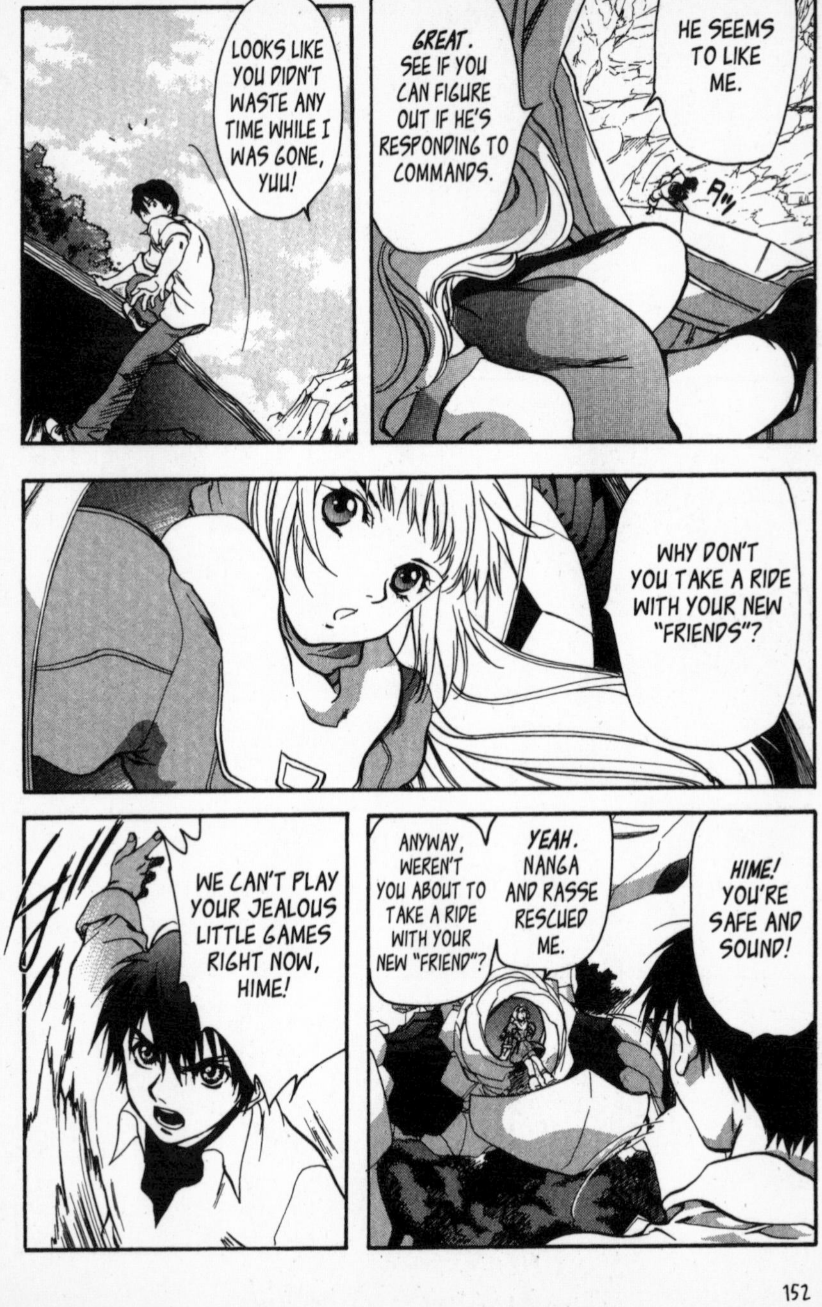
HE SEEMS TO LIKE ME.
GREAT. SEE IF YOU CAN FIGURE OUT IF HE'S RESPONDING TO COMMANDS.
LOOKS LIKE YOU DIDN'T WASTE ANY TIME WHILE I WAS GONE, YUU!
WHY DON'T YOU TAKE A RIDE WITH YOUR NEW "FRIENDS"?
HIME! YOU'RE SAFE AND SOUND!
YEAH. NANGA AND RASSE RESCUED ME.
ANYWAY, WEREN'T YOU ABOUT TO TAKE A RIDE WITH YOUR NEW "FRIEND"?
WE CAN'T PLAY YOUR JEALOUS LITTLE GAMES RIGHT NOW, HIME!

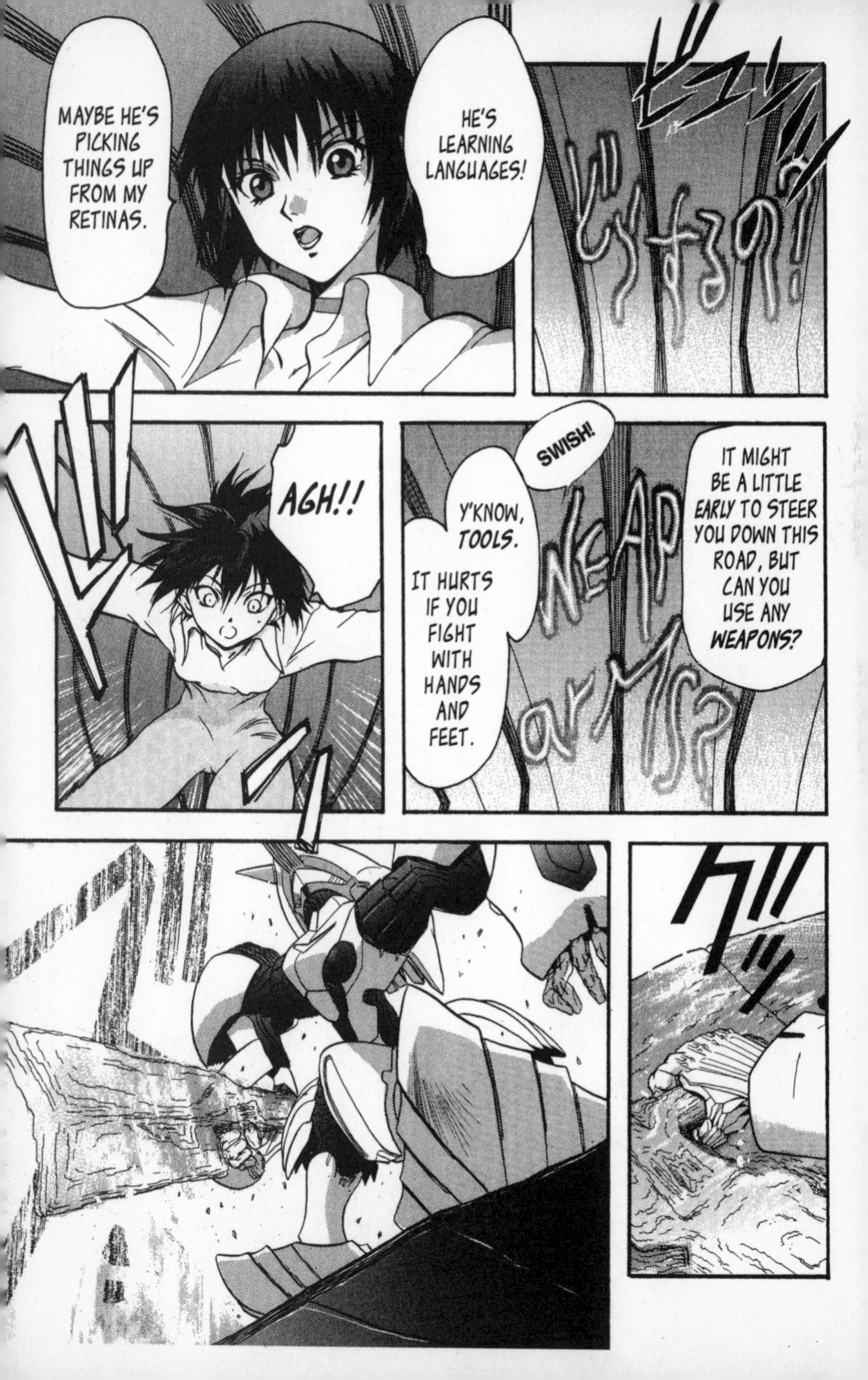
どうするの!?
HE'S LEARNING LANGUAGES!
MAYBE HE'S PICKING THINGS UP FROM MY RETINAS.
IT MIGHT BE A LITTLE EARLY TO STEER YOU DOWN THIS ROAD, BUT CAN YOU USE ANY *WEAPONS?*
arMs?
SWISH!
Y'KNOW, *TOOLS.*
IT HURTS IF YOU FIGHT WITH HANDS AND FEET.
AGH!!

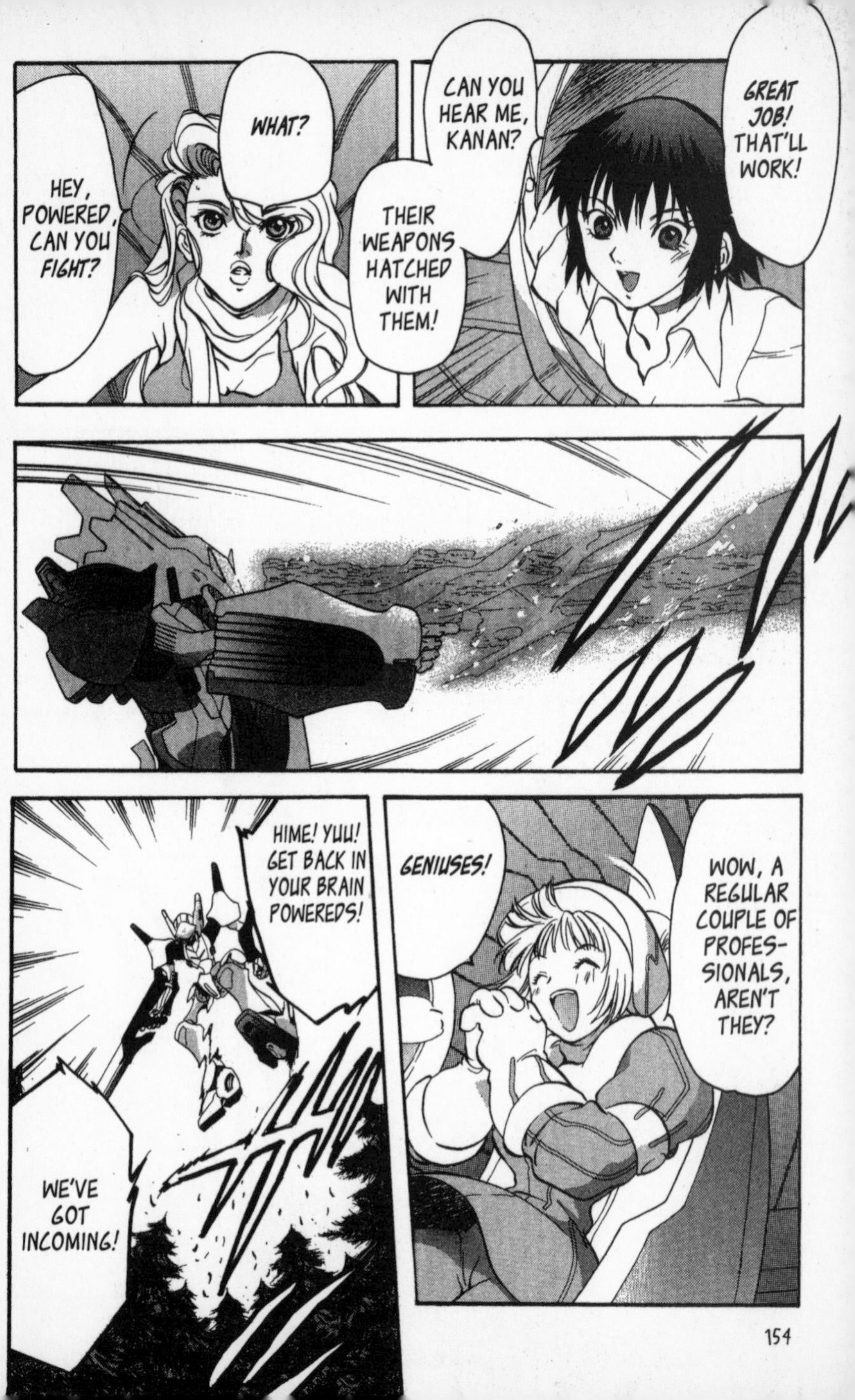
GREAT JOB! THAT'LL WORK!
CAN YOU HEAR ME, KANAN?
THEIR WEAPONS HATCHED WITH THEM!
WHAT?
HEY, POWERED, CAN YOU FIGHT?
WOW, A REGULAR COUPLE OF PROFES-SIONALS, AREN'T THEY?
GENIUSES!
HIME! YUU! GET BACK IN YOUR BRAIN POWEREDS!
WE'VE GOT INCOMING!

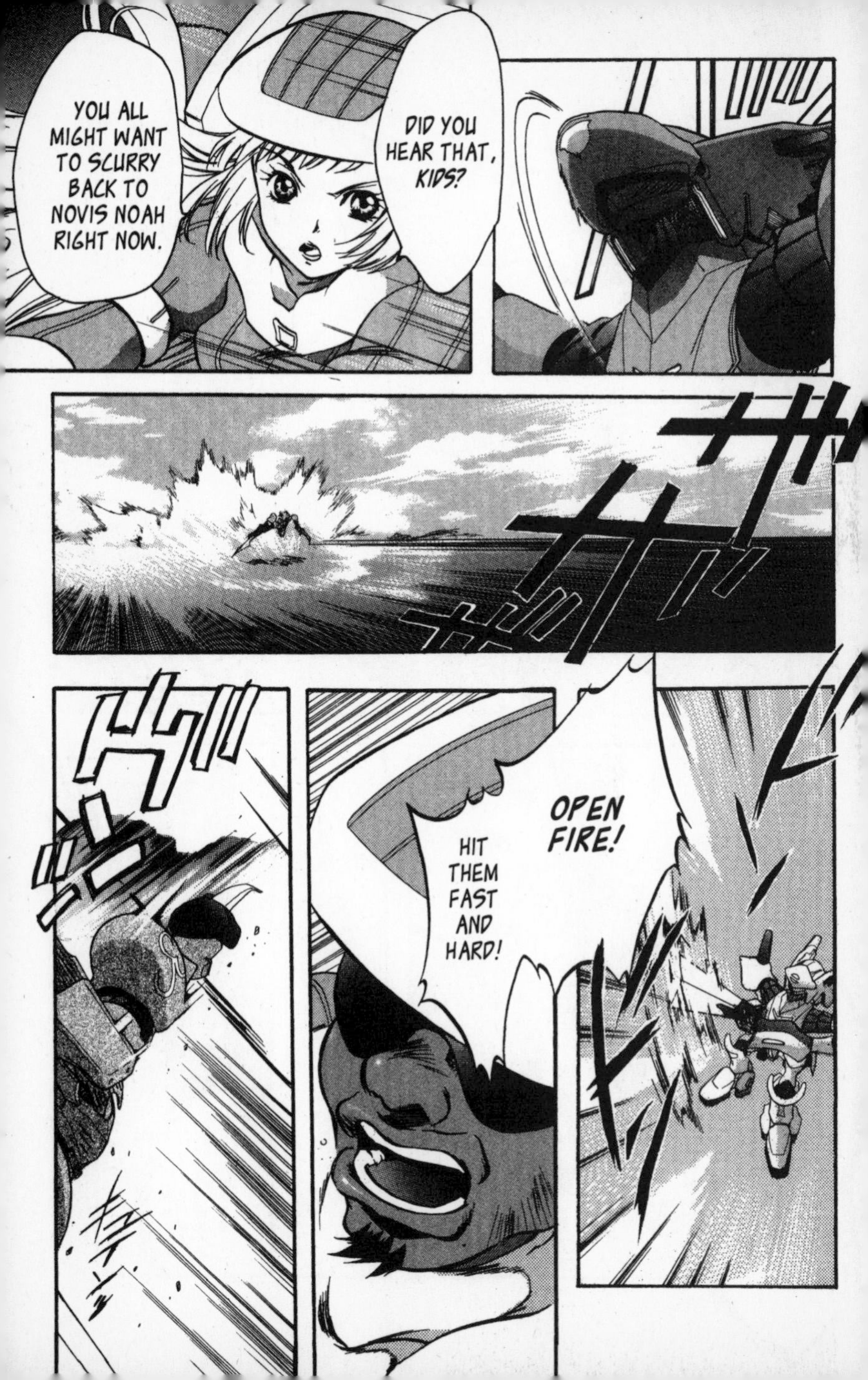
DID YOU HEAR THAT, KIDS?
YOU ALL MIGHT WANT TO SCURRY BACK TO NOVIS NOAH RIGHT NOW.
OPEN FIRE!
HIT THEM FAST AND HARD!

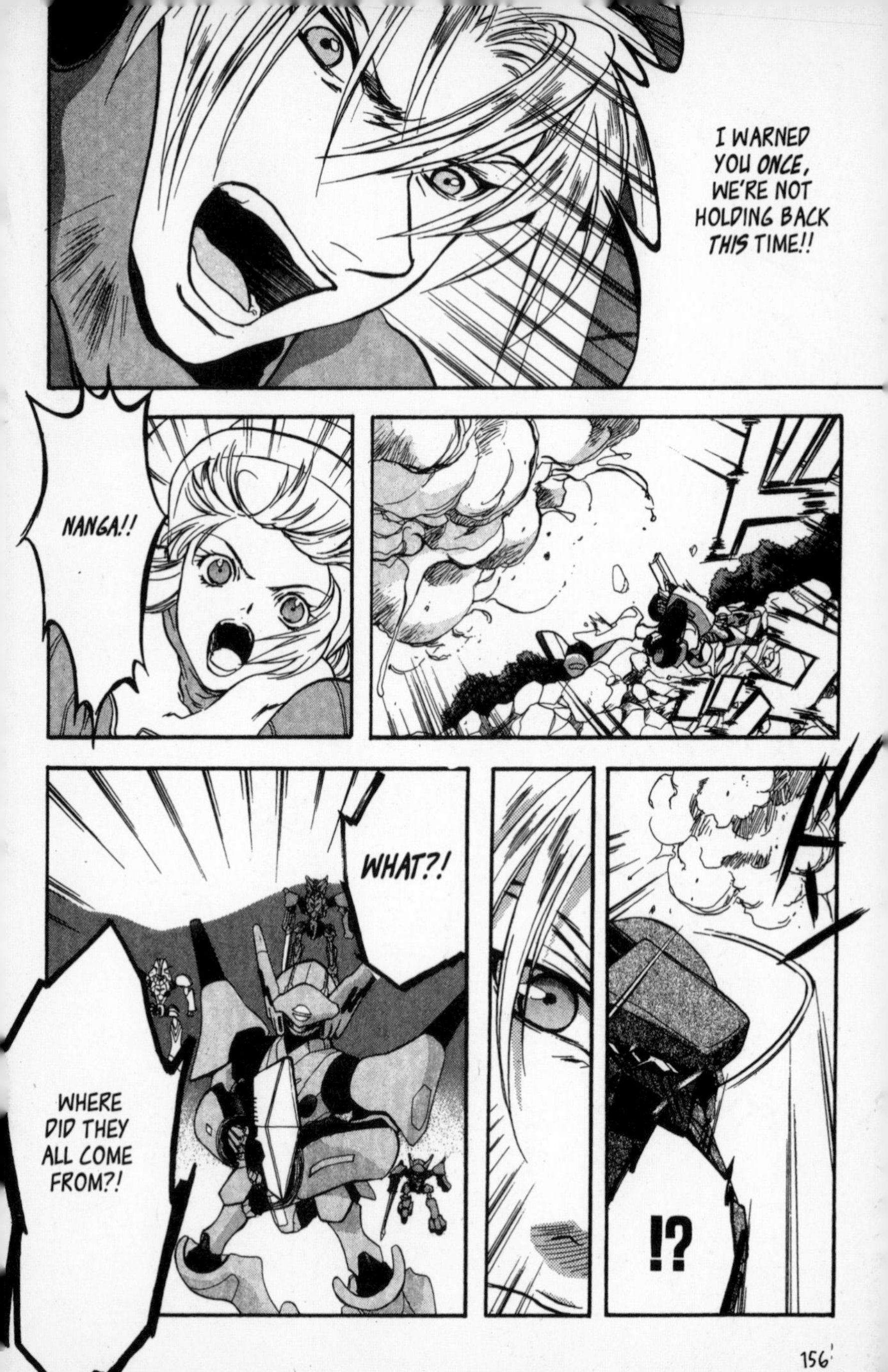
I WARNED YOU ONCE, WE'RE NOT HOLDING BACK THIS TIME!!
NANGA!!
!?
WHAT?!
WHERE DID THEY ALL COME FROM?!

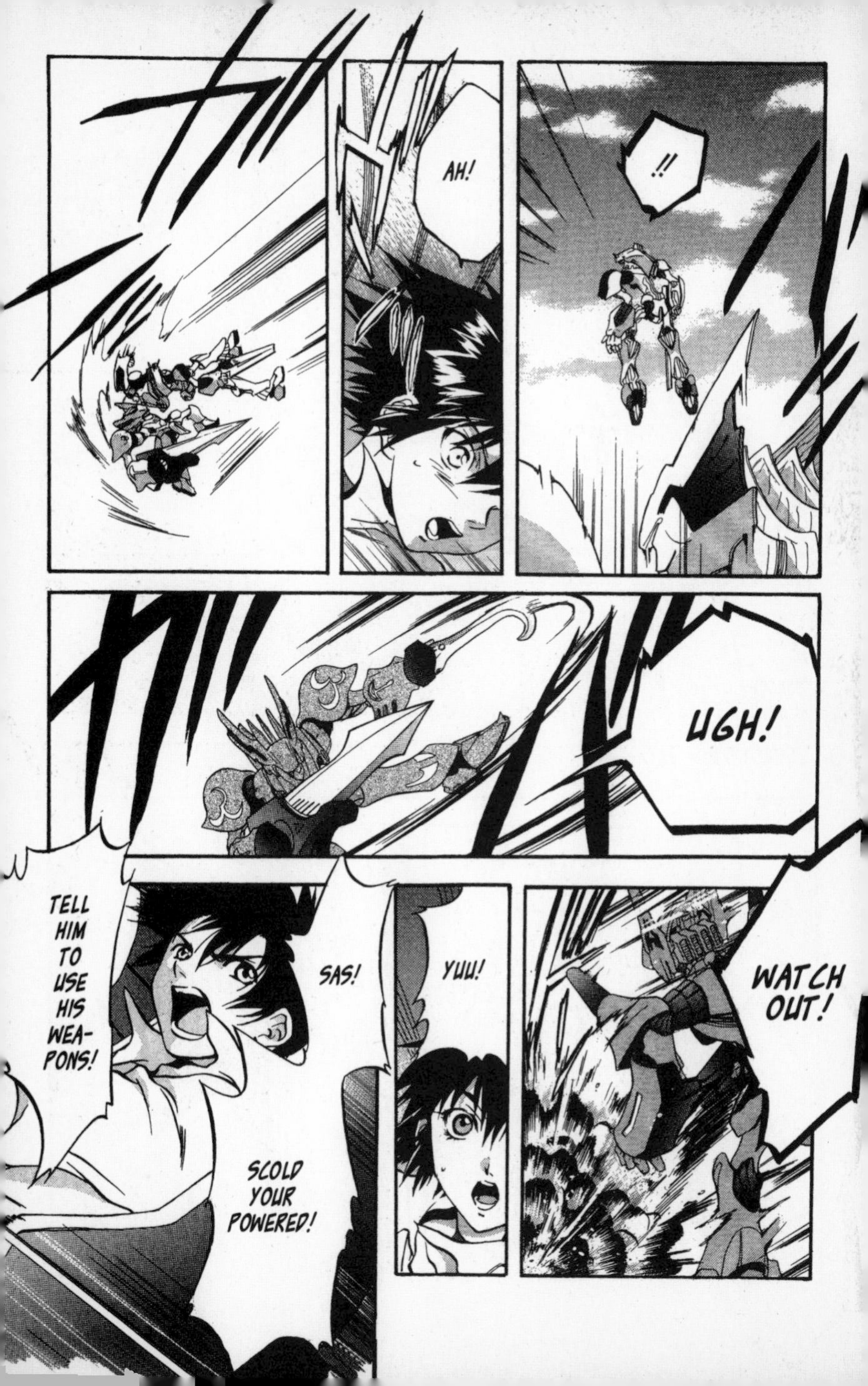
!!
AH!
UGH!
WATCH OUT!
YUU!
SAS!
TELL HIM TO USE HIS WEA-PONS!
SCOLD YOUR POWERED!

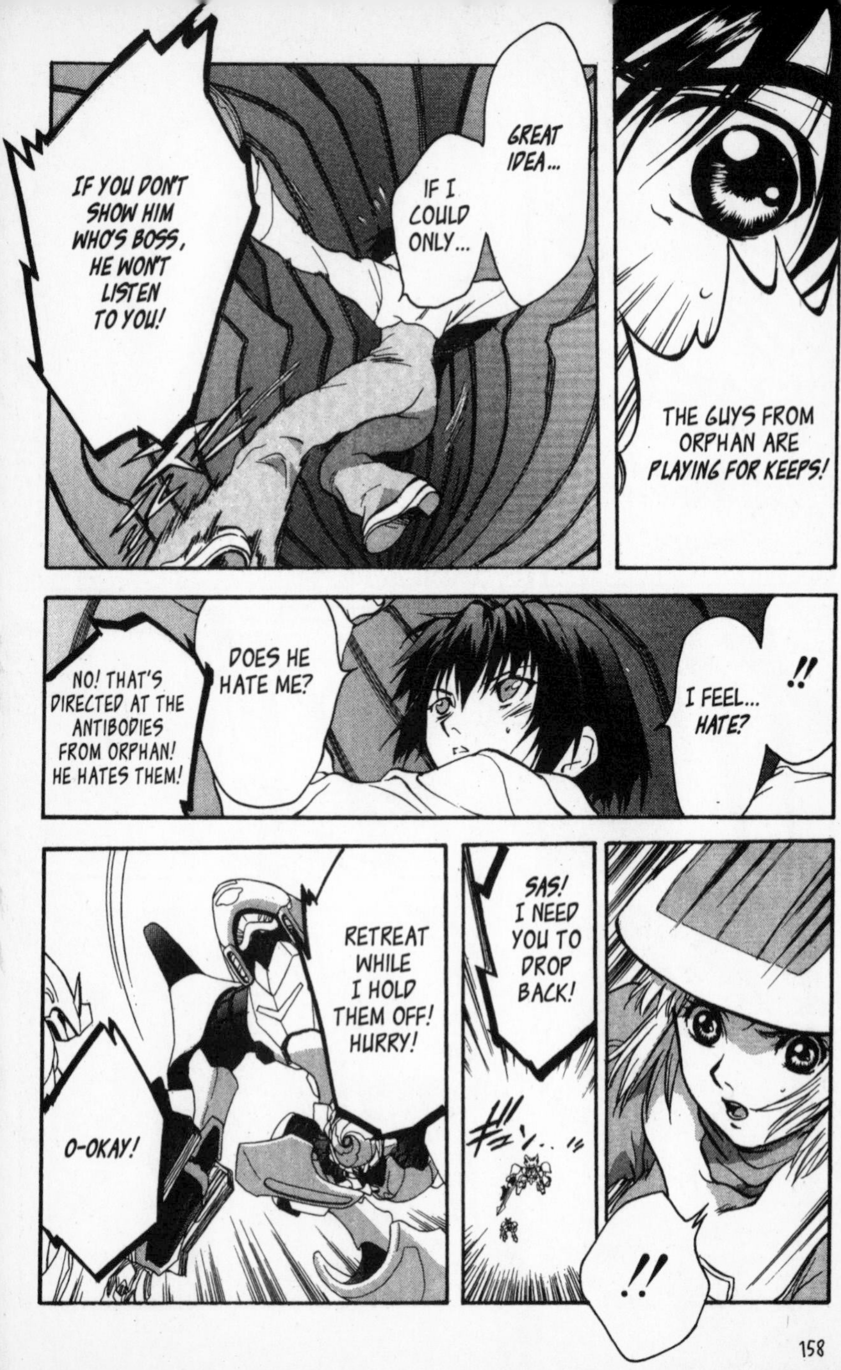
THE GUYS FROM ORPHAN ARE PLAYING FOR KEEPS!
GREAT IDEA...
IF I COULD ONLY...
IF YOU DON'T SHOW HIM WHO'S BOSS, HE WON'T LISTEN TO YOU!
!!
I FEEL... HATE?
DOES HE HATE ME?
NO! THAT'S DIRECTED AT THE ANTIBODIES FROM ORPHAN! HE HATES THEM!
!!
SAS! I NEED YOU TO DROP BACK!
RETREAT WHILE I HOLD THEM OFF! HURRY!
O-OKAY!

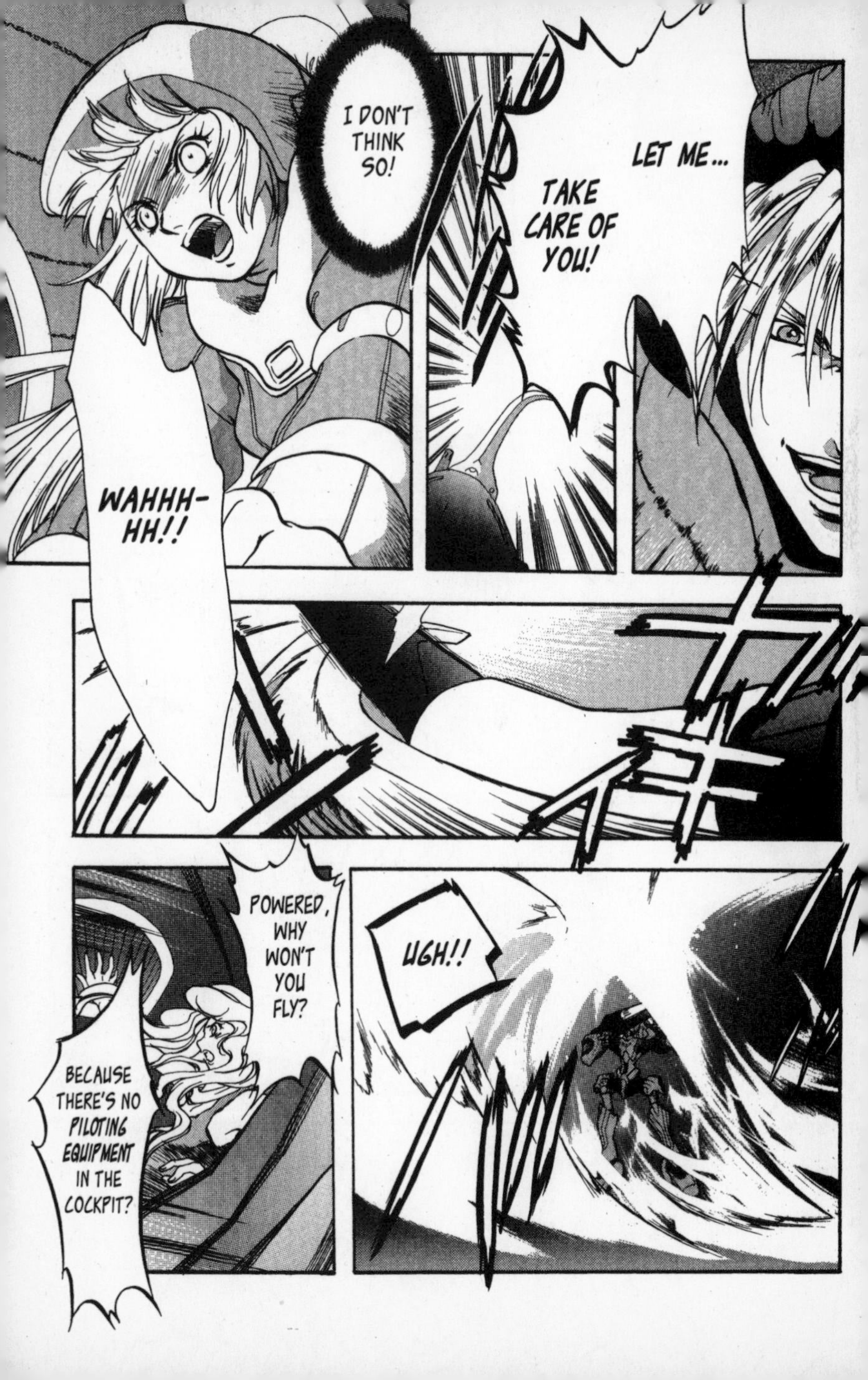
LET ME...
TAKE CARE OF YOU!
I DON'T THINK SO!
WAHHH-HH!!
UGH!!
POWERED, WHY WON'T YOU FLY?
BECAUSE THERE'S NO PILOTING EQUIPMENT IN THE COCKPIT?

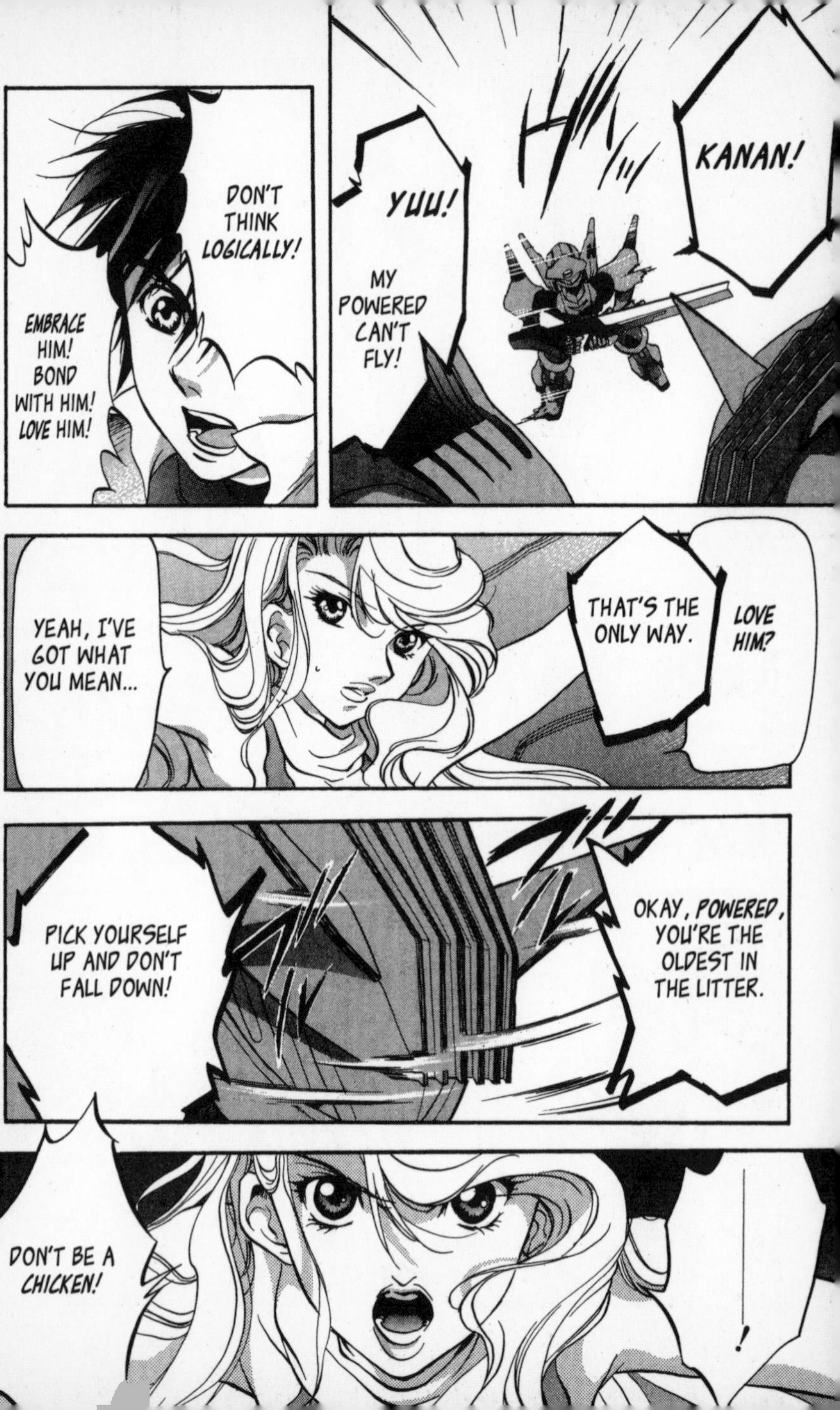
KANAN!
YUU!
MY POWERED CAN'T FLY!
DON'T THINK LOGICALLY!
EMBRACE HIM! BOND WITH HIM! LOVE HIM!
LOVE HIM?
THAT'S THE ONLY WAY.
YEAH, I'VE GOT WHAT YOU MEAN...
OKAY, POWERED, YOU'RE THE OLDEST IN THE LITTER.
PICK YOURSELF UP AND DON'T FALL DOWN!
!
DON'T BE A CHICKEN!

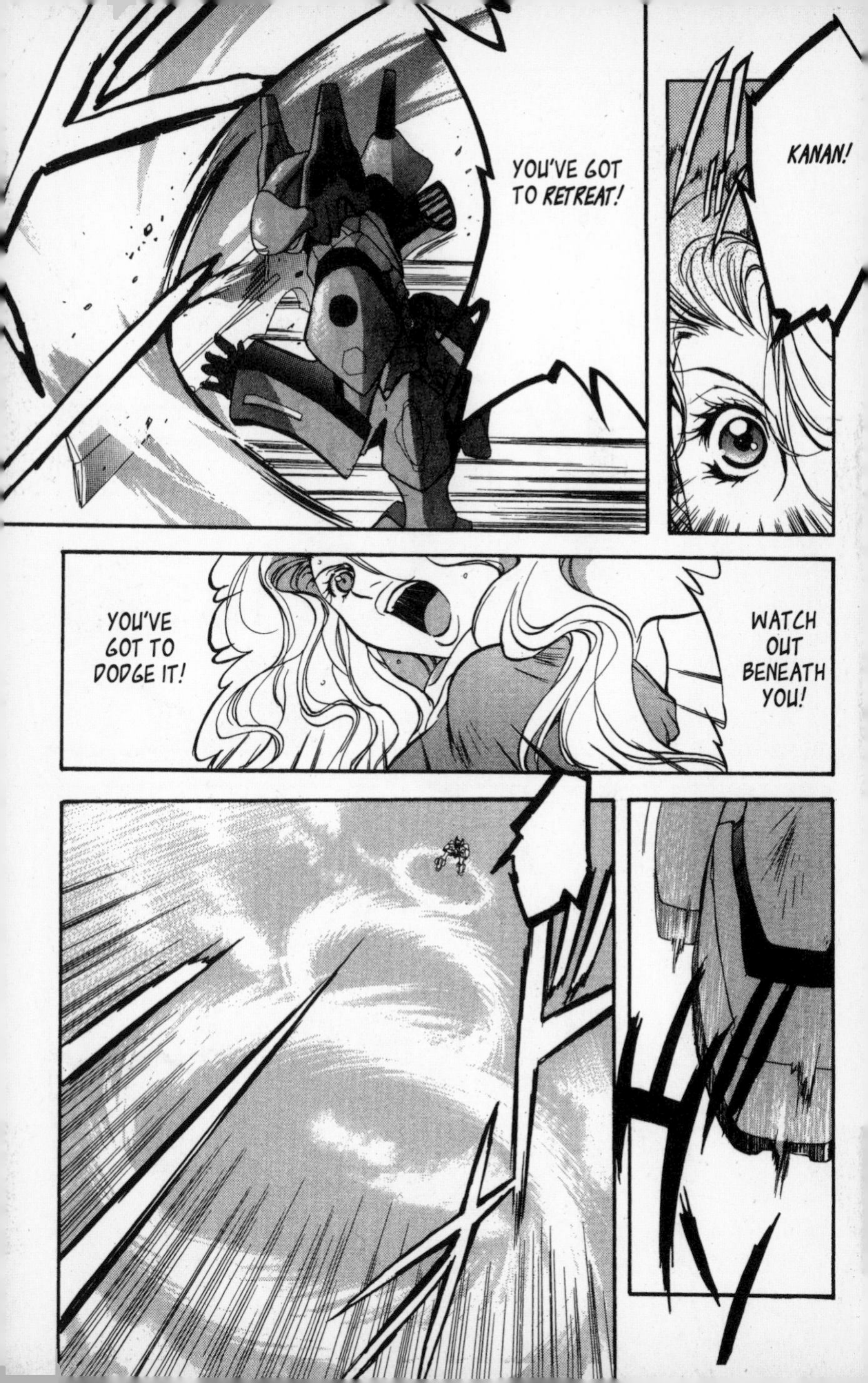
KANAN!
YOU'VE GOT TO RETREAT!
WATCH OUT BENEATH YOU!
YOU'VE GOT TO DODGE IT!

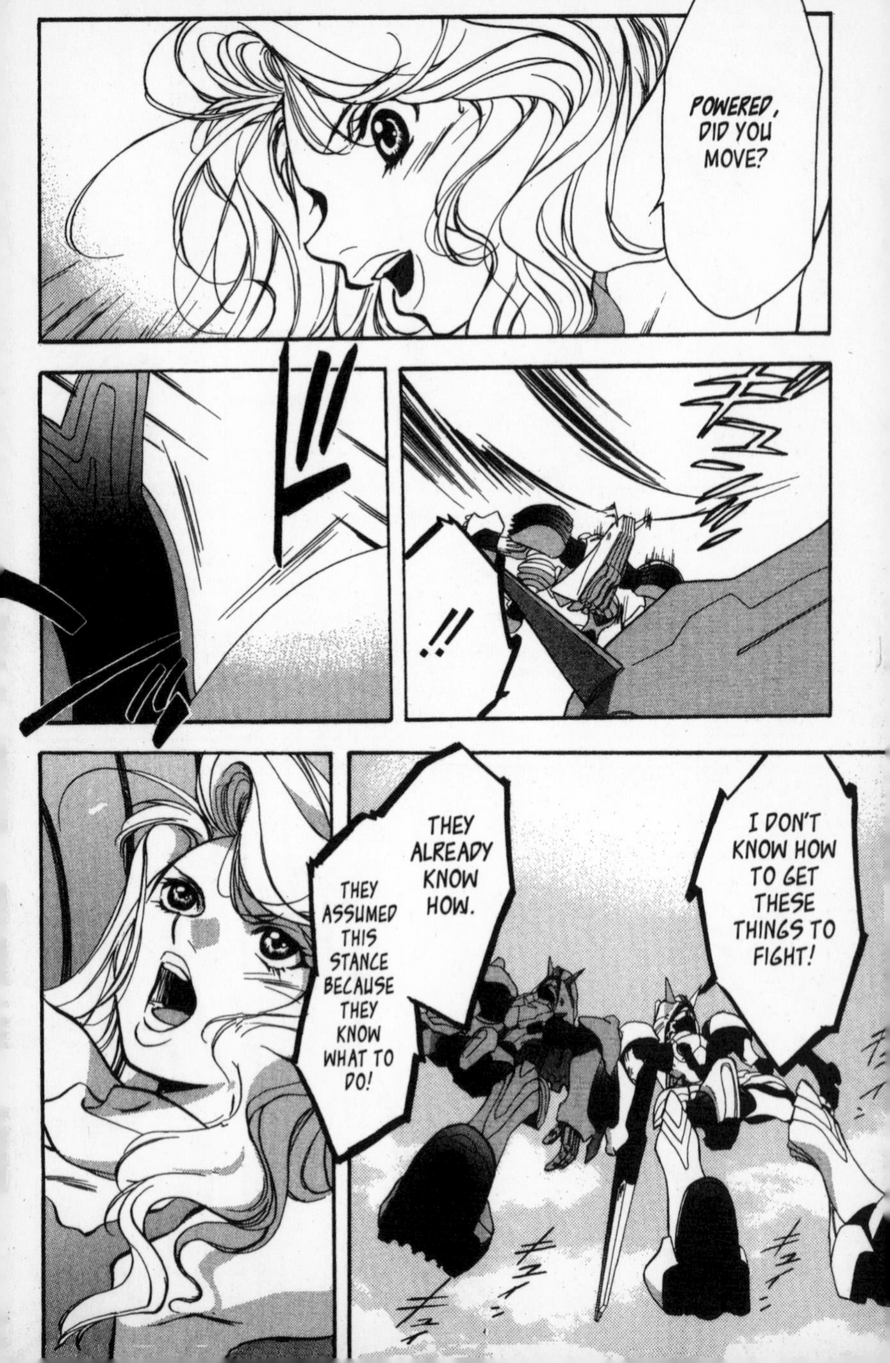
POWERED, DID YOU MOVE?
!!
I DON'T KNOW HOW TO GET THESE THINGS TO FIGHT!
THEY ALREADY KNOW HOW.
THEY ASSUMED THIS STANCE BECAUSE THEY KNOW WHAT TO DO!

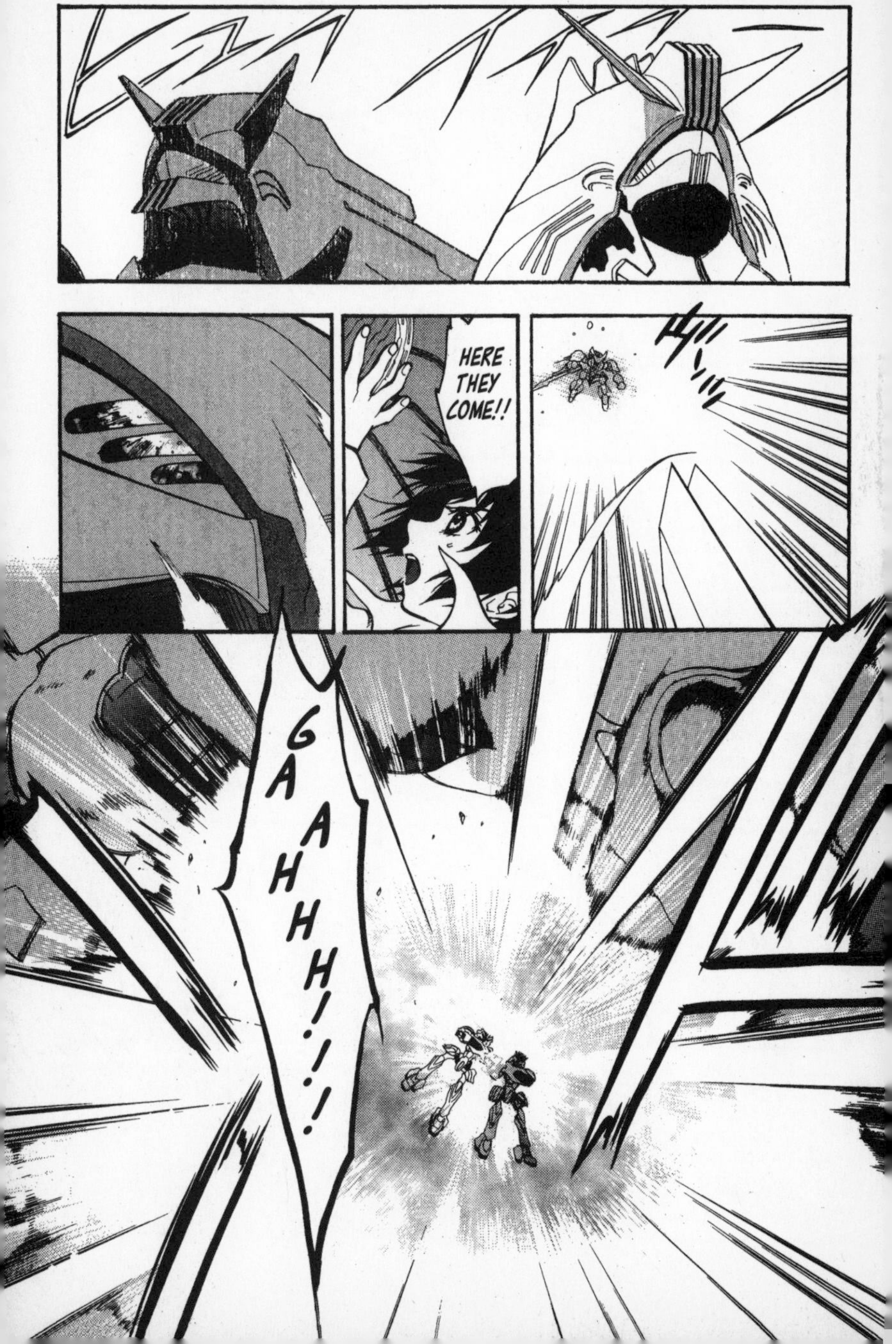
HERE THEY COME!!
GAAHHH!!!!

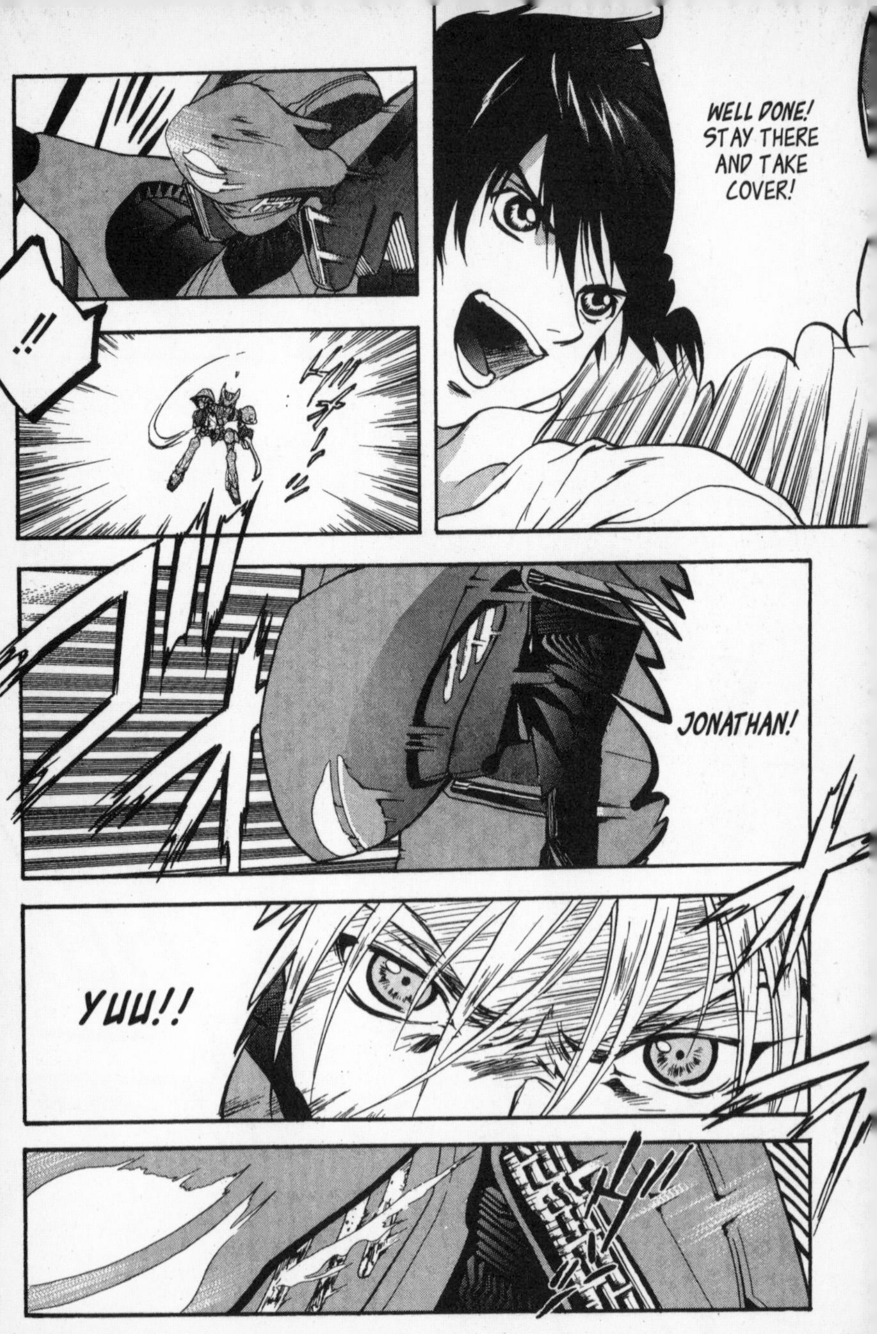
WELL DONE! STAY THERE AND TAKE COVER!
!!
JONATHAN!
YUU!!

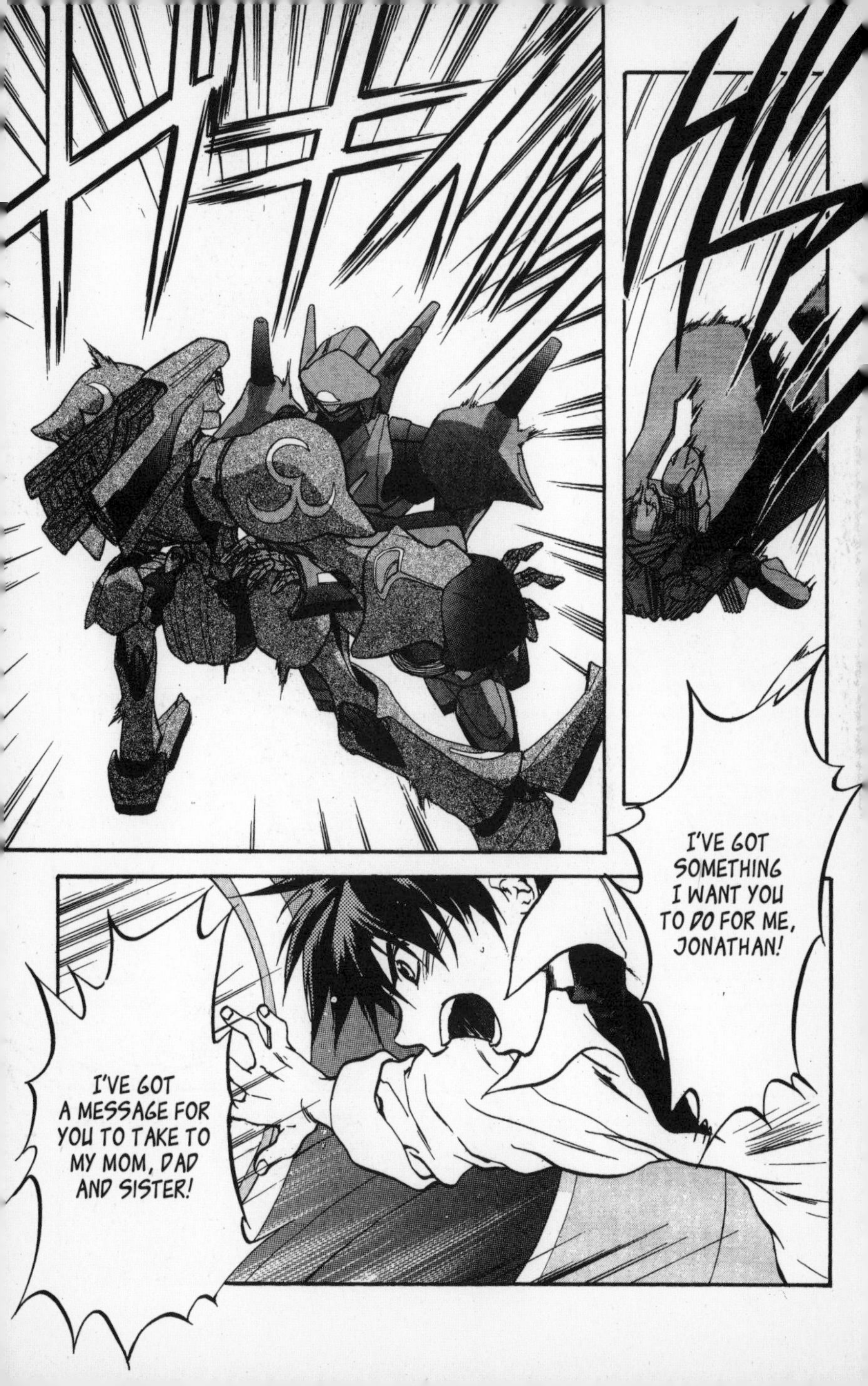
I'VE GOT SOMETHING I WANT YOU TO DO FOR ME, JONATHAN!
I'VE GOT A MESSAGE FOR YOU TO TAKE TO MY MOM, DAD AND SISTER!

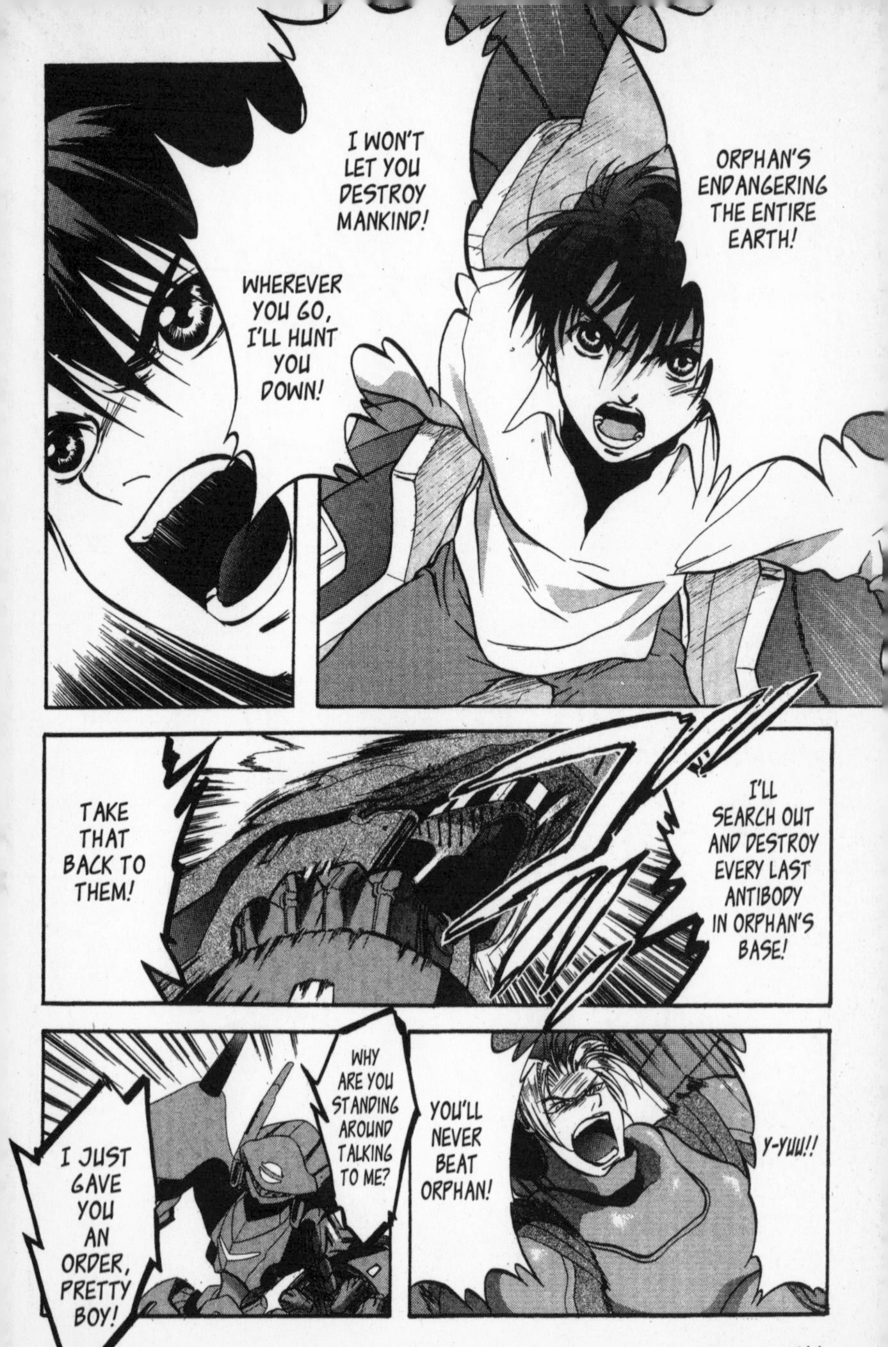
ORPHAN'S ENDANGERING THE ENTIRE EARTH!
I WON'T LET YOU DESTROY MANKIND!
WHEREVER YOU GO, I'LL HUNT YOU DOWN!
I'LL SEARCH OUT AND DESTROY EVERY LAST ANTIBODY IN ORPHAN'S BASE!
TAKE THAT BACK TO THEM!
Y-YUU!!
YOU'LL NEVER BEAT ORPHAN!
WHY ARE YOU STANDING AROUND TALKING TO ME?
I JUST GAVE YOU AN ORDER, PRETTY BOY!

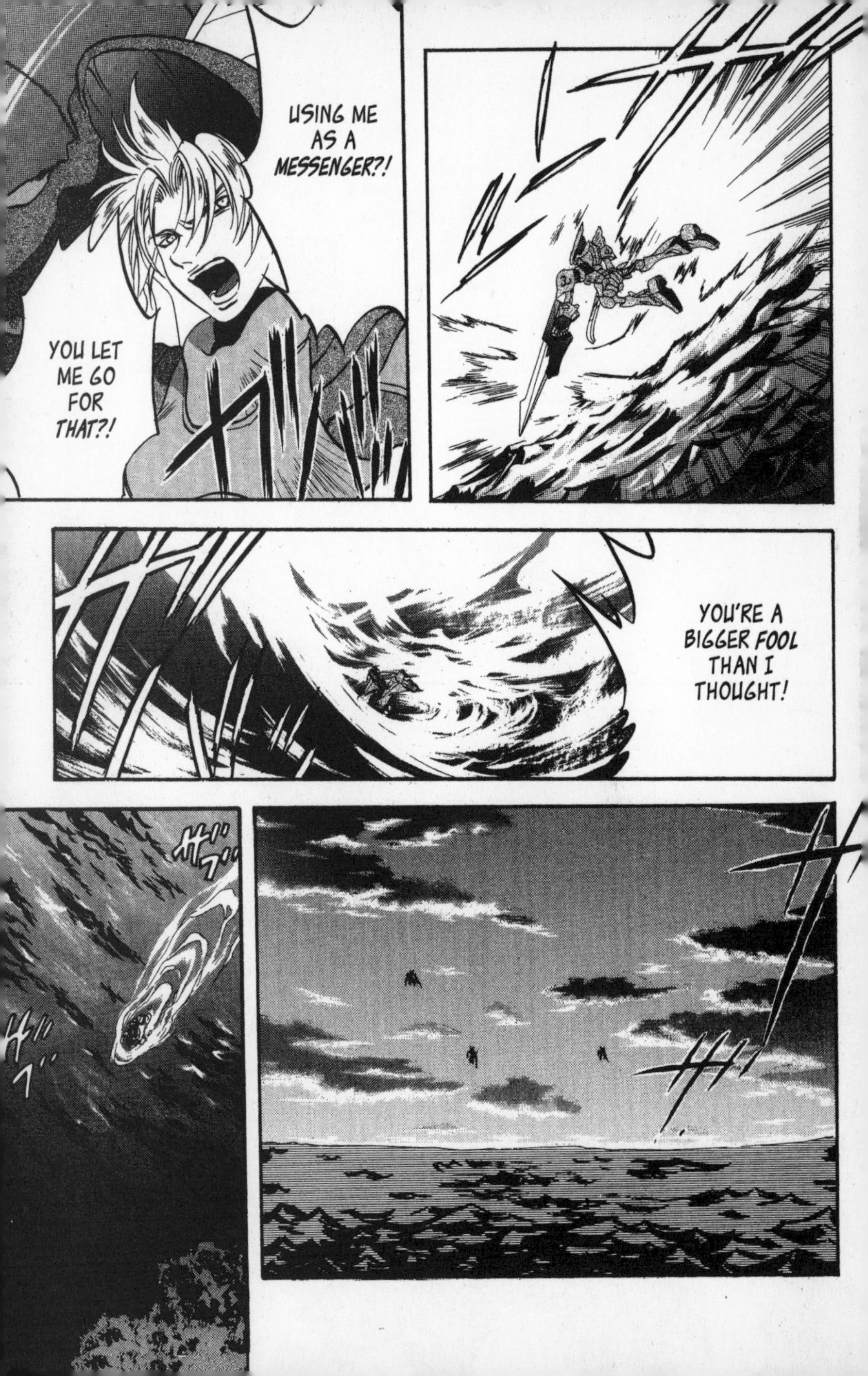
USING ME AS A MESSENGER?!
YOU LET ME GO FOR THAT?!
YOU'RE A BIGGER FOOL THAN I THOUGHT!

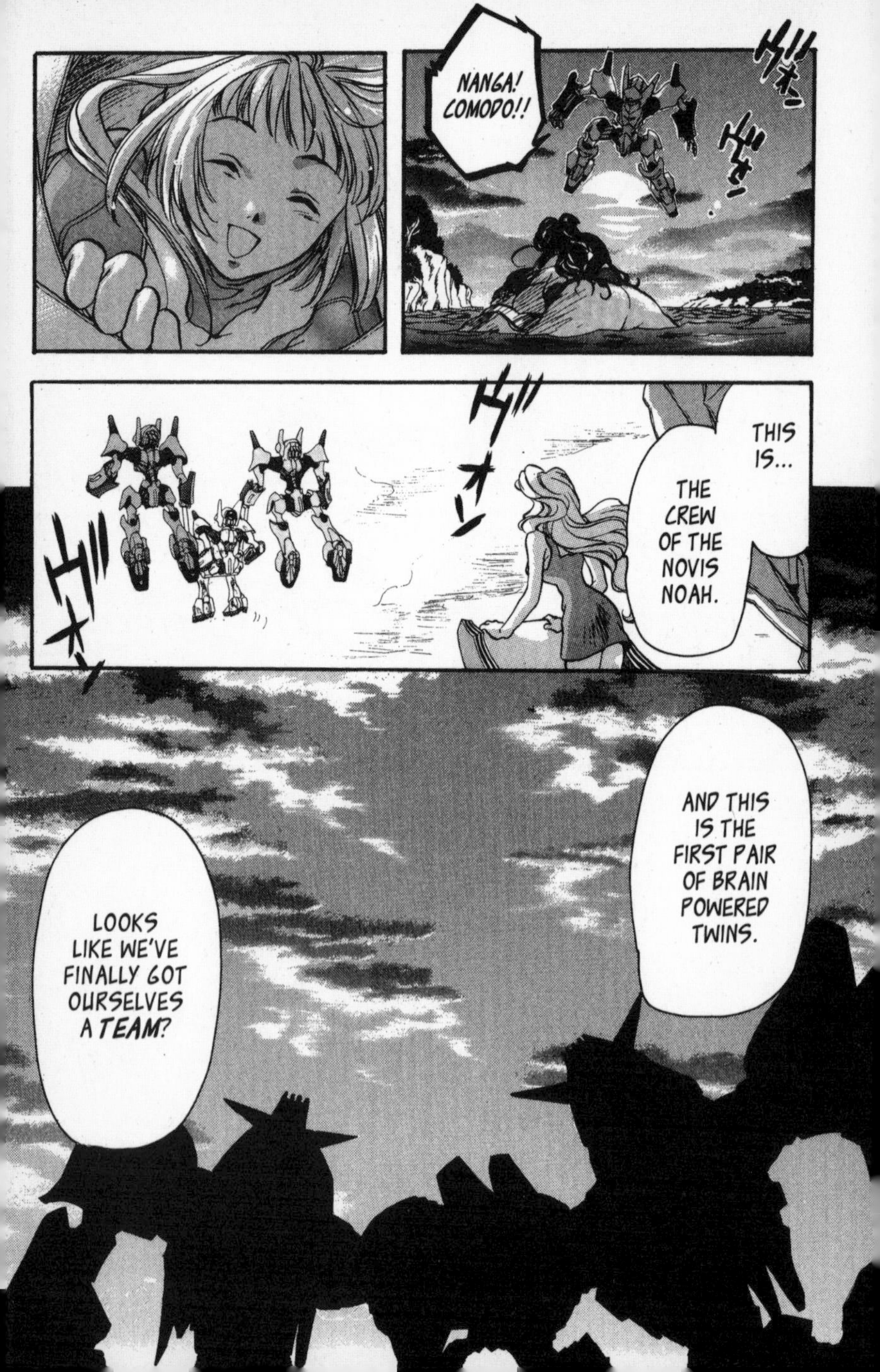
NANGA! COMODO!!
THIS IS...
THE CREW OF THE NOVIS NOAH.
AND THIS IS THE FIRST PAIR OF BRAIN POWERED TWINS.
LOOKS LIKE WE'VE FINALLY GOT OURSELVES A *TEAM*?

BRAIN POWERED

ROUGH CREATION DATA COLLECTION

KANAN GIMOSU

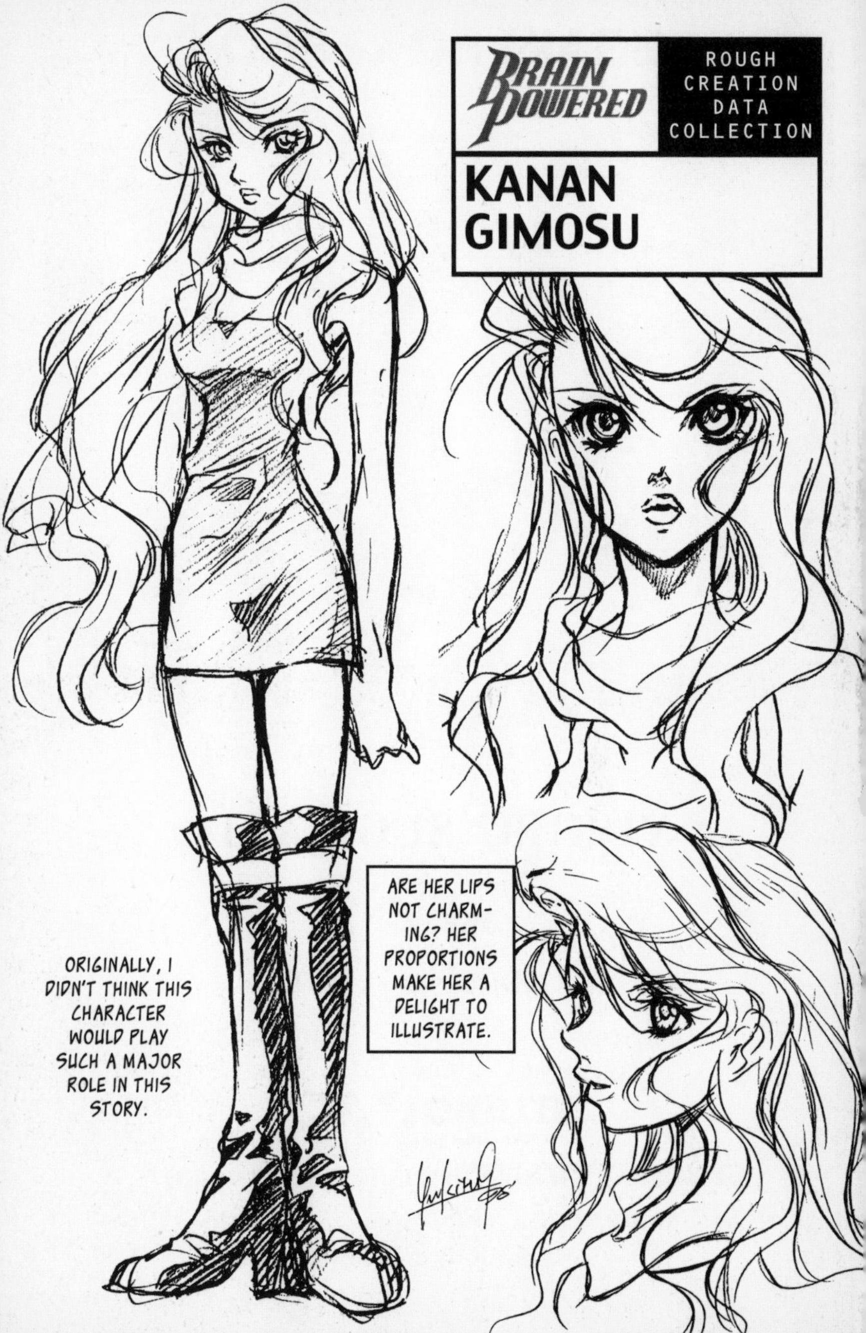
ORIGINALLY, I DIDN'T THINK THIS CHARACTER WOULD PLAY SUCH A MAJOR ROLE IN THIS STORY.
ARE HER LIPS NOT CHARM-ING? HER PROPORTIONS MAKE HER A DELIGHT TO ILLUSTRATE.

BRAIN POWERED

YUKIRU SUGISAKI

STAFF

MAMORU SUGISAKI

T·NAITOU R·WATANABE S·SHIMOZATO

A·NAKAMURA J·OKU M·OKUNO

STUDIO YS
YUKIRU SUGISAKI

SPECIAL THANKS: YOSHIYUKI TOMINO

Y·NONOGUCHI M·INOMATA M·NAGANO

Y·KAWAGUCHI & SUNRISE

IN THE NEXT VOLUME OF

BRAIN POWERED

Plot twists and dark secrets abound as Yuu adjusts to his new life on the Novis Noah. When scientists flock to the great battleship for the Organic Engine Conference, the sinister Reclaimer Jonathan sneaks onto the Novis Noah, intent on taking over the ship. Captain McCormick proves to be little help--her hands are already full dealing with the mysterious B Plate. However, the greatest threat comes from Orphan itself, as the massive underwater ship begins to surface. What does this mean for the fate of humanity? Earth's entire future is thrown into question as the exciting tale of Brain Powered continues!

ON SALE SOON!

ONE VAMPIRE'S SEARCH FOR
Revenge and Redemption...
REBIRTH
By: Woo
Joined by an excommunicated exorcist and a spiritual investigator, Deshwitat begins his bloodquest. The hunted is now the hunter.
GET REBIRTH
IN YOUR FAVORITE BOOK & COMIC STORES NOW!
T
TEEN
AGE 13+
© 1998 Lee Kang-Woo. All rights reserved. First Published in Korea in 1998 by Daiwon C.I. Inc. English translation rights in North America, UK, NZ and Australia arranged by Daiwon C.I. Inc.
TOKYOPOP is a registered trademark of Mixx Entertainment, Inc.
www.TOKYOPOP.com

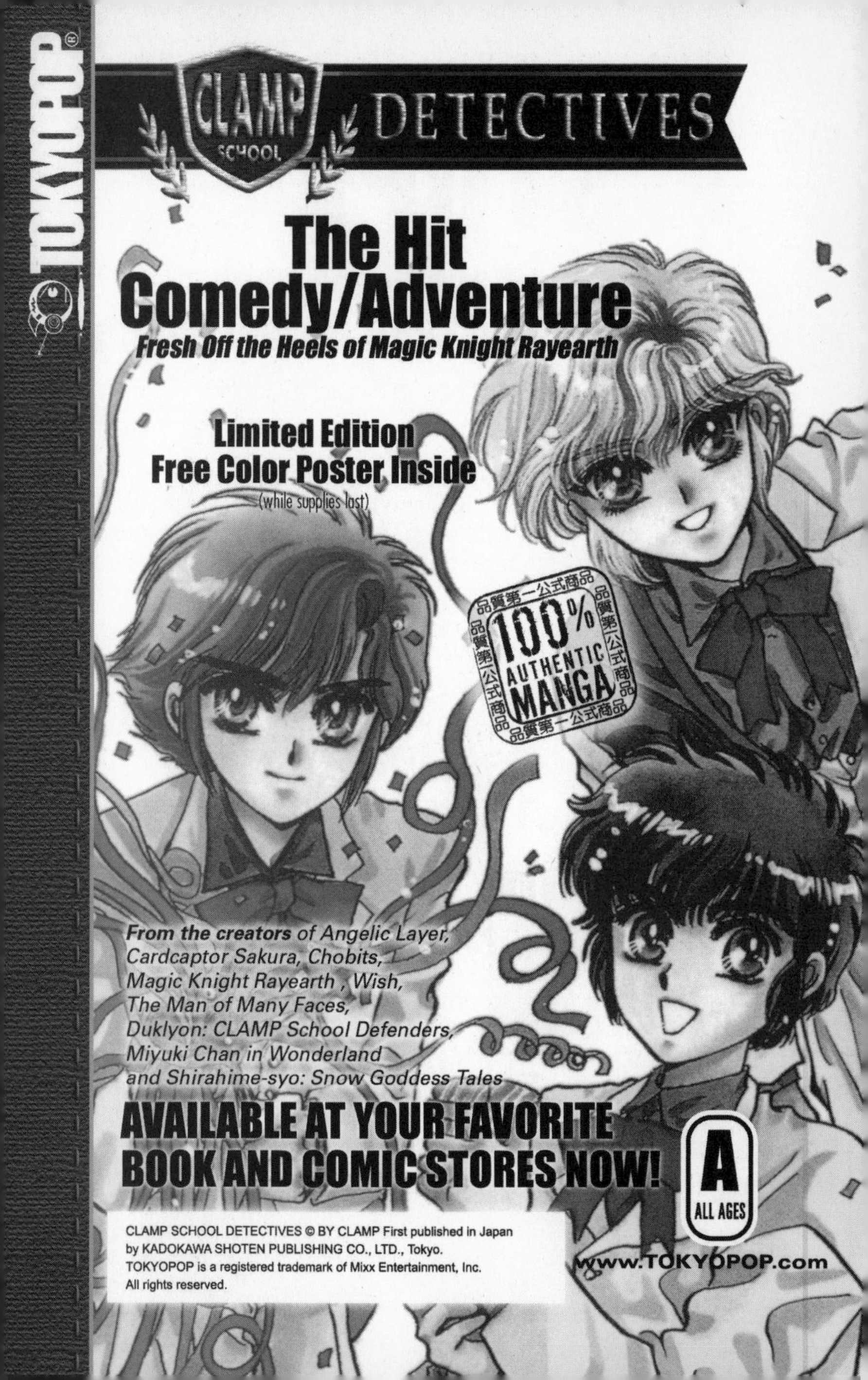
TOKYOPOP®
CLAMP SCHOOL DETECTIVES
The Hit
Comedy/Adventure
Fresh Off the Heels of Magic Knight Rayearth
Limited Edition
Free Color Poster Inside
(while supplies last)
品質第一公式商品
100%
AUTHENTIC
MANGA
From the creators of Angelic Layer,
Cardcaptor Sakura, Chobits,
Magic Knight Rayearth , Wish,
The Man of Many Faces,
Duklyon: CLAMP School Defenders,
Miyuki Chan in Wonderland
and Shirahime-syo: Snow Goddess Tales
AVAILABLE AT YOUR FAVORITE
BOOK AND COMIC STORES NOW!
A
ALL AGES
CLAMP SCHOOL DETECTIVES © BY CLAMP First published in Japan
by KADOKAWA SHOTEN PUBLISHING CO., LTD., Tokyo.
TOKYOPOP is a registered trademark of Mixx Entertainment, Inc.
All rights reserved.
www.TOKYOPOP.com

STOP!

This is the back of the book.
You wouldn't want to spoil a great ending!

This book is printed "manga-style," in the authentic Japanese right-to-left format. Since none of the artwork has been flipped or altered, readers get to experience the story just as the creator intended. You've been asking for it, so TOKYOPOP® delivered: authentic, hot-off-the-press, and far more fun!

DIRECTIONS

If this is your first time reading manga-style, here's a quick guide to help you understand how it works.

It's easy... just start in the top right panel and follow the numbers. Have fun, and look for more 100% authentic manga from TOKYOPOP®!